Butterworths Commercial Court and Arbitration Pleadings

Butterworths Commercial Court and Arbitration Pleadings

General Editors

Charles Macdonald QC MA (Oxon)
One of her Majesty's Counsel, Quadrant Chambers; Recorder; Member of the Panel of Lloyd's Salvage Arbitrators

Chirag Karia MA (Cantab), LLM (University of California, Berkeley)
Barrister, Quadrant Chambers; Attorney (California)

Tottel
publishing

quadrant
chambers

Tottel Publishing, Maxwelton House, 41-43 Boltro Road, Haywards Heath, West Sussex, RH16 1BJ

A CIP Catalogue record for this book is available from the British Library.

ISBN 1-84592-036-8

Typeset in Great Britain by Phoenix Photosetting
Printed and bound in Great Britain by CPI Bath

Preface

When reviewing 'Advocacy in the Magistrates' Court' by James Welsh, for *Counsel* magazine in March 2004, Matthew Scott wrote:

> '. . . [in this book] almost no aspect of magistrates court criminal advocacy is too dull to escape attention . . .'

It is the fear of the undersigned that the same may be said, *mutatis mutandis*, of our book on the art of pleading. If it has merit, that is thanks to the contributions of our colleagues who found time in their busy practices to produce examples of that art; and, in the view of the undersigned practitioners, to Jane Jarman whose excellent text on the use of language provides an entertaining lecture.

There are of course already in print other books of precedents, and very good books they are. But surprisingly perhaps, there are few which try to tell the reader how to draft a pleading well. There may be a parallel here with the comparatively small number of books on the art of advocacy, perhaps because, as we suggest in Chapter 1, the only way to learn how to plead is to do it. Some techniques can however be learned, and we have tried to give guidance about these, in addition to including reflections on the correct and effective use of English. Solicitors acting as advocates are already familiar in commercial arbitration, and we are entering an era when they will increasingly plead in the higher courts. We hope they, along with practising barristers, will find this book useful.

The various sets of precedents in this book are prefaced by assumed facts, something which the traditional precedent books leave to be deduced but which we thought would be helpful to set out in advance.

It may be objected that some of the content does not consist of pleadings: the chapters on jurisdictional challenges, search and freezing orders and arbitration applications, for example, comprise largely draft statements; while the precedents in Chapters 17 and 18 are certainly not pleadings in the traditional sense. However, we have not felt too narrowly constrained by our title. We hope that all the precedents will be of some help. We have eschewed skeleton arguments, however, as they largely consist of arguments on the evidence and law relevant to the particular dispute.

We offer thanks to our publishers, Tottel Publishing and to LexisNexis UK, for their patience and support, and for preparing the index. Paul Sayers and Cheryl Prophett deserve special mention. The law is intended to be stated (where it is stated at all) as of 1 February 2005.

Charles Macdonald QC
Chirag Karia
Quadrant Chambers
February 2005

Contents

Table of Statutes

Paragraph references printed in **bold** type indicate where the Act is set out in part or in full.

Table of Statutory Instruments

Paragraph references printed in **bold** type indicate where the Act is set out in part or in full.

Table of Cases

A

B

C

D

E

F

I

J

K

Q

R

S

T

U

V

W

PART I

Introduction

CHAPTER 1

Introduction

Charles Macdonald QC
Chirag Karia
Jane Jarman

The purpose of this book

1.1 This book is intended to be, not a work of scholarship, but a practical guide to those who wish to know how to plead a case in the Commercial Court[1] or in a City of London commercial arbitration. The editors hope its readership will include trainee solicitors, pupil barristers, the younger practitioners in the relevant fields and practitioners in the Commercial Court generally. Although this opening chapter will offer some suggestions, it is probably true to say that the only way to learn to plead is to do it. The precedents in the later chapters will, we hope, help the reader to do that.

In CPR 58.1(2), a commercial claim is defined as:

> 'any claim arising out of the transaction of trade and commerce and includes any claim relating to–
> (a) a business document or contract;
> (b) the export or import of goods;
> (c) the carriage of goods by land, sea, air or pipeline;
> (d) the exploitation of oil and gas reserves or other natural resources;
> (e) insurance and re-insurance;
> (f) banking and financial services;
> (g) the operation of markets and exchanges;
> (h) the purchase and sale of commodities;
> (i) the construction of ships;
> (j) business agency; and
> (k) arbitration.'

This is a wide field and the book will not set out to provide exhaustive coverage of all the many types of commercial action or arbitration, but it aims to offer precedents of pleadings for the major or common types. Guidance will be offered on what makes a good pleading, rather than a bad one. The drafting of Notices of Appeal will be included. In addition, there will be assistance in the preparation of the more important Part 23 applications and their supporting evidence; in drafting Case Memoranda and Lists of Issues for use in the Commercial Court; and in drafting Part 36 and Calderbank offers 'without prejudice save as to costs'.

1 Including, where the precedents are apposite, e.g. in carriage of goods by sea claims, the Admiralty Court.

What the book does not set out to do

1.2 It would be beyond the scope of a technical handbook on pleading to provide a guide to Commercial Court or arbitration practice generally. The practice of the Commercial Court is comprehensively covered in the *Practice Direction – Commercial Court* supplementing CPR Part 58 and in the *Admiralty & Commercial Courts Guide*. In addition, there are excellent textbooks which perform this purpose to which reference may be made[1].

Nor is this volume a guide to all the court's many case management powers or to all CPR provisions relating to pleadings (such as the rules relating to times of service, amendment or striking out).

It does not address itself to pleadings generally or to their history or comparative context[2].

Finally, and least of all, is it an account of the relevant substantive law relating to a given cause of action or defence. An attempt will however be made to draw to the reader's attention any aspect of the substantive law which has particular reference to the way in which a case might be pleaded.

1 For example, Colman, Lyon and Hopkins *Practice and Procedure of the Commercial Court* (5th edn, 2002); Ambrose and Maxwell *London Maritime Arbitration* (2nd edn, 2002); Mustill and Boyd *Commercial Arbitration* (2nd edn).

2 A full discussion of these matters can be found in Bullen and Leake and Jacob's *Precedents of Pleadings* (15th edn).

Why 'pleadings'?

1.3 To some ears the expression 'pleading' may have a dated ring. The CPR no longer refer to pleadings but to 'statements of case'[1], defined as 'particulars of claim', 'defence' and 'reply'[2]. This terminology is now used in the Commercial Court so strictly speaking there is no longer any such thing as a 'Commercial Court pleading'. However, the expression 'pleading' is still used in the *London Maritime Arbitrators' Association Terms* (2002)[3] and in its *Small Claims Procedure and Commentary* (2002). It appears also in Lloyd's Procedural Rules for arbitrations under *Lloyd's Standard Form of Salvage Agreement No Cure No Pay* ('LOF 2000')[4]. Lawyers still widely use and understand the word 'pleading', to refer not just to a physical document but also to the art, science or skill of setting out in a short, lucid and compelling form the essential elements of a case. So the editors, while mindful of the valuable reforms introduced by the CPR, will use the expression 'pleading' in this work.

1 CPR 16.

2 CPR 16.4, 16.5, 16.7.

3 See for example the Second Schedule, paras 1, 2, 3 and 5.

4 In Rule 3(c).

The purpose of pleadings

1.4 Case law tells us that:

> 'The purpose of the pleadings is to define the issues and to give the other party fair notice of the case which he has to meet'
> (per Lord Hoffmann for the House of Lords in *Barclays Bank plc v Boulter* [1999] 1 WLR 1919 at 1923F).

The minimum technical task that the pleading must perform is, therefore, to set out the facts amounting to the relevant cause of action (or defence) and to give the opposing party notice of one's case. This summation entails identifying (characterising) that cause of action[1]. That is not necessarily the same thing as pleading a point of law. As will be seen, there is even today no strict technical requirement to plead points of law. There is simply a permission to do so. However, omitting to plead a relevant point of law is:

> 'not ... a convenient course normally to be followed',

as Buckley J drily remarked in *Independent Automatic Sales Ltd v Knowles and Foster* [1962] 1 WLR 974 at 981, because it may result in the other side being taken by surprise by the point of law[2]. The editors suggest therefore that a point of law (especially a crucial one) should always be pleaded as a matter of good practice, in effect as part of the function of giving notice of one's case.

In *McPhilemy v Times Newspapers Ltd* [1999] 3 AER 775, Lord Woolf MR said that statements of case are required to mark out the parameters of the case that is being advanced by each party. It is important that they identify the issues and the extent of the dispute between the parties. They should state concisely the general nature of each party's case. The need for extensive detail and particulars has been reduced by the requirement that witness statements must (later) be exchanged. In the majority of proceedings, identification[3] of the documents upon which a party relies, together with copies of the party's witness statements, will make the detail of the nature of the case the other side has to meet obvious. This reduces the need for particulars in order to avoid being taken by surprise.

In court proceedings the trend is, therefore, intended to be in favour of brevity of the pleadings, with the detail being fleshed out in witness statements that follow on later.

Although Lord Woolf was not dealing particularly with the Commercial Court, the tradition of brevity has historically been enshrined in the procedural rules used in the Commercial Court. Under the former RSC, Commercial Court pleadings were given the snappy names 'Points of Claim', 'Points of Defence', etc[4]. As will be seen, the aim of keeping the pleadings in commercial cases short and concise is still a formal part of the court's procedure.

The pleadings served in litigation are the touchstone for decisions on issues of admissibility and relevance of evidence. Faced with a heated debate as to whether a particular witness should testify, or a particular document should be adduced, the tribunal will, as a starting point, turn to the pleadings to ascertain the issues to which it is said to be relevant.

1 As in 'in breach of contract', 'negligently', 'in breach of a duty of care owed as a bailee for reward', etc. In practice, this is invariably done.
2 Per Lord Hoffmann in *Boulter* at p 1923C. This was stated, even though by 1999 skeleton arguments had been in use for many years. It makes sense because a point of law asserted only in a skeleton argument served close to trial may indeed result in surprise, and not be conducive to open justice and early settlement.
3 NB not attachment to, or service with, the pleading – this will be mentioned further below.
4 It may even be that in some days long gone, Commercial Court pleadings actually were brief. But by the late twentieth century, they were typically at least as elaborate as any other pleading, if not more so, by which time the expressions 'Points of Claim', etc had become largely ironic. The LMAA Terms still use the expression 'points of claim', etc – see below.

CHAPTER 2

Commercial Court Pleadings: Technical Requirements and Effective Communication

Charles Macdonald QC
Chirag Karia
Jane Jarman

Technical requirements

Commercial Court pleadings: the relevant rules

2.1 The rules of court relating to Commercial Court pleadings are a combination of basic CPR provisions (some modified in their application to the Commercial Court), provisions of CPR 58 and provisions of the *Admiralty & Commercial Courts Guide* ('the Guide'). Save where they are modified by CPR 58 or the Guide, the CPR apply to the Commercial Court[1].

In case of need there is no substitute for consulting these sources but it may be helpful to the reader to have the most important provisions set out below in what is hoped to be an orderly and suitably edited form.

1 CPR 16 PD1.2; CPR 58.3.

The provisions

2.2 CPR 16.4 provides:

'(1) Particulars of claim must include–
  (a) a concise statement of the facts on which the claimant relies;
  (b) if the claimant is seeking interest, a statement to that effect and the details set out in paragraph (2);
  (c) if the claimant is seeking aggravated damages or exemplary damages[1], a statement to that effect and his grounds for claiming them;
  (d) if the claimant is seeking provisional damages, a statement to that effect and his grounds for claiming them; and
  (e) such other matters as may be set out in a practice direction[2].

(2) If the claimant is seeking interest he must–
  (a) state whether he is doing so–
    (i) under the terms of a contract;
    (ii) under an enactment and if so which; or
    (iii) on some other basis and if so what that basis is; and
  (b) if the claim is for a specified amount of money, state–
    (i) the percentage rate at which interest is claimed;
    (ii) the date from which it is claimed;

(iii) the date to which it is calculated, which must not be later than the date on which the claim form is issued;

(iv) the total amount of interest claimed to the date of calculation; and

(v) the daily rate at which interest accrues after that date.

(Part 22 requires particulars of claim to be verified by a statement of truth)'

CPR 16.5 provides:

'(1) In his defence, the defendant must state–

(a) which of the allegations in the particulars of claim he denies;

(b) which allegations he is unable to admit or deny, but which he requires the claimant to prove; and

(c) which allegations he admits.

(2) Where the defendant denies an allegation–

(a) he must state his reasons for doing so; and

(b) if he intends to put forward a different version of events from that given by the claimant, he must state his own version.

(3) A defendant who–

(a) fails to deal with an allegation; but

(b) has set out in his defence the nature of his case in relation to the issue to which that allegation is relevant,

shall be taken to require that allegation to be proved.

(4) Where the claim includes a money claim, a defendant shall be taken to require that any allegation relating to the amount of money claimed be proved unless he expressly admits the allegation.

(5) Subject to paragraphs (3) and (4), a defendant who fails to deal with an allegation shall be taken to admit that allegation ...

(Part 22 requires a defence to be verified by a statement of truth)'

CPR 16.7 provides:

'(1) A claimant who does not file a reply to the defence shall not be taken to admit the matters raised in the defence.

(2) A claimant who–

(a) files a reply to a defence; but

(b) fails to deal with a matter raised in the defence,

shall be taken to require that matter to be proved.

(Part 22 requires a reply to be verified by a statement of truth)'

In the Practice Direction accompanying Part 16, the following provisions (or parts of provisions) are most relevant to pleading in the Commercial Court:

'7.2 Where a claim is brought to enforce a right to recover possession of goods the particulars of claim must contain a statement showing the value of the goods.

7.3 Where a claim is based upon a written agreement:

(1) a copy of the contract or documents constituting the agreement should be attached to or served with the particulars of claim ..., and

(2) any general conditions of sale incorporated in the contract should also be attached (but where the contract is or the documents constituting the contract are bulky this practice direction is complied with by attaching or serving only the relevant parts of the contract or documents).

7.4 Where a claim is based upon an oral agreement, the particulars of claim should set out the contractual words used and state by whom, to whom, when and where they were spoken.

7.5 Where a claim is based upon an agreement by conduct, the particulars of claim must specify the conduct relied on and state by whom, when and where the acts constituting the conduct were done.

...

8.2 The claimant must specifically set out the following matters in his particulars of claim where he wishes to rely on them in support of his claim:

(1) any allegation of fraud,
(2) the fact of any illegality,
(3) details of any misrepresentation,
(4) details of all breaches of trust,
(5) notice or knowledge of a fact,
(6) details of unsoundness of mind or undue influence,
(7) details of wilful default, and
(8) any facts relating to mitigation of loss or damage.

...

9.1 Where a claim is for a sum of money expressed in a foreign currency it must expressly state:

(1) that the claim is for payment in a specified foreign currency,
(2) why it is for payment in that currency,
(3) the Sterling equivalent of the sum at the date of claim, and
(4) the source of the exchange rate relied on to calculate the Sterling equivalent.

9.2 A subsequent statement of case must not contradict or be inconsistent with an earlier one; for example a reply to a defence must not bring in a new claim. Where new matters have come to light the appropriate course may be to seek the court's permission to amend the statement of case ...

...

13.1 The defendant must give details of the expiry of any relevant limitation period relied on.

...

13.3 A party may:

(1) refer in his statement of case to any point of law on which his claim or defence, as the case may be, is based,
(2) give in his statement of case the name of any witness he proposes to call, and
(3) attach to or serve with this statement of case a copy of any document which he considers necessary to his claim or defence, as the case may be ...[3].'

The Guide addresses particulars of claim at Section C. The more important provisions are as follows:

> 'C1.1
>
> (a) Particulars of claim, the defence and any reply must be set out in separate consecutively numbered paragraphs and be as brief and concise as possible.
>
> (b) If it is necessary for the proper understanding of the statement of case to include substantial parts of a lengthy document the passages in question should be set out in a schedule rather than in the body of the case.
>
> (c) The document must be signed by the individual person or persons who drafted it, not, in the case of a solicitor, in the name of the firm alone.
>
> C1.2
>
> (a) Particulars of claim, the defence and also any reply must comply with the provisions of rules 16.4 and 16.5 ...
>
> (b) The requirements of PD16 paras 8.4 to 9.1 (which relate to claims based upon oral agreements, agreements by conduct and Consumer Credit Agreements and to reliance upon evidence of certain matters under the Civil Evidence Act 1968) should be treated as applying to the defence and reply as well as to the particulars of claim.
>
> (i) full and specific details must be given of any allegation of fraud, dishonesty, malice or illegality; and
>
> (ii) where an inference of fraud or dishonesty is alleged, the facts on the basis of which the inference is alleged must be fully set out.
>
> (d) Any legislative provision upon which an allegation is based must be clearly identified and the basis of its application explained.
>
> (e) Any provision of the Human Rights Act 1998 (including the Convention) on which a party relies in support of its case must be clearly identified and the basis of its application explained[4].
>
> (f) Any principle of foreign law or foreign legislative provision upon which a party's case is based must be clearly identified and the basis of its application explained.
>
> C1.3
>
> (a) PD16 para 7.3 relating to a claim based upon a written agreement should be treated as also applying to the defence, unless the claim and the defence are based on the same agreement.
>
> (b) In most cases attaching documents to or serving documents with a statement of case does not promote the efficient conduct of the proceedings and should be avoided.
>
> (c) If the documents are to be served at the same time as a statement of case they should normally be served separately from rather than attached to the statement of case.
>
> (d) Only those documents which are obviously of critical importance and necessary for a proper understanding of the statement of case should be attached to or served with it. The statement of case must itself refer to the fact that documents are attached to or served with it.

(e) An expert's report should not be attached to the statement of case and should not be filed with the statement of case at the Registry.

C1.4

If a statement of case exceeds 25 pages (excluding schedules), a summary, not exceeding 4 pages, must also be filed and served. The summary should cross-refer to the paragraph numbering of the full statement of case ...

C1.5

Parties serving statements of case should bear in mind that the court will take into account the length of the document served when considering any application by another party for further time within which to respond.

C1.6

Particulars of claim, a defence and any reply must be verified by a statement of truth ...'

Finally appendix 4 of the Guide provides as follows:

'The following principles apply to all statements of case ...:

1. The document must be as brief and concise as possible.
2. The document must be set out in separate consecutively numbered paragraphs and sub-paragraphs.
3. So far as possible each paragraph or sub-paragraph should contain no more than one allegation.
4. The document must deal with the case on a point by point basis to allow a point by point response.
5. Where particulars are given of any allegation or reasons given for a denial, the allegation or denial should be stated first and the particulars or reasons for it listed one by one in separate numbered sub-paragraphs.
6. Any party wishing to advance a positive case should set that case out in the document; a simple denial is not sufficient.
7. Any matter which, if not stated, might take another party by surprise should be stated.
8. Where they will assist:
   (i) headings should be used; and
   (ii) abbreviations and definitions should be established and used, and a glossary annexed.
9. Contentious headings, abbreviations and definitions should not be used. Every effort should be made to ensure that headings, abbreviations and definitions are in a form that will enable them to be adopted without issue by the other parties.
10. Particulars of primary allegations should be stated as particulars and not as primary allegations.
11. If it is necessary to rely upon a substantial amount of detailed factual information or lengthy particulars in support of an allegation, these should be set out in schedules or appendices.
12. Particular care should be taken to set out only those factual allegations which are necessary to support the case. Evidence should not be included.

13. A response to particulars set out in a schedule should be set out in a corresponding schedule.
14. [Is the same as the Guide, Section C1.1(b)].
15. Contentious paraphrasing should be avoided.
16. [Is the same as the Guide, Section C1.1(c)].'

1 In the Commercial Court such a claim is rare.

2 See below.

3 CPR 16 PD13.3(3) goes on to provide that such an attachment may include an expert's report, but this provision does not apply to the Commercial Court: see the Guide, Section C1.3(e) below. The Guide also discourages the attachment of documents to or serving them with the particulars of claim: see Section C1.3(b).

4 See also the CPR 16 PD15.

Discussion

2.3 Perhaps the most striking feature of the above provisions, especially those of the Guide, is that they are of a highly prescriptive nature. They go into such details as how paragraphs and sub-paragraphs are to be used[1] and the use to be made of abbreviations[2]. It may be fair to say that so long as the reader studies and closely follows the provisions, he will be in possession of a complete pleading manual. Most of the provisions are self-explanatory. However, comments on a few of the topics covered may be of use.

1 The Guide, Annex 4, paras 3 and 5.

2 The Guide, Annex 4, para 8.

Being concise

2.4 It will have been noted that considerable emphasis is placed in the provisions on the virtue of brevity. Three provisions[1] enjoin it directly and eight others encourage it[2] in various ways. The provisions obviously recognise that some Commercial Court litigation is complex and large scale and that long pleadings are inevitable in these instances. In such cases, the provisions as to schedules are relevant. But as a general rule, the pleader should be looking for economy of expression. This will lighten the task of the tribunal and enhance the impact of the pleaded case. Under contemporary court practice, tribunals are almost always tasked with a considerable volume of pre-reading before an application or trial. This reading will include more discursive documents such as skeleton arguments. For many tribunals however, the pleadings are the first port of call, since by defining the issues they presage what can (and cannot) properly be addressed in a skeleton argument or witness statement. It is therefore tactically important to present to the court your client's pleaded case in a clear and short form. A good practice, which can easily be followed by drafting with a word processing programme, is to read and re-read your completed draft looking only (or mainly) for ways to shorten it. You will usually find that it is possible to do so without affecting the sense.

In addition to being economically expressed, your pleading should be organised and systematic. Have an overall plan in mind, and follow it, for example:

'INTRODUCTION AND PARTIES
[REPRESENTATION]
[COLLATERAL WARRANTY]
CONTRACT
TERMS
BREACH
[UNTRUTH OF REPRESENTATION]
LOSS
PRAYER'

Specific allegations/denials (paragraphs) and particular supporting facts/reasons (sub-paragraphs) should be framed within the overall plan. The person reading the pleading should always know where he/she is going. NEVER just have a rambling narrative of factual events, ending with an attempt to draw them into a cause of action.

Strive to achieve balance. If your client's central complaint relates to defective goods, and he has a subsidiary complaint about late delivery involving a much lower loss, do not plead the main claim in two lines and devote five pages to how the delay occurred. Leave the reader in no doubt as to the focus of your case.

1 CPR 16.4(1)(a); the Guide, Section C1.1(a) and appendix 4, para 1.
2 The Guide, Section C1.1(b), C1.3(b) to (d), C1.4, C1.5 and appendix 4, paras 11 and 12.

Statements of truth

2.5 In court proceedings[1], all pleadings must be verified by a statement of truth, and this is true of the Commercial Court as of others[2]. It is worth noting a special procedure which applies if your client is an insurer using the name of the assured to bring or defend a claim, which is a common situation in the Commercial Court. In general, a statement of truth must be signed by the party or his legal representative[3]. In the Commercial Court, a party may apply for permission that a statement of truth may be signed by a person other than one of those. The application may be made after the issue of the claim form. The case where insurers are subrogated to the rights of the party in respect of the claim is instanced. If there is more than one insurer using rights of subrogation, the lead insurer may sign (provided that his capacity is made clear) and the court may also order that one or more of the parties signs[4]. The circumstances where the last order may be made are not defined but an example might be where the parties are also claiming deductibles in their own right. Section C1.9 expressly deals only with a situation where:

> 'insurers are conducting proceedings on behalf of many claimants and defendants',

but it is submitted that the procedure may also be apt where there is one (nominal) party who has several underwriters. A pleading which is not verified by a statement of truth is liable to be struck out, and its contents cannot be used as evidence (22 PD4.1 to 4.4). Unless the draftsperson will also be the verifying legal representative, the editors suggest that it would be a wise course to include in any draft the appropriate statement of truth wording, accompanied by a note drawing attention to the need for it to be completed.

1 The position is different in arbitrations – see below.
2 This is distinct from the requirement that the pleading be signed by the person who has drawn it up – this will be discussed below.
3 CPR 22.1(6). In this context the 'legal representative' usually means a firm of solicitors, signing as such and not as an individual pleader or draftsperson.
4 The Guide, Section C1.8, C1.9.

Stonewalling defences

2.6 Defences which are merely 'skeletal' and simply put the claimant to proof, without asserting a positive case, are no longer permitted under the CPR. Defendants are now required to plead what their real case is, including giving reasons for a denial. This feature is specifically addressed in the Guide, appendix 4, paras 5 and 6, so must presumably be regarded as especially important in a commercial case.

Admissions

2.7 A related topic is the sometimes tricky question of when to make an admission on the pleadings. The philosophy of the CPR is that parties ought to make sensible admissions at an early stage in order to narrow the issues and save costs. Nevertheless, the editors counsel some caution before (say) drafting a defence which contains admissions. Once made, admissions can be difficult to withdraw. If it is a clear case, the relevant admission should be made; but it is a wise precaution for the draftsperson to include an explanatory note accompanying the draft seeking (in effect) express instructions to make any important concession. This is an aspect which can usefully be kept under review as the case develops. For example, in a carriage of goods by sea claim it may be unwise for a carrier defendant to admit title to sue in the defence; but after disclosure (and/or service of witness statements) it may become clear that title to sue will be proved. Such a situation can be managed by either a holding denial, or an equivocal plea under CPR 16.5(1)(b), followed in due course by a suitable admission.

Attaching the contract

2.8 It is now an express requirement of the CPR[1] that where a claim is based upon a written agreement (a very common situation in the Commercial Court) the agreement must be attached to or served with the particulars of claim. If the defence in the Commercial Court relies on a distinct agreement, the same applies[2]. 'General conditions of sale incorporated[3] into the contract' must also be attached or served[4]. If the documents are bulky they can be edited. Although the CPR refer specifically to general conditions of *sale*, it may be sensible to attach or serve any adhesion terms[5] on which reliance is to be placed. This requirement has slightly confined the pleader's hand, in that it used to be possible, when acting for a defendant, to choose tactically whether it was better to set out individual terms[6] in the pleading without their context, or to annex the full terms which would reveal their context, perhaps to the detriment of one's case. Since, however, long contract documents can be edited, considerations of this sort may continue to arise in some cases. In any event, if the pleadings raise issues on adhesion terms which are in very small print, it is desirable to set out the key parts in the body of the pleading, in addition to attaching or serving the terms, in the interests of legibility.

1 CPR 16 PD7.3(1).
2 The Guide, Section C1.3(a).
3 Presumably this means 'allegedly incorporated'.
4 16 PD7.3(2).
5 Such as the small print of a bill of lading, the *RHA Standard Conditions of Carriage* and the like.
6 Or even extracts from terms.

Pleading fraud

2.9 The Guide[1] reinforces the CPR requirement[2] that any allegation of fraud[3] must be specifically pleaded with full and specific details. The Code of Conduct of the Bar of England and Wales (2000) provides at para 704:

> 'A barrister must not ... draft any statement of case ... containing:
>
> ...
>
> (c) any allegation of fraud unless he has clear instructions to make such allegation and has before him reasonably credible material which as it stands establishes a prima facie case of fraud ...'

Solicitors (or indeed para-legals or any other pleader) would be well advised to take para 704 as a guide. The requirement that there be before the pleader reasonably credible material which as it stands establishes a prima facie case of fraud is relatively new. On the one hand, 'material' is a wider concept than 'evidence' (though usually the material will be admissible as evidence). On the other hand, the material has to be reasonably credible; it has to establish a case of fraud which would be upheld in the absence of any other or different evidence; and it has to do so as it stands and not e.g. after disclosure which might be hoped or expected to produce confirmatory evidence[4]. Historically, English pleaders have been slow to allege fraud and these tough requirements make it harder to do so. Appropriate care must be taken before any such allegation is made. At the preparation stage the requirement is not that counsel should necessarily have before him evidence in admissible form but that he should have material of such a character as to lead responsible counsel to conclude that serious allegations could properly be based upon it (*Medcalf v Weatherill* [2002] UKHL 27).

1 Section C1.2(b)(i).
2 16 PD8.2(1).
3 Or dishonesty, malice or illegality.

4 This is a particular application of the general principle that in an adversarial system of litigation, a claim should not be brought unless the claimant is in a position to plead the facts on which he relies: *Hytrac Ltd v Conveyors International Ltd and Others* [1983] 1 WLR 44 at p 47H per Lawton LJ.

Naming witnesses

2.10 The CPR[1] permit (and may be said to encourage) the naming in a pleading of any witness whom the party proposes to call. There is nothing in the Guide to discourage this course. The editors, however, suggest that it will not generally be helpful, or indeed wise, to do so. Witnesses have a habit of retracting, or at any rate not turning up at the trial. Naming a witness in the pleading, only to find later that your client cannot serve a statement from him, is giving a hostage to fortune. It is not inconceivable that naming a witness in the pleading could be the right course. For example, a party's case may be supported by a former employee of the other party who is in a position to give very damaging relevant evidence about the other party's internal workings. It may be as well for the other party to be told this (if he does not know already). But as a rule, it is probably not desirable to name your witnesses in the pleading.

1 16 PD13.3(2).

Attaching documents

2.11 The question of attaching contracts to the pleading has been discussed above. As to other documents, there is a clear divergence between the CPR generally on the one hand and Commercial Court practice on the other hand. Under the CPR the attachment of other documents is permitted, if not encouraged[1]. Under the Guide it is definitely discouraged[2]. This is no doubt a reflection of the fact that most commercial actions are heavily documented. A pleading accompanied by numerous probative documents would be unwieldy and expensive to copy. It is highly likely that all the attachments would be duplicated in evidence in due course. No court in a hurry[3] will read beyond the body of the pleading anyway. There may, however, be cases where the attachment of a short 'killer' document[4] is a valid exercise. If so, it is not forbidden. Decisions of this sort obviously have to be made on a case by case basis. In general, the practice of attaching or serving documents with the pleading should be avoided.

1 CPR 16 PD13.3(3). Although in *McPhilemy* Lord Woolf referred to the 'identification' of documents in the statement of case, one suspects he may have had in mind their attachment or service, as envisaged by 16 PD13.3(3).

2 The Guide, Section C1.3(b) and appendix 4, para 12.

3 E.g. pre-reading for a CMC.

4 Such as a letter from the other party containing damaging admissions.

Signature by the draftsperson[1]

2.12 It is a specific and repeated requirement that a Commercial Court pleading be signed by the person who has drafted it[2], and not (where the pleading has been settled by a solicitor or a solicitor's employee) in the name of the firm. In *Clarke v Marlborough Fine Art* [2002] 1 WLR 1731, Patten J said (at para 21):

> 'It was never proper for a case to be pleaded unless it had some evidence to support it. The practice of requiring a pleading to be settled and signed by counsel was intended to operate as a confirmation to the court that the professional rules of conduct had been observed by counsel when deciding whether or not to advance a particular claim.'

The Commercial Court attaches importance to this practice and has effectively extended it to members of the Law Society who settle pleadings in the Commercial Court[3]. It appears to operate as a separate safeguard from the requirement that there be verification by a statement of truth, which can be given in the name of a firm.

1 The editors are not sure that such a word as 'draftsperson' exists but they strive as ever for political correctness.
2 The Guide, Section C1.1(c) and appendix 4 para 16.
3 There is a small but important point for solicitors/trainees to note here. Counsel's drafts are often transmitted by email and as such can easily be altered by the recipient. There is no objection to altering counsel's draft without his/her permission, but if the solicitor does this the draft is no longer counsel's and counsel's signature should be removed and that of the solicitor in person substituted before service.

Pleading foreign law[1]

2.13 It is common for the Commercial Court to have to adjudicate upon obligations which are governed by a foreign law. In many of these cases, the matter is argued and decided on the basis of the presumption that in the absence of evidence to the contrary, the relevant foreign law is taken to be the same as English law. The pleader should, however, be alert to the possibility that a foreign law[2] can be asserted in his client's favour, in that it is relevant and more beneficial to him in its effect in the particular case than is English law. In the English court, foreign law is a question of fact[3]. It must be pleaded like any other fact upon which a party relies. This will entail setting out any relevant foreign legislative provisions and/or case law together with brief contentions as to their alleged effect[4]. If a foreign law is pleaded against the defendant, his pleader should take care to address the issue specifically so as to avoid admitting the content of the foreign law[5].

1 A full discussion of this topic can be found in Dicey and Morris *The Conflict of Laws* (13th edn) at ch 9.
2 Including a foreign law time bar under the Foreign Limitation Periods Act 1984.
3 Albeit one usually proved by the expert evidence of suitably qualified foreign lawyers.
4 The Guide, Section C1.2(f).
5 CPR 16.5(3).

Headings, abbreviations and definitions

2.14 Even in quite a straightforward case, it is often useful to adopt headings such as 'Introduction and parties'; 'Contract'; 'Terms'; 'Breach' and so on.

Headings should not be contentious. Thus in a sea carriage dispute a useful heading might be 'Structural seaworthiness of the mv MARINER'; whereas the heading 'The mv MARINER: Ship of Shame' would be regarded as contentious. Abbreviations are also a very valuable tool. They are especially useful for describing parties, particularly where there are many parties, several parties with similar sounding names or Part 20 proceedings[1]. They are often clearer than using the terms 'the Claimants' and 'the Defendants'. In a simpler case, parties can be designated by their functions (as in 'the Owners', 'the Builders', etc). In a more complex case, use initials and/or acronyms (such as 'SIPCO' for Shell International Petroleum Co Ltd, 'SITCO' for Shell International Trading Co Ltd, etc). But be consistent: if you have used an acronym throughout, the prayer should not be made by 'the Claimants'.

1 Where the claimant is also the defendant by counterclaim or the like.

Anticipating the other side's case

2.15 This is an aspect which is not raised by the court provisions, except in the sense that they no longer recognise any pleading after the reply[1]. In a strict technical sense, your pleading should set forth what it has to set forth in order to establish a cause of action, and no more. Depending upon what is said in the defence, it may be necessary to serve a reply. It is not only technically superfluous, but may be dangerous, for the claimant to anticipate what is perceived to be a likely defence. It may, for example, raise an issue that the opposition had not thought of or one which for reasons of their own the defendants have decided to drop. But if (a) there has been extensive pre-action correspondence; (b) as a result the claimant knows that a particular point is almost certain to be raised in the defence (such a defence based on standard terms); and (c) the claimant has a strong or very strong case in reply (such as one based on Unfair Contract Terms Act 1977), it may be tactically justified for the claimant to set out his stall on that aspect in the particulars of claim. Each case has to be assessed separately.

1 Under the RSC it was possible with leave to serve after the reply a rebuttal pleading called a 'rejoinder' and after that even a 'surrejoinder'.

Arbitration

2.16 As a generality it can be said that much of the pleading practice of the Commercial Court can be transposed directly into arbitrations. There are, however, some differences to which reference will be made. By way of source, the Arbitration Act 1996, s 34 provides:

> '(1) It shall be for the tribunal to decide all procedural and evidential matters, subject to the right of the parties to agree any matter.
>
> ...
>
> (3) Procedural and evidential matters include–
>
> ...

(c) whether any and if so what form of written statements of claim and defence are to be used, when these should be supplied and the extent to which such statements can later be amended;

...'

Institutional rules

2.17 In principle, the parties to an arbitration are therefore free to agree terms as to pleadings, failing which the tribunal will decide the matter. In practice, most English arbitrations take place in the City of London pursuant to rules published by institutional bodies. Of these, the set of rules most familiar to Commercial Court practitioners is the London Maritime Arbitrators' Association Terms (2002) ('the LMAA Terms') and their provisions as to pleadings will be set out below with some comments. Other sets of rules exist, with their own provisions as to pleadings[1].

1 E.g. the UNCITRAL Arbitration Rules, arts 18–20 and 22; the ICC Rules of Arbitration 1998, art 18 and 19; the LCIA Rules, art 15.

The LMAA Terms

2.18 Term 12 provides as follows:

'(a) It shall be for the tribunal to decide all procedural and evidential matters subject to the right of the parties to agree any matter. However, the normal procedure to be adopted is as set out in the Second Schedule ...

THE SECOND SCHEDULE

ARBITRATION PROCEDURE

1. The normal procedure (which shall apply unless the parties agree otherwise) requires service of claim submissions. If, exceptionally, formal pleadings are thought appropriate (e.g. in more complicated references) special permission must be obtained from the tribunal. Whether claim submissions or points of claim are served, they must set out the position of the claimants in respect of the issues that have arisen between the parties as clearly, concisely and comprehensively as possible, and must always be accompanied by all supporting documentation relevant to the issues between the parties.
2. Except in unusual cases ... defence submissions or, if the tribunal has permitted formal pleadings, points of defence (and counterclaim, if any) with all documentation relevant to the issues between the parties (other than that disclosed by the claimants) are to be served 28 days after receipt of the claim submissions or points of claim. ...
3. Submissions in reply or, if the tribunal has permitted formal pleadings, points of reply are to be served 14 days after service of submissions or points of defence unless there is also a defence to a

counterclaim, in which case [time is extended]. Any reply to the defence and counterclaim must be served within 14 days thereafter.

...

5. All submissions and pleadings must be set out in numbered paragraphs.
6. Bare denials in response to an allegation will not be acceptable. If an allegation is denied, reasons must be given and if appropriate a positive contrary case put forward.

...

11. In appropriate cases the tribunal may order the service of a statement of truth signed by an officer or by the legal representative of a party confirming the accuracy of any submissions ...'

Discussion: claim submissions

2.19 The LMAA Terms distinguish between two types of pleading, claim submissions and formal pleadings (points of claim, etc). Claim submissions typically take the form of a letter to the tribunal (copied to the other party) which sets out the party's claim in (usually) a more discursive and less disciplined style than is used in a formal pleading. Claim submissions may or may not be drafted by a lawyer, and the Terms are no doubt intended to accommodate the many simpler cases where lawyers never become involved, and there is no oral hearing, but a decision on documents after written submissions by the lay parties. It does however happen that a lawyer (more often a solicitor than a barrister) is instructed to prepare claim submissions. The only overt requirements are, as set out above, that they should use numbered paragraphs and that in defence they should be forthcoming and not skeletal. The editors see no reason to dictate, therefore, how the individual practitioner should choose to draft claim (or defence) submissions in an LMAA arbitration. However, it is submitted that:

(a) the same basic approach should be used as set out in the Guide for commercial claims;
(b) cross references to the accompanying evidence should be given; and
(c) as the matter may proceed to a hearing on documents alone, it may be appropriate to conclude with an argumentative section, more akin to a Skeleton Argument, which would not have a place in a formal pleading.

Formal pleadings

2.20 These are usually settled by lawyers, often by counsel, and the usual practice is to track the practice of the Commercial Court.

Accompanying documents

2.21 The LMAA Terms take the opposite line to the Guide in that they positively require the claim submissions/points of claim to be accompanied by all supporting documentation, and the defence submissions/points of defence to be accompanied by all relevant[1] documentation. In this they go further even than the CPR, since 16 PD13 permits but does not require this. In the context of a reference run on submissions, where there may be no oral hearing, this makes sense. If there are to be formal pleadings and it is considered to be more appropriate to conduct the reference as if it were a Commercial Court action with a separate disclosure process, it is open to the parties to reach agreement to that effect, varying the LMAA Terms.

1 Reading the whole of paras 1 and 2 of the Second Schedule, there appears to be no distinction between 'supporting' and 'relevant', i.e. this is supposed to be the disclosure process.

Statements of truth

2.22 By contrast to the position in court, these are not normally required but they can be ordered[1].

1 Second Schedule, para 11.

The LMAA Small Claims Procedure

2.23 This is a fast and low cost arbitration procedure before a sole arbitrator, generally on documents only. Paragraphs 2(a) and 5(a) to (c) of the Procedure provide for the exchange of 'letters' of claim, defence, etc accompanied by all relevant documents and evidence including expert evidence. As the Procedure is intended for use where the claim does not exceed US$50,000 and the recoverable legal costs are capped, it is submitted that lawyers are unlikely to be involved in the drafting of these letters.

A general topic: drafting pleadings and the use of Notes

2.24 The pleader should always put the draft before the client (lay or professional as the case may be) for approval before service. In doing so, it will often be appropriate for the pleader to include, or provide as a companion, a Note explaining the draft. It is not possible to list exhaustively what topics any given Note should cover but two common problems are as follows.

Whether for a court case or in arbitration, it is often the case that the pleader must draft on the basis of assumptions as to facts which are not clear from his instructions, but as to which reasonable inferences may tentatively be drawn. In such a case, it is essential to draw to the attention of the professional or lay client that this is being done. How it is done is a matter of personal style. A clear footnote in the draft may be enough, but the use of a different typeface or some other form of highlighting is recommended. It may be better to list the assumptions in an accompanying document, and to sign the draft: 'Settled, subject to my accompanying Note' (or similar words).

Another judgment which may have to be made is whether the pleader ought to volunteer advice to the effect that a given point is very unlikely to succeed. It may be that the pleader has specific instructions to set it out, in which case (within the limits of propriety) the draft should do so. But if it is fairly bad (or appears to be so on the material which is available) it may be wise to give a restrained warning to this effect; otherwise the pleader may be accused later of having implicitly indicated that it is valid.

It is important, at all sorts of levels, for your pleading to be written in good English. Help with this is given below.

Use of English and effective communication

2.25 Lawyers have a bad reputation for using impenetrable legalese: to their clients and each other. Despite being members of a profession that is capable of a high level of linguistic acuity, a great deal of legal writing is so confusing that it almost constitutes a private dialect[1]. The documentation produced may not only be dull, but positively misleading. Furthermore, imprecise language increases the risk that a client may make an allegation of professional negligence against their lawyer on the basis that advice was not communicated to them with sufficient clarity[2]. Yet 'use of English' is one of the most straightforward elements to master when learning to draft effective and persuasive pleadings.

The Commercial Court provides a forum for the resolution of litigation that is often of a complex nature. Furthermore, such litigation is often accompanied by documentation that is voluminous and highly technical. Given this context, the aim of the practitioner must be to draft persuasive pleadings and allied documentation, which serve to illuminate the issues in dispute, rather than exacerbate an already difficult situation. Pleadings and other written submissions are growing in importance in the Civil Courts of England and Wales and have been a feature of Commercial Court procedure for many years[3]. Pleadings constitute a form of advocacy. It is imperative that the focus is on a brevity and efficiency of approach, so that all parties can focus on the main issues in dispute, thereby reducing the risk of incurring unnecessary costs.

Whilst an awareness of the technical aspects of pleading in the Commercial Court is important, the draftsperson should also be sensitive to his or her use of language. There are various techniques of 'hidden persuasion' which can be deployed by the draftsperson to add colour and interest to a lengthy narrative or to ameliorate the impact of a damaging admission[4]. The following pages provide both some useful tips on effective use of English when drafting, and guidance on how to recognise lexical 'sleight of hand' in an opponent's pleading. You must take account not only of what is said, but how it is said.

1 See Martin Cutts *The Plain English Guide* (1996) and the quotation from the chairperson of 'Clarity' the Campaign for Plain English.

> 'Why do lawyers write so that no-one can understand them? They say it is because they need to be precise, and their language has been honed by centuries of litigation. But this

is baloney. The real reason is that, although they are paid for their skill with words, most lawyers are dull and clumsy writers who have not broken the habits that they learned as students' (Cutts, p 140).

2 The vast majority of claims against solicitors emanate not from bad legal advice but rather as a result of lack of effective communication about non-legal matters. See the guidance on effective communication in the Law Society's Lexcel Standard, for instance.

3 Note the pro forma Application Notice under the CPR, and the possibility of an application being dealt with on paper. Many lawyers are still suspicious of this type of application, preferring to 'have their say' at a hearing. This type of submission is used frequently in the European inquisitorial system.

4 See Vance Packard *The Hidden Persuaders* (1959), a classic work on the advertising industry, which provides an interesting analysis of the use of persuasive language.

Effective drafting: general advice

2.26 The pleading is a critical document, and summarises the salient points of the case. It should be a persuasive document; able to engage and maintain the interest of the reader. You will appreciate that when taking over a file for the first time, many litigation solicitors will reach for the pleadings to provide a convenient synopsis of the issues in dispute. The pleadings constitute a truly 'multifunctional' document. Therefore, consider the following when drafting:

- *Consider your audience and their needs.* The pleading will be considered by the Judge and by opposing counsel and solicitors together with their client. Consider the impact of a calm and cogent piece of drafting on that opponent. A particularly compelling argument may have a considerable effect on the resolve of Claimant or Defendant that his or her own legal team may find difficult to counter. The same is true of an expert witness. The pleadings always form part of a well-prepared set of instructions to an expert witness, and provide an opportunity to 'speak' to an expert retained by an opponent. If that expert considers your argument more compelling than that of those instructing him, that sympathy may find a way into the report, albeit implicitly. Your pleading may pass into the hands of a myriad of different experts and advisors. They may be subject to time pressure, they may not be legally qualified, or given the international element the audience may be based abroad[1]. As a result, a pleading, which aids understanding without recourse to an overly legalistic approach, will find favour with such an audience.
- *Consider the material.* What is the best way to present the information? Lawyers tend to be 'narrative centric' and choose to describe disputes in words. They may even be actively hostile to other forms of communication on the basis that they are imprecise. However, often a table or diagram will create a more powerful image than many pages of narrative. For example, it may show how a pension scheme failed with more precision and impact. Think about the case, and the best way in which to communicate your message. Words may not be enough. An 'Excel spreadsheet' may be a better format on occasion. This approach may resonate with experts and clients in particular, as well as Judges and Arbitrators, as you seek to use methods of description with which they

feel comfortable, rather than forcing them to struggle with 'legal translation'.

- *Technical requirements.* Be alive to specific drafting points appropriate to the court or tribunal involved. The *Admiralty & Commercial Courts Guide* is very prescriptive, in particular, in relation to drafting. For instance, if the Statement of Case exceeds 25 pages then a summary, not exceeding four pages must be prepared, filed and served on all relevant parties. The Guide forces brevity upon the draftsperson, even in the most complex cases. It is profoundly irritating for the Judge if the rules are not observed, as inevitably, it will take longer to read and absorb the information in an unduly prolix and often confused document that does not follow the norm. It can also be demoralising for the draftsperson when all his or her hard work is dismissed as irrelevant verbiage. The function of the Guide is to assist the draftsperson, not as a form of constraint[2].
- *Drafting points in arbitrations.* You will appreciate that the position in relation to arbitration is different from that in the Commercial Court. It is wrong to say that there are no specific rules, but certainly there is greater room for manoeuvre when drafting Points of Claim for arbitration[3]. There is a greater emphasis on the use of Scott Schedules, and it is possible to plead matters of law and evidence, as well as material facts. The arbitral tribunal has considerable discretion to specify what it requires in a pleading. Make sure that you capitalise on this freedom, by being in a position to make a suggestion that will guide the Arbitrator to your preferred method of communication. For instance, elsewhere in this chapter, you will consider various lexical techniques that may take the 'sting' out of a damaging admission. If an Arbitrator has ordered a diagrammatic representation of a particular issue, it may be more difficult for your opponent to obfuscate in the pleading, and draw a veil over a difficult issue.

1 This situation is particularly acute in arbitration. The Arbitrator may not be legally qualified, but a specialist in the relevant area of activity. For instance, many of the Chartered Arbitrators on the ARIAS scheme are reinsurance practitioners rather than lawyers.

2 For detailed advice on drafting statements of case in the Commercial Court see appendix 4 of the *Admiralty & Commercial Courts Guide* (2002) together with CPR 58. The Guide can be found at the homepage of the Court Service at www.courtservice.gov.uk or by visiting the Commercial Court Registry in the Royal Courts of Justice. There are a number of Mercantile Courts throughout England and Wales, together with the Central Mercantile Court in London. The *Mercantile Court Guide* can also be found on the Court Service website. The advice on drafting is exactly the same; the differences relate to matters of procedure.

3 Consider the discretion in Arbitration Act 1996, s 34(2)(c).

Effective management of sentence structure

2.27 How do you communicate a complex issue, which may be subject to a number of qualifications and exceptions? The main problem, endemic to legal writing, is the long sentence that tries to cover too many points. The fear is that the use of a full stop will create uncertainty, and signal the end of that particular argument. It almost seems that a full stop could be fatal to an argument on causation. However, the converse is true. Proper attention to sentence construction can pay dividends without disappearing in a labyrinth of sub-clauses.

Some general advice on sentence structure and management[1]:

- *Keep the majority of the sentences short.* Many books on style and creative writing state that about 20 words per sentence is a comfortable maximum. Such prescriptive advice can, however, be a little constraining and there is no need to stop mid sentence on the basis of a word count! It is best to say that if your sentence has reached over 40 words you have probably lost your reader along the way. Your reader will suffer information overload and quickly lose interest.
- *Use a list.* Can you use a list to 'chop' the sentence into more manageable chunks? A list can be speed read more easily, and is more memorable, graphically, than a simple narrative.
- *Use full stops.* It sounds simple, but read through your draft again, and put in a full stop where you see a natural break. Consider whether it will make life easier for your reader. In particular, look for rogue conjunctions such as '*and*' or '*but*'. You may find that a full stop is even more appropriate. There are other miscreant formulations that almost demand a sub-clause. Familiar culprits include '*while*', '*whilst*', '*despite*' and '*although*', all much beloved of lawyers. The best advice is to use a full stop and start another sentence. You can use words such as '*so*', '*further*' or '*however*', if you feel that you need to signpost the linkage with the preceding sentence.
- *Vary sentence length and alternate the rhythm of the document.* Few writers (not just lawyers) pay attention to this technique. Mix short sentences with longer ones, to avoid a staccato effect and break up the material effectively[2].
- *Use one sentence to convey one idea.* Use each sentence to communicate one specific idea together with perhaps one 'gloss' on that issue.
- *Sub-clauses and double negation.* Steer away from sub-clauses within the narrative[3] and double negatives. Double negation, in particular, can be distracting to the reader. If you feel that you may fall into a double negative trap, you may find that you actually need to utilise the full stop.
- *Prune the sentence or start again!* Read the sentence and try to 'prune out' unnecessary words. Try to use a list or the other techniques described here. If you cannot prune, then be willing to scrap the sentence and start again.

1 Some of this guidance comes from the Plain English Campaign. Consult the website at www.plainenglish.co.uk for further information.

2 Try this exercise. Take just one paragraph from the daily editorial in a publication such as *The Times* and analyse the manner in which the writer breaks up the material, particularly by use of varying sentence length. The end result is, hopefully, a lively piece of writing, which maintains the reader's interest. Legal writing should aim for the same result.

3 For advice on sub-clauses and how best to manage them in page layout, see **para 2.31** below.

Word choice[1]

2.28 You must be sensitive to the language that you use when drafting Statements of Case. Remember that your word choice will have to do most of the work for you when communicating in writing. All of the subtle nuances of emphasis and expression, deployed when speaking, are absent. Use a thesaurus when drafting, to try to find the exact word that you should use. Your sensibilities have to be particularly acute when drafting legal documents. For instance, imagine that you are drafting Particulars of Claim in a medical product liability case. You need to choose your words carefully. Was the medicine promoted as a '*cure*' for a particular condition (which is unlikely) or was the claim rather more limited? Could other words be more appropriate, such as '*ameliorate*', '*soothe*', '*provide relief from*'. Sloppy drafting of Particulars of Claim can result in a denial, and a damaging Part 18 request. Imprecise language can provide a defendant with an escape route, which will damage the credibility of your case without good reason. It is not semantic pedantry; it is *strategic* word choice. A number of other linguistic traps are set out below:

- *Irritators/dogmatic language*. Ironically, dogmatic language and irritators are often used to make a case seem stronger, but they have the opposite effect. They are considered to be overly emotive, especially in a commercial context, although often it is the client who agitates for such language to be used. Try to discourage their use, and avoid such language in your own draft. It can be counterproductive. Consider the following formulations – 'the schedule is *clearly* wrong', 'the account was *obviously* inaccurate'. Do the words 'clearly' and 'obviously' add anything to the central message?
- *Fillers*. These are often seen to be legal 'terms of art' but they detract from the main argument and can seem pompous. The problem is that, when one is new to pleading, it is comforting to seek refuge in such linguistic padding. It simply 'looks right'. However, do the terms '*it is suggested that*' or '*it is submitted that*' really add anything to the pleading? Overuse of such terms may actually weaken your case, especially if they prevent the reader getting to the 'meat' of your argument. Implicitly, they may also indicate that you doubt your own case, and will admit a contrary view.
- *Latin phrases*. Avoid at all costs unless they are truly terms of art that are generally understood.
- *Avoid the passive voice*. The received advice is that the use of positive language is to be preferred over the passive voice. Active verbs give a sense of movement and interest, and tend to hold the attention of the reader. People tend to favour the active voice when speaking. Therefore, we say '*I am going to the shops*' rather than '*the shops are being visited by me*'. Consider the following formulation in a professional negligence case: '*Mr Smith did not advise the Claimant as to the terms of the lease*' or '*The Claimant was not advised as to the terms of the lease*'.

  The active voice is more definitive in terms of who is to blame; Mr Smith failed to advise. In the passive voice, this point is omitted. Mr Smith is not identified. The result is clear. If you wish to put your case in the strongest terms, use the active formulation as much as possible. It is clearer, and forces your opponent to deal with a specific (and perhaps difficult) point. Use the passive when you are less sure of your ground, where you wish to disguise an admission, protect the identity of an individual or to give the impression that nothing of import has occurred. It can be useful, on occasion, for that very reason[2].

- *Overuse of normalisations and abstract nouns.* Legal writing is littered with examples of the use of normalisations. In short, a normalisation occurs when a simple verb is converted into a noun, which then requires support from another verb to make sense. It is the name of something that is not a physical object, but rather a process or an emotion. For instance, a lawyer who writes that '*I have now had sight of the expert report*' rather than '*I have now seen the expert report*' uses a normalisation. Normalisations are often used with the passive.

  Therefore, the normalisation and the passive voice in:

  '*Notification has been received from the Architects that they wish to issue a Certificate of Satisfactory Completion*',

  can be converted to the active voice in:

  '*The architects have informed us that they wish to issue a Certificate of Satisfactory Completion*'.

  Use of the passive voice plus normalisations can equate to very dull language. The passive tends to be boring, bordering on the soporific. It can give the impression that nothing at all is happening[3].

1 For an excellent analysis of legal language see Martin Cutts *The Plain English Guide* (1996) pp 140–147, which provides numerous examples of 'legalese'.

2 See **para 2.32** below.

3 The normalisation is 'notification' and the passive is 'has been received'. There are some other examples of normalisations in *Language Toolkit: Practical advice on English grammar and usage* (2001) ed Jonathan Law. This type of formulation is useful on occasion. It is simply a matter of appropriate usage. See **para 2.29** below on persuasive drafting.

Persuasive drafting

2.29 The *Admiralty & Commercial Courts Guide* provides some very helpful, and at times prescriptive, advice for lawyers when drafting pleadings in Commercial Court disputes. For instance, the Guide specifies a page limit for pleadings, a summary when that limit is exceeded, and the use of non-contentious headings that can be adopted by an opponent[1]. However, there is still considerable latitude even within that structure. You must order and prioritise your case so that it is presented in the best possible light. A 'scattergun' technique will give the impression that the onus is on the reader to 'sort it out'.

- *Foundation, logic and chronology.* Facts should normally be presented chronologically, but this is not always the case. There may be occasions on which you wish to deviate from the norm. Consider the persuasive effect of the structure when drafting. Normally, the best points should be addressed first.
- *Grouping.* If you can group associated facts together, they will have greater impact than if they are separated out, scattered throughout the pleading. Again this may mean that you deviate from a strictly chronological approach.
- *Positive language.* The use of positive language can be quite insidious. Even lawyers can be lulled into a false sense of security by the use of

positive language. Compare the varying impact of the following alternative drafts of a paragraph in a professional indemnity claim:

'*The payment was not received and therefore it was not possible to complete the transfer*' (negative);

'*If the payment had been received it would have been possible to complete the transfer*' (positive).

The difference is subtle, but the negative formulation is rather bland. The positive formulation carries with it the implication that this was a simple issue, and the only bar to completion was the lack of the payment. The facts remain the same. Payment was not received and therefore completion could not take place. However, the narrative colour of the draft has changed, and use of the positive formulation lightens the message. Such subtlety of narrative colour may be important in some cases to add to the overall impact that the writer seeks to convey.

- *Lists*. We have already discussed the use of lists in pleadings. Consider using a list, especially when you need to break up complex issues. It is usually easier to read at speed, is more easily remembered, and can be located in the pleading very quickly. It is also useful when navigating the pleading later in the case and providing references in skeleton arguments, case management conference and written submissions. It is always easier to take the Judge to paragraph 13.1.2, rather than '*halfway down page 13*'.
- *Steal their best arguments*. Consider introducing and then dismissing difficult issues, before your opponent gets to them. If you do so you can control and manage the issue. Consider delivering difficult information in the passive voice. There is very little that your opponent can do in such cases. They may wish to retaliate, but they may resort to the empty dogmatisms and irritators discussed earlier, which may damage their case in any event.
- *'Blocking'*. Think about using a 'blocking' technique when structuring the pleading. Consider the following formulations to structure a response:
  - 'if (which is denied)' – to plead an alternative case;
  - 'save that' – to preface a limited admission. To provide even more 'distance' from the admission, consider coupling this form with a normalisation and passive voice;
  - 'as to paragraph x'.

  The only caveat is that you must be careful when using sub-paragraphs that you do not confuse your reader in a maze of sub-clauses. If you use a listing technique (together with legal outline numbering) rather than simple narrative, you should be safe.

1 The Guide, appendix 4.

Definitions

2.30 This is particularly important when drafting in very technical areas. For instance, some of the definitions used in reinsurance contracts may be impenetrable to a non-specialist. It may be necessary to provide a definition in a glossary attached to the pleading, but remember:

- once you have defined a term in a pleading, make sure that you use it consistently throughout;
- if you use an abbreviation or an acronym, again, that must be used consistently;
- make sure that the definitions and abbreviations that are used can be easily adopted by your opponent. They should not be contentious (see appendix 4 of the Guide).

Clear page layout

2.31 The Guide gives guidance on these issues. If you are a solicitor, your firm may also have a Commercial Court standard pleading template. Check that it complies with appendix 4 to the Guide. If so, you must use it without amendment.

When drafting, remember that the reader may be using a highlighter pen to aid understanding, and 'Post It' notes to navigate around the document. The advice given in the Guide attempts to limit the occasions on which the reader is confronted by a block of closely typed small text. Refer to the Guide for specific issues, but the following are important points to bear in mind:

- *Typeface.* Although a standard typeface is not specified, most law firms and chambers use a limited number of typefaces available in software packages. As a general rule, the serif types, such as Times New Roman and Garamond, are classical and authoritative. The Times New Roman typeface is that preferred by national newspapers such as *The Times.* The sans serif types, such as Helvetica are plain and direct and are often used in application forms and information sheets, and are effective when using 'Excel spreadsheets'. The most prevalent now within the legal profession is Times New Roman[1]. As a result, it is likely to find favour with a reader who uses the same typeface.
- *Size.* Usually 12 point for text.
- *Spacing.* 1.5 rather than single spacing.
- *Headings.* Make sure that they are not contentious, and ensure that a page break does not split the heading from the subject matter.
- *Numbering.* Legal 'outline' numbering is probably the best. It is easier on the eye to navigate 13.1.1.2 rather than 13(1)(a)(i). Again, this form is easier to use when addressing an opponent or a Judge.
- *Pagination.* A surprising number of pleadings are not paginated. They should be paginated, normally at the bottom of the page in the centre.
- *Chronologies.* Chronologies are underrated, but if well drafted, they can be an invaluable tool and summary. They can bring into bold relief periods of inactivity in a case that could otherwise remain hidden within a narrative. Chronologies are often 'travelling' documents in the Commercial Court, meaning that they are often agreed by the parties, and 'added to' during the life of the case. The format is set out in the Guide[2].

1 Times New Roman is fast becoming the typeface of choice worldwide. Recently, the US government changed the typeface of official documents from Courier to Times New Roman.

2 See Part 1, appendix 9 of the Guide for guidance on the preparation of skeleton arguments, and Part 2 for chronologies and indices. In complex cases, a dramatis personae may be required.

Difficult areas

2.32

- *Pleading to a badly written Statement of Case.* This is a perennial problem for a Defendant. The challenge is often to move the dispute to more helpful legal terrain, whilst at the same time, dealing with the allegations put by the Claimant. It is difficult, if not impossible, to start again, and there are limited opportunities to change the structure of the document. However, there is some latitude to plead additional facts, which undermine the Claimant's case, and put forward an affirmative defence. Consider formulations such as '*If it is the Claimant's case that …*' or '*In so far as the Defendant understands the Claimant's case to be …*' to draw attention to what may be very 'flabby' drafting. It is true that such comments border on the dogmatic, and so such a technique should be used sparingly, and only in response to the most grotesque examples.
- *Proper use of the passive voice.* Although use of the more active voice is preferred, the passive voice can be very useful.
  - When making an admission, if you seek to protect the identity of the person involved, or at least blur the responsibility for the act (i.e. '*the Defence was not served*' (passive) rather than '*Mrs Jones did not serve the Defence*').
  - The passive can be diplomatic – the active voice can be too direct, and can draw attention to the wrongdoer (the identity of Mrs Jones is protected in the example above).
  - The passive can gloss over areas where the facts are ambiguous, or of facts of which the writer is unsure (compare '*Mr Jones did not post the letter to Mr Smith*' with '*Mr Smith did not receive a letter*').
  - The passive can leave room for manoeuvre, and can obviate the need for an embarrassing amendment to a pleading. For instance, if Mr Jones can prove that he did post the letter, it will be necessary to remove the allegation, which cannot be sustained. If you are unsure, use the passive, but be aware that an astute opponent will appreciate this reticence emanates from a lack of firm evidence. Be alert to such techniques when you consider any pleading, or indeed any document. Look at the language used, not just the 'facts'. What does the language tell you about the writer's agenda?
  - Consider the use of the passive voice in circumstances where the active voice is too hostile. You may need to convey difficult information, without exacerbating the situation further by inappropriate language. Lawyers do this all the time out of professional courtesy. Consider the differing impact of the following statements: '*The Claimant has failed to comply with the order*' and '*The Claimant has disobeyed the order*'. Same information, different impact.

Drafting pro forma documents in the Commercial Court

2.33 The pro forma documents used in the Commercial Court have something of a 'Cinderella' status, and are often relegated to a quick box-ticking exercise.

The main documents are[1]:

- Case Management Information Form;
- Case Memorandum;
- List of Issues;
- Progress Monitoring Information Sheet.

However, they offer an opportunity to put your case briefly and in a targeted fashion. The pro forma documents give ample opportunity to use the techniques discussed elsewhere in this chapter. For instance, when completing the Progress Monitoring Information Sheet, it may be necessary to make liberal use of the passive, if it has not been possible to finalise an expert report.

1 See the Guide, para D5 to D8, for details of the Case Management Information Form and list of issues that should be drafted. See the Guide, para D12.2, and appendix 12 for the standard Progress Monitoring Information Sheet.

Punctuation advice[1]

2.34 The classic definition of punctuation is:

> 'the use of symbols not belonging to the alphabet to indicate intonation and meaning not otherwise conveyed in written language.'[2]

The function of punctuation is, to an extent, a device that mirrors the techniques that we use in everyday speech, to alter pitch, emphasis and to indicate pauses. The comment that 'Punctuation makes possible the clear presentation of the written language'[3] is particularly appropriate. Sadly, if punctuation is correct, no one notices. If it is incorrect, it is all they notice. Bad punctuation can let you down, detract from the case, irritate the reader and possibly change the meaning of the sentence. A detailed analysis of punctuation is outside the scope of this work. However, set out below is a short checklist that deals with the most common points of contention and mistake.

1 A detailed analysis of punctuation is outside the scope of this work, although there are several useful texts, including those set out below.

2 Quoted in Graham King *Good Punctuation* (2004) p 1. This book, although not the only one available by any means, provides a lively guide to a dry subject. Another useful work is Loreto Todd *Punctuation* (1995). Both books provide a detailed guide to punctuation outside the scope of this work. For an entertaining read, try the now ubiquitous book Lynne Truss *Eats Shoots and Leaves* (2003).

3 Quoted in Graham King *Good Punctuation* (2004) p 1.

Apostrophe

2.35 The apostrophe is easily the most contentious punctuation mark, so much so that its eventual demise seems assured. In reality, most people are so confused that they either leave it 'floating' above the text or refuse to use it at all. However, the rules are fairly straightforward, and even some of the more enigmatic uses can be as easily mastered.

The Apostrophe is used to indicate:

- *Possession*. It indicates the possessive case and comes before the 's' in the singular form and in plural nouns that do not end in 's'. Therefore, you would write '*The expert's reports*' (one expert, more than one report). It comes after the 's' in plural nouns ending in 's' as in '*the experts' reports*' (many experts, many reports). Check this type of formulation when dictating a pleading.
- *Contraction*. It indicates that the word or phrase has been contracted by the writer, as in *shouldn't, wouldn't, wasn't*. The use of '*it's*' deserves a mention on its own. '*It's*' is used as a contraction for '*it is*' or '*it has*'. Its, as a possessive pronoun, never takes an apostrophe. The same is true of *yours, theirs* or *whose*. Think about the apostrophe use in the sentence '*Whose 'Who's Who' am I reading?*'.
- *The enigmatic apostrophe*. Check the correct form when pleading. You may find that the official name of your client actually omits the apostrophe that normally would form part of the name, e.g. *Barclays Bank* not *Barclay's Bank* or, where it is included, as in *Lloyd's of London*. Check on official usage, which is often enigmatic. Sometimes the use of an apostrophe is part of traditional usage. Therefore, to use an everyday example from the London Underground, you have *Earl's Court* but *Barons Court*[1].

1 See other examples quoted in Graham King *Good Punctuation* (2004) p 133 such as King's College, London but St Andrews University.

Round brackets and square brackets

2.36 Brackets are used in normal punctuation to add further information, to clarify or comment on a point or to provide an illustration. They are of two main types, and have very different uses:

- Round brackets () as a parenthesis and to enclose information, to give references. If there is no other alternative, the round bracket can be used to break up a complicated sentence.
- Square brackets [] are used to enclose an explanation that is not normally part of the sentence, but is rather an authoritative or editorial comment. It is unlikely to be a popular feature of Commercial Court pleadings, except to enclose the adverb *sic* (from the Latin word *sicut* meaning 'just as') to show that the quotation is exactly as in the original, including any mistake, however glaring.

You may come across brace brackets {} or angle brackets <> in technical documents and expert reports. If you need to quote from such documents, make sure that you reproduce such brackets exactly, as they often have a specific function. Do not substitute square or round brackets.

Capitalisation

2.37 It is difficult to give a definitive guide to capitalisation. It is straightforward to state that capital letters should be used to mark the beginning of a sentence. The problem concerns the capitalisation of various nouns and names. Capital letters are used for personal and proper names, historical events and periods, the titles of books and newspapers, and for the names of institutions. They also tend to be used for trademarks, such a Coca-Cola or for abbreviations such as MA, or Dlitt. It is better to look up the specific usage in a good dictionary or textbook. Outside the most straightforward uses practice varies so widely that it is impossible to be definitive[1].

1 There is a useful guide in Graham King *Good Punctuation* (2004) pp 17–23 and in Laws (ed) *Language Toolkit* (2001) pp 92–94.

Comma

2.38 The comma is the most subtle and versatile punctuation mark. It is used as a separator between parts of a sentence. One problem endemic to much legal writing is the overuse of the comma. Make sure that the rhythm of the sentence is not disturbed by over use of the comma. It may be grammatically correct, but it is difficult to read as well as being disjointed.

The absence of a comma can also change the meaning of a sentence. For instance, the parents who read an advertising flyer for a nursery at which their children would be able to learn about '*painting, drawing, music, French drama and sport,*' may have been disappointed when their offspring failed to demonstrate a working knowledge of Racine! The flyer should have included a comma after the word French. The absence of the comma has changed the sense of the sentence.

The most common uses of the comma include:

- Itemising words: e.g. – '*please forward all drawings, records, reports, and day books* ...'.
- As a form of parenthesis – e.g. '*the actuary was, arguably, too inexperienced to provide such a report*'.
- Enclosing commas to help the reader navigate a difficult sentence.
- To separate contrasting conjunctions – e.g. '*Counsel asked the witness whether, if the Claim Form had been served within the limitation period, the claim would have been settled?*'.
- The 'Oxford' comma – be aware of the debate about the use of the Oxford comma. Many editors advise that the Oxford or serial comma (the use of a comma before 'and' (e.g. 'a, b and c' not 'a, b, and c'))[1] should be avoided. Commentators now believe that a comma before 'and' in a list is unnecessary, unless there is a possibility of ambiguity.

The comma is a subtle and versatile punctuation mark, and can assist the reader to assimilate complex information. When editing check your draft make sure that you check for ambiguity in use of the comma, which may change the sense of your draft.

1 See Graham King *Good Punctuation* (2004) p 55.

Semicolon

2.39 The semicolon is the least used of the punctuation marks. It is a shame that the semicolon has fallen out of favour as it is effective in changing the pace and rhythm of a sentence, if used correctly. It forms a midpoint between a comma and a full stop. You choose to use a semicolon; it is not obligatory. However, correct usage can add balance and finesse to prose. It has four main uses:

- To connect ideas and clauses that are closely related – e.g. '*The blueprints to the recording studio show the mixing desk to the left of the soundproofed door; the tape deck is to the right*'.
- To separate and manage 'word lists' that otherwise would contain too many commas – e.g. '*The dispute resolution team includes Harold Chambers, construction; Trisha Greaves, media law; Margaret Rose, professional indemnity, and Jane Bickleigh, arbitration services.*'.
- To emphasise contrast and promote balance – it is for this reason that the semicolon is often found in political speeches and rhetoric as shown in a well-known letter from President Kennedy to Nikita Khrushchev: '*What your Government believes is its own business; what it does in the world is the world's business.*'.
- To connote a significant pause before an adverb to add emphasis to your draft – e.g. '*The component was posted to the incorrect address; moreover it was damaged in transit.*'.

In the context of pleadings, the semicolon is often used at the end of a sub-paragraph.

Colon

2.40 One of the main functions of the colon is to lead the reader from one idea to its logical conclusion. It is a type of 'flag' to herald the conclusion. The colon has suffered concerted attack from the dash in the media in recent years. However the colon, rather than the dash, is still the preferred punctuation mark in pleadings.

The colon has a number of functions within pleadings:

- To introduce a list – e.g. '*The architect provided the following documentation: site notes, day books, risk management assessments*'.
- To provide an explanation, example or illustration – e.g. '*The operations manager noticed the oil leak and closed the main supply valve to the factory: in compliance with the company protocol*'.
- To link opposing statements and/or provide the dramatic 'punch line' – e.g. '*The computer software used by the actuary was antiquated: it could never have provided the detail required*'.

- To introduce a subtitle – e.g. '*The First Agreement: The efficacy of the exclusion clause*'.
- To introduce direct speech or other quotations – e.g. '*The expert witness stated: "The calculation is correct"*'.

Three-dot ellipsis

2.41 The three-dot ellipsis ... is used in pleadings to indicate either:

- a missing word; or
- the omission of matter which is considered to be irrelevant.

There are other uses of the ellipsis. For instance, novelists and playwrights tend to use it when writing disjointed speech. It has a limited use in a legal context. Be aware that the ellipsis is limited to three dots. Most software programmes appreciate this limit; anything more is overkill[1].

1 Note that some publishers and writers insert a fourth ellipsis mark when a sentence ends with an ellipsis.

The use of a Dictaphone to draft pleadings

2.42 Most lawyers prefer to use a Dictaphone when drafting letters, documents and pleadings, as it is possible to speak seven times more quickly than the average person can write or type. Secretaries often prefer this form of drafting, as it is quicker to audio type than to spend hours trying to decipher illegible handwriting. It is convenient to dictate even when using a precedent. However, it is important to appreciate the pitfalls inherent in this method, and to avoid them.

- Plan before you dictate. The Dictaphone may lull you into a false sense of security, and you may produce a rambling, repetitive and disorganised document.
- Be aware that you are more likely to use fillers, irritators, dogmatisms, and adopt a conversational tone when dictating. Your secretary may appreciate the emphasis in your voice, but that may not translate into the finished document. Pay special attention, when reviewing your draft, to word choice, punctuation and use of the passive and active voice.
- You may not pay due attention to important structural matters, such as layout and the proper use of lists and tables. When you edit your draft pleading, consider whether some of the narrative can be removed and replaced with a table, diagram, Scott Schedule or other representation.
- Make sure that you print the document off to check it and edit. You will not be able to see the totality of the document on a computer screen, and may find it difficult to cross check to other parts of the text.

Use of automatic 'spellchecker'

2.43 Most software packages include some form of 'spellchecker'. Used correctly, this tool is invaluable, and provides a quick and easy check on typographical errors. However, it is a blunt instrument when it comes to correction of grammatical errors. Do not depend on it in relation to punctuation and grammar, as some of the corrections are of dubious validity in the context of legal pleadings. This is not a deficiency in the programme, merely an understandable limitation of the software. Do not follow it unquestioningly. It could make a correction that fundamentally changes the sense of part of the pleading.

Layout of the later chapters

2.44 In **Chapter 3** and following, a number of precedents are offered. In each chapter a short summary of the legal principles most material to the pleading will be set out, followed by a set of assumed facts and the specimen drafts.

Summary

2.45 No pleading should ever leave your hands unless it performs its minimum technical function of disclosing a cause of action (or defence), giving notice to the other party of the case it has to meet and being compliant with the applicable rules and guidelines. It should however do more. It should be orderly, concise, elegant and forceful. It should be balanced. It should read well as prose. In many cases, it will be your tribunal's first port of call, and the last document he or she checks before issuing a judgment or award. We hope the precedents and notes below will help you to achieve these goals.

PART II

Commercial Court Pleadings

CHAPTER 3

Shipping – Charterparties

Time Charterparties:
Michael Howard QC
Robert Thomas

Voyage Charterparties:
Lionel Persey QC
Nigel Jacobs

TIME CHARTERPARTIES

Law

3.1 A time charterparty is effectively a contract for the hire of a vessel whereby the owner of the vessel agrees with the charterer to render the latter services for a given period by the owner's vessel and the master and crew employed by him. The charterer usually pays 'hire' which is based on an agreed daily rate. No special form is required for such a charter contract and the usual rules on the formation of contracts apply. In fact, it is not uncommon for such contracts to be made orally and evidenced by a telex or faxed 'recap' setting out the terms agreed. There are, however, a number of standard forms which are very commonly used. The most common of these is New York Produce Exchange Form (often referred to as the 'NYPE' form) which will almost invariably be amended or supplemented by additional provisions agreed by the parties. It is to be noted, however, that what is 'hired' is the use or availability of the space on board the vessel. Generally speaking, the shipowner retains possession of the ship, though the Master will often acquire possession of goods shipped on board by or on behalf of the charterer. (In the case of time charters 'by demise', there *is* a transfer of possession but this type of time charter is usually used for specialised purposes, such as the financing of new buildings, and not for ordinary international trade. Where, as is usual, a demise charter also involves the charterer finding his own crew, it is known as a 'bareboat charter'.)

There are a number of specialist texts dealing with time charters and the issues arising from the standard forms and reference should be made to these for a detailed discussion of the law[1].

Plainly, a wide variety of disputes may arise under a time charter. The pleadings set out below address two of the more common types of claim. They have been set in the Commercial Court, although in all such cases the Admiralty Court has jurisdiction, and in the case of most (but not all) standard form time charters there is an arbitration clause.

In the first, shipowners are seeking to recover compensation for the damage caused to their vessel when she grounded in the approaches to the berth to which charterers had ordered her to proceed under the terms of the charter. In this instance, the claim is brought for breach of an express warranty that the port/berth to which the vessel was ordered was safe, although it is to be noted that, even in the absence of such an express term, a similar term may be implied into a time charter. Shipowners also claim pursuant to an indemnity which is commonly implied into the NYPE charter against the consequences of complying with the charterers' orders and directions given under the employment clause (clause 8). It is, however, yet to be settled whether, on facts such as the present, the latter offers the claimant better prospects of success than the claim for breach of the warranty of safety.

It should be noted that in order to bring a successful claim under either the warranty of safety (whether express or implied) or the implied indemnity under the employment clause, the claimant is not required to prove the fault (e.g. negligence) of the defendant charterers. In other words, the warranty and indemnity are simply mechanisms by which risk is allocated to one or other party for certain events. This point is, however, sometimes lost on charterers when assessing the merits of such claims. Equally, the reader should be aware that safety is not limited to physical safety and that relevant dangers can include those created by a particular political situation.

It is equally clear that the liability of charterers is not open-ended. For instance, the prospective safety of the port is to be judged at the time that the order to proceed to that port is given. Thus, charterers will not (without more) be liable for damage caused by a state of unsafety arising subsequent to the order. Likewise, charterers are not liable for every danger of navigation. The classic definition of a safe port or berth is to be found in the judgment of Sellers LJ in *The Eastern City* [1958] 2 Lloyd's Rep 127 at p 131 '... a port will not be safe unless, in the relevant period of time, the particular ship can reach it, use it and return from it without, in the absence of some abnormal occurrence, being exposed to a danger which cannot be avoided by good navigation and seamanship...'. As this passage makes plain, charterers are also not liable for damage caused by an abnormal occurrence at the port but only by the features, attributes or qualities of the port itself.

The second pleading reflects the very common types of claim where there is a dispute between the parties as to the amount of any outstanding hire which often involve counterclaims by charterers that there has in fact been an overpayment. It also reflects the fact that in some cases, the refusal to pay hire may lead the shipowners to terminate the contract on the basis of an alleged repudiation of the contract by the charterers.

By their very nature, such hire disputes will usually turn on one or more of a wide variety of issues relating to the operation of the vessel and the nature and effect of various provisions of the charter (such as the off-hire clause) in light of what are often disputed facts. As such, it is difficult to give generally applicable guidance on pleading the various disputes which are likely to arise.

From the point of view of the pleader, however, it is worth noting that the true nature of the underlying disputes (and thus what evidence, factual or expert may be required) is sometimes obscured when the parties simply rely in their respective pleadings on their own hire statements without expanding upon the issues which have led to various deductions to be made or expenses claimed. At best, this results in the disputes only becoming apparent in the latter stages of the pleadings (e.g. in Reply or Defence to Counterclaim, etc) and may at worst result in the issues being obscured.

Equally vexed is the question of what (if any) documentation should be appended to the statement of case. Attaching a copy of the relevant charter makes it easier for the reader to appreciate the clauses in their context and to consider the charter as a whole. However, such charters can be substantial in size and the majority of clauses irrelevant. All time charters contain jurisdiction clauses of one sort or another. Of those where the parties agree English jurisdiction, some make disputes subject to the jurisdiction of the English High Court, though the majority contain arbitration clauses. In arbitrations under the Rules of the London Maritime Arbitrators Association, the Rules provide (LMAA Rules 2002, Sch 2, para 1) that all relevant documents have to be attached. In practice, this is taken to mean that the whole of the charterparty should be attached to the Submissions. The practice in the High Court is not uniform, but compliance with the rules of court implies a different practice. In cases referred to the jurisdiction of the English High Court, the Commercial Court will have jurisdiction. The Guide at C1.2 and C1.3 has the effect of incorporating the relevant paragraphs of the CPR, including CPR 16.4.1(e), which in turn refers to 16 PD7. That Practice Direction, especially 7.3 requires the party to attach a written agreement if one is relied on, but, if the agreement is bulky, to attach only the *relevant* parts.

1 See, e.g. *Wilford Time Charters* (LLP, 5th edn) and *Scrutton on Charterparties* (Sweet & Maxwell, 20th edn) and *Davis on Bareboat Charters* (LLP, 1st edn).

Pleading

Assumed facts

3.2 Unsafe Berth/Port Claim. The Claimants' vessel was chartered to the Defendants on the terms of an amended NYPE 1946 form. She loaded a cargo of grain in Vancouver and proceeded towards Indonesia pending orders as to the discharge port. On 9 February 2004, Charterers designated Jakarta as the discharge port. Following a period at anchor just outside the port, the vessel was finally given orders to proceed to berth on the evening of 27 February 2004. The Owners allege that, as she proceeded to the berth, she struck a submerged obstruction in the main navigation channel which caused damage to her hull. Charterers deny that this was the case and contend that if the damage happened at Jakarta at all, it was due to the vessel leaving the navigation channel.

Hire/Withdrawal Claim. The Claimants' vessel was chartered to the Defendants on the terms of an amended NYPE 93 form. Following payment of the first seven instalments of hire, problems arose at the port of [...] which had been designated for discharge, when a stevedore was injured by one of the vessel's cranes. As a result, the local port authorities prohibited discharge and detained the vessel. This, in turn, resulted in Charterers putting the vessel off-hire, maintaining that the injury was caused by the defective nature of the cranes. Owners maintained that this was not the case and that the injury was caused by stevedore negligence, for which Charterers were responsible under the terms of the charterparty. When Charterers refused to pay hire, Owners served anti-technicality notices under the charter and when no payment was forthcoming withdrew the vessel from the Charterers' service. Due to the fact that Charterers had sub-chartered the vessel, this caused them to lose the hire which would have been payable under the sub-charter until the end of the charter period.

Claim No ....

IN THE HIGH COURT OF JUSTICE
QUEEN'S BENCH DIVISION
COMMERCIAL COURT[1]

B E T W E E N:

Claimants

- and -

Defendants

PARTICULARS OF CLAIM[2]

---

1 The Claimants were at all material times the owners of the bulk carrier 'STURDY' ('the vessel').

2. By a time charter on an amended NYPE 1946 form dated 24th November 2003 ('the charter') the Claimants agreed to charter the vessel to the Defendants for the period and upon the terms more particularly identified in the said charter.

3. The charter, to which the Claimants will refer as may be necessary for its full terms and the precise effect thereof, included the following (among other) express provisions:

'One Timecharter trip via safe port(s), safe berth(s) . . . intention Bulk Wheat from Vancouver to Indonesia

. . .

8. … the Captain (although appointed by the Owners) shall be under the orders and directions of the Charterers as regards employment and agency. . .

. . .

11. . . . the Charterers shall furnish the Captain from time to time with all requisite instructions and sailing directions, in writing . . .'

4. In the premises, the Defendants warranted the safety of any port, berth or place to which the vessel was ordered to proceed during the course of the charter.

5. Further, it was an implied term of the charter, such a term to be implied in order to give business efficacy thereto and/or as reflecting the common intentions of the parties and/or by law, that the Defendants would indemnify the Claimants against the consequences of the Master complying with the Defendants' orders.

6. The vessel was duly delivered to the Defendants and in accordance with their instructions loaded a cargo of grain at Vancouver for carriage to Indonesia.

7. Following the vessel's departure from Vancouver bound for Indonesia, by a telex sent on or about 9th February 2004, the Defendants instructed the vessel to proceed to Jakarta as the discharge port.

8. In accordance with the Defendants' orders, the vessel duly proceeded to Jakarta, arrived off the port and anchored at about 13:00 hrs on 26th February 2003.

9. After a period waiting at anchor, the vessel received instructions to berth late in the evening of 27th February 2003. She duly proceeded towards her berth along the designated approaches assisted at all material times by local pilots. However, as she did so, at about 23:10 hrs the vessel was struck and damaged by an underwater obstruction in a position a little to the North of the breakwater.

PARTICULARS

[*Set out the extent of the damage suffered.*]

10. The aforesaid damage was caused by the Defendants' breach of charterparty in ordering the vessel to proceed to Jakarta which was not a safe port or place.

PARTICULARS

10.1 The Claimants will rely on the fact that that vessel was damaged as aforesaid by an underwater obstruction whilst proceeding to her berth as sufficient evidence of the unsafety of the port;

10.2 Further or alternatively, there was no or no proper system in place at the port to check and/or monitor the safety of the approaches to the port and/or to warn traffic using the approaches of any such danger as might exist. In particular, but without prejudice to the generality of the foregoing:

[*Set out particular features of the port systems which are inadequate.*]

11. By reason of the matters aforesaid, the Claimants have suffered loss and damage as set out in Appendix 'A' served herewith.

12. Further or alternatively, the Defendants are liable to indemnify the Claimants in respect of the aforesaid loss and damage pursuant to the implied term set out at paragraph 5 above, the said loss and damage being the consequence of complying with the Defendants' orders to discharge at Jakarta.

13. Further, the Claimants claim interest pursuant to section 35A of the Supreme Court Act 1981 at such rate for such period as the Court considers just.

AND the claimants claim:

(1) US$, alternatively damages.

(2) Interest pursuant to section 35A of the Supreme Court Act 1981.

(3) Costs.

Served the day of by [ ]. Solicitors for the Claimants.

Statement of Truth

I believe that the facts stated in these Particulars of Claim are true

Full name ....

Signed: ....

Position held: ....

Date ....

<u>Appendix 'A' to the Particulars of Claim</u>

<u>Schedule of Claimants' Loss and Damage</u>

[E.g.]

(a) Cost of repairs.

(b) Additional bunkers used as a result of the damage to the vessel and the need for repairs.

(c) Loss of Hire during repair period.

<u>**TOTAL**</u>

Claim No ....

IN THE HIGH COURT OF JUSTICE
QUEEN'S BENCH DIVISION
COMMERCIAL COURT[3]

B E T W E E N:

Claimants

- and -

Defendants

D E F E N C E

---

1. Paragraph 1 is not admitted.

2. Paragraphs 2 and 3 are admitted. The Defendants will refer to the charterparty therein referred to for its full terms and the precise effect thereof.

3. As to paragraph 4:

   3.1 On the true construction of the charter, the Defendants' obligation was to order the vessel only to ports or berths which, at the time when the order was given, were prospectively safe;

   3.2 Save to the extent the same is consistent with paragraph 3.1 above, the same is denied.

4. No admissions are made as to paragraph 5. Further and in any event, the Defendants will contend that if any indemnity is properly to be implied into charter (as to which no admissions are

made) the same does not, on its true construction, extend the Defendants' obligations in relation to the safety of the port(s) or berth(s) beyond those contained in the express provisions of the charter.

5. Paragraphs 6 and 7 are admitted and averred. The Defendants deny that the port was prospectively unsafe as at the time that they sent the said telex on 9th February 2004.

6. Paragraph 8 is admitted.

7. As to paragraph 9:

   7.1 It is admitted that the vessel waited at anchor and following the receipt of instructions from the port authority proceeded towards her designated berth shortly before 22:40 hrs on 27th February 2003 under pilotage;

   7.2 It is denied that the vessel struck an underwater obstruction in the position alleged. It is further not admitted that the vessel struck an underwater obstruction at all during her approach to the berth;

   7.3 If (which is not admitted) the vessel struck any underwater obstruction during her approach to the berth, then the Defendants will say she did so outside the designated channel and that any loss or damage arising therefrom was caused by the negligence of the vessel's Master and/or pilot in allowing the vessel to stray outside the said channel;

   7.4 Further and in any event, no admissions are made as to the damage allegedly suffered and the Claimants are put to strict proof of the same.

8. Paragraph 10 is denied. Without prejudice to the generality of the foregoing denial, the Defendants will say as follows:

   8.1 As stated in paragraph 7 above, it is not admitted that the vessel struck an underwater object whilst approaching the port and, if she did, she did so outside the designated channel;

   8.2 Further or alternatively, if (which is denied) the vessel struck an underwater obstruction in the designated channel on the night of 27th February 2003 as alleged, the same is no evidence of the prospective unsafety of the vessel when orders were given on 9th February 2003;

   8.3 Further or alternatively, the port was safe in that it had a proper system in place to check and/or monitor the safety of the approaches to the port and/or to warn traffic using the approaches of any such danger as might exist. In particular, but without prejudice to the generality of the foregoing:

   [*Set out particulars of the port systems in place.*]

9. Without prejudice to the fact that they are not liable for the same, the Defendants make no admissions as to the items of loss and damage claimed in paragraph 11 and set out in Appendix 'A' and the Claimants are put to strict proof of the same.

10. As to paragraph 12:

    10.1 As stated above, it is denied that the implied indemnity (if any) imposes any obligations on the Defendants in relation to the safety of the port(s) or berth(s) beyond those contained in the express provisions of the charter;

10.2 In the premises, since the Defendants are not liable to the Claimants pursuant to the express terms of the charter, it is denied that they are liable to the Claimants pursuant to the alleged indemnity;

10.3 Further or alternatively, the Defendants will in any event contend if necessary that any damage suffered by the vessel on the occasion alleged was not caused by the Defendants' orders.

11. Paragraph 13 is noted.

12. Save in so far as is expressly admitted or not admitted above, each and every allegation in the Particulars of Claim is denied as if the same were individually set out and traversed seriatim.

Served the day of by [ ]. Solicitors for the Claimants.

Statement of Truth

I believe that the facts stated in these Particulars of Claim are true

Full name ....

Signed: ....

Position held: ....

Date ....

Claim No ....

IN THE HIGH COURT OF JUSTICE
QUEEN'S BENCH DIVISION
COMMERCIAL COURT[4]

B E T W E E N:

Claimants

- and -

Defendants

PARTICULARS OF CLAIM

---

1. By a time charter on an amended NYPE 93 form dated 24th November 2003 ('the charter') the Defendants agreed to charter the Claimants' vessel 'STURDY' ('the vessel') for a period of six months, 15 days more or less in charterers' option.

2. The charter provided (amongst other things) that:

'7. Charterers to Provide
The Charterers, while the Vessel is on hire, shall provide and pay for all the bunkers ... shall pay for port charges ... all communication expenses ..., pilotages, towages, agencies, commissions ... and all other usual expenses ...

8. Performance of Voyages
... the Charterers shall perform all cargo handling, including but not limited to loading, stowing, trimming, lashing, securing, dunnaging, unlashing, discharging and tallying, at their risk and expense ...

9. Bunkers

(a) The Charterers on delivery and the Owners on redelivery, shall take over and pay for all fuel and diesel oil remaining on board the Vessel as hereunder. The Vessel shall be delivered with .... metric tons of fuel at the price of US$...... per ton; .... tons of diesel oil at the price of US$...... per ton. The vessel shall be redelivered with: .... tons of fuel oil at the price of .... per ton; .... tons of diesel oil at the price of .... per ton.

10. Rate of Hire . . .

The Charterers shall pay for the use and hire of the said Vessel at the rate of $13,500 US currency daily, per 15 days, commencing on and from the day of her delivery . . . hire shall continue until the hour of the day of her redelivery in like good order and condition, ordinary wear and tear excepted . . .

. . .

. . .

11. Hire Payment

(a) Payment

. . . Payment of Hire shall be made so as to be received by the Owners or their designated payee in United States Currency, in funds available to the Owners on the due date, 15 days in advance . . . Failing the punctual and regular payment of the hire, or on any fundamental breach whatsoever of this Charter Party, the Owners shall be at liberty to withdraw the Vessel from the service of the Charterers without prejudice to any claims they (the Owners) may otherwise have on the Charterers.

. . .

At any time after the expiry of the grace period provided in Sub-Clause 11(b) hereunder and while the hire is outstanding, the Owners shall, without prejudice to the liberty to withdraw, be entitled to withhold the performance of any and all of their obligations hereunder and shall have no responsibility whatsoever for any consequences thereof in respect of which the Charterers hereby indemnify the Owners and hire shall continue to accrue and any extra expenses resulting from such withholding shall be for the Charterers' account

. . .

<u>(b) Grace Period</u>

Where there is failure to make punctual and regular payment of hire due to oversight, negligence, errors or omissions on the part of the Charterers or their bankers, the Charterers shall be given by the Owners five clear banking days . . . written notice to rectify the failure and when so rectified within those five days following the Owners' notice, the payment shall stand as regular and punctual.

Failure by the Charterers to pay the hire within five days of their receiving the Owners' notice as provided herein, shall entitle the Owners to withdraw as set forth in Sub-Clause 11(a) above . . .

. . .

<u>29. Crew Overtime</u>

In lieu of any overtime payments to officers and crew for work ordered by the Charterers or their agents, the Charterers shall pay the Owners, with the hire . . . per month or pro rata . . .'

3. The vessel was duly delivered to the Defendants pursuant to the charterparty and the Defendants have subsequently paid the first seven instalments of hire. However, the Defendants have

wrongfully refused and failed to pay any instalments thereafter, in particular, the 8th and 9th instalments of hire.

4. In light of the Defendants' refusal to pay the 8th hire instalment which fell due on or before 16th April 2004, on 17th April 2004, the Claimants served notice on the Defendants pursuant to clause 11(b) of the charterparty requiring payment to be made. Despite service of this notice, no payment was received, whether within the five day grace period provided for in clause 11(b) or at all.

5. Further, no payment was made by the Defendants in respect of the 9th hire instalment which fell due on or before 1st May 2004. Accordingly, on 2nd May 2004, the Claimants served a further notice on the Defendants pursuant to clause 11(b) of the charter requiring payment of both the 8th and 9th hire instalments and reserving the Claimants' rights to withdraw the Vessel in the event that the outstanding hire was not paid.

6. In the absence of payment by the Defendants of any part of the outstanding hire, the Claimants, as they were entitled to do, withdrew the Vessel from the Defendants' service on 8th May 2004.

7. Further or alternatively, the Defendants' failure to pay hire constituted a repudiatory breach of the charter which breach the Claimants accepted by withdrawing the vessel from the Defendants' service.

8. Accordingly:

    8.1 There is due and owing from the Defendants to the Claimants hire in the sum of US$[. . . .] together with [. . . .] in respect of bunkers and [. . . .] in respect of crew overtime, as evidenced by the attached hire statement provided to the Defendants on 10th May 2004;

8.2 In addition, further sums are due and owing pursuant to the terms of the charterparty, particulars of which will be provided in due course;

8.3 Further, the Claimants have suffered additional loss and damage as result of the Defendants' wrongful actions and/or breach of contract in failing to pay hire.

9. Further, the Claimants claim interest pursuant to section 35A of the Supreme Court Act 1981 at such rate for such period as the Court considers just.

AND the claimants claim:

(1) US$, alternatively damages.

(2) Interest pursuant to section 35A of the Supreme Court Act 1981.

(3) Costs.

Served the day of by [ ]. Solicitors for the Claimants.

Statement of Truth

I believe that the facts stated in these Particulars of Claim are true

Full name ....

Signed: ....

Position held: ....

Date ....

Claim No ....

IN THE HIGH COURT OF JUSTICE
QUEEN'S BENCH DIVISION
COMMERCIAL COURT[4]

B E T W E E N:

Claimants

- and -

Defendants

DEFENCE AND COUNTERCLAIM

Paragraphs 1 and 2 are admitted. The charterparty, to which the Defendants will refer as may be necessary for its full terms and the precise effect thereof, further provided as follows:

> '2. Delivery
> … The Vessel on her delivery shall be ready to receive cargo with clean-swept holds and tight, staunch, strong and in every way fitted for ordinary cargo service . . .
>
> . . .
>
> 6. Owners to Provide
> The Owners . . . shall maintain the Vessel's class and keep her in a thoroughly efficient state in hull, machinery and equipment for and during the service. . .
>
> . . .

13. <u>Space Available</u>
(a) the whole reach of the Vessel's holds, decks and other cargo spaces . . . shall be at Charterers' disposal . . .

. . .

17. <u>Off Hire</u>
In the event of loss of time from deficiency and/or default of officers or crew or deficiency of stores, fire, breakdown of, or damages to hull, machinery or equipment . . . or by any other similar cause preventing the full working of the Vessel, the payment of hire and overtime, if any, shall cease for the time thereby lost . . . All bunkers used by the Vessel while off hire shall be for the Owner's account . . .'

2. As to paragraph 3:

2.1 It is admitted and averred that the Defendants have paid the first seven instalments of hire in accordance with the terms of the charter and that they have failed to pay any other sums to the Claimants. No such other sums were due or payable;

2.2 At 17:30 hrs on 15th April 2004, the day before the 8th instalment of hire fell due, the vessel was detained by the authorities in the port of [. . .] where the vessel was discharging pursuant to the Defendants' orders. The authorities detained the vessel due to the unsafe condition of her cranes which resulted in injury to one of the stevedores;

2.3 The vessel remained under detention until 08:00 hrs on 7th May 2004 by which time satisfactory repairs had been carried out by the Claimants;

2.4 In the premises, pursuant to clause 17 of the charter, the Vessel was off-hire from 17:30 hrs on 15th April until 08:00 hrs on 7th May and no hire is due or payable for the said period;

2.5 In fact, the Defendants have overpaid the Claimants in the sum of US$[. . .] as set out in the attached hire statement provided to the Claimants on 10th May 2004.

3. As to paragraphs 4 and 5:

3.1 It is admitted that the Claimants purported to serve a notices pursuant to clause 11(b) of the charter on or about 17th April and 1st May 2004 and it is further admitted that no further payment was made by the Defendants following the service of either notice;

3.2 For the reasons set out above, no further sums were due or owing to the Claimants and, in the premises, each of the notice was wrongly served and/or invalid.

4. As to paragraph 6:

4.1 It is admitted and averred that the Claimants purported to withdraw the vessel from the Defendants' service on or about 8th May 2004;

4.2 By reason of the fact (as stated above) that no sums were due and owing to the Claimants, the said withdrawal was wrongful and/or a repudiatory breach of contract which was accepted by the Defendants by a fax dated 11th May 2004.

5. For the reasons set out above (namely that no sums were due and owing to the Claimants), it is denied that the Defendants were in repudiatory (or any other) breach of contract as alleged in

paragraph 7 and it is denied that the Claimants had any right to withdraw the vessel, whether as alleged therein or at all.

6. Save in so far as is expressly admitted or not admitted above, each and every allegation in the Particulars of Claim is denied as if the same were individually set out and traversed seriatim.

7. For the reasons set out above, it is denied that there are the alleged or any sums due and owing to the Claimants and/or that the Claimants are entitled to the relief claimed, or any relief.

COUNTERCLAIM

8. Paragraphs 1 to 5 above are repeated.

9. In the premises, there is due and owing to the Defendants on the balance of the hire account the sum of US$[. . .].

10. Further or alternatively, by reason of the Claimants' wrongful repudiation of the charter, the Defendants have suffered loss and damage.

PARTICULARS

[E.g.]

The Defendants had sub-chartered the Vessel to [B & Co] at the rate of US$15,000 per day. But for the Claimants' repudiatory breach of contract the Defendants would have continued to earn hire under the sub-charter until [date].

In the premises, the Defendants have suffered loss in the amount of US$. . .

11. Further or alternatively, the Claimants were in breach of clause 1 and/or 2 of the charter in that (as stated above) the vessel had

defective cranes and/or her cranes became defective during the course of the charter. By reason of the said defects, injury was sustained by one of the stevedores, to whom the Defendants have been obliged to pay compensation in the amount of US$[. . .]. In the premises, the Defendants claim the said sum as damages.

12. Further, the Defendants claim interest pursuant to section 35A of the Supreme Court Act 1981 at such rate for such period as the Court considers just.

AND the defendants counterclaim:

(1) US$, alternatively damages.

(2) Interest pursuant to section 35A of the Supreme Court Act 1981.

(3) Costs.

Served the day of by [ ]. Solicitors for the Defendants.

Statement of Truth

I believe that the facts stated in this Defence and Counterclaim are true

Full name . . . .

Signed: . . . .

Position held: . . . .

Date . . . .

1 This claim may also be brought in the Admiralty Court.
2 This statement of case is loosely based on that in *The Marinicki* [2003] 2 Lloyd's Rep 655.
3 This claim may also be brought in the Admiralty Court.
4 This claim is technically within the jurisdiction of the Admiralty Court, but would normally be brought in the Commercial Court if it was not referred to arbitration.

VOYAGE CHARTERPARTIES

Law

3.3 A voyage charterparty is a contract to carry specified goods on a defined voyage or voyage. The most common form of voyage charterparty in use is the Gencon form although the standard form will almost always be subject to additional provisions (of which the most important may be the 'Clause Paramount' or variation thereof). A detailed study of the law relating to voyage charterparties is beyond the scope of this chapter[1].

The pleadings set out below deal with particular disputes which frequently arise in relation to voyage charterparties.

In the 'Freight/Demurrage' pleading, the shipowner is seeking to recover freight and demurrage. The shipowner's remuneration for the carriage is by freight, in contrast, for example, to the payment of daily hire under a standard time charterparty. The precise basis upon which freight is calculated and earned depends upon the terms of the charterparty: for example, it may be earned on the quantity of cargo loaded or discharged and may be payable on shipment or delivery. Claims (whether liquidated or unliquidated) for damages for breach of charterparty cannot generally be set off in diminution or extinction of a claim for freight[2]. Demurrage represents a sum agreed by the charterer to be paid as liquidated damages for delay beyond a stipulated time for loading and discharging (known as lay-days or laytime) or a reasonable time for loading and discharging[3]. The voyage charterparty itself will usually contain detailed provisions as to the commencement of laytime and demurrage and the circumstances in which time is not to count towards laytime and demurrage. Apart from any specific contractual provision, delay caused by the fault of the shipowner or for those for whom the shipowner is responsible and which deprives the charter of access to the vessel will not generally count towards laytime or time on demurrage.

In the second set of pleadings, the charterer is claiming for cargo damage. The voyage charterer is often also the owner of the cargo. The standard form of Gencon does not incorporate the Hague or Hague-Visby Rules or the United States Carriage of Goods By Sea Act 1936 but may do so through a 'Clause Paramount' or variation thereof. In the absence of such a provision, the liability of the shipowner may be limited to 'personal' default in contrast to Article III, Rule 1 of the Hague or Hague-Visby Rules.

1 See further, *Voyage Charters* (LLP, 2nd edn) and *Scrutton on Charterparties* (Sweet & Maxwell, 20th edn).
2 See *Aries Tanker Corporation v Total Transport* [1977] 1 Lloyd's Rep 334.
3 See further, Schofield *Laytime and Demurrage* (4th edn).

Pleading

Assumed facts

3.4 The shipowners, Lady Eleanor S.A. ('the Owners'), have agreed to charter their vessel the 'LADY ELEANOR' to Sophie Chartering Inc ('the Charterers') for the carriage of a cargo of wheat from Cape Town to Antwerp. The Owners claim is for (a) outstanding freight and (b) demurrage earned in respect of delay during the course of discharge. The Charterers contend that there is no liability for demurrage primarily because periods of delay at Antwerp were the Owners' fault and because the Owners' calculation has taken into account a Sunday. As regards the freight claim, the Charterers dispute the Owners' calculation and have already tendered the amount which (they allege) is due and owing. In accordance with CPR 37.3, the amount tendered must be paid into court in order to be effective.

In the second pleading, the Charterers claim for damage to their cargo. The Charterers rely upon the condition of the cargo upon discharge (damaged by sea water) as well as the defective condition of the hatch covers. The Owners deny liability on the grounds of heavy weather and say that condition of the hatch covers was not the result of any personal default on their part.

Freight/Demurrage

Claim No ....

IN THE HIGH COURT OF JUSTICE
QUEEN'S BENCH DIVISION
COMMERCIAL COURT

B E T W E E N:

LADY ELEANOR S.A.

Claimants

- and -

SOPHIE CHARTERING INC

Defendants

PARTICULARS OF CLAIM

---

1. By a Voyage Charterparty on an amended Gencon form dated 21st December 2003 ('the Charterparty'), the Claimants, as Owners, agreed to charter the 'LADY ELEANOR' ('the vessel') to the Defendants, as Charterers, for the carriage of a cargo of wheat in bulk from Cape Town to Antwerp.

2. The Charterparty, to which the Claimants will refer for its full terms and effect, provided (*inter alia*) as follows:

   '[Box] 13. Freight rate (also state whether freight prepaid or payable on delivery) (Cl.4)
   US$50 per mt.
   80% prepaid; 20% on delivery

[Box] 16. Laytime (if separate laytime for load and discharge is agreed, fill in (a) and (b). If total laytime for load. and discharge, fill in (c) only (Cl.6)

(a) Laytime for loading: 72 hours

(b) Laytime for discharging: 72 hours

(c) Total laytime for loading and discharging.

[Box] 20. Demurrage rate and manner payable (loading and discharging) (Cl.7)

US$6,000 per day or pro rata to be paid into the Owners' designated freight account

PART II

4. Payment of Freight

(a) The freight at the rate stated in Box 13 shall be paid in cash calculated on the intake quantity of cargo.

(b) *Prepaid.* If according to Box 13 freight is to be paid on shipment, it shall be deemed earned and non-returnable, Vessel and/or cargo lost or not lost.

Neither the Owners nor their agents shall be required to sign or endorse bills of lading showing freight prepaid unless the freight due to the Owners has actually been paid.

(c) *On delivery.* If according to Box 13 freight, or part thereof, is payable at destination it shall not be deemed earned until the cargo is thus delivered. Notwithstanding the provisions under (a), if freight or part thereof is payable on delivery of the cargo the Charterers shall have the option of paying the freight on delivered weight/quantity provided such option is declared before breaking bulk and the weight/quantity can be ascertained by official weighing machine, joint draft survey or tally.

Cash for Vessel's ordinary disbursements at the port of loading to be advanced by the Charterers, if required, at highest current rate of exchange . . .

6. Laytime

**(a) Separate laytime for loading and discharging*

The cargo shall be loaded within the number of running days/hours as indicated in Box 16, weather permitting, Sundays and holidays excepted, unless used, in which event time actually used shall count.

The cargo shall be discharged within the number of running days/hours as indicated in Box 16, weather permitting, Sundays and holidays excepted, unless used, in which event time used shall count.

**(b) Total laytime for loading and discharging*

The cargo shall be loaded and discharged within the number of total running days/hours as indicated in Box 16, weather permitting, Sundays and holidays excepted, unless used, in which event time used shall count.

(c) Commencement of laytime (loading and discharging)

Laytime for loading and discharging shall commence at 13:00 hrs, if notice of readiness is given up to and including 12:00 hrs, and at 06:00 hrs next working day if notice given during office hours after 12:00 hrs. Notice of readiness at loading port to be given to the Shippers named in Box 17 or if not named, to the Charterers or their agents named in Box 18. Notice of readiness at the discharging port to be given to the Receivers or, if not known, to the Charterers or their agents named in Box 19.

If the loading/discharging berth is not available on the Vessel's arrival at or off the port of loading/discharging, the Vessel shall be entitled to give notice of readiness within ordinary office hours on arrival there, whether in free pratique or not, whether customs cleared or not. Laytime or time on demurrage shall then count as if she were in berth and in all respects ready for loading/discharging provided that the Master warrants that she is in fact ready in all respects. Time used in moving from the place of waiting to the loading/discharging berth shall not count as laytime . . .

7. Demurrage

Demurrage at the loading and discharging port is payable by the Charterers at the rate stated in Box 20 in the manner stated in Box 20 per day or pro rata for any part of a day. Demurrage shall fall due day by day and shall be payable upon receipt of the Owners' invoice . . .'

3. Pursuant to the Charterparty the vessel proceeded to Cape Town where it duly loaded a cargo of 11,642 mts of wheat pursuant to a Bill of Lading No. 1 dated 1st January 2004.

4. Pursuant to Box 13 and clause 4 of the Charterparty, the Defendants duly paid the sum of US$465,680 which represented 80% of the total freight (namely US$582,100) in respect of the cargo.

5. The vessel arrived at Antwerp on Thursday 22nd January 2004. Notice of Readiness was tendered at 14:00 hrs on the same day. In the premises and pursuant to clause 6(c), laytime for the discharge of the cargo commenced at 06:00 hrs on Friday 23rd January and expired at 06:00 hrs on Monday 26th January.

6. However, wrongfully and in breach of Charterparty the Defendants did not complete discharge until 11:25 hrs on Friday 30th January 2004.

7. In the premises the vessel was on demurrage from 06:00 hrs on 26th January until 11:25 hrs on 30th January, a period of four days 5 hours 25 minutes (4.23 days) and the sum of US$25,380 is due and owing from the Defendants to the Claimants. [*Or set out the demurrage calculation in a Schedule.*]

8. However, wrongfully and in breach of Charterparty the Defendants have failed and/or refused to pay the sum of US$25,380 or any part thereof.

9. Further upon completion of discharge and delivery of the cargo, the 20% balance of freight became due and owing from the Defendants to the Claimants in the sum of US$116,420.

10. However, wrongfully and in breach of Charterparty, the Defendants have failed and/or refused to pay the sum of US$104,778 or any part thereof and the sum of US$104,778 remains due and owing.

11. The Claimants will claim interest on these amounts pursuant to the Supreme Court Act 1981, section 35A, at such rate and for such period as the Court may consider appropriate.

AND the claimants claim:

(1) Under paragraphs 8 and 10 respectively US$25,380 (in respect of demurrage) and US$104,778 (in respect of freight) or alternatively damages;

(2) Under paragraph 11 interest pursuant to of the Supreme Court Act 1981, section 35A;

(3) Costs.

[Statement of Truth, etc][1]

Claim No ....

IN THE HIGH COURT OF JUSTICE
QUEEN'S BENCH DIVISION
COMMERCIAL COURT

B E T W E E N:

LADY ELEANOR S.A.

Claimants

- and -

SOPHIE CHARTERING INC

Defendants

D E F E N C E

---

1. Paragraphs 1 and 2 of the Particulars of Claim are admitted. The Charterparty, to which the Defendants will also refer for its full terms and effect, further provided (*inter alia*).

2. Paragraphs 3 and 4 of the Particulars of Claim are admitted.

3. As regards paragraph 5 of the Particulars of Claim:

    3.1 It is admitted that the vessel arrived at Antwerp on Thursday 22nd January and purported to tender Notice of Readiness at 14:00 hrs on the same day.

    3.2 However, it is denied that the Notice of Readiness tendered was valid whether as alleged or at all. Upon her arrival at Antwerp the vessel failed Port State Control as a result of the following deficiencies which were required to be remedied before the vessel was entitled to berth. [*Set out the particular respects which render the Notice of Readiness ineffective.*]

3.3 At 07:30 hrs on Monday 26th January the vessel passed Port State Control and the Claimants tendered a Notice of Readiness at 08:00 hrs. In the premises, and pursuant to clause 6(c) of the Charterparty, laytime for the discharge of the cargo commenced at 13:00 hrs on 26th January and expired at 13:00 hrs on 29th January 2004.

3.4 In any event, even if laytime commenced at 06:00 hrs on Friday 23rd January, it did not expire until 06:00 hrs on Tuesday 27th January. Pursuant to clause 6 of the Charterparty Sunday is excepted unless used and no work was in fact carried out on Sunday 25th January 2004.

4. As regards paragraphs 6–8 of the Particulars of Claim:

4.1 It is admitted that the vessel did not complete discharge of the cargo until 11:25 hrs on Friday 30th January 2004.

4.2 It is denied that the vessel was on demurrage for a period of 4.23 days whether as alleged or at all.

4.3 The discharge of the vessel should have been completed by (at the latest) 13:00 hrs on 29th January, namely the expiry of laytime. The failure and/or inability of the vessel to complete discharge within this time was caused by fault of the Claimants, their servants or agents, in that it was not possible to open the hatch covers and to discharge the cargo on 27th January as a result of their defective condition.

4.4 Further or alternatively if, contrary to the Defendants' primary case as set out under (4.3) above the vessel was on demurrage, the vessel was in any event only on demurrage from 13:00 hrs on 29th January to 11:25 hrs on 30th January, a period of 0.93 days. In the premises, the sum of US$5,604 was due and owing from the Defendants to the Claimants in respect of demurrage.

4.5 Save as aforesaid paragraphs 6–8 of the Particulars of Claim are denied.

5. As regards paragraphs 9–11 of the Particulars of Claim:

5.1 Upon discharge of the cargo and pursuant to clause 4(c) of the Charterparty, the Defendants declared their option to pay freight on the delivered weight of cargo as ascertained by the official weighing machine. The delivered weight of the cargo was determined as 11,108 mts and the freight due in respect thereof was US$555,400.

5.2 In the premises, the balance of freight due and owing to the Claimants is US$89,720, namely US$555,400 – US$465,680. The Defendants tendered the amount of US$89,720 to the Claimants on 5th February 2004 and paid the money into Court pursuant to CPR Part 37.3.

5.3 Save as aforesaid paragraphs 9–11 of the Particulars of Claim are denied.

6. In the premises, it is denied that the Claimants are entitled to the relief claimed in the Particulars of Claim or at all.

7. Save as is admitted or not admitted each and every allegation contained in the Particulars of Claim is denied.

[Statement of Truth, etc][1]

Cargo Claim

<u>Claim No ....</u>

<u>IN THE HIGH COURT OF JUSTICE</u>
<u>QUEEN'S BENCH DIVISION</u>
<u>COMMERCIAL COURT</u>

B E T W E E N:

SOPHIE CHARTERING INC

<u>Claimants</u>

- and -

LADY ELEANOR S.A.

<u>Defendants</u>

PARTICULARS OF CLAIM

---

1. By a Voyage Charterparty on an amended Gencon form dated 21st December 2003 ('the Charterparty'), the Claimants, as Charterers, agreed to charter the 'LADY ELEANOR' ('the vessel') from the Defendants, as Owners, for the carriage of a cargo of wheat in bulk from Cape Town to Antwerp.

2. The Charterparty, to which the Claimants will refer for its full terms and effect, provided (*inter alia*) as follows:

   '2. Owners' Responsibility Clause
   The Owners are to be responsible for loss or damage to the goods or for delay in delivery of the goods only in case the loss, damage or delay has been caused by personal want of due diligence on the part of the Owners or their Manager to make the Vessel in all

respects seaworthy and to secure that she is properly manned, equipped and supplied, or by the personal act or default of the Owners or their Manager . . .

(Additional Clause 20)

Vessel to have clean and dry holds to charterers' satisfaction and to be suitable in all respects for the loading and carriage of wheat in bulk.'

3. Pursuant to the Charterparty the vessel proceeded to Cape Town where it duly loaded a cargo of 11,642 mts of wheat pursuant to a Bill of Lading No. 1 dated 1st January 2004.

4. The Claimants were at all material times the charterers of the vessel and/or the owners and/or shippers of the cargo.

5. In the premises, the Defendants owed the Claimants a contractual duty of care and/or a duty of care as carriers and/or bailees for reward:

    5.1 to take reasonable care of the cargo whilst the cargo was in its possession and control, and

    5.2 to deliver the cargo in the same good order and condition as upon shipment.

6. Upon arrival of the vessel at Antwerp and discharge of the cargo it was discovered that substantial quantity of cargo had been damaged by sea water.

PARTICULARS

[*Set out the nature and extent of the cargo damage*]

7. The damage was caused by the Defendants' breach of Charterparty and/or duty and/or negligence in that:

7.1 The holds were not suitable in all respects for the loading and carriage of wheat in bulk; and/or

7.2 The Defendants, their servants or agents, failed to take reasonable care of the cargo whilst the cargo was in its possession and control; and/or

7.3 The Defendants, their servants or agents, failed to deliver the cargo in the same good order and condition as upon shipment.

PARTICULARS

7.3.1 Without prejudice to the burden of proof (which rests upon the Defendants as bailees for reward), the Claimants will rely upon the condition of the cargo upon discharge as sufficient evidence of the Defendants' breach of contract and/or duty and/or negligence.

7.3.2 Further or alternatively:

7.3.2.1 The packing of the hatch covers was old and wasted so that it was unable to create a proper seal of the hatch covers and to prevent the ingress of sea water into the holds;

7.3.2.2 The hatch covers were corroded and/or insufficiently secure to withstand the ordinary weather conditions which the vessel experienced during the course of the voyage;

[*Set out here any further specific particulars as to why the holds were unsuitable.*]

8. Further or alternatively, wrongfully and/or in breach of clause 2 of the Charterparty, the damage was caused by the personal want of due diligence on the part of the Defendants or their managers to make the vessel seaworthy and/or by the personal act or default of the Defendants or their managers.

PARTICULARS

[*Set out any specific allegations in relation to breach of the Owners' personal obligations for breach of clause 2, e.g.:*

(a) The Defendants had no or no proper system for ensuring the upkeep of the hatch covers.

(b) Hatch cover inspections were random and infrequent.

(c) Hatch cover maintenance was not fully addressed in the vessel's SMS manual.

(d) In August 2003, Class noted that the hatch covers were 'severely deteriorated due to years of neglect'.]

9. By reason of these matters the Claimants have suffered loss and damage amounting to [*amount*].

PARTICULARS

[*Set out the nature and extent of the financial loss and damage including any consequential loss claims.*]

10. The Claimants will claim interest on these amounts pursuant to the Supreme Court Act 1981, section 35A, at such rate and for such period as the Court may consider appropriate.

AND the claimants claim:

(1) Under paragraphs 9 [*amount*] or alternatively damages;

(2) Under paragraph 10 interest pursuant to of the Supreme Court Act 1981, section 35A;

(3) Costs.

[Statement of Truth, etc][1]

Claim No ....

IN THE HIGH COURT OF JUSTICE
QUEEN'S BENCH DIVISION
COMMERCIAL COURT

B E T W E E N:

SOPHIE CHARTERING INC

Claimants

- and -

LADY ELEANOR S.A.

Defendants

D E F E N C E

---

1. Paragraphs 1 and 2 of the Particulars of Claim are admitted. The Charterparty, to which the Defendants will also refer for its full terms and effect, further provided (*inter alia*):

   '… [a]nd the Owners are not responsible for loss, damage or delay arising from any other cause whatsoever, even from the neglect or default of the Master or crew or some other person employed by the Owners on board or ashore for whose acts they would, but for this clause, be responsible, or from unseaworthiness of the Vessel on loading or commencement of the voyage or at any time whatsoever.'

   [*Set out any further specific terms of the Charterparty which are relied upon.*]

2. Paragraph 3 of the Particulars of Claim is admitted.

3. No admissions are made as to paragraph 4 of the Particulars of Claim. The Claimants are put to strict proof of their alleged title to sue.

4. Paragraph 5 of the Particulars of Claim is denied. The duties owed by the Defendants to the Claimants were set out in the Charterparty.

5. No admissions are made as to paragraph 6 of the Particulars of Claim and as to how much wetting (if any) was caused by sea water.

6. Paragraphs 7 and 8 of the Particulars of Claim are denied. It is denied that any alleged damage was caused by the Defendants' breach of Charterparty and/or duty whether as alleged or at all.

7. Further or alternatively if, which is not admitted, any cargo was damaged by sea water, any such damage was caused by perils of the sea, namely heavy weather experienced during the voyage, for which the Defendants are not responsible pursuant to clause 2.

PARTICULARS

[*Give details of the heavy weather conditions encountered during the course of the voyage.*]

8. Further or alternatively, any alleged loss and damage was not caused by any personal want of due diligence on the part of the Defendants or their managers to make the vessel seaworthy and/or to secure that the vessel was properly manned, equipped and supplied, or by the personal act or default of the Defendants or their managers.

PARTICULARS

8.1 In August 2003, the Defendants carried out extensive repairs to the vessel and her hatch covers whilst the vessel was in dry-dock in Lisbon.

8.2 Following the repairs, in September 2003, the vessel was subject to and passed her special survey free of recommendations.

8.3 Following the special survey, the vessel performed two laden voyages (for the carriage of foodstuff in bulk) from Lisbon to Hong Kong and thereafter from Singapore to Durban. During the course of neither voyage did the cargo sustain any damage nor was there any sea water ingress into the holds.

8.4 At no stage did the master or officers of the vessel inform the Defendants that the hatch covers were in a defective condition or that there was sea water ingress into the vessel's holds.

8.5 [Any further particulars to demonstrate the absence of personal fault.]

8.6 In the premises, it is denied that any alleged loss and damage was not caused by any personal want of due diligence on the part of the Defendants or their managers to make the vessel seaworthy and/or to secure that the vessel was properly manned, equipped and supplied, or by the personal act or default of the Defendants or their managers.

9. Save that it is denied that the Defendants acted in breach of Charterparty and are liable to the Claimants whether as alleged in

paragraphs 9 and 10 of the Particulars of Claim, no admissions are made to as to any alleged loss and damage suffered by the Claimants.

10. In the premises it is denied that the Claimants are entitled to the relief claimed in the Particulars of Claim or at all.

11. Save as is admitted or not admitted each and every allegation contained in the Particulars of Claim is denied.

[Statement of Truth, etc][1]

1 Statement of truth, etc as set out in **para 3.2** of this chapter.

CHAPTER 4

Shipping – Bills of Lading

Simon Rainey QC
Ruth Hosking

CARGO CLAIMS

Law

4.1

> 'A bill of lading is a document issued by a carrier by sea to a shipper of goods acknowledging the receipt by the carrier on board a named vessel (or for subsequent shipment on board) of the goods described therein and containing an undertaking to deliver the goods at the place of delivery to the shipper or named consignee or to his order or assigns, subject to the terms and conditions set out in or incorporated into the document. It represents the right to possession of the goods and therefore, if an 'order' bill, allows traders to deal with the goods while they are at sea, the carrier automatically attorning to the holder on the terms of the bill[1].'

Bills of lading vary greatly in their type, in the circumstances in which and for which they are issued and in their form. They may therefore be 'charterparty' bills, bills of lading issued under a voyage or time charterparty relating to the vessel on which the goods have been shipped or 'liner' bills issued by the carrier in a liner service. They may be 'order' bills under which the goods are to be delivered to the person named in the bill as consignee or to his order so that the bill can be negotiated or they may be 'straight bills' under which the goods can only be delivered to a named party. They may be issued for one sea voyage or for a transit involving carriage by land as well as by sea in various stages, the 'combined transport' or 'multi-modal' bill. They may be issued on well-known industry-wide or recommended forms, such as the BIMCO 'Conlinebill' or the 'Congenbill', or on a particular carrier's or line's house forms.

For present purposes, however, any bill of lading can be regarded as ordinarily having three functions all of which need to be borne in mind when drafting a claim or defence:

(1) a receipt issued by the carrier for the goods shipped;
(2) a contract of carriage between the carrier and the shipper or others interested in the goods; and
(3) a document of title which gives certain parties the right to possession of the goods and which may be negotiable.

Similarly, for present purposes, any bill of lading will usually consist of a printed form consisting of two sides with, on the face, spaces left for the entry of the details of the goods shipped, the voyage, the date of shipment and the signature of the person issuing the bill and, on the reverse, printed standard terms and conditions which may vary greatly in length and nature.

The width of this topic prevents any more than a very basic introduction to some of the more common problems facing the pleader in a bill of lading cargo claim. Reference should in all cases be made to one of the leading textbooks: the most recent of which is *Carver on Bills of Lading* (Treitel, Reynolds, 2001); see also chapter 18 of Cooke et al *Voyage Charters* (2nd edn, 2001); *Scrutton on Charterparties*, Boyd, Burrows, Foxton (20th edn, 1996). For a looseleaf encyclopaedia of common forms and types of bills of lading with a full commentary see too Gaskell *Contracts for the Carriage of Goods*.

For the purposes of this book, the very common situation of a bill of lading issued under a charterparty (other than a charter by demise) is considered. In this situation, the pleader is likely to encounter four issues particular to bill of lading cargo claims:

(1) Who is the carrier?
(2) Who can sue for loss or damage to the goods?
(3) What are the relevant terms of the contract of carriage?
(4) What does the bill of lading evidence as to the condition of the goods when shipped?

1 This definition is taken from Cooke et al *Voyage Charters* (2nd edn, 2001), para 18.1. See also *Borealis AB v Stargas Ltd (The Berge Sisar)* [2001] 1 Lloyd's Rep 663 per Lord Hobhouse at para 18ff.

Who is the carrier?

4.2 In the case of a charterparty bill of lading, the identification of the person who has accepted the contractual responsibility for the damage of the goods is complicated by the fact that the owners of the carrying vessel may not have issued the bill of lading; this may have been issued by the charterers of the vessel, or by one of the various charterers of the vessel if the vessel (as is common) is the subject of a chain of sub-charterparties both time and voyage charters. Is it an 'owners' bill' or a 'charterers' bill'?

The answer lies in the analysis of the external form of the bill (is it a charterers' house or company form or is it on the owners' form), of the terms of the bill of lading in so far as they contain any express term which purports to identify the carrier and of the form and terms in which it has been signed, stamped and issued, usually in a box left for the dating and signing of the bill of lading on the face of the bill where the shipment details are recorded. The resolution of these different factors to arrive at the correct construction of the bill of lading is often difficult and, as the cases demonstrate, can turn on small differences in the wording from one bill of lading to another bill of lading. To take some examples:

(1) where a bill is issued on a sub-time charterers' house form and was signed by agents '*for the master*', the bill was held to be an owners' bill[1];

(2) where a bill was issued on a liner service house form and was signed by the line's agents in the signature box worded '*in witness whereof the master of the vessel has signed*' with the words '*as agents for the line as carriers*' and '*as agents for the carrier (the line)*', the effect of the signature even in these terms was held to be overridden by two printed clauses on the reverse of the bill, one of which identified the carrier as the owner and the other (a 'demise clause') stating that the line was not the principal and that the contract was with the owner or demise charterers of the vessel[2];

(3) however, where a bill was issued by charterers' agents with typed words stating charterers to be 'carriers', signed '*for and on behalf of the master*' and with a clause identifying owners as carriers, the bill was held to be a charterers' bill notwithstanding the printed clause[3].

In the recent decision of *The Starsin*[4], the House of Lords considered the correct approach where the bill of lading was similar to the second example above and where the courts below were divided as to whether the signatures and typed wording should prevail over the printed 'identification of carrier' clauses (as in the third example) or vice versa (as in the second example). It held that in so far as there were inconsistencies between statements on the face of the bill and general descriptions elsewhere, it was common sense that greater weight should attach to terms that the parties had chosen to include in the contract than to pre-printed terms on the reverse of the bill. Accordingly, the House of Lords agreed with Rix LJ's dissenting judgment in the Court of Appeal for essentially the reasons he gave and held that the signatures and typed wording should prevail over the printed 'identification of carrier' clauses on the reverse of the bill.

1 *The Rewia* [1991] 2 Lloyd's Rep 325.
2 *The Flecha* [1999] 1 Lloyd's Rep 612.
3 *The Hector* [1998] 2 Lloyd's Rep 287; compare *The Ines* [1995] 2 Lloyd's Rep 144.
4 [2003] 1 Lloyd's Rep 571; Times Law Reports, 17 March 2003.

Who is entitled to sue the carrier?

4.3 In the case of every bill of lading, it is necessary to identify the person who is entitled to sue the carrier in respect of the loss or damage to the goods (or otherwise for breach of the bill of lading contract). This question of 'title to sue' is invariably focused on by the carrier when considering its defences to see if the claim can be defeated on this simple ground.

The law as it relates to bills of lading issued before 16 September 1992 was highly complex. For bills issued after that date the relevant law is principally found in the Carriage of Goods by Sea Act 1992. That Act introduces the concept of the 'lawful holder' of a bill of lading. The lawful holder is entitled to sue on the contract contained in or evidenced by the bill of lading whether or not he has suffered the loss or damage and simply by virtue of being the lawful holder: Carriage of Goods by Sea Act 1992, s 2(1). The main categories of people who qualify as 'lawful holder' under Carriage of Goods by Sea Act 1992, s 5(2) are a consignee named in the bill of lading who is in possession of the bill and a person who is in possession of the bill by virtue of the completion, by delivery to him of the bill of lading, of the endorsement of that bill to him.

The important point to note is that the transfer of the bill of lading from shipper to lawful holder and from lawful holder to any further lawful holder has the effect of extinguishing the rights of the transferor: Carriage of Goods by Sea Act 1992, s 2(5). Therefore, there can only be one person entitled to sue at the time the claim is brought, either the original shipper if the bill has not been transferred, or the ultimate transferee and lawful holder if it has been. In the case of the original shipper, there may be collateral rights which survive the transfer of the bill: as to this see the textbooks referred to above.

What are the terms of the contract of carriage?

4.4 Where the shipper sues on a bill of lading, while it is possible that the bill of lading is not the relevant contract of carriage since it is issued as a mere receipt of goods where the goods have been shipped under a pre-existing contract or booking note[1], 'it is rarely questioned in practice that the bill of lading accurately records the terms of the contract' between shipper and carrier[2].

Where the bill of lading has been issued by the owners of the vessel to the charterers of the vessel because they are the shippers of the goods or is held by the charterers as the consignees of them, then the ordinary rule is that in the charterers' hands the bill of lading is merely a receipt for the goods and the relevant contract of carriage is that set out in the charterparty between owners and charterers[3].

These two special cases apart, in the hands of the shipper, consignee or indorsee the bill of lading will usually contain and evidence the terms of the contract of carriage. Two common questions arise as to what are the terms and conditions of the bill of lading contract.

The first is whether the bill of lading incorporates the terms of any charterparty under which it was issued. Many bills contain some form of incorporation provision as part of their printed terms, e.g. '*all terms, conditions and exceptions of the charterparty referred to on the face are incorporated herein*'. However, narrower or different formulations are often found: '*freight and other terms as per charterparty dated [...]*'. It is necessary to identify the relevant incorporating words in the bill and then construe these to see what charter terms are apt to be incorporated (see for examples of the different results which may be produced: *Scrutton on Charterparties* (20th edn) pp 77–79).

The general rule is that however wide the words of incorporation used, they will still incorporate only those terms of the charterparty which relate directly to the core obligations under the bill of lading namely the shipment, carriage and delivery of the goods and the payment of freight[4]. Even if the incorporation provision is apt to comprise the charter term in question, if the charter term when written out in the bill of lading requires verbal manipulation to make it 'fit' in the bill of lading context, the term may be rejected even if it is directly germane to the core obligations under the bill. A bill which incorporates '*all the terms whatsoever of the charterparty*' was held not to incorporate a charter term 'Charterer shall pay demurrage' and 'Owner shall have an absolute lien on the cargo for freight, dead freight and demurrage' because of the need to manipulate the term 'charterer' to read 'bill of lading holder'[5].

A common feature of an incorporation provision is that it refers to '*the charterparty dated [...]*' but fails to identify it by date or otherwise. Which charter, if any, is incorporated? If there is only one charterparty, then it will be effectively incorporated notwithstanding the absence of specific identification and whether it is a time or voyage charter. If there is a head charter between owners and charterers and then successive sub-charters, the general rule is that the incorporation is presumed to be that of the head charter because that is the only charter to which the owner is party[6], at least where the carrier is the owner not the charterer[7]. This presumption may be displaced where the head charter is a time charter and there is a voyage charter covering the bill of lading carriage voyage[8].

The second common question is whether the bill of lading incorporates or is otherwise subject to the Hague or Hague-Visby Rules, respectively being the Rules adopted by an International Convention in 1924 and the 1924 Rules as amended by a further International Convention in 1968, which regulate the rights and liabilities of sea carriers under bills of lading contracts. Space does not permit any analysis of the application of the Rules or their content for which reference must be made to ch 85 of Cooke et al *Voyage Charters* (2nd edn, 2001); *Scrutton on Charterparties* (20th edn); ch 9 of *Carver on Bills of Lading* (2001) and Tetley *Marine Cargo Claims* (3rd edn, 1988)[9].

In very broad outline, as a matter of English law, Carriage of Goods by Sea Act 1971, s 1, the Hague-Visby Rules have 'force of law' with the result that the English court is bound to give effect to the Rules as to bills of lading falling within the Rules where the Rules provide they are to apply, irrespective of any choice of proper law or jurisdiction clause in the bill of lading[10]. The Hague-Visby Rules provide that they are to apply compulsorily in the case of international carriage by sea, where the goods were shipped in a contracting state or if the bill of lading was issued in a contracting state, irrespective of the place of discharge: see Article X of the Rules. Even if neither condition is satisfied the Rules apply compulsorily if the bill of lading expressly provides for the Rules to govern the contract: see Carriage of Goods by Sea Act 1971, s 1(6). If none of the criteria for compulsory application are satisfied, then it is a question of the construction of the bill of lading terms (and of any terms incorporated into the bill from any charterparty) as to whether the earlier

Hague or later Hague-Visby Rules apply. Many bills of lading contain provisions incorporating the Hague Rules (or local legislation in other countries giving effect to them, e.g. the US Carriage of Goods by Sea Act 1936) or incorporate similar provisions in charterparties; these provisions are usually referred to as '*Clauses Paramount*' and even the single reference to '*Clause Paramount incorporated herein*' may be effective[11].

The scheme of both sets of Rules is to impose a code of duties and liabilities on sea carriers together with a codified set of exceptions from liability. Article III, Rule 1 of both sets of Rules requires the carrier to exercise due diligence to provide a seaworthy vessel while Article III, Rule 2 requires the carrier to carry out properly and carefully any operation for which he is responsible in relation to the goods. Article IV, Rule 2 sets out exceptions to liability such as perils of the sea, fire, insufficiency of packing, inherent vice. Reference to the Rules, both in terms of how they are incorporated and what provisions are relied upon, is a standard part of any bill of lading pleading where the Rules apply. The incidence of the burden of proof on the cargo claimant and the defending carrier in respect of particular alleged breaches of the Hague or Hague-Visby Rules, is important and should be correctly reflected in the pleading.

In outline:

(a) For an alleged breach of duty to provide a seaworthy vessel under Article III, Rule 1 the claimant must allege and prove that the loss or damage resulted from unseaworthiness; once unseaworthiness causative of the loss or damage is proved, the carrier must prove that he exercised due diligence to make the vessel seaworthy and that the loss could not have been prevented by due diligence[12]. While it is not necessary therefore for the claimant to allege a want of due diligence in the claim and it can simply traverse any case of due diligence which the carrier pleads in its defence or join issue with it in its reply, it is common for the claimant to plead not only the unseaworthiness and the loss caused by it but also want of due diligence[13].

(b) For an alleged breach of Article III, Rule 2 and the duty to care properly for the cargo the position is more complex. By analogy with bailment, the goods owner needs only to allege that the goods were shipped in a certain quantity and in a sound condition and were not delivered in that quantity and/or condition or were not delivered at all[14]. However by analogy with ordinary cases of breach of duty/negligence, it would be necessary for the goods owner to allege and prove the breach of duty (even if reliance can be placed on the maxim *res ipsa loquitur*)[15]. The better practice, it is suggested, is to rely on the loss or damage to the goods as in bailment but to add where possible an allegation of breach of duty as specifically particularised as the information available to the claimant permits. The carrier must, to escape liability, allege and prove the operation of an excepted peril under Article IV, Rule 2 and that no non-excepted peril operated. Where two perils, one excepted and one not, apply, the carrier must identify what part of the loss or damage was caused by the excepted peril; if he cannot do so, the exception is ineffective[16]. If the carrier alleges and proves the operation of an excepted peril, the burden probably passes to the claimant to prove want of care by the carrier in order to displace the exception[17].

1 *Pyrene v Scindia Navigation Co* [1954] 2 QB 402, per Devlin J at pp 419, 424.
2 Cooke et al *Voyage Charters* (2nd edn, 2001) para 18.46.
3 *President of India v Metcalfe* [1969] 2 QB 123; [1970] 1 QB 289.
4 *Miramar Shipping v Holborn Oil (The Miramar)* [1984] AC 676; *Thomas v Portsea Steamship Co* [1912] AC 1.
5 *The Miramar*. See also *The Northern Progress (No. 2)* [1996] 2 Lloyd's Rep 319 and *The Spiros C* [2000] 2 Lloyd's Rep 312.
6 *The San Nicholas* [1976] 1 Lloyd's Rep 8.
7 *Lignell v Samuelson* (1921) 9 Lloyd's List Rep 361.
8 *The SLS Everest* [1981] 2 Lloyd's Rep 389; *The Heidberg* [1994] 2 Lloyd's Rep 287.
9 The 4th edition is due out in 2007. Chapter 1 of the 4th edition deals with the Rules and can be viewed at http://tetley.law.mcgill.ca/maritime.
10 See Carriage of Goods by Sea Act 1971, s 1(2), (3) and (6) and *The Hollandia* [1983] 1 AC 565.
11 See for consideration of clauses paramount and the Hague Rules *The Agios Lazarus* [1976] QB 933; *Lauritzen Reefers v Ocean Reef Transport Ltd SA (The Bukhta Russkaya)* [1997] 2 Lloyd's Rep 744 and *Seabridge Shipping v Orssleff's EFTF* [1999] 2 Lloyd's Rep 685.
12 Article IV, Rule 1 of the Rules; *The Torenia* [1983] 2 Lloyd's Rep 210; *The Polessk* [1996] 2 Lloyd's Rep 40; *The Eurasian Dream* [2002] 1 Lloyd's Rep 719.
13 Cf per Scrutton LJ in *Madras Electrical Supply Co v P & O Steam Navigation Co* (1924) 18 Lloyd's List Law Report 93 at p 96: 'the difficulty which has always perplexed practitioners in the Commercial Court and will perplex them to the end of time.'
14 See *The Torenia* [1983] 2 Lloyd's Rep 210; *Gosse Millard v Canadian Government Merchant Marine* [1927] 2 KB 432 and [1929] AC 223 (HL). See also *The Polessk* [1996] 2 Lloyd's Rep 40 at p 45, per Clarke J.
15 Suggested in Cooke et al *Voyage Charters* (2nd edn, 2001) at paras 85.112–85, 113.
16 *The Torenia* [1983] 2 Lloyd's Rep 210.
17 *The Flowergate* [1967] 1 Lloyd's Rep 1; *The Eurasian Dream* [2002] 1 Lloyd's Rep 719.

What does the bill evidence about the goods shipped?

4.5 The usual form of bill of lading contains a typed section on the face of the bill describing the goods shipped. Normally the bill will qualify this with some form of printed rubric such as '*received in apparent good order and condition*' or '*said to be*' or '*weight, quantity contents unknown*'. The words '*apparent good order and condition*' refer to the goods being accepted by the carrier as being in a good condition externally as apparent on reasonable inspection and properly packaged for the voyage with no obvious insufficiency of packing[1]. Statements as to quantity and weight in a bill may amount to conclusive evidence against the carrier of such matters[2] but it is rare to find such statements without qualifying words of wide effect. Such qualifying words will usually be effective[3].

1 *Silver v Ocean Steamship Co* [1930] 1 KB 416.
2 Article III, Rule 4 of the Hague-Visby Rules; Carriage of Goods by Sea Act 1971, s 4.
3 *Noble Resources v Cavalier Shipping* [1996] 1 Lloyd's Rep 642.

Pleading

Assumed facts

4.6 Ferro-Espana S.A. are the consignees of a cargo of steel coils shipped on board the vessel 'MALADROITE' at Mumbai, India, for carriage to and delivery at Santander, Spain in respect of which two bills of lading were issued. The vessel (owned by Les Armateurs Reunis S.A.) was under a time-trip charter to Ferrous and Non-Ferrous Impex AG.

During the voyage, the vessel encountered very heavy weather around the Cape of Good Hope. On arrival at Santander, the cargo was found to have suffered wetting damage and to have shifted in the holds causing dents and distortion. The consignees incurred additional discharge expenses as a result and were unable to use the steel coils for their intended purpose of manufacturing motor cars.

Particulars of Claim

<u>Claim No ………….</u>

<u>IN THE HIGH COURT OF JUSTICE</u>
<u>QUEEN'S BENCH DIVISION</u>
<u>COMMERCIAL COURT</u>

B E T W E E N:

FERRO-ESPANA S.A.

<u>Claimant</u>

- and -

LES ARMATEURS REUNIS S.A.

<u>Defendant</u>

PARTICULARS OF CLAIM

---

1. By two bills of lading ('the bills of lading') issued at Mumbai, India numbered 00-1 and 00-2, dated 14th February 2005 and signed by or on behalf of the master of the vessel, the Defendant by their servants or agents acknowledged shipment on board their vessel 'MALADROITE' ('the vessel') of a cargo of 5,500 metric tons of galvanised steel coils ('the cargo') in apparent good order and condition for carriage to and delivery at Santander, Spain.

2. The Claimant was at all material times the owner of the cargo and is the lawful holder of the bills of lading.

3. The bills of lading contained or evidenced contracts of carriage between the Claimant and the Defendant. They provided in so far as is relevant as follows:

'All terms, conditions, liberties and exceptions of the charterparty as dated overleaf are herewith incorporated.

Clause Paramount. This bill of lading and the carriage thereunder shall be governed by the Hague Rules (or if the Hague-Visby Rules are applied to it by any relevant local law, by the Hague-Visby Rules).'

4. The vessel was chartered by the Defendant to Ferrous and Non-Ferrous Impex AG under a charterparty dated 1st January 2005 on the London form ('the charterparty'). The charterparty provided by clause 37 as follows:

'The Owners shall be responsible for segregation of steel coils and for tomming and chocking as necessary. Charterers to pay for all costs of additional dunnaging.'

Clause 37 was incorporated into the bills of lading pursuant to the incorporation provision referred to in paragraph 3 above.

5. Further, the Defendant was under a duty to the Claimant as bailee and/or carrier for reward and/or was under a contractual duty of care to be implied into the contracts of carriage contained in or evidenced by the bills of lading to take reasonable care of the cargo and to deliver at Santander in the same good order and condition in which it was in on shipment at Mumbai.

6. Further or alternatively, the contract of carriage contained in or evidenced by the bill of lading was subject to and incorporated the Hague Rules, which provide as follows:

'Article III, rule 1

The carrier shall be bound before and at the beginning of the voyage, to exercise due diligence to–

(a) Make the ship seaworthy;

(b) . . .

(c) Make the holds . . . and all other parts of the ship in which goods are carried, fit and safe for their reception, carriage and preservation.

Article III, rule 2

Subject to the provisions of Article IV, the carrier shall properly and carefully load, handle, stow, carry, keep, care for and discharge the goods carried.'

7. The vessel completed loading on or about 14th February 2005 and sailed from Mumbai on 16th February 2005.

8. The vessel arrived at Santander on 28th March 2005 and discharge of the cargo was commenced on 29th March 2005, completing on 3rd April 2005.

9. In breach of duty and/or contract the Defendant failed to deliver the cargo at Santander in the same condition in which it had been in on shipment at Mumbai but delivered a large part of it damaged.

<u>PARTICULARS</u>

9.1 There was friction damage on the surface of 127 coils;

9.2 there was torsional deformation on the surface of 136 coils;

9.3 there was structural deformation in the inner diameter of 118 coils caused by pressure damage;

9.4 all of the coils loaded in the vessel's hold No. 2 (497 coils or some 50% of the total cargo) were severely spotted with sea water with the bottom most coils in the hold rusted on their leading surface and edges.

10. Further or alternatively, the damage was caused by the negligence of the Defendant, their servants or agents and/or by the Defendant's failure properly and carefully to load, stow, carry, care for and discharge the cargo in breach of contract and/or duty and in breach of Article III, Rule 2 of the Hague Rules and/or by the Defendant's failure properly to separate the coils and to tom and chock the same sufficiently for the voyage in breach of contract and clause 37 of the charterparty incorporated in the bills of lading.

PARTICULARS

10.1 The Claimant relies upon the fact that the cargo was discharged in a damaged condition as sufficient evidence of the Defendant's breach of contract and/or duty.

10.2 Further or alternatively, the friction and deformation damage referred to in paragraph 9.1 to 9.3 above is consistent with improper stowage of the cargo and insufficient segregation of the cargo in the hold, and of improper or insufficient tomming and chocking to brace the cargo against movement when exposed to the ordinary incidents of sea carriage.

10.3 Further, the rust damage referred to in paragraph 9.4 above is consistent with the failure by the Defendant properly to close or secure the hatch covers to hold No. 2.

11. Further or alternatively, the damage referred to in paragraph 9.4 above was caused by the Defendant's breach of contract and/or duty and or Article III, Rule 1 of the Hague Rules in failing to

exercise due diligence to make the ship seaworthy at the commencement of the voyage from Mumbai and, in particular, to make hold No. 2 fit for the reception, carriage and preservation of the cargo stowed in it.

PARTICULARS

11.1 The hatch covers to hold No. 2 were in poor repair, in particular all of the packing rubbers to the seats and panels were perished and/or cracked and two of the panels' lids did not sit true when the same were closed.

11.2 As a result sea water was able to enter hold No. 2.

11.3 Without prejudice to the burden of proof upon the Defendant, the Claimant will rely upon the condition of the hatch covers as evidence of the Defendant's failure to exercise due diligence.

12. By reason of the damage to the cargo the Claimant has suffered loss and damage and been put to expense.

PARTICULARS

12.1	The market value of the damaged cargo if in sound condition (based on its intended use for the manufacture of motor cars)	US$1,250,000
12.2	The value of the damaged cargo in its delivered condition (fit for use only in the canning/packaging industry)	US$310,725
Loss		**US$939,275**

12.3	Storage of damaged cargo pending disposal (20 days at US$2,000 per day)	US$40,000
	Total:	**US$970,275**

13. Further the Claimant claims and is entitled to interest pursuant to section 35A of the Supreme Court Act 1981 on the damages found to be due at such rate and for such period as the Court shall think fit.

AND the Claimants claim:

(1) US$970,275, alternatively damages.

(2) Interest.

[Statement of Truth, etc][1]

Defence

Claim No ....

IN THE HIGH COURT OF JUSTICE
QUEEN'S BENCH DIVISION
COMMERCIAL COURT

B E T W E E N:

FERRO-ESPANA S.A.

Claimant

- and -

LES ARMATEURS REUNIS S.A.

Defendant

D E F E N C E

---

1. Save that no admissions are made as to the apparent good order and condition of the cargo on shipment at Mumbai, paragraph 1 of the Particulars of Claim is admitted.

2. Paragraph 2 of the Particulars of Claim is not admitted and the Claimant is put to strict proof of its title to sue.

3. Paragraph 3 of the Particulars of Claim is admitted.

4. As to paragraph 4 of the Particulars of Claim, the charterparty and the term at clause 37 thereof are admitted. It is denied that clause 37 was incorporated into the bills of lading.

5. Paragraph 5 of the Particulars of Claim is not admitted. The Claimant is put to proof.

6. Paragraph 6 of the Particulars of Claim is admitted and averred. The Hague Rules further provide by Article IV, rules 1 and 2:

   '1. Neither the carrier nor the ship shall be liable for loss or damage arising or resulting from unseaworthiness unless caused by want or due diligence on the part of the carrier to make the ship seaworthy . . .

   2 Neither the carrier nor the ship shall be responsible for loss or damage arising or resulting from:

   (c) perils of the sea

   . . .

   (n) insufficiency of packing.'

7. Paragraphs 7 and 8 of the Particulars of Claim are admitted.

8. Paragraph 9 of the Particulars of Claim is denied. Without prejudice to the generality of the foregoing denial or to the burden of proof on the Claimant, the cause of any damage to the cargo observed at Mumbai was as set out in paragraphs 9 and/or 10 and/or 11 below.

9. The alleged damage to the cargo arose or resulted from insufficiency of packing which left the cargo unable to withstand the ordinary incidents of the voyage and/or the stowage for sea carriage of a steel coil cargo.

PARTICULARS

9.1 The coils were all wrapped in kraft paper which bore the notation 'waxed kraft paper – do not tear or break' and 'protective coil around steel coil – unstrap with great care'.

9.2 In fact the kraft paper was unwaxed or unwaxed in places such that, during loading and while the same was on the quayside, the cargo was exposed to moisture leading to spotting during light drizzle which fell for 20 minutes during the loading of the cargo for hold No. 2.

9.3 The Defendant will refer to the result of silver nitrate tests on the wetted paper at Santander which showed that the same was fresh and not salt water.

9.4 Further the coils were not wrapped in a protective coil but simply in binding straps which meant that the same were prone to torsional flexing and were unable to withstand coils being stowed on top of each other.

9.5 For the avoidance of doubt and by reason of the labels and markings on the wrappings of the coils at Mumbai, the insufficiency in packing was not and could not reasonably have been apparent to the vessel's deck officers during loading[2].

10. Further or alternatively, the alleged damage to the cargo arose or resulted from perils of the sea.

PARTICULARS

10.1 When rounding the Cape of Good Hope between 1st or 2nd March 2005 the vessel experienced SW winds force 10 with very heavy seas.

10.2 The vessel was hove to for two days with severe pitching and rolling. Damage was sustained to her forward mast derrick post and various ladders and companionways were damaged or lost.

10.3 Any movement of cargo (or ingress of sea water) was due to the exceptional nature of the weather, wind and sea conditions at this time.

11. Paragraph 10 of the Particulars of Claim is denied. Further or alternatively if, which is denied, the vessel was unseaworthy as alleged or at all the Defendant will contend that, before and at the beginning of the voyage they exercised due diligence to make the ship seaworthy and hold No. 2 fit for the reception and carriage of the cargo.

PARTICULARS

11.1 All hatch covers and packing rubbers were inspected every six months and were renewed and repaired as necessary in accordance with the manufacturer's (MacGregor) guidelines.

11.2 At Mumbai before loading the hatch cover to holds No. 1 and 2 were subjected to pressure hose testing and were found staunch and watertight, all packing rubbers were greased and all cleats and locking bars checked for true running/ sealing.

12. Paragraph 11 of the Particulars of Claim is not admitted.

13. Paragraph 12 of the Particulars of Claim is noted.

14. It is accordingly denied that the Claimant is entitled to the relief claimed or to any relief against the Defendant.

[Statement of Truth, etc][1]

1 Statement of truth, etc as set out in **Chapter 3, para 3.2**.

2 This needs to be pleaded because insufficiency of packing which was obvious to the ship gives rise to an estoppel against the ship if bills of lading were issued attesting to the 'apparent good order and condition' of the cargo: see *Silver v Ocean Steamship Co* [1930] 1 KB 416 and **para 4.5**, footnote 1 above.

GENERAL AVERAGE

Law

4.7 The Marine Insurance Act 1906, s 66(2) defines general average in the following way:

> 'There is a general average act where any extraordinary sacrifice or expenditure is voluntarily and reasonable made or incurred in time of peril for the purpose of preserving the property emperilled in the common adventure.'

The section codifies a long established rule of law. The legal consequences of a general average are similarly codified: see Marine Insurance Act 1906, s 66(3) which provides:

> 'where there is a general average loss, the party on whom it falls is entitled, subject to the conditions implied by maritime law, to a rateable contribution from the other parties interested and such contribution is called a general average contribution.'

In the nineteenth century the principles and practices of general average were largely codified by internationally agreed sets of rules which came to be known as the 'York-Antwerp Rules'. 'The current revision of the York-Antwerp Rules is the 1994 Rules. The York-Antwerp Rules are the starting point for any consideration of what is and is not a general average act, sacrifice or expenditure and what heads of loss, damage and expense are and are not allowable in general average. They consist of seven lettered 'Rules', Rules A to G, and 22 roman numbered Rules dealing (by accretion) with common problems in average adjustment. In addition, there are 'Rules of Practice' of the Association of Average Adjusters. The full text of these can be found in the leading texts: see below.

The provisions of the bill of lading will very often contain an express term which provides for the adjustment of general average in accordance with a specific revision of the York-Antwerp Rules, today 2004 (but on some older forms still that of 1974). Alternatively, by incorporating the terms of a charterparty, the bill of lading will often incorporate the corresponding charterparty provision for the adjustment of general average.

The typical context in which general average arises under a bill of lading is where a carrying vessel which has issued bills of lading experiences some casualty or breakdown. This first, necessitates the making of what is said to be a general average sacrifice involving cargo (e.g. jettisoning cargo) or more usually the incurring of general average expenditure (e.g. the engaging of salvage tugs or the putting into a port of refuge) on the vessel owner's part. Secondly, the casualty or breakdown gives rise to a claim by the holder of the bill for breach of the contract of carriage by the carrier; where the cause of the casualty or breakdown said by the owner to give rise to the general average act is alleged by the holder of the bill to be some defect or fault for which the owner is responsible, thereby defeating the claim for general average. An example is found below in the facts assumed for the specimen pleading.

The topic of general average is too broad for any more than a very brief outline to be given here: the leading text remains Lowndes and Rudolf *General Average and the York-Antwerp Rules* (12th edn, 1997). A handy overview of the relevant principles is given by Hudson *The York-Antwerp Rules: principles and practice of general average adjustment* (1996)[1]. For present purposes the most common rules of general average encountered in the pleading of bill of lading in the typical context referred to above are Rules A and D, dealing respectively with the requirements to be met for entitlement to general average and the impact upon a claim for contribution of the claimant's fault.

1 For a comparison of the provisions of the 1974, 1994 and 2004 York-Antwerp Rules see Francis Rose, *General Average: Law and Practice* (2nd edn, 2005).

Rule A: Entitlement to general average

4.8 Rule A defines general average giving rise to entitlement to claim contribution in terms similar to those employed by Marine Insurance Act 1906, s 66(2), as follows:

> 'There is a general average act when, and only when, any extraordinary sacrifice or expenditure is intentionally and reasonably made or incurred for the common safety for the purpose of preserving from peril the property involved in a common maritime adventure.'

The pleading of a claim in general average should address each element of the definition of a general average act.

(i) There must be an 'extraordinary sacrifice or expenditure'. Where the general average act involves some action affecting the cargo, such as jettisoning deck cargo to improve ship stability or the flooding of cargo holds with water to prevent loss of ship and cargo by fire, the requirement of 'extraordinariness' is usually self-apparent. Where the act affects the carrying vessel, more difficult questions sometimes arise: whereas the beaching of a sinking vessel to save ship and cargo is self-evidently 'extraordinary', the use of the vessel's CO_2 and fire extinguishing materials to save ship and cargo is the ordinary use of the vessel's plant as would be the ordinary use of her engines and fuel by running astern for a long period to keep a vessel off a reef. Numbered Rule XX deals with the specific problem of damage to main engines and draws a broad distinction between damage caused in attempting to refloat once aground (allowable) and while afloat (not allowable).

(ii) The sacrifice or expenditure must be 'intentional'. This excludes sacrifices done accidentally which otherwise would qualify as allowable in general average. The sacrifice must therefore be done deliberately although the fact that there is no practical alternative to doing what is done does not disqualify the act in general average provided it is done with specific intent. An example is given in the facts assumed for the pleading set out below.

(iii) The sacrifice or expenditure must be reasonably made or incurred. What is reasonable will be a question of fact in each case given the circumstances prevailing. Given that most general average cases arise in circumstances of urgency and imminent peril, provided the sacrifice is not one which it is obvious was one which was unnecessary or extravagant the requirement will be satisfied. However, in cases of medium- and long-term peril a more considered approach to various courses of action taken, may well be an issue in the case.

(iv) The sacrifice or expenditure must be made for the common safety to preserve the property from peril. The satisfaction by a claimant of the requirement of a peril or danger confronting the whole of the property provided in the common maritime adventure can usually be answered by asking whether, in the absence of the alleged sacrifice or action taken, the ship and cargo would have been in substantial danger of loss within a sufficiently immediate timescale. The danger or peril must be a real one facing ship *and* cargo: if a peril is feared which does not in fact exist the Rule is not satisfied. Similarly, while the peril need not be immediate (e.g. a vessel without power is exposed to danger from weather or grounding which may be long-term only), it must operate within a reasonably finite period. Most importantly, the peril must confront all of the property on the adventure. Perils facing only ship or only cargo which are avoided do not qualify in general average.

Once the requirements of Rule A are made out, the claimant in general average is entitled to contribution from the other interests involved in the maritime adventure. The two main interests are the ship and her equipment and the cargo on board the ship (freight at risk is another class of interest which may be noted). Contribution is calculated, usually in a general average adjustment carried out by specialist adjusters, on the basis of the value of each interest at the time and place where the common maritime adventure comes to an end. To give a simple example: if the ship sustains damage to preserve ship and cargo in the sum of £100,000 and if the value of the interest are ship £1,000,000 and cargo £2,000,000, then ship claims a two third, contribution from cargo, i.e. £66,666.66. Individual cargo interests bear this contribution pro rata to the value of their cargo to that owned by other cargo interests. If the ship sustains damage and cargo is lost then both ship and cargo are entitled to contribution from each other calculated in the same way.

Rule D: The effect of the claimant's fault

4.9 A common problem in bill of lading claims arises where it is alleged by the defendant to a claim in general average that the state of affairs which gave rise to the peril against which the sacrifice was made or the expenditure was incurred to preserve the property was caused by or resulted from the claimant's own fault. A typical example is where a ship suffers a main engine breakdown exposing ship and cargo to the risk of stranding; the ship engages a salvage tug to hold her off the shore until the engines are fixed and her owners claim the cost of so doing in general average from cargo interests; the cargo interests allege that the main engine broke down due to the shipowners' poor maintenance or the unseaworthiness of the vessel.

Rule D provides that where the fault is 'actionable', while there is no effect on the general average character of the sacrifice or expenditure claimed, the defendant nevertheless may rely upon that fault as a defence to the claim:

> 'Rights to contribution in general average shall not be affected though the event which gave rise to the sacrifice or expenditure may have been due to the fault of one of the parties to the adventure, but this shall not prejudice any remedies or defences which may be open against or to that party in respect of such fault.'

The test for 'actionable' fault is whether or not the claimant would be legally liable to the defendant (in the above example, the cargo owners) for loss or damage to the cargo which would have resulted from the state of affairs giving rise to the peril if no general average act had taken place[1]. To consider the example above: if the salvage tug had not been engaged and the ship had stranded with loss of the cargo, would the cargo owner have recovered that loss in law from the shipowner on the basis of actionable fault in respect of ship's engines? In the bill of lading context, the legal position under the contract of carriage has to be analysed. If the shipowner has the benefit of an exemption clause or statutory defence, for example, under the Hague-Visby Rules or Carriage of Goods by Sea Act 1971, then it is not legally liable to the cargo owner and, even if otherwise 'at fault', since that fault is not actionable because of the exemption clause, the shipowners' right to general average contribution is unaffected[2].

1 *Tempus Shipping Co Ltd v Louis Dreyfus & Co* [1931] AC 762; *The Makedonia* [1962] P 190. See also *Goulandris v Goldman* [1958] 1 QB 74.
2 *The Carron Park* (1890) 15 PD 203; *Goulandris v Goldman* [1958] 1 QB 74.

Pleading

Assumed facts

4.10 The tanker 'DEUX FOIS', owned by Shuttle Tankers S.A., experienced a main engine failure off Sicily while on a laden voyage from Constanza to Rotterdam. She was carrying a cargo of 10,000 metric tons of crude oil under two bills of lading which were transferred by the shippers to the holders of the bill of lading, Crude Oil Import-Export B.V.

She engaged salvage assistance from Italo-British Salvors SpA whose tug 'MR STANDFAST' held the vessel off the coast while repairs were effected. The vessel resumed passage but shortly afterwards her steering motor sustained a hydraulic failure which locked the rudder to port. While repairs were being effected the vessel grounded in shallow water on the coast off Salerno.

She sustained significant bottom damage and required to be refloated. The owners entered into a further salvage contract with the same salvors whose tug 'RICHARD HANNAY' effected the refloatation. The owner claimed general average in respect of the two salvage services rendered by the tug and the cost of repairs at the Mendoza yards, Portugal. The cargo interests alleged that the vessel's main engine and steering motor were unseaworthy.

Particulars of Claim

Claim No ....

IN THE HIGH COURT OF JUSTICE
QUEEN'S BENCH DIVISION
ADMIRALTY COURT

B E T W E E N:

SHUTTLE TANKERS S.A.

Claimant

- and -

CRUDE OIL IMPORT-EXPORT B.V.

Defendant

PARTICULARS OF CLAIM

---

1. The Claimant is, and at all material times was, the owner of the motor tanker 'DEUX FOIS' ('the vessel').

2. Between 29th March and 1st April 2005 the vessel loaded a cargo of two parcels of crude oil, the first of 4,000 metric tons and the second of 6,000 metric tons ('the cargo') at Constanza for carriage to and delivery at Rotterdam.

3. The master for and on behalf of the Claimant acknowledged receipt of the cargo by two bills of lading each dated 1st April 2005 and numbered C-01 and C-02 in respect of the first and second parcels of cargo respectively ('the bills of lading').

4. The Defendant was at all material times the owner of the cargo and was and is the lawful holder of the bills of lading.

5. It was an express term of the contract of carriage contained in or evidenced by the bills of lading that '*General Average* (if the same should arise) to be adjusted in London, York-Antwerp Rules 1994 to apply to the adjustment.'

6. Further or alternatively, the bills of lading expressly incorporated all terms, conditions, liberties and exceptions of the charterparty dated 11th March 2005 between the Claimants and Traders Limited. The charterparty provided (*inter alia*): 'GA per York-Antwerp Rules 1994; to be adjusted in London'.

7. Whilst on a voyage from Constanza to Rotterdam and on 5th April 2005 at 10:17 hrs (all times in these Particulars of Claim are given as UTC + 1), the vessel suffered a main engine failure off Syracuse (Siracusa), Sicily in Cape Passero at a position 36°43' N, 14°52' E. The weather conditions were poor with winds S-SE force 7 to 8 (with gales forecast) and with a heavy Southerly swell.

8. The vessel was in danger of running aground on the Denti di Passero reef with consequent risk of total loss of the vessel and cargo.

9. The Claimant engaged salvage assistance under a lump sum salvage contract dated 5th April 2005 made with Italo-British Salvors SpA ('the salvors'). The salvage tug 'MR STANDFAST' was mobilised from Valetta, Malta and made fast to the vessel at 12:40 hrs and held the vessel until repairs could be made to the main engine. These were completed at 0137 hrs.

10. At about 05:14 hrs on 6th April 2005 the vessel suffered a steering tele-motor failure while 10 miles off to the east of Castellamare di Gallo, Sicily. Attempts were made to repair the steering motor and to go over to manual steering but the rudder locked in a starboard heading. The weather conditions were winds SE to E, force 6 gusting

to 7 and the vessel was encountering strong Easterly currents of some 3 to 4 knots.

11. The vessel was in danger of running aground on the rocky coast between Marsala and Castellamare di Gallo, Sicily, with consequent risk of the total loss of the vessel and the cargo.

12. The Claimant was unable to engage any salvage or other tug assistance within a time sufficient to prevent the vessel from grounding. The master accordingly put the vessel aground off Palermo at slow speed to prevent the vessel from being carried on to the rocky coast referred to above and to preserve the vessel and cargo from loss. The vessel grounded on a soft bottom of sand and mud.

13. On 7th April 2005, the Claimant engaged the salvors to refloat the vessel under a further lump sum contract of the same date. The vessel was refloated on 8th April 2005 by the tug 'RICHARD HANNAY'. On refloatation the vessel was found to have sustained some setting up of her bottom plates and internals in way of frames 43 and 76 on her portside.

14. In saving the vessel and the cargo from common danger as set out above, the vessel incurred general average loss and expenditure:

    14.1 In respect of the preservation of the vessel from grounding on 5th April 2005, the Claimant incurred a salvage charge of £150,000 of which £100,000 is attributable to cargo under the York-Antwerp Rules 1994; and

    14.2 In respect of the preservation of the vessel from grounding on 6th April 2005 and from stranding thereafter, the Claimant incurred repair costs for the bottom damage sustained by the vessel of £500,000 and salvage charges of £210,000 of which £400,000 and £140,000 respectively are attributable to cargo under the York-Antwerp Rules.

15. Full details of the matters referred to in paragraph 14 are set out in the general average adjustment prepared by GA Counsellors Inc dated 11th May 2005 in London, a cargo of which has always been provided to the Defendant.

16. By reason of the matters set out above the Defendant is liable to contribute the sum of £640,000 in general average but wrongfully and in breach of contract it has failed to do so.

17. The Claimant claims interest pursuant to section 35A of the Supreme Court Act 1981 on the sum of £640,000, alternatively damages, at Base Rate + 1% for such period as the Court sees fit.

AND the Claimant claims:

(1) £640,000, or alternatively damages;

(2) A declaration that the Defendant is liable to contribute in general average.

(3) Interests as set out in paragraph 17 above.

[Statement of Truth, etc][1]

Defence

Claim No ....

IN THE HIGH COURT OF JUSTICE
QUEEN'S BENCH DIVISION
ADMIRALTY COURT

B E T W E E N:

SHUTTLE TANKERS S.A.

Claimants

- and -

CRUDE OIL IMPORT-EXPORT B.V.

Defendants

D E F E N C E

---

1. Paragraphs 1 to 6 inclusive of the Particulars of Claim are admitted.

2. The bills of lading further expressly incorporated that they were subject to the Hague-Visby Rules.

3. The Hague-Visby Rules provide (*inter alia*):

   'Article III, rule 1

   The carrier shall be bound before and at the beginning of the voyage, to exercise due diligence to–

   (a) Make the ship seaworthy;

Article IV, rule 1

Neither the carrier nor the ship shall be liable for loss or damage arising from unseaworthiness unless caused by want of due diligence on the part of the carrier to make the ship seaworthy . . . the burden of proving the exercise of due diligence shall be on the carrier or other person claiming exemption under this Article.'

4. It is admitted that the vessel suffered a main engine failure in the circumstances set out in paragraph 7 of the Particulars of Claim.

5. In breach of contract and Article III Rule 1 of the Hague-Visby Rules, the vessel was not seaworthy at the beginning of the voyage from Constanza as a result of which the vessel's main engine experienced the failure on 5th April 2005.

PARTICULARS

5.1 One or more of the main engine bearing shells had exceeded the permitted maximum running hours well before the voyage to Constanza and should have been changed over with new shells.

5.2 The main engine failure was a seizure caused by the breaking of one or more bearing shells.

6. Save in that no admissions are made as to the alleged repairs to the vessel's main engine paragraphs 8 and 9 of the Particulars of Claim are admitted.

7. It is admitted that the vessel suffered a steering failure in the circumstances set out in paragraph 10 of the Particulars of Claim as a result of which the vessel's rudder was locked to starboard.

8. In further breach of contract and of Article III Rule 1 of the Hague-Visby Rules, the vessel was not seaworthy at the beginning of the voyage from Constanza as a result of which the vessel's steering motor failed on 6th April 2005.

<u>PARTICULARS</u>

8.1 A cleaning rag was left in the lubricating oil sump of the steering motor at some stage prior to the voyage. The rag was drawn into the lubricating oil system blocking a filter and causing a blockage.

8.2 The blockage triggered a low-level alarm cut-out which immobilised the steering motor.

9. Paragraph 11 of the Particulars of Claim is admitted.

10. Save in that it is admitted that the Claimants were unable to engage salvage or towage assistance and that the vessel grounded off Palermo on a sandy bottom, paragraph 12 of the Particulars of Claim is denied. The grounding of the vessel was not the result of any act or decision by the master of the vessel but was caused unintentionally by the vessel attempting to maintain steerage and to keep clear of the coast but by being set aground by the vessel's rudder being locked to starboard combined with the continued working of her main engines and the acting of the current of the vessel.

11. Paragraph 13 of the Particulars of Claim is admitted.

12. As to paragraph 14 of the Particular of Claim, the alleged general average sacrifice and expenditure was caused by the Claimant's breaches of contract as set out above. In the circumstances and pursuant to Rule D of the York-Antwerp Rules 1994, the Claimant is not entitled to recover a contribution in general average.

13. Further or alternatively, the Defendant relies upon the breaches of contract as a defence by way of set-off and/or the Claimant's claim fails for circuity of action in that by reason of the Claimant's breaches of contract the Defendant is entitled to damages in the amount of any general average contribution paid by them to the Claimant.

14. Further or alternatively, if the steering motor failure was not caused by the Claimant's breach of contract as set out above, the Claimant is not entitled in any event to general average contribution in respect of the damage to the vessel sustained as a result of the grounding off Palermo. That grounding was not the result of an intentional act on the part of the vessel but arose by accident or force of circumstance as set out in paragraph 10 above and, accordingly, was not a general average act.

COUNTERCLAIM

15. Paragraphs 1 to 13 above are repeated.

16. If, which is denied, the Defendant is liable to pay the alleged contribution to the Claimant, the Defendant counterclaims any sum for which it is liable to the Claimant as damages for breach of contract.

17. The Defendant further claims, if appropriate, interest pursuant to section 35A of the Supreme Court Act 1981 at such rate and for such period as the Court thinks fit.

AND the Defendant claims:

(1) Damages for breach of contract;

(2) Interest.

[Statement of Truth, etc][1]

1 Statement of truth, etc as set out in **Chapter 3, para 3.2**.

DANGEROUS CARGO

Law

4.11 At common law the shipper of goods which are dangerous to the carrying vessel or to other cargo on board her is obliged, by virtue of an implied term of the contract of carriage to give notice to the carrier of the characteristics of the goods which is sufficient to enable the carrier, first, to decide whether or not to carry the goods at all and, secondly, if it will carry them, to take all necessary and appropriate precautions for the safe carriage of the goods and for the safety of the ship and other cargo. It will therefore be an implied term of every bill of lading contract of carriage governed by English law. The leading cases are *Brass v Maitland* (1856)[1] and *The Giannis NK* (1998)[2]. In *Brass v Maitland,* a cargo of casks of bleaching powder was shipped in defective casks. The carrier was unaware of the highly corrosive nature of the cargo or that the casks leaked. It recovered its liability to other cargo owners as damages from the shippers. In *The Giannis NK*, the majority of the Court of Appeal held that a shipper was under an absolute duty to give notice of the dangerous characteristics of the goods shipped, whether or not the shipper knew or ought to have known of those characteristics. The majority view was confirmed by the House of Lords in *The Giannis NK*, albeit obiter. If it is the Claimant's case that the shipper did know or ought to have known it is always advisable to plead this expressly.

Goods can be 'dangerous goods' for the purposes of the common law implied obligation in a variety of different ways. Many goods are now classified as dangerous goods by the International Maritime Organisation Code regulating the carriage of dangerous cargoes, the 'International Maritime Dangerous Goods Code' or 'IMDG Code', which contains detailed safety requirements for carriage. Other cargoes, while not so classified, may be dangerous to ship or cargo if carried. The notice to be given in each case may vary. For goods which are listed in the IMDG Code it will usually suffice to give the carrier the IMO class number and the specific goods identification number which will enable the carrier to ascertain all relevant characteristics and typical carriage precautions. For other goods the notice must be sufficient to enable the carrier to appreciate the real characteristics of which is being shipped. Where a cargo is well known to be 'dangerous', e.g. crude oil or coal, if the particular type of cargo presents special dangers beyond those which are inherent in ordinary crude oil or coal cargoes, the notice must alert the carrier to these if it is to be sufficient[3]. The 'danger' posed by a cargo may extend beyond the obvious physical dangers of fire, explosion, corrosion or noxious taint to the risks of special cleaning or decontamination[4] or to the risks of danger to the ship in terms of detention, arrest or delay[5].

Where the bill of lading incorporates or is subject to the Hague or Hague-Visby Rules, the question of cargoes which present certain types of physical danger is regulated by the express terms of Article IV, Rule 6 of the Rules. This provides as follows:

'Goods of an inflammable, explosive or dangerous nature to the shipment whereof the carrier, master, or agent of the carrier has not consented with knowledge of their nature and character, may at any time before discharge be landed at any place, or destroyed or rendered innocuous by the carrier without compensation, and the shipper of such goods shall be liable for all damages and expenses directly or indirectly arising out of or resulting from such shipment.

If any such goods shipped with such knowledge and consent shall become a danger to the ship or cargo they may in like manner be landed at any place or destroyed or rendered innocuous by the carrier without liability on the part of the carrier except to general average if any.'

The first point to note about Article IV, Rule 6 is that it confers an express right to indemnity upon the carrier with the potential benefit of not having to establish a claim for breach of contract in terms of recoverable damages[6]. Since it extends only to physically dangerous goods (the term 'dangerous' does not take its character from the preceding words 'inflammable, explosive' and applies to all physical dangers (e.g. beetle infestation)) it does not affect the position at common law in relation to wider risks and dangers. It is an open question whether the *Brass v Maitland* implied term has any independent existence in relation to physical dangers where Article IV, Rule 6 applies[7].

The second is that it requires the carrier not to have 'consented' to the shipment 'with knowledge of their nature and character'. As the editors of Cooke on *Voyage Charters* (2nd edn, 2001)[8], to which text reference should be made for a detailed account of the law relating to the shipment of dangerous goods, state:

'The relevant knowledge may be "actual" or it may be constructive in the sense of knowledge which the carrier and crew ought to possess. Were it otherwise there would be a premium on ignorance. The constructive knowledge imported to the carrier is that of the ordinary experienced and skilful carrier of goods of the general kind shipped: it does not extend to that of the "expert chemist" but it is not confined to "what is universally known"[9].'

It is very common in the pleading of a claim for the shipment of dangerous goods without notice for the claim to be put not only on the basis of the breach of an implied obligation not to ship without notice (coupled, where the Hague or Hague-Visby Rules apply and Article IV, Rule 6 is appropriate to the cargo in question with an allegation of breach of this provision) but also upon the basis of an implied warranty that the goods were safe for carriage in the ordinary way. As the editors of Cooke on *Voyage Charters* point out 'This formulation amounts to much the same thing'[10] but it emphasises that the breach lies in the act of shipping the goods without notice.

Under the Carriage of Goods by Sea Act 1992 (considered above in relation to cargo claims), provision is made not only for the transfer to the lawful holder of the bill of lading of rights of suit against the carrier but it is also provided by s 3(1) that where a person becomes a lawful holder and has rights of suit vested in him under s 2(1) that person 'shall become subject to the same liabilities under that contract as if he had been party to that contract' in certain cases, for example where he takes or demands delivery of the goods from the carrier[11]. This is explained by s 3(3) to be 'without prejudice to the liabilities under the contract of any person as original party to the contract'. In the case of the shipment of dangerous goods, the carrier will usually have a claim against the shipper and it seems, where s 3(1) applies, also against the lawful holder of the bill of lading under which the goods were shipped[12].

1 (1856) 6 E&B 470.
2 *Effort Shipping v Linden Management (The 'Giannis NK')* [1998] 1 Lloyd's Rep 337.
3 See, e.g. *The Atlantic Duchess* [1957] 2 Lloyd's Rep 54: butanised crude oil; *The Athanasia Comminos* [1990] 1 Lloyd's Rep 277: gassy coal; *The Fiona* [1993] 1 Lloyd's Rep 257, affirmed [1994] 2 Lloyd's Rep 506: high sulphur fuel oil.
4 *The Berge Sund* [1993] 2 Lloyd's Rep 453.
5 *Mitchell Cotts v Steel* [1916] 2 KB 610: rice cargo exposing the vessel to detention at port of discharge.
6 *The Eurus* [1998] 1 Lloyd's Rep 351 (CA).
7 See *The Fiona* [1993] 1 Lloyd's Rep 257 where such existence was doubted. Cf the approach of the Court of Appeal in *The Giannis NK* [1994] 2 Lloyd's Rep 171.
8 See ch 6, para 6.46ff (common law); ch 85, para 85.409ff (Hague Rules).
9 Cooke on *Voyage Charters* (2nd edn, 2001) para 85.417.
10 Cooke on *Voyage Charters* (2nd edn, 2001) para 6.49.
11 See the detailed provisions set out in Carriage of Goods by Sea Act 1992, s 3(1).
12 See the discussion in Cooke on *Voyage Charters* (2nd edn, 2001) paras 18.98–18.99.

Pleading

Assumed facts

4.12 Pericula Coal and Coke Inc shipped a cargo of steam coal at Tuapse on 1 January 2005 for carriage to and delivery at Immingham under a bill of lading issued by the master of the vessel 'INFELIX' owned by Bulk Carriers S.A. The coal gave off very large quantities of methane and as a result the coal loaded in the hold spontaneously combusted during the voyage leading to serious damage to the vessel. The vessel continued to the port of discharge where the remnants of the cargo were taken delivery of by the consignees of the cargo and the lawful holders of the bill of lading, the Humber and Tees Electricity Generating Board. The vessel underwent temporary and then permanent repairs.

Particulars of Claim

Claim No ....

IN THE HIGH COURT OF JUSTICE
QUEEN'S BENCH DIVISION
COMMERCIAL COURT

B E T W E E N:

BULK CARRIERS S.A.

Claimant

- and -

(1) PERICULA COAL AND COKE INC

(2) HUMBER AND TEES ELECTRIC GENERATING BOARD

Defendant

PARTICULARS OF CLAIM

---

1. On or about 1st January 2005, the First Defendant tendered for shipment and shipped aboard the Claimant's vessel 'INFELIX' ('the vessel') at Tuapse a cargo described by the First Defendants on the bill of lading presented to the master for signature as '15,000 metric tons of Russian No. 1 steam coal' ('the cargo').

2. By a bill of lading dated 1st January 2005 at Tuapse and numbered 'TUA-1' ('the bill of lading') the Claimant acknowledged receipt of the cargo for shipment to and delivery at Immingham. The bill of lading contained and evidenced the contract of carriage between the Claimant as carrier and the First Defendant as shippers.

3. It was a term of the contract of carriage implied by operation of law that the First Defendant would not ship, or tender for shipment on board the vessel, goods which were dangerous to carry without giving express notice of that fact and/or of the characteristics of the cargo to the Claimant.

4. Further, the bill of lading expressly incorporated the Hague Rules. Accordingly, the contract of carriage was subject to Article IV, Rule 6 of the Hague Visby Rules which provides in so far as material as follows:

   'Goods of an inflammable, explosive or dangerous nature to the shipment whereof the carrier, master, or agent of the carrier has not consented with knowledge of their nature and character, may at any time before discharge be landed at any place, or destroyed or rendered innocuous by the carrier without compensation, and the shipper of such goods shall be liable for all damages and expenses directly or indirectly arising out of or resulting from such shipment.'

5. Further or alternatively, by their shipment of the cargo the First Defendant impliedly warranted that the cargo was fit and safe for the carriage in the ordinary way. In reliance on this warranty, the Claimant agreed to carry the cargo and to issue the bill of lading and the contract of carriage was subject to the implied warranty by operation of law.

6. In breach of contract and/or the implied warranty the First Defendant shipped the cargo on board the vessel without giving notice of the fact that the same was dangerous and/or the cargo as shipped was not fit and safe for carriage in the ordinary way.

<u>PARTICULARS</u>

6.1 The cargo gave off large volumes of methane gas;

6.2 By the process of decomposition and the production of methane gas, the coal was liable to spontaneous combustion or ignition at ordinary carriage temperatures and in ordinary coal carriage ventilation conditions.

7. The Claimant, their servants or agents, did not know nor ought they to have known of the characteristics or nature of the cargo as set out in paragraph 6.

8. The Claimant will contend (in so far as it is necessary for them to do so) that the First Defendant knew or ought to have known of the matters set out in paragraph 6 as the producers and exporters of the cargo.

9. As a result of the dangerous nature of the cargo, the cargo loaded in hold No. 3 of the vessel gave off large quantities of methane gas and on 10th January 2005 spontaneously combusted, leading to an explosion which blew off the hatch covers and caused damage to the vessel.

10. The resultant fire was extinguished by the crew and the vessel proceeded to Immingham.

11. By reason of the above the Claimant has suffered loss and damage and has been put to expense.

<u>PARTICULARS</u>

11.1	Cost of temporary repairs to hatch covers at Teesport to enable the vessel to proceed to Lisbon for permanent repairs.	US$197,000
11.2	Cost of permanent repairs by Lisnave SA at Lisbon to damage to hatch covers and hold interior.	US$1,393,000

11.3 Cost of digging out remaining cargo clinker in hold No. 3 at Immingham and of disposal of the same. US$17,500

US$1,607,500

12. At Immingham the Second Defendant who was at all material times the lawful holder of the bill of lading presented the bill of lading and took delivery of the remaining cargo loaded in holds 1, 2 and 4 (amounting to some 12,747 metric tons).

13. Pursuant to section 3(1) of the Carriage of Goods by Sea Act 1992 the Second Defendant became subject to the same liability under the contract of carriage contained in or evidenced by the bill of lading, as the shipper, as if it had been the original party to it.

14. The First and/or Second Defendants are therefore liable to the Claimant in damages for breach of contract in the sum set out in paragraph 11 above.

15. Further or alternatively, pursuant to the implied term or Article IV, Rule 6 of the Hague Rules, the Claimant is entitled to be indemnified by the First and/or Second Defendants in respect of such sums.

16. Further the Claimant claims interest pursuant to section 35A of the Supreme Court Act 1981 at such rate and for such period as the Court thinks fit.

AND the Claimant claims against the Defendants:

(1) Damages and/or an indemnity in the sums set out at paragraph 11.

(2) Interest as set out in paragraph 16.

[Statement of Truth, etc][1]

Defence

Claim No ....

IN THE HIGH COURT OF JUSTICE
QUEEN'S BENCH DIVISION
COMMERCIAL COURT

B E T W E E N:

BULK CARRIERS S.A.

Claimant

- and -

(1) PERICULA COAL AND COKE INC

(2) HUMBER AND TEES ELECTRIC GENERATING BOARD

Defendant

DEFENCE OF THE FIRST DEFENDANT[2]

---

1. Paragraphs 1 to 5 of the Particulars of Claim are admitted.

2. Paragraph 6 of the Particulars of Claim is denied. The First Defendant will say as follows:

    2.1 It is admitted that the cargo gave off quantities of methane gas and, if not properly ventilated, was liable to spontaneous combustion;

    2.2 These characteristics are common to all cargoes of coal in general and steam coal in particular whether of Russian or other origin.

    2.3 The Claimant was or ought to have been well aware of the characteristics from the statement on the bill of lading that the cargo was 'Russian No. 1 Steam Coal';

2.4 The First Defendant will refer to *Thomas on Stowage* (4th edn) p 364 which describes coal as a commodity 'liable to spontaneous hearing' and with a 'risk of explosion from the accompanying release of marsh gas', i.e. methane;

2.5 In the circumstances the cargo was shipped with due and proper notice to the Claimant of its characteristics.

3. By reason of the matters set out above, paragraph 7 of the Particulars of Claim is denied.

4. Paragraph 8 of the Particulars of Claim is admitted.

5. As to paragraph 9 of the Particulars of Claim, it is admitted that there was an explosion in hold No. 3 as a result of spontaneous combustion. This was an ordinary risk and incident of the carriage of coal which the Claimants accepted.

6. Paragraph 10 of the Particulars of Claim is admitted.

7. Paragraph 11 of the Particulars of Claim is not admitted; the Claimant is put to proof of the alleged loss, damage and/or expense.

8. Paragraphs 12 and 13 of the Particulars of Claim make no case against the First Defendant who, accordingly, does not plead thereto.

9. In so far as they allege liability on the part of the First Defendant, Paragraphs 14 and 15 of the Particulars of Claim are denied.

10. Paragraph 16 of the Particulars of Claim is noted.

11. It is accordingly denied that the Claimant is entitled to the relief alleged or to any relief against the First Defendant.

[Statement of Truth, etc][1]

1 Statement of truth, etc as set out in **Chapter 3, para 3.2**.

2 The defence of the Second Defendant would be likely to be similar save for any issues as to the operation of the Carriage of Goods by Sea Act 1992, s 3(1) and for questions of a possible Part 20 claim against the First Defendant, e.g. if the Second Defendant was the buyer of the cargo from the First Defendant and sought to allege breach of the sale contract resulting in its liability to the Claimant.

CHAPTER 5

Shipping – Marine Insurance

Nevil Phillips
Nichola Warrender
Stewart Buckingham

Law

5.1 This short introduction to the law of marine insurance is not intended to be exhaustive or comprehensive, but is provided merely as an outline intended to aid an appreciation of those matters which will be of significance or relevance to any marine insurance pleading. For a more detailed consideration of the law of marine insurance, reference should be made to the leading texts on the subject, including *Chalmer's Marine Insurance Act 1906*; *Arnould on The Law of Marine Insurance and Average* (16th edn); *O'May on Marine Insurance*; Rose *Marine Insurance: Law and Practice*; Thomas et al *Modern Law of Marine Insurance*.

The policy

5.2 The starting point for any marine insurance claim under English law is the Marine Insurance Act 1906 (MIA 1906) which codified the law of marine insurance.

A contract of marine insurance is inadmissible in evidence unless contained in or evidenced by a marine policy in accordance with MIA 1906, s 22. Further, a marine policy must indicate the name of the assured thereunder or of the person effecting the cover on his behalf (MIA 1906, s 23), together with the subject matter insured (MIA 1906, s 26).

Insurable interest

5.3 The effect of MIA 1906, s 6(1) is that, in order to recover under a marine policy, the assured must demonstrate that at the time of any alleged loss they had an insurable interest in the subject of the insurance (e.g. a ship or cargo). Insurable interest is defined in MIA 1906, s 5: every person has an insurable interest who is interested in a marine adventure (s 5(1)); a person is interested in a marine adventure where he stands in any legal or equitable relation to the adventure or to any insurable property at risk therein, in consequence of which he may benefit by the safety or due arrival of insurable property, or may be prejudiced by its loss, or damage thereto, or by the detention thereof, or may incur liability in respect thereof (s 5(2)). Examples of persons having an insurable interest in a marine policy are the owner or mortgagee of a ship or cargo (by reference to their property or beneficial interest: s 14), an officer or member of the crew of a vessel (by reference to their entitlement to wages: s 11), the intended recipient of freight (by reference to their concern for the performance of a voyage: s 12) and charterers (by reference to their payment of hire and interest in sub-chartering). It is unusual for a claim under a marine policy to fail for want of an insurable interest, not least because no policy may be effected in the absence (at the time of taking out the policy) of an existing interest or a legitimate expectation that such an interest will be acquired prior to any loss[1].

1 See *Mark Rowlands Ltd v Berni Inns Ltd* [1986] QB 211 per Kerr LJ at p 228.

The loss

5.4 Absent express provision within the policy as to the losses which the insurer agrees to cover, a policy is taken to cover any loss proximately caused by a peril insured against (s 55(1)). Losses which are not covered include any loss attributable to the wilful misconduct of the assured (although, unless the policy otherwise provides, any loss proximately caused by a peril insured against, even though the loss would not have happened but for the misconduct or negligence of the master or crew is covered: s 55(2)(a)), any loss proximately caused by delay (even if the delay is caused by a peril insured against: s 55(2)(b)), and ordinary wear and tear, ordinary leakage and breakage, inherent vice or nature of the subject matter insured, or any loss proximately caused by rats or vermin, or any injury to machinery not proximately caused by maritime perils (s 55(2)(c)).

Loss may be total or partial. Any loss other than a total loss is a partial loss (s 56(1)). A total loss may be either an actual total loss, or a constructive total loss (s 56(2)). Thus a policy which insures against 'total loss' alone will nevertheless permit a claim for constructive total loss[1]. Where there is a constructive total loss, the assured may either treat the loss as a partial loss, or abandon the subject matter insured to the insurer and treat the loss as if it were an actual total loss (s 61). Where the assured brings an action for a total loss and the evidence proves only a partial loss, they may, unless the policy otherwise provides, recover for a partial loss (s 56(4)).

Where the subject matter insured is destroyed, or so damaged as to cease to be a thing of the kind insured, or where the assured is irretrievably deprived thereof, there is an actual total loss (s 57(1)). A total loss may be established albeit that the subject still exists (for example, in cases of capture, seizure and condemnation)[2].

There is a *constructive* total loss where the subject matter insured is reasonably abandoned on account of its actual total loss appearing to be unavoidable, or because it could not be preserved from actual total loss without an expenditure, which would exceed its value when the expenditure had been incurred (s 60(1)). In this regard, a constructive total loss will be established where the assured is deprived of the possession of his ship or goods by a peril insured against, and (a) it is unlikely that he can recover the ship or goods, as the case may be, or (b) the cost of recovering the ship or goods, as the case may be, would exceed their value when recovered (s 60(2)(i)), where (in the case of damage to a ship), she is so damaged by a peril insured against that the cost of repairing the damage would exceed the value of the ship when repaired (s 60(2)(ii)), and where (in the case of damage to goods), the cost of repairing the damage and forwarding the goods to their destination would exceed their value on arrival (s 60(2)(iii)). Thus, a constructive total loss may be established where the prudent uninsured shipowner would consider the damage worth repairing[3]. However, the provision of notice of abandonment is a condition precedent to a claim for constructive total loss (s 62(1)) unless the circumstances of the loss would have the result that such notice was redundant as to permit or amount to the excusal or waiver of such notice (s 62(7))[4].

1 See *Adams v McKenzie* (1863) 32 LJCP 92.
2 *Cossman v West* (1887) 13 App Cas 160.
3 See *MacBeth & Co Ltd v Maritime Insurance Co Ltd* [1908] AC 144; *The Medina Princess* [1965] 1 Lloyd's Rep 361.
4 See *Kastor Navigation Co Ltd v AGF MAT* [2003] 1 Lloyd's Rep 296.

The burden of proof

5.5 Where an assured alleges that a loss was caused in a manner for which underwriters are responsible, underwriters are entitled by way of defence to say 'We require this case to be strictly proved, and admit nothing'; they are not obliged to put forward some affirmative case of their own as to the cause of the loss. Where such is the defence, the onus remains throughout upon the claimants to establish the case they are alleging[1]. However, if underwriters adopt this course, they are limited in the manner in which they can approach the case brought against them[2].

Thus, where underwriters simply put the assured to proof of their allegation that a loss was caused by an insured peril and advance no positive case of their own as to the cause of the loss, the position is as follows:

(1) Underwriters are entitled to:
   (a) cross-examine the assured's witnesses in order to demonstrate that the loss did not occur in the manner alleged by the assured;
   (b) cross-examine the assured's witnesses in order to demonstrate the possibility or probability that the damage was caused by some other means (e.g. ask the assured's expert if he has considered the possibility that the loss was caused by something other than the alleged peril);
   (c) call evidence of their own in order to disprove the evidence called by the assured (i.e. in order to show that the loss was not caused in the manner alleged).
(2) However, underwriters are not entitled to:
   (a) call evidence merely going to the credibility of the assured's witnesses;

(b) call evidence not directed at disproving evidence called by the assured, but directed at establishing an affirmative case as to an alternative cause which has not been pleaded;

(c) plead no affirmative case as to an alternative cause and, after all the evidence, invite the court or tribunal to infer that the true cause of the damage was something different from that alleged.

(3) Accordingly, there is a very fine line between what underwriters are legitimately entitled to do and what they are not permitted to do[3]. The critical observation is that, if underwriters simply put the assured to proof, they must not actively contend that an unpleaded cause was the cause of the damage.

In contrast, where underwriters seek to advance a positive defence (such as scuttling or non-disclosure), they will bear the burden of proving the same.

In the case of a defence of scuttling (MIA 1906, s 55(2)(a)), and while formally it is the case that underwriters must prove their case on the balance of probabilities, the standard of proof is linked to the gravity of the allegation. In this regard, and given that an allegation of scuttling is tantamount to an allegation of fraud or wilful misconduct, the standard of proof which rests upon underwriters in proving the allegation will be greater than that upon the assured seeking to prove their claim under the policy[4].

In the case of alleged non-disclosure (MIA 1906, ss 17–20), underwriters must adduce evidence to establish that a critical fact was not disclosed. In this regard, they must identify the risk to which it is contended the alleged non-disclosure is material[5]. However, once underwriters discharge the evidential burden of establishing a prima facie case of non-disclosure, the evidential burden shifts in the ordinary way to the assured in order to establish that the alleged material fact *was* disclosed[6].

1 See *Regina Fur Company Ltd v Bossom* [1958] 2 Lloyd's Rep 425 per Lord Evershed MR at p 428 and Sellers LJ at p 434.

2 See generally *Regina Fur Company Ltd v Bossom* [1958] 2 Lloyd's Rep 425 per Lord Evershed MR at p 428 and Sellers LJ at p 434; *Roselodge Ltd v Castle* [1966] 2 Lloyd's Rep 113 per McNair J at p 119; *The Dias* [1972] 2 QB 625 per Sachs LJ at p 636, Buckley LJ at p 640 and Cairns LJ at p 647; *The Popi M* [1985] 1 WLR 948 per Lord Brandon; *Morris v London Iron and Steel Co Ltd* [1988] QB 493 per May LJ at p 504; *The Marel* [1994] 1 Lloyd's Rep 624 per Dillon LJ at p 627; *The Milasan* [2000] 2 Lloyd's Rep 458 per Aikens J; and *The Vergina* [2001] 2 Lloyd's Rep 719 per Aikens J.

3 See *Roselodge Ltd v Castle* [1966] 2 Lloyd's Rep 113 per McNair J at 119.

4 See *The Gloria* (1936) 54 Ll L Rep 35 per Branson J at p 50; *The Ikarian Reefer* [1995] 1 Lloyd's Rep 455 per Stuart-Smith LJ at 459; *The Delphine* [2001] 2 Lloyd's Rep 542 per Toulson J at p 544.

5 See *The Elena G* [2001] 2 Lloyd's Rep 387 per David Steel J at p 382; *International Management Group (UK) Ltd v Simmonds* [2004] Lloyd's Rep IR 247 per Cooke J.

6 See *Glicksman v Lancashire and General Assurance Co Ltd* [1925] 2 KB 593, [1927] AC 139.

Pleading issues

5.6 Plainly, the purposes of a pleading is for each party clearly and precisely to set out its case in order that the other party knows and understands the case which it has to meet. General guidance in this regard may be obtained from **Chapter 2** of this work, CPR 16 and 16 PD, together with more specific guidance with regard to the Admiralty and Commercial Courts in CPR 58.5, 58.10, and 58.11, CPR 61 and the *Admiralty & Commercial Courts Guide*, section C.

On the part of the assured or claimant, and in the light of the matters stated above, this requires that the following are clearly pleaded and particularised as necessary.

(1) Details of the policy of marine insurance, including the subject insured, the insurable risk and any insured value.
(2) The interest of the assured or claimant in the subject insured and the policy.
(3) The occurrence and extent of any loss insured under the policy.
(4) The fact that the cause of the loss was an insured peril.
(5) Compliance with any condition precedent to a right to recover under the policy.
(6) The refusal or failure of underwriters to make payment under the policy.
(7) The consequent right to payment or indemnity under the policy or damages in the alternative.
(8) Any claim to interest.
(9) Any claim as to costs.

On the part of underwriters, while there is no obligation to plead references to evidence, appropriate particulars must be provided of any defence in circumstances where underwriters do otherwise than simply put the assured or claimant to proof. Such particulars might therefore include reference to evidence where underwriters contend that inferences should be drawn from such evidence[1]. In this regard, the following matters must be included:

(1) Full particulars of any scuttling allegation[2].
(2) Full particulars of any alleged non-disclosure[3].
(3) Full particulars of any alleged failure to comply with a condition precedent.
(4) Full particulars of the circumstances which give rise to the application of an exception within the policy.

1 See *The Michael* [1978] 1 WLR 411.
2 See *The Dias* [1972] 2 QB 625.
3 See *The Elena G* [2001] 2 Lloyd's Rep 387 per David Steel J at p 382; *International Management Group (UK) Ltd v Simmonds* [2004] Lloyd's Rep IR 247 per Cooke J.

Pleading: Total loss

Assumed facts

5.7 The Claimants, ABC Limited, were the owners of a passenger ferry, 'THE SUNSHINE EXPRESS'. The ferry was built in 1980 and bought in 1984 for US$5m. Since then she had been managed by ABC (Management) Limited and operated under a ferry service between Algeciras and Ceuta in the summer months from May to September. ABC Limited was effectively owned and controlled by Mr A, who was also one of three directors of ABC (Management) Limited along with his two brothers.

In 1984 'THE SUNSHINE EXPRESS' had been the sole vessel operating this service but in 1997, a rival company, the XYZ Corporation had commenced a ferry service operating high-speed catamarans, which significantly reduced the journey time. From 1998, ABC Limited's profits from 'THE SUNSHINE EXPRESS' had dwindled whilst their operating costs had steadily increased primarily due to higher maintenance costs. From 2000 onwards, ABC Limited were making a loss in operating the ferry service. They had tried but failed to sell 'THE SUNSHINE EXPRESS' initially for US$1.8m but reducing the price to US$1.5m in December 2001. This had been motivated in part by the fact that from July 2002 onwards, in order to continue operating to and from Morocco, 'THE SUNSHINE EXPRESS' would be required to comply with new safety regulations (The New Safety Regulations 2002).

In March 2002, ABC Limited insured 'THE SUNSHINE EXPRESS' with PQR Insurance Co. Limited for 12 months with an agreed value of the vessel of US$3m on terms which covered the risks of perils of the seas and negligence by any person whatsoever.

At this time, 'THE SUNSHINE EXPRESS' was at anchor at Cadiz for the winter season. She had been dry-docked and inspected by her classification society on 1 March 2002 whose surveyor found the vessel to be seaworthy. However, all of the necessary works for her to comply with the new safety regulations had not yet been carried out. Further, the ferry sailing schedules from Algeciras to Ceuta for the summer season 2002 had not yet been agreed with the port authorities or printed. At Cadiz, ABC (Management) Limited through Mr A had just hired three new crew (a master, his son as the engineer, and one other) to replace the former crew of seven, all of whom had been employed on 'THE SUNSHINE EXPRESS' since 1990 and had not been told of their replacement until the end of March 2002.

On 1 April 2002, with the new crew on board at about 05:30 hrs 'THE SUNSHINE EXPRESS' sank about 15 miles off the coast of Cadiz in the course of a voyage to Algeciras for the summer season. The crew were picked up by a passing fishing vessel and returned to Cadiz, where they were reunited with all of their personal possessions, which had been left behind on the quayside when they set off for Algeciras.

On 1 April 2002, PQR Insurance Co Limited were advised by ABC Limited that 'THE SUNSHINE EXPRESS' had been lost and that a claim on the policy of insurance would be made. It was admitted that 'THE SUNSHINE EXPRESS' had been lost in calm sea and good weather but asserted that she sank because all of the sea water valves located in the engine room had been opened and the stern vehicle ramp had been left open on leaving Cadiz.

In investigating the loss, PQR Insurance Co Limited interviewed the crew, one of whom, Mr Squealer said that he had no relevant experience on ferries but had been offered a lot of money to take the job with ABC (Management) Limited. In his signed statement, Mr Squealer said that before leaving the port of Cadiz he had noticed that they had left the stern vehicle ramp open but had been told by the master not to close it. Further, an expert advised PQR Insurance Co Limited that the ingress of water via the sea valves in the engine room would not have been sufficient by itself to sink 'THE SUNSHINE EXPRESS'.

PQR Insurance Co Limited rejected the claim and ABC Limited brought an action against them under the policy.

Particulars of Claim: Hull claim under marine insurance policy

Claim No ....

IN THE HIGH COURT OF JUSTICE
QUEEN'S BENCH DIVISION
COMMERCIAL COURT

B E T W E E N:

ABC LIMITED

Claimants

- and -

PQR INSURANCE CO. LIMITED

Defendants

PARTICULARS OF CLAIM

---

1. The Claimants are and were at all material times the Owners of the ferry 'THE SUNSHINE EXPRESS' ('the Vessel').

2. By a policy of marine insurance contained in or evidenced by Certificate No. 01/A/007/03052004/01/02 dated 3rd March 2002 ('the Policy') and subscribed by the Defendants to the extent of 100% the Vessel was insured at a value of US$3m against the perils specified therein, including perils of the seas and negligence of any person whatsoever, for a period of 12 months beginning on 30th March 2002.

3. The Claimants were at all material times fully interested in the Policy and will refer to the same for its full terms and effect.

4. On 1st April 2002, while insured under the Policy and in a position about 15 miles off the coast of Cadiz, the Vessel sank and was lost as a result of the fortuitous entry of sea water into the Vessel through sea valves in the engine room being mistakenly opened and/or the stern vehicle ramp being mistakenly left open by the Vessel's crew.

5. In the premises, the Vessel became a total loss by perils of the seas and/or the negligence of the Vessel's crew during the currency of the Policy.

6. On 1st April 2002, and in accordance with the terms of the Policy, the Claimants notified the Defendants of the sinking of the Vessel and that she had become a total loss.

7. As a result of the matters set out above, the Defendants became liable under the Policy to pay to the Claimants the sum of US$3m (being the value thereunder).

8. Wrongfully and in breach of contract the Defendants have failed and refused to pay the value under the Policy and/or US$3m and/or any sum to the Claimants.

9. As at the date of these Particulars of Claim, the sterling equivalent to US$3m amounts to £4.8m based on a US Dollar: Pound Sterling rate of US$1 = £1.60. The claim is made in US Dollars, that being the currency of the agreed value of the Vessel.

10. Further the Claimants are entitled to and claim interest, pursuant to section 35A of the Supreme Court Act 1981, upon the sum of US$3m at a rate of 6% per annum from 14th April 2002 to date

amounting to US$360,000 and thereafter at a daily rate of US$493.15 to judgment herein or sooner payment, alternatively on such other sum as the Court shall find due and/or at such rate and for such period as the Court shall think just.

AND the Claimants claim:

(1) US$3m, or alternatively damages.

(2) Interest pursuant to section 35A of the Supreme Court Act 1981 [and/or the inherent jurisdiction of the Court].

(3) Costs.

[Statement of Truth, etc][1]

Defence: Scuttling

Claim No ....

IN THE HIGH COURT OF JUSTICE
QUEEN'S BENCH DIVISION
COMMERCIAL COURT

B E T W E E N:

ABC LIMITED

Claimants

- and -

PQR INSURANCE CO. LIMITED

Defendants

D E F E N C E

---

1. Save as appears from the matters stated below, the Defendants join issue with the Claimants upon their Particulars of Claim as if the same were here set out in full and specifically not admitted or denied.

2. All references herein to paragraph numbers are to the numbered paragraphs within the Particulars of Claim unless otherwise stated.

3. Paragraphs 1 to 3 of the Particulars of Claim are admitted. The Defendants will refer to the Policy for its full terms and effect.

4. Save that it is admitted that on 1st April 2002, during the currency of the Policy, the Vessel sank so as to be totally lost 15 miles off

the coast of Cadiz, and save in so far as appears from paragraph 5 below, paragraph 4 is denied.

5. The Defendants will contend that the Vessel was, with the knowledge and/or connivance of the Claimants, wilfully cast away and/or otherwise disposed of by her master and crew. Prior to disclosure and without prejudice to the Defendants' right to rely upon other matters at trial, the Defendants will say as follows.

PARTICULARS

5.1 The sinking of the Vessel was deliberate. In this regard, the Defendants will rely upon, *inter alia*, the following facts and matters:

5.1.1 The Vessel sank in calm sea and weather conditions.

5.1.2 The Vessel sank only one month after having been dry-docked and surveyed, inspected and passed by her classification society.

5.1.3 All of the Vessel's sea valves in the engine room had been opened as the result of a deliberate act with the intention of bringing about the sinking and loss of the Vessel and not (as the Claimants contend) a result of negligence on the part of any party.

5.1.4 The stern vehicle ramp of the Vessel had been left open as the result of a deliberate act and not (as the Claimants contend) a result of negligence on the part of any party. In this regard, the master knew before leaving the port of Cadiz that the stern vehicle ramp had been left open but ordered the crew not to close it. Further, and in any event, there was no reason to open the stern vehicle ramp at Cadiz.

5.2 It is an obvious and/or inevitable inference that the sinking of the Vessel was caused with the connivance and/or knowledge of the Claimants when regard is had, *inter alia*, to the following matters:

5.2.1 The crew had no reason to sink the Vessel of their own volition.

5.2.2 The crew had only recently been employed onboard the Vessel, and the Claimants (through Mr A, who was the beneficial owner and/or the controlling mind and/or alter ego of the Claimants, and who was also a director of ABC (Management) Limited) had the opportunity to arrange a deliberate sinking and/or loss with the crew of the Vessel.

5.2.3 At the time of the casualty in April 2002:

5.2.3.1 The ferry sailing schedules from Algeciras to Ceuta for the summer season commencing in May 2002 had not yet been agreed with the port authorities nor printed.

5.2.3.2 The crew who had been hired for the summer season had no personal possessions on board the Vessel.

5.2.3.3 The Claimants had taken no steps to ensure that the Vessel complied with The New Safety Regulations 2002 despite having just come out of dry-dock. In order to do so would have required the Vessel to cease operating to Ceuta midway through the summer season of 2002.

5.2.4 The Vessel was some 22 years old in 2002. Attempts to sell the Vessel had been made since about 2000 but had been unsuccessful.

5.2.5 The Claimants were in financial difficulties and the Vessel's ferry service was making a loss.

5.2.6 The Vessel was insured for US$3m but the market value of the Vessel at the time of the casualty was unlikely to have exceeded US$1.5m.

The Defendants reserve the right to add to and/or amend these particulars on disclosure.

6. In the premises, save that it is admitted that in sinking the Vessel became a total loss, paragraph 5 is denied.

7. Without prejudice to the matters stated above, paragraph 6 is admitted.

8. In the premises, it is denied that the Defendants are liable to pay the sum of US$3m or any sum to the Claimants under the Policy or otherwise. The loss was not due to any insured peril and the Defendants are under no liability in respect thereof whether as alleged or at all. Accordingly, save that the Defendants have lawfully refused to pay the Claimants the sum of US$3m or any sum, paragraphs 7 and 8 are denied.

9. Without prejudice to the foregoing, in so far as there is a valid claim under the Policy (which is denied), the same is payable in US dollars and the exchange rates to which reference is made are applicable.

10. In the premises, it is denied that the Claimants are entitled to the relief claimed or any relief against the Defendants.

[Statement of Truth, etc][1]

1 Statement of truth, etc as set out in **Chapter 3, para 3.2**.

Pleading: Partial loss

Assumed facts

5.8 The Claimants, XYZ Limited, were the owners of 360 drums of menthol crystals packed in container No. TTNU 270893-3 ('the Goods') carried on board the 'WINTER EXPRESS' in March 2004 from Mumbai to Felixstowe. The Goods were carried pursuant to bill of lading No. 9560JNP06140. The Goods were insured under a policy of marine insurance No. 00MP00726G dated 1 March 2004.

Prior to loading, the shippers of the Goods instructed the carrier to keep the Goods below water level, under-deck, away from the engine room and any other heat source. On 12 March 2004 the container was loaded immediately adjacent to the vessel's No.4 lower wing tank starboard and the vessel proceeded to the port of discharge, namely Felixstowe and arrived on or about 17 April 2000.

On opening the container, it was discovered that the contents had shifted to varying degrees with drums having partially toppled over and that there was a large amount of menthol webbing on and around the drums. XYZ Limited alleged that the damage (which affected 293 of the 360 drums) was caused by the Goods being subjected to high temperatures during carriage, causing the menthol crystals to evaporate and reform in the large amounts of webbing noted on inspection. Insurers declined liability on the basis that the damage was caused due to insufficient packing or exposure to excessive temperatures prior to shipment.

Particulars of Claim: Cargo claim under marine insurance policy

Claim No ....

IN THE HIGH COURT OF JUSTICE
QUEEN'S BENCH DIVISION
COMMERCIAL COURT [ADMIRALTY COURT]

B E T W E E N:

XYZ LIMITED

Claimants

- and -

PQR INSURANCE CO LIMITED

Defendants

PARTICULARS OF CLAIM

---

1. By a policy of marine insurance No. 00MP00726G dated 1st March 2004 ('the Policy'), the Defendants agreed to insure 360 drums of menthol crystals packed in container No. TTNU 270893-3 ('the Cargo') against the perils set out therein including perils of the sea for a voyage from Mumbai to Felixstowe on board the vessel 'WINTER EXPRESS' ('the vessel') sailing from Mumbai on or about 12th March 2004.

2. The Policy, to which the Claimants will refer for its full terms, meaning and effect, incorporated the Institute Cargo Clauses (A) which provided amongst other provisions as follows:

'Clause 1

This insurance covers all risks of loss of or damage to the subject matter insured except as provided in Clauses 4, 5, 6 and 7 below'.

'Clause 16

It is the duty of the Assured and their servants and agents in respect of loss recoverable hereunder

16.1 to take such measures as may be reasonable for the purpose of averting or minimising such loss and

16.2 to ensure that all rights against carriers, bailees or other third parties are properly preserved and exercised

and the Underwriters will in addition to any loss recoverable hereunder reimburse the Assured for any charges properly and reasonably incurred in pursuance of these duties.'

3. The Claimants were at all material times the Owners of the Cargo and therefore fully interested in the Cargo and in the Policy.

4. Prior to loading, the shippers of the Cargo instructed the carrier to keep the Cargo below water level, under-deck, away from the engine room and any other heat source.

5. On or about 12th March 2004 the Cargo was loaded on board the Vessel in bay 23 of hold No. 4, level 02, position 07. The container was loaded immediately adjacent to the vessel's No. 4 lower wing tank starboard.

6. The Vessel proceeded to the port of discharge, namely Felixstowe and arrived on or about 17th April 2004.

7. On opening the container, it was discovered that the contents had shifted to varying degrees with drums having partially toppled over and that there was a large amount of menthol webbing on and around the drums.

8. As a result, the Claimants reasonably attempted to minimise their loss by arranging for the container to be cleaned and the sound drums of menthol crystals to be recovered. In so doing, the Claimants incurred charges of £50,000.

9. In the premises, pursuant to clause 16 of the Institute Cargo Clauses (A), the Claimants are entitled to recover from the Defendants the sum of £50,000 incurred in taking reasonable measures for the purpose of averting or minimising loss.

10. Further, upon discharge, it was discovered that the Cargo had suffered heat damage.

<u>PARTICULARS</u>

The best particulars that the Claimants can provide at this stage are provided without prejudice to their right to provide further particulars following disclosure.

10.1 The cargo was subjected to high temperatures during the voyage.

10.2 As a result, the menthol crystals evaporated and reformed in the large amounts of webbing noted on inspection.

11. The damage to the Goods occurred during the currency of the Policy by reason of a peril or perils insured against, namely perils of the sea.

PARTICULARS

11.1 Contrary to the express instructions given by the shippers of the cargo, the cargo was placed adjacent to the vessel's No. 4 lower wing tank starboard, a source of heat.

11.2 Steam heating is applied to the fuel oil contained in such tanks to reduce the viscosity of the oil to enable it to be pumped to the engine room for consumption.

11.3 It was the positioning of the container next to the fuel oil tank that was the source of heat which caused damage to the cargo.

12. By the reason of the matters set out above, the Claimants have suffered loss and damage, together with expense in the sum of £50,000, by reason of a peril insured against and are entitled to be indemnified against the same by the Defendants.

PARTICULARS OF LOSS

12.1	Sound arrived value of damaged cargo	£134,704.77.
12.2	Expenses	£50,000.

13. Wrongfully, and in breach of contract, the Defendants have failed to pay this sum or any part thereof to the Claimants.

14. Further, the Claimants are entitled to and claim interest pursuant to section 35A of the Supreme Court Act 1981 [and/or the inherent jurisdiction of the Court] for such period and at such rate as the Court considers just.

AND the Claimants claim:

(1) The sum of £134,704.77 and £50,000, alternatively damages.

(2) Interest pursuant to section 35A of the Supreme Court Act 1981 [and/or the inherent jurisdiction of the court].

(3) Costs.

Filed and served this day of 2004

[Statement of Truth, etc][1]

Defence: Cargo claim under marine insurance policy

Claim No ....

IN THE HIGH COURT OF JUSTICE
QUEEN'S BENCH DIVISION
COMMERCIAL COURT [ADMIRALTY COURT]

B E T W E E N:

XYZ LIMITED

Claimants

-and-

PQR INSURANCE CO. LIMITED

Defendants

D E F E N C E

---

1. Save as expressly admitted or not admitted, each and every allegation contained in the Claimants' Particulars of Claim is denied.

2. Paragraphs 1 and 2 are admitted.

3. The Policy also incorporated the following express provisions of the Institute Cargo Clauses (A):

   '*Clause 4*

   In no case shall this insurance cover:

   4.1 ...

   4.2 ...

4.3 loss damage or expense caused by insufficiency or unsuitability of packing or preparation of the subject matter insured (for the purpose of this Clause 4.3 "packing" shall be deemed to include stowage in a container or lift van but only when such stowage is carried out prior to attachment of this insurance or by the Assured or their servants)'

4. No admissions are made as to paragraph 3 to 7.

5. As to paragraphs 8 and 9, the 360 drums of menthol crystals were packed in the container without sufficient strapping and/or dunnage to enable the Cargo to withstand the ordinary incidents of the voyage. Further, prior to shipment, the container had failed to be adequately packed with dry ice.

6. In the premises, if, which is not admitted, the Claimants incurred charges in respect of cleaning the container and recovering the sound drums, the same was caused by the inherent vice of the Cargo and/or the insufficiency or unsuitability of the packing. The Claimants are further put to strict proof that the costs of cleaning the container fall within the terms of the Policy.

7. No admissions are made as to paragraph 10.

8. As to paragraph 11, the damage to the Cargo was caused prior to loading in that the container had been stored in the dockyard at Mumbai for a period of 10 days prior to shipment without any refrigeration. If, which is not admitted, the Cargo suffered heat damage, any loss of menthol was caused by sublimation prior to shipment. In the premises, the alleged loss or damage was caused by the inherent vice of the Cargo and, pursuant to the Marine Insurance Act 1906, s 55(2)(c), the Defendants are not liable in respect of the same.

9. Without prejudice to the foregoing, no admissions are made as to paragraph 12.

10. Further and alternatively, and without prejudice to the foregoing, if (which is denied) the Defendants are liable under the Policy as alleged or at all, pursuant to the Marine Insurance Act 1906, s 71(3) the Defendants are liable only to the extent of such proportion of the insured value of the Cargo as the difference between the gross sound and damaged values at the place of arrival bears to the gross sound value.

11. Save that it is admitted that the Defendants have not paid the amount claimed, paragraph 13 is denied for the reasons set out above.

12. Paragraph 14 is noted but denied.

Filed and served this day of 2004

[Statement of Truth, etc][1]

1 Statement of truth, etc as set out in **Chapter 3, para 3.2**.

CHAPTER 6

Carriage of Goods by Road and Air

Carriage of goods by road:
John Russell

Carriage of goods by air:
Matthew Reeve

CARRIAGE OF GOODS BY ROAD

Law

6.1 Most international carriage of goods by road within Europe is governed by the Convention on the Contract for the International Carriage of Goods by Road ('the CMR')[1]. The CMR has the force of law by virtue of the Carriage of Goods by Road Act 1965. The CMR is set out in the Schedule to that Act.

A detailed analysis of the CMR is beyond the scope of this work, but in broad terms the scheme of the CMR is as follows:

- The carrier is liable for the total or partial loss of the goods and for damage to the goods occurring between the time when he takes over the goods and the time of delivery, as well as for any delay in delivery[2].
- There are certain exceptions to liability[3] (for example default of the claimant; inherent vice; circumstances which the carrier could not avoid and the consequences of which he was unable to prevent).
- The compensation payable by the carrier is calculated by reference to the value of the goods at the place and time at which they were accepted for carriage[4]. In addition, carriage charges, Customs duties and other charges incurred in respect of the carriage of the goods shall be refunded in full in case of total loss and in proportion to the loss sustained in case of partial loss[5].
- The carrier is entitled to limit his liability to 8.33 SDRs per kilo of gross weight of the goods[6]. The right to limit applies only to the compensation payable under art 23(1), and not to the other refundable items under article.
- The right to limit will be lost if the loss, damage or delay was caused by the carrier's wilful misconduct or equivalent default[7].
- Where the carriage is governed by a single contract, but the carriage is in fact performed by successive road carriers, each of the carriers is responsible for the performance of the whole operation, the second carrier and each successive carrier becoming a party to the contract of carriage, under the terms of the consignment note, by reason of his acceptance of the goods and the consignment note[8].
- However, the claimant can sue only the first carrier, the last carrier, or the carrier performing that portion of the carriage during which the event causing the loss, damage or delay occurred ('the actual carrier')[9].

- It should be noted that while a failure to comply with the formalities, such as the issuance of a consignment note, will not, in general, affect the liability of the first contracting carrier, successive carriers are only liable to the claimant if a consignment note has been issued and this has been accepted with the goods by the successive carrier.
- A detailed regime for claims between carriers in the case of successive carriage is set out in arts 37 to 40. In addition to this regime, sub-contracts within the successive carriage chain may themselves be primary CMR contracts.
- There are strict time limits for commencement of claims[10].

Where the carriage is not governed by the CMR – principally domestic carriage within the UK – the likelihood is that the carriage will be governed by the carrier's standard terms and conditions, which, in the case of UK carriers, will usually be, or will be modelled on, the Road Haulage Association Conditions of Carriage ('the RHA conditions') or the British International Freight Association Standard Trading Conditions ('the BIFA conditions')[11].

1 The abbreviation 'CMR' is the acronym for the French title of the convention: 'Convention relative au Contrat de Transport International de Marchandises par Route'.
2 Article 17(1).
3 Article 17(2)–(5).
4 Article 23(1).
5 Article 23(4). A common feature in CMR claims is a claim for tobacco and alcohol duty payable following the theft of such goods. The House of Lords in *Buchanan v Babco* [1978] AC 141 held that such duty is recoverable from the carrier under art 23(4) as being an 'other charge incurred in respect of the carriage of the goods'. However, this is not universally accepted in other jurisdictions, and the Court of Appeal has recently cast some doubt on the *Buchanan* decision, stating, in *Sandeman Coprimar v Transitos y Transportes Integrales* [2003] QB 1270 that: 'We do not consider that the [*Buchanan*] decision should be applied any more widely by the courts of this country than respect for the doctrine of precedent requires'.
6 Article 23(3).
7 Article 29.
8 Article 34.
9 Article 36.
10 Articles 32, 39(4).
11 The most recent RHA conditions are the 1998 conditions, and the most recent BIFA conditions are the 2000 conditions. However, it is not always the most recent conditions which are incorporated (some carriers continue to use stationery referring to prevision editions of the RHA or BIFA conditions, for example), and so this needs to be checked in each case.

Some issues to be considered before drafting

6.2 *Does the CMR apply?* – As indicated above, most international carriage will be governed by the CMR: Article 1(1) of the CMR provides that,

> 'This Convention shall apply to every contract for the carriage of goods by road in vehicles for reward, when the place of taking over of the goods and the place designated for delivery, as specified in the contract, are situated in two different countries, of which at least one is a contracting country, irrespective of the place of residence and the nationality of the parties'[1].

However, there are certain exceptions, and in the case of multimodal transport there may be an issue as to whether the contract is in fact a contract for carriage by road at all[2].

Do the English courts have jurisdiction? – See, e.g. art 31 of the CMR, Council Regulation (EC) No 1348/2000 of 29 May 2000 (the Brussels Regulation), and CPR Part 6III.

Who should be named as claimants? – At the pleading stage the sensible, pragmatic approach is to seek permission to name as claimants any party that might possibly be interested in the goods – sender, consignee, any other possible owner, and, if the goods were insured under a policy which may be governed by a foreign law pursuant to which the insurer gains rights to sue in his own name, the insurer. It is a very rare case where adding claimants will cause any increase in costs, so there is no downside to multiple joinder.

Who should be named as defendants? – This is potentially more difficult, as joining defendants unnecessarily is likely to increase costs, which the claimants may eventually have to pay. Attempts should be made in advance of the issuance of proceedings to gain agreement from the potential defendants as to their status (agent or carrier; and as to first, performing and last carrier). If agreement is not reached the prudent course is to join all possible defendants.

Keeping options open – Often, when Particulars of Claim are being drafted, the precise relationship between the various bodies engaged on the carriage side will be unclear. There may be limited documentation available until disclosure (or indeed at all), and potential defendants may not volunteer information. It is prudent therefore to plead all possible alternative cases, to avoid the need for subsequent amendments.

1 The following are the contracting countries: Austria, Belarus, Belgium, Bosnia and Herzegovina, Bulgaria, Croatia, Czech Republic, Denmark, Estonia, Finland, France, Georgia, Germany, Greece, Hungary, Iran, Ireland, Italy, Kazakhstan, Kyrgyzstan, Latvia, Lithuania, Luxembourg, Macedonia, Moldova, Morocco, Netherlands, Norway, Poland, Portugal, Romania, Russian Federation, Slovakia, Slovenia, Spain, Sweden, Switzerland, Tajikistan, Tunisia, Turkey, Turkmenistan, United Kingdom, Uzbekistan and Yugoslavia.

2 See *Quantum v Plane Trucking* [2002] 1 WLR 2678.

Specimen statements of case

Known facts

6.3 Alpha (an English company) sell a consignment of computer chips, worth US$500,000 and weighing 10 kg to Bravo (a German company). The goods are insured by Charlie (Dutch underwriters). It is not clear what law the policy is governed by, at this stage. Alpha contact their usual freight forwarders, Delta and tell them that the consignment is to be carried from Alpha's premises in London to Bravo's premises in Frankfurt. Delta collect the goods and carry them to their London hub. They contact Echo, a major road haulier, and instruct Echo to carry the goods from the London hub to Bravo's premises in Frankfurt. Echo in turn instruct an owner/driver, Mr Foxtrot, to carry the goods. It is not clear whether Mr Foxtrot is an employee of Echo, or an independent contractor. Delta issue a CMR consignment note naming Delta as sender, Bravo as consignee and Echo as carrier. Mr Foxtrot collects the goods and the consignment note and sets off in an unmarked white van. The goods are sitting in the back of the van. Shortly afterwards, while driving down a quiet side road, a car stops in front of the van. Two men jump out waving guns. They open Mr Foxtrot's door, pull him out of the seat, and drive off. The goods are never recovered.

The statements of case

6.4 The specimen statements of case are: Particulars of Claim, first defendant's Defence, Reply, and Part 20 Particulars of Claim by the first defendant against the second and third defendants. This is not a complete set of statements of case, for example there is no Defence for the second or third defendants, but the form of their Defences would broadly follow the pattern of the first defendant's (though clearly some arguments might not be available to them).

Particulars of Claim

<u>Claim No ....</u>

<u>IN THE HIGH COURT OF JUSTICE</u>
<u>QUEEN'S BENCH DIVISION</u>
<u>COMMERCIAL COURT</u>

B E T W E E N:

(1) ALPHA

(2) BRAVO

(3) CHARLIE

<u>Claimants</u>

- and -

(1) DELTA

(2) ECHO

(3) FOXTROT

<u>Defendants</u>

PARTICULARS OF CLAIM

---

1. At all material times the first and/or second claimants were the owners of and/or were entitled to immediate possession of a consignment of computer chips ('the goods').

2. By a contract of carriage made on or about [date] between the first and/or second claimants and the first and/or second and/or third defendants the first and/or second and/or third defendants agreed

to carry the goods for reward from the first claimant's premises in London and/or from the first defendant's premises in London, to the second claimant's premises in Frankfurt, Germany.

3. The provisions of the Convention on the Contract for the International Carriage of Goods by Road as set out in the Schedule to the Carriage of Goods by Road Act 1965 ('the CMR') have the force of law in relation to the said carriage.

4. The CMR, to which the claimants shall refer in full, provides *inter alia* as follows:

'*Article 17*

(1) The carrier shall be liable for the total or partial loss of the goods and for damage thereto occurring between the time when he takes over the goods and the time of delivery, as well as for any delay in delivery.

Article 27

(1) The claimant shall be entitled to claim interest on compensation payable. Such interest, calculated at five per centum per annum, shall accrue from the date on which the claim was sent in writing to the carrier, or, if no such claim has been made, from the date on which legal proceedings were instituted.

Article 34

If carriage governed by a single contract is performed by successive road carriers, each of them shall be responsible for the performance of the whole operation, the second carrier and each succeeding carrier becoming a party to the contract of carriage, under the terms of the consignment note, by reason of his acceptance of the goods and the consignment note.

Article 36

Except in the case of a counter-claim or a set-off raised in an action concerning a claim based on the same contract of carriage, legal proceedings in respect of liability for loss, damage or delay may only be brought against the first carrier, the last carrier or the carrier who was performing that portion of the carriage.'

5. The first and/or second and/or third defendants took over the goods and the CMR consignment note on or about [date].

6. In the premises, the first and/or second and/or third defendants became bailees of the goods.

7. On or about [date] while the goods were being carried by the third defendant they were stolen and they have not been recovered.

8. In the premises, the first and/or second and/or third defendants are liable for the loss of the goods pursuant to article 17 of the CMR. The first and/or second defendants were the first carrier and the second and/or third defendants were the performing and/or last carrier.

9. Further or alternatively, the loss of the goods was caused by the first and/or second and/or third defendants' breach of contract and/or breach of their duties in bailment and/or by the negligence of the third defendant, for whose acts the second defendant is vicariously liable. Without prejudice to the burden of proof which is on the defendants, the first and/or second and/or third defendant and/or those for whose acts and omissions they were responsible failed to take reasonable care of the goods as follows:

PARTICULARS

9.1 Providing information about the consignment and the route to the thieves. The claimants will contend that the fact that the thieves targeted an unmarked van carrying a high value cargo demonstrates that they were provided with such information.

9.2 Carrying the goods in an ordinary van. The goods should have been carried in a proper security van and/or in a secure locked box (for which the driver did not have the key) which was securely fixed to the van.

9.3 Failing to fit a panic button in the van.

9.4 Failing to fit a satellite tracking device in the van.

9.5 Driving with the driver's door unlocked.

10. By reason of the matters aforesaid the first and/or second claimants have suffered loss and damage:

PARTICULARS

10.1 Value of the goods: US$500,000

11. Further or alternatively, the third claimants were the insurers of the goods. To the extent that the rights of action of the first and/or second claimants have passed by operation of law or otherwise to the third claimants, the third claimants rely on the matters set out above.

12. Further the claimants are entitled to and claim interest to be assessed pursuant to article 27 of the CMR and/or section 35A of the Supreme Court Act 1981.

AND the claimants claim:

(1) Compensation pursuant to the CMR; and/or

(2) Damages; and

(3) Interest.

[Statement of Truth, etc][1]

Defence

<u>Claim No ....</u>

<u>IN THE HIGH COURT OF JUSTICE</u>
<u>QUEEN'S BENCH DIVISION</u>
<u>COMMERCIAL COURT</u>

B E T W E E N:

(1) ALPHA

(2) BRAVO

(3) CHARLIE

<u>Claimants</u>

- and -

(1) DELTA

(2) ECHO

(3) FOXTROT

<u>Defendants</u>

DEFENCE OF FIRST DEFENDANT

---

1. In this statement of case, unless the contrary appears:

   1.1 References to paragraph numbers are to the paragraphs of the Particulars of Claim;

   1.2 The terminology used in the Particulars of Claim is adopted.

2. Save for the admissions and denials in this Defence, no admissions are made as to any matters in the Particulars of Claim and the claimants are required to prove the same.

3. Paragraph 1 is not admitted.

4. As to paragraph 2, it is admitted that on or about [date] the first defendant agreed with the first and/or second claimants to carry the goods from the first claimant's premises in London to the first defendant's premises in London, and thereafter to arrange the carriage of the goods from its premises to the premises of the second claimant in Frankfurt. The first defendant, as agent for the first and/or second claimants only, entered into a contract of carriage with the second and/or third defendants for the said carriage from its premises to the premises of the second claimant. Save as aforesaid paragraph 2 is denied.

5. As to paragraph 3, it is denied that the CMR had any application to the contract between the first and/or second claimants and the first defendant as it was not a contract of international carriage by road.

6. Paragraph 4 is admitted, but the terms of the CMR are not relevant to the claim against the first defendant.

7. The first defendant's standard terms and conditions were incorporated into the contract between the first and/or second claimants and the first defendant. The said terms, provided, *inter alia*, as follows:

> *'Clause 10. The [first defendant] shall not be liable in any circumstances whatsoever for any sum in excess of £100.'*

8. If, which is denied, the first defendant contracted to carry the goods from London to Frankfurt, then it is admitted that the CMR applied to the said carriage.

9. The CMR provides, *inter alia*, as follows:

   '*Article 17*

   (2) *The carrier shall however be relieved of liability if the loss, damage or delay was caused by the wrongful act of neglect of the claimant, by the instructions of the claimant given otherwise than as the result of a wrongful act or neglect on the part of the carrier, by inherent vice of the goods or through circumstances which the carrier could not avoid and the consequences of which he was unable to prevent.*

   Article 23

   (3) *Compensation shall not, however, exceed 8.33 units of account per kilogram of gross weight short.*'

10. As to paragraph 5, it is admitted that the first defendant collected the goods from the first claimant's premises on [date]. It is denied that the first defendant took over the consignment note.

11. As to paragraph 6, it is admitted that the first defendant became a bailee of the goods when it collected them from the first claimant's premises. The first defendant fulfilled its duties as a bailee, and ceased to be a bailee, when it delivered them safely to the second and/or third defendants for the carriage from its premises to Frankfurt.

12. Paragraph 7 is admitted.

13. As to paragraph 8, it is denied that the first defendant is liable as alleged or at all, and it is denied that the first defendant was the first carrier for the purposes of the CMR.

14. Paragraph 9 is denied.

15. Further or alternatively, any liability of the first defendant to the claimants is limited to the sum of £100 by virtue of clause 10 of the first defendant's standard terms and conditions.

16. Further or alternatively, if, contrary to the first defendant's primary case, the CMR applies:

    16.1 The first defendant is relieved of liability pursuant to article 17(2) as the goods were lost through circumstances which the first and/or second and/or third defendants could not avoid and the consequences of which they were unable to prevent; and/or

    16.2 The compensation payable is limited pursuant to article 23(3) to 8.33 SDRs per kilo. The claimants are required to prove the weight of the goods.

17. As to paragraph 10, it is denied that the first defendant is liable to the claimants as alleged or at all. The value of the goods is not admitted and the claimants are required to prove the same.

18. No admissions are made as to paragraph 11.

19. The claimants' claim, and claim to interest, are denied.

[Statement of Truth, etc][1]

Reply

<u>Claim No ....</u>

<u>IN THE HIGH COURT OF JUSTICE</u>
<u>QUEEN'S BENCH DIVISION</u>
<u>COMMERCIAL COURT</u>

B E T W E E N:

(1) ALPHA

(2) BRAVO

(3) CHARLIE

<u>Claimants</u>

- and -

(1) DELTA

(2) ECHO

(3) FOXTROT

<u>Defendants</u>

REPLY TO THE DEFENCE OF THE FIRST DEFENDANT

---

1. In this statement of case, unless the contrary appears:

    1.1 References to paragraph numbers are to the paragraphs of the first defendant's Defence;

    1.2 The terminology used in the Particulars of Claim is adopted.

2. Save for the admissions and denials in this statement of case, and save in so far as the first defendant's Defence is inconsistent with matters pleaded the Particulars of Claim (in which case the Defence is denied, and the matters pleaded in the Particulars of Claim are repeated), no admissions are made as to any of the matters pleaded in the first defendant's Defence, and the first defendant is required to prove the same.

3. As to paragraph 7, it is denied that the first defendant's standard terms and conditions were incorporated into the contract between the claimant and the defendant.

4. Further or alternatively, article 41(1) of the CMR provides:

> *'Subject to the provisions of article 40, any stipulation which would directly or indirectly derogate from the provisions of this Convention shall be null and void . . .'*

In the premises, clause 10 of the first defendant's standard terms and conditions is null and void.

5. Further or alternatively, clause 10 is unenforceable as it fails to satisfy the test of reasonableness for the purposes of the Unfair Contract Terms Act 1977.

6. As to paragraph 16.1, it is denied that the goods were lost through circumstances which the first and/or second and/or third defendants could not avoid and the consequences of which they were unable to prevent. If the first and/or second and/or third defendants had not failed to exercise reasonable care as alleged in paragraph 9 of the Particulars of Claim the goods would not have been lost.

7. As to paragraph 16.2, article 29 of the CMR provides:

> *'The carrier shall not be entitled to avail himself of the provisions of this chapter which exclude or limit his liability or which shift the burden of proof if the damage was caused by his wilful misconduct or by such default on his part as, in accordance with the law of the court or tribunal seised of the case, is considered as equivalent to wilful misconduct*
>
> *The same provision shall apply if the wilful misconduct or default is committed by the agents or servants of the carrier or by any other persons of whose services he makes use for the performance of the carriage, when such agents, servants or other persons are acting within the scope of their employment.'*

8. The claimant's primary case as set out in paragraph 9.1 of the Particulars of Claim is that an agent or servant of the first and/or second and/or third defendants or some other person of whose services they made use for the performance of the carriage provided the thieves with information about the carriage of the goods. This constituted wilful misconduct or equivalent default, and accordingly it is denied that the first defendant is entitled to limit its liability in accordance with the CMR.

9. Further or alternatively, the decision to carry the goods in an ordinary van which did not have a secure box and/or panic button and/or tracking device constituted wilful misconduct or equivalent default. Whoever took this decision knew that it was seriously wrong and/or that it would increase the risk of the goods being lost and/or took the decision with reckless indifference to the consequences.

[Statement of Truth, etc][1]

Part 20 Particulars of Claim

Claim No …………

IN THE HIGH COURT OF JUSTICE
QUEEN'S BENCH DIVISION
COMMERCIAL COURT

B E T W E E N:

(1) ALPHA

(2) BRAVO

(3) CHARLIE

Claimants

- and -

DELTA

First defendant/ Part 20 claimant

ECHO

Second defendant/ First Part 20 defendant

FOXTROT

Third defendant/ Second Part 20 defendant

FIRST DEFENDANT'S PART 20 PARTICULARS OF CLAIM AGAINST SECOND AND THIRD DEFENDANTS

---

1. The claimants have claimed compensation pursuant to the CMR and/or damages from the first defendant.

2. The first defendant had denied liability to the claimants.

3. If, contrary to the first defendant's denial of liability, the first defendant is found liable to the claimants, then the first defendant claims against the second and/or third defendants as follows.

4. Article 37 of the CMR provides as follows:

   'Article 37

   A carrier who has paid compensation in compliance with the provisions of this Convention, shall be entitled to recover such compensation, together with interest thereon and all costs and expenses incurred by reason of the claim, from the other carriers who have taken part in the carriage, subject to the following provisions:

   (a) the carrier responsible for the loss or damage shall be solely liable for the compensation whether paid by himself or by another carrier;

   (b) when the loss or damage has been caused by the action of two or more carriers, each of them shall pay an amount proportionate to his share of liability; should it be impossible to apportion the liability, each carrier shall be liable in proportion to the share of the payment for the carriage which is due to him;

   (c) if it cannot be ascertained to which carriers liability is attributable for the loss or damage, the amount of the compensation shall be apportioned between all the carriers as laid down in (b) above.'

5. If, contrary to the first defendant's pleaded Defence, it is liable as first CMR carrier to pay compensation to the claimants, it is

entitled to recover such compensation, any interest thereon, and all costs and expenses incurred by reason of the claim from the second and/or third defendants who were the carriers responsible for the loss of the goods.

6. Further or alternatively, if, contrary to the first defendant's pleaded Defence, it contracted with the first and/or second claimants to carry the goods, then the first defendant as sender entered into a sub-contract with the second and/or third defendants which sub-contract was a contract of carriage for the carriage of the goods from London to Frankfurt and which was itself subject to the provisions of the CMR. The first defendant repeats the claimant's Particulars of Claim against the second and third defendants, mutatis mutandis.

7. Further or alternatively, the second and third defendants are liable to the claimants in respect of the same damage as the first defendant is liable to the claimants for, and the first defendant is entitled to and claims an indemnity or contribution pursuant to the Civil Liability (Contribution) Act 1978.

AND the first defendant claims:

(1) Compensation, interest, costs and expenses pursuant to the CMR.

(2) Damages.

(3) Interest.

(4) An indemnity or contribution pursuant to the Civil Liability (Contribution) Act 1978.

[Statement of Truth, etc][1]

1 Statement of truth, etc as set out in **Chapter 3, para 3.2**.

CARRIAGE OF GOODS BY AIR

Law

The Warsaw Convention

6.5 The carriage of goods by air is largely regulated by a series of international treaties, starting with and based on the Warsaw Convention 1929 ('Convention for the Unification of Certain Rules relating to International Carriage by Air') which have been given the force of law in the United Kingdom by statute. There is no single applicable treaty text. Depending on the circumstances of the case, one of the following versions of the Warsaw Convention will usually apply:

(1) The unamended Warsaw Convention, 1929, given the force of law as Sch 2 to the Carriage by Air (Application of Provisions) Order 2004 (SI 2004/1899) (the 'unamended Warsaw Convention').

(2) The Warsaw Convention as amended at The Hague, 1955, given the force of law as Sch 1 to the Carriage by Air Act 1961 (as amended) (the 'Hague-Warsaw Convention').

(3) The Warsaw Convention as amended by Montreal Additional Protocol No 1 of 1975, given the force of law as Sch 3 to the Carriage by Air (Application of Provisions) Order 2004 (SI 2004/1899) (the 'MAP1 Convention').

(4) The Warsaw Convention as amended at The Hague and as further amended by Montreal Additional Protocol No 4 of 1975, given the force of law as Sch 1A to the Carriage by Air Act 1961(as amended) (the 'MP4 Convention').

(5) The Montreal Convention 1999, which restated the Warsaw Convention with revisions, given the force of law in the United Kingdom, with effect from 28 June 2004, as Sch 1B to the Carriage by Air Act 1961 (as amended) (the 'Montreal Convention')[1].

The first four versions above are all supplemented by the provisions of the Guadalajara Convention 1961, which has been given the force of law in the United Kingdom as the Schedule to the Carriage by Air Act (Supplementary Provisions) Act 1962 and Part B of Sch 2 of the Carriage by Air (Application of Provisions) Order 2004 (SI 2004/1899). The provisions of the Guadalajara Convention are restated in the body of the Montreal Convention, with minor drafting changes.

1 See the Carriage by Air Acts (Implementation of the Montreal Convention 1999) Order 2002 (SI 2002/263).

Carriage for reward/gratuitous carriage/carriage by an air transport undertaking

6.6 Each version of the Warsaw Convention is expressed (by art 1(1)) to apply only to carriage performed by aircraft for reward or to gratuitous carriage by aircraft performed by an air transport undertaking[1]. Accordingly, where loss is suffered in the course of gratuitous carriage by air by a person other than an air transport undertaking, the claimant should make his or her claims under the general law, including bailment, contract and tort.

1 A business is an 'air transport undertaking' if it has provided carriage for reward in the past and continues to offer to do so: *Gurtner v Beaton* (1990) 1 S & B Av R VII/499; affirmed on other grounds [1993] 2 Lloyd's Rep 369.

The selection of the correct treaty version

6.7 The selection of the applicable treaty, in cases of international carriage of cargo by air, depends upon the places of departure and destination provided for in the contract of carriage. Each treaty is expressed to apply to 'international carriage' of cargo and, in each case, art 1(2) gives (with some slight differences in wording) a definition of international carriage which applies it to carriage in which, according to the agreement between the parties, the place of departure and the place of destination (whether or not there be a break in the carriage or a transhipment) are situated either within the territories of two states who are parties to that treaty, or are within the territory of a single party to the treaty if there is an agreed stopping place within the territory of another state, even if that state is not a party. The nationality of the aircraft and the nationality and place of residence of the parties to the contract of carriage are irrelevant. It is, therefore, important to identify the places of departure and destination provided for in the contract of carriage and to determine to which treaty version the states in which those places are situated are a party. Where the respective states in which the places of departure and destination are situated are party to more than one of the relevant treaties, the later version applies[1].

The Carriage by Air (Parties to Convention) Order 1999 (SI 1999/1313) identifies the states who are parties to the unamended Warsaw Convention, the Hague-Warsaw Convention and the MAP1 Convention, and the dates when they became parties. The Carriage by Air (Parties to Protocol No 4 of 1975) Order 2000 (SI 2000/3061) performs the same function in respect of the MP4 Convention. At the date of writing, there was no similar English statutory provision identifying the parties to the Montreal Convention[2].

1 See, in the case of the Montreal Convention, art 55.
2 This information may be available on the website of the International Civil Aviation Organisation at www.icao.org.

Non-international carriage

6.8 A version of the Montreal Convention is given the force of law as Sch 1 to the Carriage by Air (Application of Provisions) Order 2004 (SI 2004/1899) (as amended). It applies to carriage for reward or by an air transport undertaking not falling within the meaning of 'international carriage' above (because it is performed entirely within the United Kingdom or other British territory or because it is international carriage between the United Kingdom and a state which is not a party to any version of the Warsaw Convention[1]).

1 The schedule does not apply carriage performed entirely within the territory of foreign state: *Holmes v Bangladeshi Biman Corpn* [1989] AC 1112, HL.

Liability for cargo

6.9 Unless otherwise indicated, the following account deals with the Hague-Warsaw Convention which has been the most commonly applicable version of the Warsaw Convention, at least until the coming into force of the Montreal Convention.

The Convention provides a system of compensation without the need for the claimant to prove fault. Under art 18(1):

> 'The carrier is liable for damage sustained in the event of the destruction or loss of, or damage to, any registered baggage or cargo, if the occurrence which caused the damage so sustained took place during the carriage by air.'

The 'carriage by air' for this purpose comprises the period during which the cargo is in the charge of the carrier, whether in an aerodrome or on board an aircraft or, in the case of a landing outside an aerodrome, in any place whatsoever (art 18(2)). It does not extend to carriage by land, by sea or by river performed outside an aerodrome, but if such carriage takes place in the performance of a contract for carriage by air for the purpose of loading, delivery or transhipment, any damage is presumed, subject to proof of the contrary, to have been the result of an event which took place during the carriage by air (art 18(3)).

So far as delay in the carriage of cargo is concerned, art 19 provides:

> 'The carrier is liable for damage occasioned by delay in the carriage by air of passengers, baggage and cargo.'

Unless the carrier has agreed to perform the carriage within a specified time, his obligation is to deliver within a reasonable time[1]. The claim for delay under art 19 arises if the carrier fails to deliver within that time.

The action for damages under the Convention may be brought by the consignor or consignee of the cargo, their principals, the owner of the cargo, or a person having an immediate right to possession of it[2].

The Convention provides an exclusive regime. In cases covered by it, claims against the carrier for damage to, or destruction or loss of, cargo and for damage caused by delay, any claim for damages can only be brought subject to the conditions and limits set out in the Convention. No recourse can be had to the common law or national laws in order to provide alternative remedies[3].

1 *Panalpina International Transport v Densil Underwear* [1981] 1 Lloyd's Rep 187.
2 *Western Digital Corpn v British Airways plc* [2001] QB 733, CA.
3 *Sidhu v British Airways plc* [1997] AC 430.

Complaints

6.10 Where cargo is damaged, the person entitled to delivery of it must complain in writing to the carrier forthwith after the discovery of the damage and, at the latest, within 14 days after receipt. Where the cargo is delayed, the written complaint must be made within 21 days of the date when the cargo was placed at the claimant's disposal (art 26(2)). If a complaint is not made in accordance with these time limits, no action can be brought against the carrier, save in the case of fraud on his part (art 26(4)).

Liability limit

6.11 The carrier's liability in respect of cargo is limited to 17 Special Drawing Rights[1] per kilogram unless the consignor has made, at the time when the package was handed over to the carrier, a special declaration of interest in delivery at destination and has paid a supplementary sum if the case so requires. In that case, the carrier will be liable to pay a sum not exceeding the declared sum unless he proves that that sum is greater than the consignor's actual interest in delivery (art 22(2)(a)). Where only part of a consignment of cargo has been damaged, the weight to be taken into account for the purposes of calculating the liability limit is only the weight of the package or packages concerned (art 22(2)(b)).

The claim against the carrier will not be subject to limits if:

(1) the cargo was loaded on board the aircraft with the consent of the carrier without a document of carriage, called an air waybill, having been made out or if the air waybill did not contain a notice, required by art 8(c), to the effect that, if the carriage involves an ultimate destination or stop in a country other than the country of departure, the Warsaw Convention may be applicable and that the Convention governs and in most cases limits the liability of carriers in respect of loss or damage to cargo (art 9); or

(2) the claimant can satisfy art 25:

> 'The limits of liability specified in Article 22 shall not apply, if it is proved that the damage resulted from an act or omission of the carrier, his servants or agents, done with intent to cause damage or recklessly and with knowledge that damage would probably result; provided that, in the case of such act or omission of a servant or agent, it is also proved that he was acting within the scope of his employment.'

The test of 'recklessness' is a subjective one and means, in this context, acting in a manner which indicates a decision to run a risk of undesirable consequences or a mental attitude of indifference to the risk[2]. As for 'knowledge that damage would probably result', imputed knowledge is not sufficient and actual knowledge is required[3].

1 A 'Special Drawing Right' is a unit of account defined by the International Monetary Fund; it is to be converted into national currency at the rate current at the date of judgment (art 22(5)).
2 *Goldman v Thai Airways* [1983] 1 WLR 1186.
3 *Nugent v Michael Goss Aviation* [2000] 2 Lloyd's Rep 222.

Other defences

6.12 Other defences available to the carrier are:

(1) that the carrier and his servants or agents have taken all necessary measures to avoid the damage or that it was impossible for them to take such measures (art 20);
(2) that the damage was caused or contributed to by the negligence of the injured person, with the result that the court may, in accordance with the provisions of its own law, exonerate the carrier wholly or partly from his liability (art 21);
(3) that the loss or damage results from the inherent defect, quality or vice of the cargo carried and the carrier has the benefit of a contractual exclusion or limitation of liability for such loss or damage (art 23).

Limitation of actions

6.13 The right to damages is extinguished if a claim is not brought within two years, reckoned from the date of arrival at the destination, or from the date on which the aircraft ought to have arrived, or from the date on which the carriage stopped (art 29).

The Montreal Convention

6.14 Much of the above description of the operation of the Hague-Warsaw Convention, in so far as it relates to liability for air cargo, applies equally to the Montreal Convention. However, the following important differences in the Montreal Convention should be noted[1]:

(1) The limit of liability of 17 Special Drawing Rights per kilogram for loss of or damage to cargo is unbreakable. There is no equivalent to art 25 in the Hague-Warsaw Convention. Nor does a failure to make out an air waybill deprive the carrier of the benefit of the liability limit.
(2) The defence that the carrier and its servants or agents have taken all necessary measures to avoid the damage (or that it was impossible for them to take such measures) is only available in answer to a claim of damage occasioned by delay. It is not available in cases of loss or damage to cargo under the Montreal Convention (see art 19).
(3) There is a new defence for the carrier. The carrier is not liable if it proves that the destruction, or loss of, or damage to, the cargo resulted from one or more of the following:
    (a) inherent defect, quality or vice of that cargo;
    (b) defective packing of the cargo by a person other than the carrier or its servants or agents;

(c) an act of war or armed conflict;
(d) an act of a public authority carried out in connection with the entry, exit or transit of the cargo (art 18(2)).

1 Many of the changes were foreshadowed in the MP4 Convention.

Pleading

Assumed facts

6.15 The facts of the example below are simple. A typical export sale agreement is made under which fragile goods have to be carried by air, the task being undertaken by Icarus Airlines Limited. The Hague-Warsaw Convention applies. Part of the cargo is damaged on the ground while in the airline's care. The issues are contributory negligence (bad packing) and limitation of liability.

Particulars of Claim

Claim No ....

IN THE HIGH COURT OF JUSTICE
QUEEN'S BENCH DIVISION
COMMERCIAL COURT

B E T W E E N:

(1) GLASSWARE LIMITED

(2) MEDITERRANEAN HOTELS INC

Claimants

- and -

ICARUS AIRLINES LIMITED

Defendant

PARTICULARS OF CLAIM

---

1. The Defendant is an international airline and, in particular, carries cargoes by air between Brighton Airport and Algiers Airport in Algeria.

2. By a contract of export sale made on [date] the First Claimant agreed to sell and the Second Claimant agreed to buy 400 lead crystal decanters for delivery at Algiers Airport ('the cargo'). At all material times the First and/or Second Claimants were the owners of the cargo and entitled to sue in respect of any damage thereto.

3. By a contract of carriage by air contained in or evidenced by an air waybill number . . . dated . . . (a copy of which is attached) the Defendant agreed to carry the cargo from Brighton Airport to Algiers Airport on [date].

4. On [date] and pursuant to the contract of carriage, the Claimant delivered the cargo, packed in 10 cartons (each containing 40 decanters and weighing . . . kilograms), at the cargo warehouse of the Defendant at Brighton Airport who accepted it for carriage to Algiers.

5. On about [date], two of the cartons containing 80 decanters were damaged in the Defendant's warehouse by an employee of the Defendant and all 80 decanters were destroyed.

6. The United Kingdom and Algeria are both high contracting parties to the Warsaw Convention as amended at The Hague, 1955, which is given the force of law as Schedule 1 to the Carriage by Air Act 1961 (as amended) ('the Hague-Warsaw Convention'). Accordingly, the carriage of the cargo was carriage to which the Hague-Warsaw Convention applied.

7. The destruction of the decanters took place in an aerodrome whilst in the charge of the Defendant and the Defendant is liable, under article 18 of the Hague-Warsaw Convention, for the Claimant's loss.

8. The Claimant claims the sound arrived value of the 80 lost decanters in the sum of £. . . . . .

9. Further the Claimants claim interest pursuant to section 35A of the Supreme Court Act 1981 at such rate and for such period as the Court thinks fit.

AND the Claimants claim:

(1) Damages.

(2) Interest pursuant to section 35A of the Supreme Court Act 1981, to be assessed.

[Statement of Truth, etc][1]

Defence

<u>Claim No ....</u>

<u>IN THE HIGH COURT OF JUSTICE</u>
<u>QUEEN'S BENCH DIVISION</u>
<u>COMMERCIAL COURT</u>

B E T W E E N:

(1) GLASSWARE LIMITED

(2) MEDITERRANEAN HOTELS INC

<u>Claimants</u>

- and -

ICARUS AIRLINES LIMITED

<u>Defendant</u>

D E F E N C E

---

1. Paragraph 1 of the Particulars of Claim is admitted.

2. Paragraph 2 of the Particulars of Claim is not admitted.

3. Paragraphs 3 and 4 of the Particulars of Claim are admitted.

4. As to paragraph 5 of the Particulars of Claim, it is admitted that one of the Defendant's warehousemen at the Defendant's warehouse at Brighton Airport dropped two cartons of the Defendant's cargo from a height of about 30 centimetres and that all of the decanters inside were destroyed.

5. Paragraphs 6 and 7 of the Particulars of Claim are admitted.

6. The destruction of the decanters was wholly caused or was contributed to by the negligence of the Claimants and the Defendant is entitled, under article 21 of the Hague-Warsaw Convention to be exonerated wholly or partly from any liability it may have.

PARTICULARS OF CONTRIBUTORY NEGLIGENCE

The decanters were each only wrapped in a single layer of paper and packed in single-layered cardboard cartons. Otherwise, they were not protected or separated from other decanters in the same carton or even from damage from minor external impacts.

7. Further or alternatively, pursuant to article 22(2)(a) of the Hague-Warsaw Convention the Defendant's liability is limited to 17 Special Drawing Rights per kilogram. The two cartons which were dropped weighed . . . kilograms. Accordingly, the Defendant's liability is limited to . . . Special Drawing Rights.

8. As paragraph 8 of the Particulars of Claim, the Defendant does not admit the value of the lost decanters.

[Statement of Truth, etc][1]

Reply

Claim No ....

IN THE HIGH COURT OF JUSTICE
QUEEN'S BENCH DIVISION
COMMERCIAL COURT

B E T W E E N:

(1) GLASSWARE LIMITED

(2) MEDITERRANEAN HOTELS INC.

Claimants

- and -

ICARUS AIRLINES LIMITED

Defendant

R E P L Y

---

1. The Claimants join issue with the Defendant on its Defence, save to the extent that it consists of admissions.

2. The Defendant's claim in paragraph 7 of the Defence to be entitled to limit its liability under article 22(2)(a) of the Hague-Warsaw Convention is denied. The Claimants will rely on article 25 and say that the destruction of the decanters resulted from an act or omission of the defendant, its servants or agents acting within the scope of their employment, either done with intent to cause damage or recklessly and with knowledge that damage would probably result and that, accordingly, the limit of liability does not apply.

PARTICULARS

The Defendant's warehouseman was ordered by his floor manager to carry the cartons containing the cargo from the door of the warehouse to racking inside. In the course of performing this task the warehouseman became engaged in an argument with a colleague and threw two of the cartons at him. In doing so he intended to destroy the decanters inside or was reckless with knowledge that they would probably be destroyed.

3. The Claimant is entitled to be compensated for the loss of the full value of the decanters which were destroyed, without limitation.

[Statement of Truth, etc][1]

1 Statement of truth, etc as set out in **Chapter 3, para 3.2**.

CHAPTER 7

Commercial Insurance – Non Marine

Kirsten Houghton

Law

7.1 The law relating to non-marine insurance is a vast subject well treated in may textbooks such as *MacGillivray on Insurance Law* (10th edn). It is not really practical to identify issues of particular interest to the pleader, save to say that litigation commonly centres on issues of breach of warranty, misrepresentation and non-disclosure. These are well illustrated in the examples below.

Unlike a warranty under the general law of contract, a warranty in insurance law is a term of the contract of insurance in the nature of a condition precedent to the liability of the insurer. Typically it is a promissory term whereby the assured promises the existence and/or continuing existence of a state of affairs. If the state of affairs does not, or ceases to, exist the insurer is discharged from liability under the policy from the date of breach.

The essential characteristics of a warranty are that it must be a term of the contract; it must be exactly complied with; it need not be material to the risk; and a breach discharges the insurer from liability on the policy even though the loss had no connection with the breach or that the breach was remedied before the loss occurred.

It is clear therefore that a warranty in a contract of insurance may give powerful protection to the insurer. If the assured dealt as a consumer for a non-business purpose (which will only rarely arise in the Commercial Court), it may be possible to challenge the warranty as an unfair non-core term under the Unfair Terms in Consumer Contracts Regulations 1999.

A very typical situation in which the pleader has to deal with a breach of warranty allegation arises where the Claimant claims under the policy; and the (or a) defence of breach of warranty is pleaded. Points worth looking at include the following:

(a) Although a warranty must be strictly complied with, that is not the same thing as construing a warranty strictly. Since the consequences of breach can be draconian, the court will tend to give a businesslike rather than a strict meaning to a warranty clause.
(b) A breach of warranty can be waived by the insurer, e.g. if he accepts a premium while aware of the facts constituting the breach.

If you are pleading in reply to an allegation of breach of warranty these aspects are worth considering.

The effect of a misrepresentation in the context of an insurance contract is broadly the same as under the general law of contract.

The duty of disclosure is however of greater peculiarity, although not unique to insurance law. Insurance contracts belong to the small number of contracts based upon the principle of utmost good faith. This must be shown by both parties, in both the pre-formation period and during the performance of the contract. In the pre-formation period the duty obliges the assured and his agent to disclose material facts and to refrain from making untrue statements when negotiating the contract.

A fact is material if it would influence a prudent insurer in fixing the premium or in deciding whether to accept the risk. In addition to falling within this class, the insurer must show that he was actually induced by the relevant non disclosure to make the contact, but the matter not disclosed need not have been decisive (*Pan Atlantic Ins Co Ltd v Pine Top Ins Co Ltd* [1995] 1 AC 501).

If the assured fails in his duty of full disclosure the insurer may on discovering the true facts elect to avoid the contract.

Points to consider if you are resisting a plea of misrepresentation or non-disclosure include:

(a) Was the matter relied upon one of fact (as opposed to a promise as to the future)?
(b) Is it a qualifying statement (such as would influence a prudent insurer)?
(c) Even if so, was the contract induced by it?
(d) Exploit the burden of proof – let the insurer prove his case, do not make unnecessary admissions.
(e) Consider whether the insurer has affirmed the contract with knowledge of the facts.

Of course if you are acting for the insurer, be aware of the above points but from the opposite perspective.

The draft Pleadings which follow illustrate how these principles of law arise in two practical cases.

Pleading: Fire Risks

Assumed facts

7.2 Clothes Shop Limited occupied 2–4 Main Street ('the Shop'). Mr Taylor was the director of Clothes Shop Limited. Mr Taylor employed Miss Button as the manageress of the Shop, and took no part in the day-to-day management of it. Clothes Shop Limited also employed Mr Tennant as its property manager. One of Mr Tennant's responsibilities was arranging insurance for the various buildings occupied by Clothes Shop Limited. He kept a copy of the policy, but did not provide the managers of the shops with copies for themselves or give them a summary of its terms.

Miss Button engaged a local handyman, Mr Sawyer, to repair the flat roof of the stock room at the back of the Shop because it was leaking. She did not ask how he intended to carry out the repair. During the course of the work, Mr Sawyer set fire to the roof with his blowtorch. He was unable to extinguish the flames, because he had not taken a fire extinguisher with him onto the roof, and the Shop was destroyed by fire.

Mr Tennant made a claim under the policy for reinstatement of the building and costs of replacement stock. Insurers declined the claim on the grounds that Clothes Shop Limited had failed to comply with a condition in the policy regarding precautions to be taken in the event that 'hot works' were undertaken at the insured premises.

Particulars of Claim

Claim No ....

IN THE HIGH COURT OF JUSTICE
QUEEN'S BENCH DIVISION
COMMERCIAL COURT

B E T W E E N:

PROPERTY INSURANCE LIMITED

Claimant

- and -

CLOTHES SHOP LIMITED

Defendant

PARTICULARS OF CLAIM

Parties

1. The Claimant ('PIL') is a limited company (registration no. UK. . . . .) which carries on the business of, amongst other things, underwriting property insurance from premises at . . . .

2. The Defendant ('CSL') is a limited company (registration no. UK. . . . .) which, amongst other things, carries on business as a ladies' fashion retailer from premises at 2–4 Main Street, Townville ('the Shop').

The Policy

3. By an agreement in writing dated 1st June 2003 ('the Policy'), a copy of which is served with this statement of case marked '**Appendix 1**'[1], in consideration for the payment by CSL of premium in the sum of £2,500 (plus Insurance Premium Tax), PIL agreed to insure the Shop and its contents against certain risks, including accidental damage by fire, for a period of 12 months commencing on 1st January 2003.

4. The following were, amongst others, express terms of the Policy:

4.1 '***Condition 3***

HOT WORK

In respect of the use of blow-lamps, propane torches or similar burning equipment, oxy-acetylene or similar burning or welding, equipment and soldering and brazing equipment the under-noted minimum precautions must be complied with on each occasion:

1. Before starting work

a) *the Assured shall appoint a competent Employee to be responsible for fire safety and for ensuring that these precautions are taken*

b) *all Employees and any sub-contractor shall be made aware of the location of office alarms and fire-fighting equipment*

c) *the competent Employee shall examine the vicinity of the place where the heat is to be applied (including the area on the opposite side of any wall or partition) and shall ensure that all combustible materials are removed to beyond a radius of 15 metres. Where such material cannot be moved it must be covered and fully protected by overlapping sheets or screens of non-combustible material*

d) *a sufficient number of suitable fire extinguishers shall be kept close to the work available for immediate use and not removed until at least one hour after the completion of the work*

2. During the progress of the work

a) *a responsible person shall work alongside each operative using the equipment solely to see that there is no outbreak of fire and that the fire-fighting equipment and extinguishers are available for immediate use'*

4.2 '***Conditions Precedent***

The due observance of the terms and conditions of this certificate relating to anything to be done or complied with by the Assured is a condition precedent to any liability of the Underwriters except in so far as it is necessary to comply with the requirements of any legislation enacted in Great Britain relating to compulsory insurance of legal liability to employees.'

The Fire

5. On 14th September 2003:

5.1 the Shop and all its contents and stock were destroyed by fire; and

5.2 CSL, by its director, Mr Taylor, made a claim under the Policy for reinstatement of the Shop and the replacement cost of the damaged contents and stock ('the Claim').

6. The fire was caused when a blowtorch being used by Mr Sawyer, a workman engaged by CSL, by Miss Button, the manageress of the Shop, to carry out repairs to a felt roof over the stockroom ignited combustible material, namely a pile of old cardboard boxes and polythene bags, on the roof.

PIL's claim

7. CSL did not comply with Condition 3 of the Policy in that:

    7.1 Before Mr Sawyer started the repairs, CSL its servants or agents:

        7.1.1 failed to appoint a competent employee to be responsible for fire safety and for ensuring that the minimum precautions set out in Condition 3 were taken;

        7.1.2 failed to make Mr Sawyer aware of the location of fire alarms and fire-fighting equipment;

        7.1.3 failed to examine the vicinity of the place where the heat was to be applied (including the area on the opposite side of any wall or partition);

        7.1.4 failed to ensure that all combustible materials, notably the cardboard boxes and polythene bags, were removed to beyond a radius of 15 metres from the source of the heat and/or to cover and fully protect them using overlapping sheets or screens of non-combustible material;

        7.1.5 failed to ensure that a sufficient number of suitable fire extinguishers were kept close to the work available for immediate use.

7.2 During the course of the work, CSL its servants or agents failed to ensure that a responsible person worked alongside Mr Sawyer solely to see that there was no outbreak of fire and that the fire-fighting equipment and extinguishers are available for immediate use.

8. By the express term set out in paragraph 4.2 above, due observance of the requirements set out in Condition 3 was a condition precedent to PIL's liability under the Policy.

9. Each of the matters set out in paragraph 7 above was a failure duly to observe the requirements of Condition 3 on CSL's part.

10. In the circumstances, PIL claims and is entitled to a declaration that it is not liable to indemnify CSL under the Policy in respect of the Claim or any part of it.

AND the claimant claims a declaration that it is not liable to indemnify CSL under the Policy in respect of the Claim or any part of it.

FRED BLOGGS

STATEMENT OF TRUTH[2]

[I believe]/[The Claimant believes] that the facts stated in these Particulars of Claim are true.[3]

Signed .... **Position or**[4]
(Legal Representative)[5] **Office held**
(if signing on behalf of a firm or company)

Print[6]
Name .... **Date**

[The Claimant's address for service is: [address]][7]

Appendix 1

[The Policy]

Defence and Counterclaim

Claim No ....

IN THE HIGH COURT OF JUSTICE
QUEEN'S BENCH DIVISION
COMMERCIAL COURT

B E T W E E N:

PROPERTY INSURANCE LIMITED

Claimant

- and -

CLOTHES SHOP LIMITED

Defendant

DEFENCE AND COUNTERCLAIM

---

1. Save where otherwise stated:

   1.1 The Defendant adopts the abbreviations used by the Claimant in the Particulars of Claim and

   1.2 References to paragraph numbers are references to the paragraphs of the Particulars of Claim.

D E F E N C E

The Parties and the Policy

2. Paragraphs 1 to 4 are admitted.

3. The following was also an express term of the Policy:

'GENERAL CONDITIONS

4. Precautions

The Assured shall take reasonable precautions to prevent personal injury to individuals and damage to property and to maintain all buildings, furnishings, ways, works, machinery, plant and vehicles in sound and safe condition.'

The Fire

4. Paragraph 5 is admitted.

5. Save that it is admitted that Miss Button engaged Mr Sawyer to carry out the repairs to the felt roof over the stockroom, CSL is unable either to admit or deny paragraph 6. CSL requires PIL to prove the cause of the fire[8].

PIL's claim

6. Paragraph 7 is admitted.

7. It is denied that CSL is in breach of conditions precedent whether as alleged in paragraphs 8 and 9 or at all.

8. On the true construction of Condition 3 and Condition 4 of the General Conditions of the Policy, CSL's obligation to comply with the 'minimum precautions' referred to therein did not arise merely because a blowtorch was used, but only if CSL had actual or constructive knowledge of the fact that Mr Sawyer intended to do so to carry out the repair[9].

9. CSL its servant and agents did not know, or have any reason to suspect, that Mr Sawyer would or might use a blowtorch to carry out the repair.

10. In the circumstances, CSL was not under any obligation to comply with Condition 3, and is not in breach of conditions precedent.

11. Accordingly, PIL has rejected the Claim wrongfully and is in breach of the Policy.

COUNTERCLAIM

12. CSL repeats its Defence.

13. By reason of PIL's breach of the Policy, CSL has suffered loss and damage.

PARTICULARS

13.1 Reinstatement of the Shop

Building cost	£350,000
Fixtures and fittings	£250,000

13.2 Replacement Stock £250,000

14. Further, the Defendant seeks and is entitled to interest pursuant to section 35A of the Supreme Court Act 1981 at such rate from such date and on such amount as the Court thinks fit.

AND the defendant counterclaims:

(1) Damages.

(2) Interest pursuant to section 35A of the Supreme Court Act 1981 to be assessed.

JOE CHAMBERS

STATEMENT OF TRUTH[10]

[I believe]/[The Defendant believes] that the facts stated in this Defence and Counterclaim are true[11].

Signed .... **Position or**[12]
(Legal Representative)[13] **Office held**
(if signing on
behalf of a firm
or company)

Print[14]
Name .... **Date**

Reply and Defence to Counterclaim

Claim No ....

IN THE HIGH COURT OF JUSTICE
QUEEN'S BENCH DIVISION
COMMERCIAL COURT

B E T W E E N:

PROPERTY INSURANCE LIMITED

Claimant

- and -

CLOTHES SHOP LIMITED

Defendant

REPLY AND DEFENCE TO COUNTERCLAIM

R E P L Y

1. Save in so far as it consists of admissions, PIL joins issue with CSL on its Defence.

2. As to paragraph 8:

   2.1 On the true construction of Condition 3, all that is required to trigger the requirement to take the minimum precautions set out is that 'hot works' are being carried out.

   2.2 Clause 10 should be construed as if it read:

   'In respect of the use of blow-lamps, propane torches or similar burning equipment, oxy-acetylene or similar burning or welding, equipment and soldering and brazing

equipment **in any case in which the Assured knew of such use, or exercising common care, would have known of such use** *the under-noted minimum precautions must be complied with on each occasion:- etc*[15]*.'*

2.3 CSL, by Miss Button, should have known:

2.3.1 that the Policy contained terms requiring minimum precautions to be taken if hot works were to be carried out, however, CSL, by its director Mr Taylor and/or its Property Manager, Mr Tennant, failed to exercise the common care which they should have by failing to ensure that the manager/esses of its shops, and in particular Miss Button, were informed of the terms of the Policy, in particular Condition 3, and

2.3.2 that Mr Sawyer intended to or might use a blowtorch to carry out the repair, however, Miss Button failed to exercise the common care which she should have by failing to ask Mr Sawyer what he was going to do; if she had done so, she would have realised that hot works were to be carried out and would have implemented the necessary precautions.

<u>DEFENCE TO COUNTERCLAIM</u>

3. It is denied that PIL is in breach of the Policy whether as alleged or at all.

4. Further and in any event, it is denied that any loss and/or damage which CSL may be found to have suffered was caused by PIL its servants or agents.

5. CSL is required to prove its alleged losses.

FRED BLOGGS

STATEMENT OF TRUTH[16]

[I believe]/[The Claimant believes] that the facts stated in this Reply and Defence to Counterclaim are true.[17]

Signed .... **Position or**[18]
(Legal Representative)[19] **Office held**
(if signing on
behalf of a firm
or company)

Print[20]
Name .... **Date**

---

1 CPR PD16 7.3(1).
2 CPR 22.1(1)(a), CPR PD22 1.1(1).
3 CPR PD22 2.1.
4 CPR PD22 3.4.
5 CPR 2.3(1), PD22 3.1(2), 3.7, 3.8, 3.10; and see 3.5 (Partners) and 3.6 (Motor Insurers' Bureau and lead insurers).
6 CPR PD22 3.10
7 CPR PD16 3.8(4)
8 CPR 16.5(1)(b)
9 *Bonner-Williams v Peter Lindsay Leisure Ltd* (27 March 2000, unreported) Richard Seymour QC (TCC).
10 CPR 22.1(1)(a), CPR PD22 1.1(1).
11 CPR PD22 2.1.
12 CPR PD22 3.4.
13 CPR 2.3(1), PD22 3.1(2), 3.7, 3.8, 3.10; and see 3.5 (Partners) and 3.6 (Motor Insurers' Bureau and lead insurers).
14 CPR PD22 3.10.
15 *Bonner-Williams v Peter Lindsay Leisure Ltd* (27 March 2000, unreported) Richard Seymour QC (TCC).
16 CPR 22.1(a), CPR PD22 1.1(1).
17 CPR PD22 2.1.
18 CPR PD22 3.4.
19 CPR 2.3(1), PD22 3.1(2), 3.7, 3.8, 3.10; and see 3.5 (Partners) and 3.6 (Motor Insurers' Bureau and lead insurers).
20 CPR PD22 3.10.

Pleading: Liability Risks

Assumed facts

7.3 The Claimant, Commission Limited, is an insurance broker. Reputable plc, a well-known insurer, has underwritten Commission's professional indemnity insurance for years. The policy runs for periods of 12 months and the annual renewal falls due on 1 January each year.

Commission's most successful employee, John Smith, had, as his most important client, John Smith Cars Limited ('JSCL'), a company owned and controlled by his father. The account was very successful, and JSCL purchased property, employer's and public liability, trader's motor and fleet and business interruption insurance using Commission as its broker, via John Smith. The account ran successfully for a number of years. During 2001, JSCL made a number of claims under its policies, all of which were handled by John Smith. The claims were settled by JSCL's insurers, and monies were paid into Commission's client account for transmission to JSCL by telegraphic transfer. Unknown to the directors of Commission, these claims had been dishonestly exaggerated by John Smith, who had a gambling habit, and some of the monies emanating from the client account had been paid to him by telegraphic transfer at the same time as the transfers to JSCL, in order to pay off his debts.

In July 2002, JSCL conducted its annual audit. The auditors noticed that there was a shortfall between the sums claimed under the insurance policies and the amounts received from Commission to pay those claims. The auditors wrote to Commission's managing director, Mr Jones, asking him to explain the discrepancies. Mr Jones conducted an investigation, and discovered that Mr Smith had handled all the claims. During the course of his investigation, Mr Jones received an anonymous note suggesting that he should have Mr Smith followed, because 'he has a problem with the gee-gees'. Mr Jones dismissed the note as idle gossip, and did not act on it, because he was convinced by Mr Smith's explanation that he was ignorant of any problems, and that the missing money must have been stolen by an employee of JSCL. Mr Jones did not appreciate the significance of transfers leaving the client account in the names of JSCL and plain John Smith.

On 1 January 2003, the professional indemnity policy was renewed for the last time. Mr Jones did not disclose the fact that he had been contacted by the auditors of a client to explain an accounting shortfall to them, nor that he conducted an investigation into the matter.

In November 2004, John Smith senior discovered his son's gambling problem and that it had been his son who had caused the losses from the company's accounts. He immediately instructed the company's solicitors, who issued a claim form against Commission, claiming an account, without any prior reference to Commission. John Smith senior then decided to negotiate a private settlement with his son. He failed, and the claim form was served on Commission in March 2004.

Commission forwarded the proceedings to Reputable and filled in a claim form. Reputable initially reserved its position and asked for further information. In response, the matters referred to above come to light. Reputable considered the matter and denied liability. Commission decided to take proceedings to claim a declaration that it was entitled to an indemnity under the professional indemnity policy.

Particulars of Claim

Claim No ....

IN THE HIGH COURT OF JUSTICE
QUEEN'S BENCH DIVISION
COMMERCIAL COURT

B E T W E E N:

COMMISSION LIMITED

Claimant

- and -

REPUTABLE PLC

Defendant

PARTICULARS OF CLAIM

Parties

1. The Claimant ('Commission') is a limited company (registration no. UK. . . . .) which carries on the business of insurance brokers from premises at. . . . .

2. The Defendant ('Reputable') is a public limited company (registration no. UK. . . . .) which carries on the business of, amongst other things, underwriting professional indemnity insurance for insurance brokers, from premises at. . . . .

The Policy

3. By an agreement in writing dated 1st January 2003 ('the Policy'), a copy of which is served with this statement of case marked

‘**Appendix 1**’[1], in consideration for the payment by Commission of premium in the sum of £10,000 (plus Insurance Premium Tax), Reputable agreed to insure Commission against errors and omissions in respect of Commission’s business as insurance brokers for a period of 12 months commencing on 1st January 2003.

4. The following were, amongst others, express terms of the Policy:

4.1 ‘***Insuring Clauses***

1. The Underwriters shall indemnify the Assured in respect of:-

(a) Claims first made against the Assured during the Period of Insurance for any negligent act, error, omission, libel, slander or defamation committed by or on behalf of the Assured or any firm with which the Assured is acting jointly.

(b) (i) Claims first made against the Assured during the Period of Insurance

(ii) Losses sustained by the Assured which they first discover during the period of insurance

in consequence of any dishonest or fraudulent act or omission of any former or present employee of the Assured other than any former or present director of the Assured.’

4.2 ‘*Excess £7,500 each and every loss*’

4.3 ‘*Legal Actions: UK*’

4.4 *'Limit of Indemnity: £1,000,000 any one claim and in all including costs and expenses.'*

4.5 ***'Conditions***

1. Precedent to their right to indemnity, the Assured shall give to the Underwriters immediate written notice of:-

(a) any claim made against the Assured

(b) any loss discovered by the Assured

(c) any circumstance of which the Assured shall become aware which may give rise to a claim

(d) the discovery by the Assured of reasonable cause for suspicion of dishonesty or fraud on the part of any former or present employee of the Assured whether or not giving rise to a claim under this Policy.'

Background

5. At all material times, Commission employed Mr John Smith ('Mr Smith') as an insurance broker.

6. Mr Smith was responsible for the account of one of Commission's clients, John Smith Cars Limited ('JSCL').

7. JSCL purchased property, employer's and public liability, trader's motor and fleet and business interruption insurance using Commission, by Mr Smith, as its broker, from various insurers.

8. During 2002, JSCL made a number of claims against its various insurance policies as set out in **Schedule 1** to this statement of case.

9. Mr Smith acted as the claims handler in relation to all the claims set out in **Schedule 1**.

10. Settlement monies were paid by the various insurers to Commission for transmission to JSCL in the amounts and on the dates shown in **Schedule 1**.

11. So far as Commission was aware, the settlement monies were forwarded in their entirety by Commission to JSCL shortly afterwards.

12. By a claim form in Claim no. HQ 109876, ('the Claim') issued on 10th December 2003 by JSCL against Commission, JSCL:

    12.1 alleges that it did not receive the settlement monies in their entirety;

    12.2 alleges that, in each case, Mr Smith, in the course of his employment by Commission, dishonestly exaggerated the claim which it had honestly made in its claim forms by approximately 20%;

    12.3 alleges that, in each case, when arranging the onward transmission of the settlement monies to it, Mr Smith dishonestly diverted approximately 40% of the total of each claim to his own bank account for his own use;

    12.4 claims an account of monies properly due to it in respect of settlement monies; and

    12.5 claims repayment of monies properly due to it in respect of settlement monies received on its behalf, but not paid to it, by Commission, together with interest and costs.

Commission's claim

13. JSCL served the Claim on Commission on 3rd March 2004.

14. If the facts and matters set out in the Claim are true, and JSCL has a valid claim against Commission, Reputable are liable (subject to the Excess and the Limit of Indemnity):

    14.1 to indemnify Commission against their liability to JSCL (if any), including any costs which may be awarded against them; and

    14.2 to pay Commission's costs of defending the proceedings bought against them by JSCL

    in accordance with the terms of Insuring Clause 1(b)(i) of the Policy.

15. Accordingly, on 3rd March 2004, Commission, by Mr Jones:

    15.1 telephoned Reputable and spoke to Mr Baker, a claims handler, and informed him of the receipt of the Claim;

    15.2 sent the Claim to Mr Baker by fax;

    15.3 filled in and faxed a claim form ('the Claim Form') provided by Mr Baker back to him; and

    15.4 sent a copy of the Claim, and the Claim Form to Mr Baker by first class post

    in accordance with Condition 1(a) of the Policy.

16. Wrongly, and in breach of the terms of the Policy, in particular Clause 1(b)(i) thereof, Reputable have refused to accept Commission's claim and/or to provide an indemnity to Commission in respect of their liability to JSCL (if any)

including any costs which may be awarded against them, and their cost of defending the proceedings brought against them by JSCL.

AND THE CLAIMANT claims:

(1) A declaration that Reputable is liable to indemnify it against the Claim made by JSCL together with any costs which may be awarded against them, and the costs of defending those proceedings.

(2) An inquiry into the amount properly due to Commission as a result of the indemnity and payment of such amount, alternatively damages.

(3) Interest pursuant to section 35 of the Supreme Court Act 1981 at such rate from such date and on such amount as the Court thinks fit[2].

FRED BLOGGS

STATEMENT OF TRUTH[3]

[I believe]/[The Claimant believes] that the facts stated in these Particulars of Claim are true[4].

Signed .... **Position or**[5]
(Legal Representative)[6] **Office held**
(if signing on
behalf of a firm
or company)

Print[7]
Name .... **Date**

[The Claimant's address for service is: [address]][8]

Schedule 1

(1) *Property Insurance* (Policy no. ABC 123 with Property Insurers Limited)

Date of Claim	23rd January 2001
Nature of Claim	Fire Damage to workshops
Amount Claimed	£150,000
Date paid	11th November 2001

(2) *Employer's Liability Insurance* (Policy no. DEF 456 with Employers' Claims plc)

Date of Claim	27th March 2001
Nature of Claim	Serious Injury to mechanic in workshop
Amount of Claim	£250,000
Date paid	29th September 2001

(3) *etc...*

Appendix 1

[The Policy]

Defence and Counterclaim

Claim No ....

IN THE HIGH COURT OF JUSTICE
QUEEN'S BENCH DIVISION
COMMERCIAL COURT

B E T W E E N:

COMMISSION LIMITED

Claimant

- and -

REPUTABLE PLC

Defendant

DEFENCE AND COUNTERCLAIM

---

1. Save where otherwise stated:

   1.1 The Defendant adopts the abbreviations used by the Claimant in the Particulars of Claim and

   1.2 References to paragraph numbers are references to the paragraphs of the Particulars of Claim.

D E F E N C E

The Parties and the Policy

2. Paragraphs 1 to 4 are admitted.

3. The following were also express terms of the Policy:

   3.1 '***Exclusions***

   The Underwriters shall not indemnify the Assured against any claim or loss arising from:-

   1. Any circumstances which may give rise to a claim and of which the Assured is aware prior to the inception of this Policy.'

   3.2 '***Conditions***

   2. In the event of a claim under Insuring Clause 1(b), the Assured shall take all possible action to sue for and obtain reimbursement from any employee concerned in such loss, or from their estate or legal representatives. The Assured shall (except as provided by law to the contrary) withhold any money which but for such fraud or dishonesty would be due to such person from the Assured or any money of such person held by the Assured for the benefit of the Underwriters, but only to the extent of the loss which they have suffered or will suffer as a result of the fraud and dishonesty of such person.'

Background

4. Paragraphs 5 to 10 are admitted.

5. Reputable is unable either to admit or deny paragraph 11. However, Reputable will assert that, in the event that the matters set out in the Claim are true:

5.1 Mr Smith knew that the settlement monies were not being forwarded to JSCL in their entirety by, at the latest by 29th September 2001; and

5.2 Mr Smith's knowledge is to be imputed to Commission because:

5.2.1 he was a senior employee

5.2.2 he was delegated with complete control of JSCL's account by Commission

5.2.3 he was authorised by Commission to give telegraphic transfer instructions in relation to Commission's client account and

5.2.4 the transfers were carried out as part of, or in conjunction with, transfers made in the ordinary course of his employment.

6. Paragraph 12 is admitted.

Commission's Claim

7. Paragraph 13 is admitted.

8. Paragraph 14 is denied.

9. The facts set out in paragraph 15 are admitted, but it is denied that those facts amount to a valid notification of a claim under the Policy.

10. It is admitted that Reputable have refused to accept Commission's claim and to provide an indemnity under the Policy. It is denied

that such refusal is in breach of the terms of the Policy, whether as alleged in paragraph 16 or at all.

Defence 1 – Material Non-Disclosure

11. The matters set out in paragraph 5 above and 22 to 24 below were material facts of which a reasonable, prudent underwriter would have wished to be informed before deciding whether, and if so on what terms, to underwrite the Policy.

12. Neither Mr Penn, the underwriter employed by Reputable who underwrote the Policy, nor any other member of Reputable's staff, was informed of any of the matters set out in paragraph 5 above and 22 to 24 below by Commission its servants or agents prior to underwriting the Policy.

13. By reason of Commission's non-disclosure of material facts, Reputable was induced to underwrite the Policy on more favourable terms than it would otherwise have done.

14. In fact, Reputable would not have underwritten the Policy, or would have underwritten it on different terms, including:

    14.1 the exclusion of any claim arising out of Mr Smith's conduct in relation to the claims set out in Schedule 1 to the Particulars of Claim and/or

    14.2 an increased premium

    if Mr Penn had been informed of the matters set out in paragraph 5 above and 22 to 24 below, or any of them.

15. In the circumstances, Reputable is entitled to, and does, avoid the Policy.

16. If, contrary to its primary case, the Court holds that Reputable is not entitled to avoid the Policy, and without prejudice to its primary case, Reputable will rely upon the facts and matters set out below in defence of the Claimant's claim.

Defence 2 – no claim made within the Period of the Policy

17. The Claim was issued on 10th December 2003, but not served on Commission until 3rd March 2004.

18. The Policy expired on 31st December 2003.

19. In the circumstances, Commission's claim was not first made until after the expiration of the Policy period and, in accordance with Insuring Clause 1(b)(i), it is not a valid claim under the Policy.

Defence 3 – Condition Precedent

20. During the course of July 2002, JSCL's auditors contacted Mr Jones and informed him that there was a shortfall between the monies claimed by JSCL and the monies paid by Commission to JSCL in settlement of those claims.

21. Subsequently, in July and August 2002, Mr Jones conducted an investigation into the causes of the alleged shortfall, but concluded that the shortfall had been caused by theft by an employee of JSCL.

22. Mr Jones' conclusions were unreasonable and incorrect. In fact:

22.1 Mr Jones should have but failed to notice that, during 2001, transfers were being sanctioned by Mr Smith from Commission's client account to:

22.1.1 John Smith Cars Limited, account no. 21222334 at Everybank plc and

22.1.2 John Smith, account no. 84859192 at Royal New Bank plc.

22.2 Further, Mr Jones should have but failed to appreciate that these transfers might suggest that the settlement monies may not have been sent to JSCL in their entirety, but were, in fact, being split between JSCL and Mr Smith.

22.3 Accordingly, Mr Jones should have, but failed to:

22.3.1 challenge Mr Smith concerning the transfers and/or

22.3.2 make any other investigations (e.g. with Commission's bank) in connection with the transfers in order to ascertain the identity of the recipient of the monies.

If he had done so, Mr Jones would have discovered that Mr Smith was dishonestly diverting the settlement monies for his own benefit.

22.4 Further, during the course of the investigation, Mr Jones was sent an anonymous note, which urged him to have Mr Jones followed, because 'he had a problem with the gee-gees'.

22.5 Mr Jones failed to act on the note, whether by having Mr Jones followed, or by investigating whether or not Mr Jones had a gambling problem or at all.

22.6 If Mr Jones had undertaken any such investigations, he would have discovered that Mr Jones had a serious gambling problem, and large debts, in excess of £200,000, as a result.

23. The matters set out in paragraph 22 to 24 above were:

23.1 circumstances of which Commission became aware and which might give rise to a claim and/or

23.2 a reasonable cause for suspicion of dishonesty or fraud on the part of one of Commission's employees.

24. Commission failed to give Reputable immediate or any written or any other notice of the facts and matters set out in paragraphs 22 to 24 above.

25. In the circumstances, Commission has failed to comply with Condition 1 of the policy, which is a condition precedent to Reputable's liability, and, accordingly, Reputable is not liable to indemnify Commission.

Defence 4 – Exclusions

26. Further or alternatively, Commission became aware of the matters set out in paragraphs 22 to 24 above prior to the inception of the Policy.

27. In the circumstances, Commission's claim under the Policy is excluded by Exclusion 1 of the Policy and, accordingly, Reputable is not liable to indemnify Commission.

COUNTERCLAIM

28. Reputable repeats its Defence.

29. By a letter dated 25th April 2004, Reputable, by its solicitors, avoided the policy and tendered a return of premium, which was refused by Commission's solicitors. Reputable remains willing and able to make a return of premium.

AND the defendant counterclaims a declaration that it is entitled to, and has, avoided the Policy.

JOE CHAMBERS

STATEMENT OF TRUTH[9]

[I believe]/[The Defendant believes] that the facts stated in this Defence and Counterclaim are true[10].

Signed .... **Position or**[11]
(Legal Representative)[12] **Office held** (if signing on behalf of a firm or company)

Print[13]
Name .... **Date**

---

1 CPR PD16 7.3(1).
2 CPR PD16.4(1)(b) and (2)(iii).
3 CPR 22.1(a), CPR PD22 1.1(1).
4 CPR PD22 2.1.
5 CPR PD22 3.4.
6 CPR 2.3(1), PD22 3.1(2), 3.7, 3.8, 3.10; and see 3.5 (Partners) and 3.6 (Motor Insurers' Bureau and lead insurers).
7 CPR PD22 3.10.
8 CPR PD16 3.8(4).
9 CPR 22.1(a), CPR PD22 1.1(1).
10 CPR PD22 2.1.
11 CPR PD22 3.4.
12 CPR 2.3(1), PD22 3.1(2), 3.7, 3.8, 3.10; and see 3.5 (Partners) and 3.6 (Motor Insurers' Bureau and lead insurers).
13 CPR PD22 3.10.

CHAPTER 8

Reinsurance

Guy Blackwood

Introduction

8.1

1. This introductory section serves to highlight a number of principles which ought to be borne in mind when pleading a statement of case in a reinsurance claim. For a comprehensive analysis of the substantive law of reinsurance contracts, please refer to the specialist texts[1].
2. As with direct insurance, in the absence of particular contractual provisions to the contrary, a claim under a reinsurance policy is a claim for unliquidated damages, not debt[2]. However, it is customary to plead an alternative claim in debt.
3. The relevant terms of the reinsurance policy, the underlying contract of insurance and the circumstances surrounding the loss should be set out in full, since a reinsurer will not be liable unless the relevant loss falls within the scope of the cover provided by the underlying policy and within the cover afforded by the contract of reinsurance[3].
4. Subject to any express contractual terms to the contrary, the limitation period is six years from the date of accrual of the cause of action[4]. The Courts have generally held, again subject to any express contractual terms to the contrary, that the reassured's cause of action against its reinsurer accrues at the time when the reassured's liability to the original assured is 'ascertained' by judgment, award or agreement[5].
5. Reinsurance contracts vary greatly in both in the scope of cover provided and in the basis of the obligation on the reinsurer to indemnify the reassured, which can either be a specified percentage of the amount insured under the original contract of insurance (proportional), or referable to particular limits and/or excess points (non-proportional).
   (a) Scope of cover:
   Facultative[6] contracts of reinsurance typically involve the reinsurance of a single risk. Treaty reinsurance frequently involves the reinsurance of many hundreds of individual risks which fall within the scope of the terms set out in the treaty itself.
   (b) Basis of indemnity:
   Under a 'proportional' contract, the reinsurer reinsures a specified percentage of the original risk (which may be 100%), typically in consideration for the receipt of the same percentage of the original premium. The percentage of the original risk retained by the reassured is known as the reassured's retention.

Under a non-proportional contract, the reinsurer's obligation to indemnify the reassured and the reassured's obligation to pay premium are calculated by reference to specified limits of indemnity and/or excess points.

6. Examples of proportional reinsurance include quota share and surplus treaties. Under a quota share treaty, generally the reinsurer is obliged to accept a specified percentage of every original risk written by the reassured which falls within the scope of the treaty (e.g. property risks) and to pay the same percentage of losses to the reassured. The reassured is obliged to pay premium to the reinsurer in an amount which is referable to the proportion of risks reinsured.
Under surplus treaties, the reassured is either obliged, or has the option to cede risks to the treaty over and above the reassured's 'retention', which is generally expressed to be a fixed sum.
7. The two most common forms of non-proportional reinsurance are excess of loss and stop-loss. By a contract of excess of loss reinsurance (which can be either facultative or treaty), the reinsurer agrees to indemnify its reassured for a loss which exceeds a specified sum (the 'excess point', also known as the reassured's retention) loss up to a maximum limit ('the limit of indemnity').
8. Excess of loss contracts frequently entitle the reassured to combine ('aggregate') its losses so as to exceed the stated excess point, in so far as such losses arise from one 'event' or 'cause'[7]. Frequently, excess of loss contracts also contain 'aggregate deductibles' which need to be eroded by losses before the reassured has a claim against its reinsurer[8].
9. There are four basic types of 'period' in excess of loss treaty reinsurance. 'Losses occurring during' contracts provide cover in respect of any loss sustained by the reassured in a given period (usually the calendar year) irrespective of when the original risk was written[9]. 'Risks attaching/incepting during' contracts cover losses arising from original risks written by the reassured in a set period of time, irrespective of when the loss occurs[10]. 'Year of account' contracts provide cover for original risks written by a reassured, and allocated by that reassured to a particular underwriting year of account. Occasionally, contracts are written which provide cover for all losses arising from 'events' occurring during a particular period.
10. Under stop-loss contracts, the reinsurer's liability is engaged when the aggregate of losses sustained by the reassured exceed a specified amount in relation to a particular class of risks. This retention is often expressed as a percentage or ratio of claims paid to premium received.
11. Contracts of reinsurance are contracts of utmost good faith[11]. If a reassured or its agent fails to disclose a material fact to its reinsurer and/or misrepresents a material fact on placement of the risk, the reinsurer may avoid the policy provided its underwriter was induced[12] to write the risk by reason of the non-disclosure/misrepresentation[13].
12. As with direct insurance, where a reinsurer is seeking to avoid a policy, particular care should be taken when pleading contractual defences to ensure that no inadvertent affirmation of the policy can be made out from

the terms of the defence itself[14]. Accordingly, in these circumstances it is suggested that the all contractual defences are expressly stated to be without prejudice to the reinsurer's right to avoid.

1 These include Barlow Lyde and Gilbert *Reinsurance Practice and the Law*, LLP Limited; *Butler and Merkin on Reinsurance Law*; O'Neill and Woloniecki *The Law of Reinsurance* (2nd edn, 2004).

2 See for example *The Fanti* [1991] 2 AC 1, 35 (HL); *Edmunds v Lloyd Italico* [1986] 1 Lloyd's Rep. 326, 327; *The Italia Express (No. 2)* [1992] 2 Lloyd's Rep 281.

3 Frequently, reinsurance contracts contain 'follow the settlements' clauses, whereby the reinsurer and reassured agree on means of proving that these requirements have been fulfilled. 'Follow the settlements' clauses vary greatly in their terms and effect, and have created a substantial body of case law; see for example *Hill v Mercantile & General Reinsurance Co* [1996] 1 WLR 1239 (HL); *Insurance Company of Africa v Scor Reinsurance Company Ltd* [1985] 1 Lloyd's Rep 312 (CA); *Commercial Union Assurance Company plc v NRG Victory Reinsurance Ltd* [1998] 2 All ER 434; *Assicurazioni Generali SPA v CGU International Insurance plc* [2003] 1 Lloyd's Rep Insurance and Reinsurance 725.

4 Section 5 of the Limitation Act 1980.

5 *Colin Baker v Black Sea and Baltic General Insurance Co Ltd* [1995] LRLR 261, 286; *Halvanon Insurance Company Ltd v Companhia de Seguros do Estado de Sao Paulo* [1995] LRLR 303, 306; *North Atlantic Insurance Co Ltd v Bishopsgate Insurance Ltd* [1998] 1 Lloyd's Rep 459, 462; see also *Charter Reinsurance Co Ltd v Fagan* [1997] AC 313 (HL) in relation to the 'ultimate net loss' clause.

6 In the context of treaty reinsurance, the term 'facultative' is also used in a second sense to refer to the optional nature of the cover as viewed from the perspective of the reassured. Hence a facultative/obligatory ('fac/oblig') treaty is a contract under which the reassured has the right to elect whether or not to cede individual risks, but the reinsurer is obliged to accept any such risks which have been ceded. As to the practice of retrospective cessions/declarations, see *Glencore v Alpina* [2004] 1 Lloyd's Rep 111 at pp 168–170.

7 In this respect, see *Axa Re v Field* [1996] 1 WLR 1026, 1035, 'an event is something which happens at a particular time, at a particular place, in a particular way ... cause is to my mind something altogether less constricted' per Lord Mustill; *Caudle v Sharp* [1995] LRLR 433 (CA); *Kuwait Airways Corporation v Kuwait Insurance Co* [1996] 1 Lloyd's Rep 664; *Mann v Lexington* [2001] 1 Lloyd's Rep 1 (CA); *Scott v Copenhagen Re* [2003] 1 Lloyd's Rep Insurance and Reinsurance 696 (CA); *Silverstein Properties Inc (and others) v Swiss Re (and others)*, 26 September 2003, United States Court of Appeals for the Second Circuit; *Lloyds TSB General Insurance Holdings v Lloyds Bank Group Insurance Co Ltd* [2003] 1 Lloyd's Rep Insurance and Reinsurance 623 (HL). As to 'sole judge' clauses, see *Brown v GIO Insurance Ltd* [1998] Lloyd's Rep Insurance and Reinsurance 201 (CA)

8 It is also important to note that in treaty excess of loss reinsurance, the number of times upon which a reassured may call upon its reinsurers to pay claims up to the limit of indemnity is generally limited ('reinstatement of cover'). Typically an excess of loss treaty will provide for two or three reinstatements of cover, upon payment of an additional premium ('reinstatement premium'). Reassured's often insure their liability to pay such reinstatement premium ('reinstatement premium protection').

9 Treaties sometimes incorporate clauses dealing with the situation where an 'event' is 'in progress' at the expiry of one policy and the inception of another; see for example clause 4, 'Overlapping Period' of the Joint Excess Loss Committee, Excess Loss Clauses 1/1/97.

10 Another species of clause, the 'interlocking clause' has the effect of pushing the reassured's claims 'vertically' by apportioning the reassured's retention and the limit of indemnity as between excess of loss treaties, in circumstances where the reassured is involved in a series of losses arising from one event affecting business allocated to two or more excess of loss treaties, which cover different periods.

11 *Pan Atlantic Insurance Co Ltd v Pine Top Insurance Co Ltd* [1995] 1 AC 501 (HL); *Assicurazioni Generali SpA v ARIG* [2003] 1 Lloyd's Rep Insurance and Reinsurance 131.

12 The test for material non-disclosure is thus two-fold: (1) Was the undisclosed fact 'material' viewed from the perspective of the hypothetical prudent underwriter (usually a matter of expert

evidence)? (2) If so, was the underwriter who wrote the policy actually induced to write the same by reason of the relevant non-disclosure (causation)?

13 In certain circumstances, the courts have been prepared to infer that a particular underwriter was induced to write the relevant policy by reason of a material non-disclosure/misrepresentation; *St Paul Fire & Marine Insurance Co Ltd v McConnell Dowell Constructors* [1995] 2 Lloyd's Rep 116, 127; *Assicurazioni Generali SpA v ARIG* [2003] 1 Lloyd's Rep Insurance and Reinsurance 131, 149.

14 As to the legal test for waiver by election (affirmation) see *ICCI v Royal Hotel* [1998] Lloyd's Rep Insurance and Reinsurance 151; *Callaghan & Hedges v Thompson* [2000] 1 Lloyd's Rep Insurance and Reinsurance 125; *Wise (underwriting Agency) Ltd v Grupo Nacional Provincial* [2004] 1 Lloyd's Rep Insurance and Reinsurance 764.

Pleading

Assumed facts

8.2 A Lloyd's Syndicate no. 1234 writes an original contract of property insurance, reference no. 789 on two adjacent skyscrapers, Tower 1 and Tower 2, in favour of Jaded Enterprises ('the Property Policy'), covering the period 1 January 1999 to 31 December 2000. The Property Policy is expressed to be subject to the laws of the Grand Court of Atlantis.

The combined limit of the indemnity under the Property Policy for both Towers is US$50m, each of the Towers being insured in an amount of US$25m.

On 1 January 2000, at 09.00 hours Tower 1 is completely destroyed by fire.

On 1 January 2000, at 10.00 hours Tower 2 is completely destroyed by fire.

On 1 December 2000, the Grand Court of Atlantis hold that Syndicate 1234 are liable to indemnify Jaded Enterprises in an amount of US$50m, being US$25m for each of the Towers on the basis that both Towers were lost by an insured peril, fire.

The Grand Court further finds that:

(1) the two fires in fact resulted from defects in the air cooling systems of the Towers, which overheated;
(2) this overheating resulted from a defective chip which had been installed in a computer which was remotely controlling the two air cooling systems from a nearby office block, the 'ZIP A1';
(3) the 'ZIP A1' failed to due to its inability to recognise dates on or after 1 January 2000 (the 'millennium bug').

Example 1: Claim in arbitration under a treaty excess of loss contract of reinsurance

Claim No ....

IN THE MATTER OF THE ARBITRATION ACT 1996

AND

IN THE MATTER OF AN ARBITRATION

B E T W E E N:

IVOR GOODBOOK

(For and on behalf of himself and all
Underwriting members of syndicate 1234
for the 2000 year of account)

Claimants

- and -

MOONSHINE RE

Respondents

POINTS OF CLAIM

---

1. By a contract of reinsurance, Policy reference no. 987, the Respondents agreed to reinsure the Claimants in consideration for the payment of premium, subscribing to a line of 100% ('the Policy').

2. The Policy contained the following, among other express terms:

'PERIOD *Losses occurring during 12 months at 1st January, 2000, local standard time at the place where the loss occurs.*

TYPE *Whole account excess of loss reinsurance*

INTEREST *To cover all business underwritten by the Reassured . . .*

LIMITS *US$25,000,000 excess of US$25,000,000 each and every loss. . .*

Full wording as Joint Excess Loss Committee Clauses 1.1.97 . . .

Joint Excess Loss Committee

EXCESS LOSS CLAUSES

1. REINSURANCE CLAUSE

1.1 In consideration of the premium to be paid to reinsurers by or on behalf of the reassured, the reinsurers hereon shall reimburse the reassured to the extent that its net loss (as defined in Clause 2 below) under business reinsured by this contract exceeds the reassured's retention but only up to the limit of reimbursement ...

1.5 It is a condition precedent to liability under this contract that settlement by the reassured shall be in accordance with the terms, conditions and exclusions of the original policies or contracts.

2. *NET LOSS*

2.1 'Net Loss' under this contract means the sum actually paid by the reassured in discharge of its liability for loss (as defined in Clause 3 below) after deduction of all salvage and recovery ...

2.2 'Payment' in these clauses requires that funds have been transferred by the payer, with 'paid' being construed accordingly.

...

3. EVENT CLAUSE

3.1 'Loss' under this contract means loss, damage, liability or expense or a series thereof arising from one event . . .

15. ARBITRATION

15.1 The parties agree that prior to recourse to courts of law any dispute between them concerning the provisions of this contract shall first be the subject of arbitration.

...

15.9 The seat of the arbitration shall be in London and the arbitration tribunal shall apply the laws of England as the proper law of this contract ...'

The original contract of insurance:

3. By a contract of insurance, policy reference no. 789 ('the Property Policy'), in consideration for the payment of premium, the Claimants agreed to insure Jaded Enterprises, subscribing to a line of 100%. The Property Policy contained the following express terms:

'PERIOD:	*24 MONTHS AT 1/1/99*
TYPE:	*PROPERTY*
SUBJECT MATTER:	*TOWER 1 AND TOWER 2, NO. 1 & 2, LIBERTY STREET, ATLANTIS CITY, ATLANTIS*

INSURED PERILS:	*ALL RISKS*
LIMIT OF INDEMNITY:	*US$25,000,000 TOWER 1*
	US$25,000,000 TOWER 2
LAW AND JURISDICTION:	*SUBJECT TO THE LAWS OF ATLANTIS AND THE EXCLUSIVE JURISDICTION OF THE GRAND COURT OF ATLANTIS.'*

The loss and judgment:

4. Towers 1 and 2 were both skyscrapers located on Liberty Street in the City of Atlantis, some 50 metres apart. On 1st January 2000, at 09:00 hrs local time Tower 1 was completely destroyed by fire. At 10:00 hrs local time on the same day, Tower 2 was completely destroyed by fire.

5. On 1st December 2000, the Grand Court of Atlantis ('the Court') held that Syndicate 1234 was liable to indemnify Jaded Enterprises Inc in an amount of US$50m, being US$25m for each of the Towers, pursuant to the terms of the Property Policy. The Court further found that:

   5.1 The two fires in fact resulted from defects in the air-cooling systems of the Towers, which overheated.

   5.2 This overheating in turn resulted from a defective chip which had been installed in a computer which was remotely controlling the two air cooling systems from a nearby office block, the 'ZIP A1'.

   5.3 The 'ZIP A1' failed to due to its inability to recognise dates on or after 1st January 2000.

6. On 10th December 2000, the Claimants duly indemnified Jaded Enterprises in the sum of US$50m.

Aggregation:

7. For the purposes of clause 3.1 of the Joint Excess Loss Committee, Excess Loss Clauses ('JELC')[1], the 'event' was the failure of the 'ZIP A1' on 1st January 2000, alternatively the inability of the 'ZIP A1' microchip to recognise dates on or after 1st January 2000.

8. In the premises, the Claimants were entitled to aggregate their losses arising from the complete destruction of Towers 1 and 2 by fire on 1st January 2000 and pursuant to clause 1 of JELC, the Respondents were liable to indemnify the Claimants in an amount of US$25m.

9. Wrongfully, and in breach of the Policy, the Respondents have failed and refused to indemnify the Claimants for the Tower 1 and 2 losses, whether in an amount of US$25m or otherwise. As a result of the Respondents' breach of the Policy, the Claimants have suffered loss and damage, in an amount of US$25m. In the alternative, the said sum of US$25m is due and owing from the Respondents to the Claimants under the Policy.

10. The Claimants are further entitled to interest on the amount of US$25m pursuant to section 49 of the Arbitration Act 1996, and claim compound, alternatively simple interest at such rate and for such period as the tribunal deems fit.

AND the Claimants claim:

(1) A declaration that, pursuant to the terms of the Policy they are entitled to aggregate their losses arising from the destruction of Towers 1 and 2 on 1st January 2000, and that they are entitled to an indemnity from the Respondents in respect of the same.

(2) The aforesaid indemnity.

(3) The sum of US$25m.

(4) Alternatively, damages in an amount of US$25m.

(5) Interest, as set out in paragraph 10 above.

(6) Costs.

(7) Such further or other relief as the Tribunal in its discretion thinks fit.

[Statement of Truth, etc][2]

Example 2: Defence and Counterclaim for avoidance in arbitration under a treaty excess of loss contract of reinsurance

Claim No ....

IN THE MATTER OF THE ARBITRATION ACT 1996

AND

IN THE MATTER OF AN ARBITRATION

B E T W E E N:

IVOR GOODBOOK

(For and on behalf of himself and all
Underwriting members of syndicate 1234
for the 2000 year of account)

Claimants

- and -

MOONSHINE RE

Respondents

POINTS OF DEFENCE
AND COUNTERCLAIM

---

1. Unless stated to the contrary, references to paragraph numbers herein are references to the numbered paragraphs of the Points of Claim. References to the Policy herein are references to the contract of reinsurance reference no. 987.

2. Paragraphs 1 to 4 are admitted.

Avoidance

3. The Respondents hereby avoid the Policy and tender return of premium in respect of the same, on the basis of the following particulars:

   3.1 On 23rd December 1999, the Respondents entered into the Policy with the Claimants.

   3.2 The Policy was a contract of utmost good faith, such that in and about the placement of the risk, the Claimants, their servants, agents and privies were obliged:

      3.2.1 to disclose to the Respondents all facts and matters which they knew and/or ought to have known in the ordinary course of their business, which were material to the risk being placed;

      3.2.2 to ensure that every material representation made to the Respondents was true.

   3.3 On or about 2nd April 1999, the Claimants sustained a loss of US$750,000 on their property account.

   3.4 On or about 21st December 1999, the Claimants sustained a loss of US$8m on their property account, in the wake of hurricane Marjorie.

   3.5 Notwithstanding the obligation to make disclosure referred to in paragraph 3.2.1 above, the Claimants, their servants, agents and privies failed to disclose any of the facts and matters referred to in paragraphs 3.3 and 3.4 above to the Respondents prior to placement of the Policy.

3.6 On 23rd December 1999, the Claimants' broker, Mr Friday of Trumpet Broking Limited presented the risk to the Respondents' underwriter, Mr Sage, with a presentation pack purporting to reflect the Claimants' underwriting results during the years 1994 to 1999. During this presentation:

3.6.1 Mr Friday drew Mr Sage's attention to page 78 of the presentation pack, which stated that the Claimants' had 'sustained no significant losses to their Property Account during the 1999 year of account'.

3.6.2 Mr Friday informed Mr Sage that the Claimants would not seek to aggregate losses on the basis that the failure of a computer chip to recognise a date constituted an 'event'.

3.7 In breach of the obligation set out in paragraph 3.2.2 above, the representations set out in paragraph 3.6 above were false:

3.7.1 As particularised in paragraphs 3.3 and 3.4 above, the Claimants actually sustained two significant losses to their property account during the 1999 year of account.

3.7.2 In this matter, the Claimants are seeking to aggregate two losses on the basis that the failure of the 'ZIP A1' chip to recognise a date constitutes a single event for the purposes of clause 3.1 of JELC.

3.8 The facts and matters set out in paragraphs 3.3, 3.4 and 3.6 above were material to the risk which was being placed with the Respondents. But for the non-disclosures and/or misrepresentations, Mr Sage would not have agreed to enter into the Policy, and/or would have only entered into the Policy on substantially different terms.

Construction

4. The remainder of the Points of Defence is without prejudice to the Respondents' case on avoidance, set out above.

5. Paragraphs 5 and 6 are admitted. By clause 4.1 of JELC:

> '*4. OVERLAPPING PERIOD*
>
> *4.1 If at the inception date shown in the schedule an event is in progress, no loss arising from that event shall be treated as occurring during the currency of this contract.*'

6. Paragraphs 7 and 8 are denied:

   6.1 The destruction of Tower 1 and Tower 2 on 1st January 2000 constituted two separate events for the purposes of clause 3.1 of JELC, even if, which is not admitted, the two fires resulted from the same originating cause.

   6.2 The inability of the 'ZIP A1' microchip to recognise dates on or after 1st January 2000 and/or the alleged failure of the 'ZIP A1' on 1st January 2000 did not constitute an 'event' for the purposes of clause 3.1 of JELC.

   6.3 Further, or alternatively, if, which is denied, the losses resulted from one event as defined by the Claimants, the same was an 'event in progress' for the purposes of clause 4.1 of JELC. In the premises, the Claimants' losses arising from the 'event' fall outside the currency of the Policy.

6.4 In the further alternative, by reason of the matters set out in paragraph 3.6.2 above, it was a term of the Policy that the Claimants were not entitled to aggregate losses on the basis that the failure of a computer chip to recognise a date constituted an 'event'.

7. In the premises:

7.1 The Claimants' two losses fall entirely within the Claimants' retention under the Policy, US$25m, and the Claimant is not entitled to aggregate the same and/or the Claimants' losses fall outside the currency of the Policy.

7.2 Paragraphs 9 and 10 are denied. It is further denied that the Claimants are entitled to interest, whether as claimed in paragraph 10 or otherwise.

COUNTERCLAIM

---

8. Paragraph 3 hereof is repeated. In the premises, the Respondents are entitled to and seek a declaration that they are entitled to avoid the Policy and/or that they have successfully avoided the same.

9. If and to the extent that the claims paid by the Respondents pursuant to the Policy exceed the sums received by the Respondents by way of premium, the Respondents seek delivery of those sums from the Claimants, plus compound, alternatively simple interest thereon pursuant to section 49 of the Arbitration Act 1996, at such rate and for such period as the Tribunal thinks fit.

AND the Respondents Counterclaim:

(1) A declaration that they are entitled to avoid the Policy and/or that they have successfully avoided the same.

(2) The taking of an account, and the payment by the Claimants of any sums found to be due to the Respondents.

(3) Interest on any such sums as are found to be due to the Respondents.

(4) Such further or other relief as the Tribunal in its discretion thinks fit.

[Statement of Truth, etc][2]

Example 3: Reply and Defence to Counterclaim for avoidance in arbitration under an excess of loss contract of reinsurance

Claim No ....

IN THE MATTER OF THE ARBITRATION ACT 1996

AND

IN THE MATTER OF AN ARBITRATION

B E T W E E N:

IVOR GOODBOOK

(For and on behalf of himself and all
Underwriting members of syndicate 1234
for the 2000 year of account)

Claimants

- and -

MOONSHINE RE

Respondents

POINTS OF REPLY
AND DEFENCE TO COUNTERCLAIM

---

1. Unless stated to the contrary, references to paragraph numbers herein are references to the numbered paragraphs of the Points of Defence and Counterclaim.

Purported avoidance:

2. As to paragraph 3:

2.1 Paragraphs 3.1–3.4 are admitted.

2.2 As to paragraph 3.5, it is admitted that the Claimants did not disclose the facts and matters particularised in paragraphs 3.3 and 3.4 on placement of the Policy. It is denied that the Claimants were in breach of any obligation owed to the Respondents in this regard.

2.3 Paragraph 3.6.1 is admitted.

2.4 Paragraph 3.6.2 is denied. In fact, Mr Friday informed Mr Sage that the Claimants would not seek to aggregate losses 'solely' on the basis of a chip failing to recognise a date correctly, but that the Claimants would seek to aggregate losses in the 'normal manner' irrespective of whether all or part of the losses were connected with a failure in electronic date recognition.

2.5 Paragraph 3.7.1 is denied:

2.5.1 The losses sustained by the Claimants on 2nd April and 21st December 1999 (which amounted to US$750,000 and US$8m respectively) were not 'significant' in the context of the placement of the Policy, which incorporated a retention of US$25m.

2.5.2 In the premises, the statement set out on page 78 of the Claimants' presentation pack was true.

2.6 Paragraph 3.7.2 is denied:

2.6.1 Paragraph 2.4 above is repeated. The statement made by Mr Friday on behalf of the Claimants was merely a statement of present intention, and was true.

2.6.2 Further, and in any event in the present matter, the Claimants are not seeking to aggregate their losses 'solely' on the basis of the failure of the 'ZIP A1' to recognise dates on or after 1st January 2000. The Claimants rely upon the unity in way (the failure of the 'ZIP A1' and overheating of the air cooling), time (the morning of 1st January 2000) and place (the Towers were some 50 metres apart and centrally controlled) in order to aggregate their losses.

2.7 As to paragraph 3.8:

2.7.1 It is denied that the facts and matters upon which the Respondents place reliance, or any thereof were material to the risk which was being placed with the Respondents.

2.7.2 The Respondents are put to strict proof as to the alleged inducement.

Construction:

3. Paragraph 5 is admitted.

4. As to paragraph 6.3, it is denied that the 'event' was an 'event in progress' for the purposes of clause 4.1 of JELC:

4.1 There was no 'event in progress' as at 00:00 hrs on 1st January 2000.

4.2 Further, or alternatively, upon a true construction of clause 4.1 of JELC, an 'event in progress' as defined therein is an 'event' which has already caused loss in the expiring year and continues to cause loss in the succeeding year. The

Claimant did not sustain any loss prior to 1st January 2000. In the premises, the Claimants' losses occurred during the currency of the Policy.

5. As to paragraph 6.4:

   5.1 The statement made by Mr Friday was in the terms set out in paragraph 2.4 above, and constituted a statement of present intention, not a contractual term of the Policy.

   5.2 If, which is denied, the Policy contained any contractual term in this regard, the same was limited to a term precluding the Claimants from aggregating losses solely on the basis of a chip failing to recognise a date correctly. For the reasons set out in paragraph 2.6.2 above, the Claimants are not thereby precluded from aggregating their losses.

6. Paragraph 7.1 is denied, for the reasons set out above.

DEFENCE TO COUNTERCLAIM

---

7. Paragraph 2 hereof is repeated. In the premises, it is denied that the Respondents are entitled to any relief, whether as claimed in paragraphs 8 and 9, or otherwise.

[Statement of Truth, etc][2]

Example 3: Claim in High Court under a facultative contract of reinsurance

Claim No ....

IN THE HIGH COURT OF JUSTICE
QUEEN'S BENCH DIVISION
COMMERCIAL COURT

B E T W E E N:

IVOR GOODBOOK

(For and on behalf of himself and all
Underwriting members of syndicate 1234
for the 2000 year of account)

Claimants

- and -

MOONSHINE RE

Defendants

PARTICULARS OF CLAIM

---

1. By a contract of reinsurance, Policy reference no. 987, the Defendants agreed to reinsure the Claimants in consideration for the payment of premium, subscribing to a line of 100% ('the Policy').

2. The Policy contained the following, among other express terms:

'Type:	*Facultative reinsurance*
Reassured:	*Ivor Goodbook Syndicate 1234*
Original: Assured:	*Jaded Enterprises*

Period:	*Twenty four (24) months from 1st January 1999*
Terms:	*Coverage as original policy reference no. 789 for Towers 1 and 2*
Sum insured:	*US$50m*
Reassured's Retention:	*US$1m for each Tower*

This contract shall be subject to English law and the exclusive jurisdiction of the English Courts.'

The original contract of insurance

3. By a contract of insurance, policy reference no. 789 ('the Property Policy'), in consideration for the payment of premium, the Claimants agreed to insure Jaded Enterprises, subscribing to a line of 100%. The Property Policy contained the following express terms:

'PERIOD:	*24 MONTHS AT 1/1/99*
TYPE:	*PROPERTY*
SUBJECT MATTER:	*TOWER 1 AND TOWER 2, NO. 1 & 2, LIBERTY STREET, ATLANTIS CITY, ATLANTIS*
INSURED PERILS:	*ALL RISKS*
LIMIT OF INDEMNITY:	*US$25,000,000 TOWER 1* *US$25,000,000 TOWER 2*
LAW AND JURISDICTION:	*SUBJECT TO THE LAWS OF ATLANTIS AND THE EXCLUSIVE JURISDICTION OF THE GRAND COURT OF ATLANTIS.'*

The loss and judgment:

4. Towers 1 and 2 were both skyscrapers located on Liberty Street in the City of Atlantis, some 50 metres apart. On 1st January 2000, at 09:00 hrs local time Tower 1 was completely destroyed by fire. At 10:00 hrs local time on the same day, Tower 2 was completely destroyed by fire.

5. On 1st December 2000, the Grand Court of Atlantis held the Syndicate 1234 was liable to indemnify Jaded Enterprises in a total amount of US$50m, comprised of US$25m for each of the Towers, pursuant to the terms of the Property Policy.

6. On 10th December 2000, the Claimants duly indemnified Jaded Enterprises in the sum of US$50m.

7. By reason of the matters aforesaid, the Claimant has suffered reinsured loss and damage and is entitled to an indemnity from the Defendants in an amount of US$48m. Wrongfully, and in breach of the Policy, the Defendants have failed and refused to indemnify the Claimants for the Tower 1 and 2 losses, whether in an amount of US$48m or otherwise. As a result of the Defendants' breach of the Policy, the Claimants have suffered loss and damage in an amount of US$48m. In the alternative, the said sum of US$48m is due and owing from the Defendants to the Claimants under the Policy.

8. The Claimants are further entitled to interest on the amount of US$48m pursuant to section 35A of the Supreme Court Act 1981, and claim interest at such rate and for such period as the Court deems fit.

AND the Claimants claim:

(1) A declaration that they are entitled to be indemnified by the Defendants.

(2) The aforesaid indemnity.

(3) The sum of US$48m.

(4) Alternatively, damages in an amount of US$48m.

(5) Interest, as set out in paragraph 8 above.

(6) Costs.

(7) Such further or other relief as the Court in its discretion thinks fit.

The Claimants believe that the facts stated in the Particulars of Claim are true.

Example 4: Claim in High Court under a quota share treaty contract of reinsurance

Claim No ....

IN THE HIGH COURT OF JUSTICE
QUEEN'S BENCH DIVISION
COMMERCIAL COURT

B E T W E E N:

IVOR GOODBOOK

(For and on behalf of himself and all
Underwriting members of syndicate 1234
for the 2000 year of account)

Claimants

- and -

MOONSHINE RE

Defendants

PARTICULARS OF CLAIM

---

1. By a contract of reinsurance, policy reference no. 987, the Defendants agreed to reinsure the Claimants in consideration for the payment of premium, subscribing to a line of 100%.

2. The contract contained the following, among other express terms:

'Reassured: *Ivor Goodbook Syndicate number 1234*

Period: *As from 1st January 1999*

	Continuous contract always open in respect of risks attaching on and after 1st January 1999
	. . .
Type:	*Property Quota Share Treaty*
Class:	*All business underwritten by the Reinsured and classified by them as property business*
Quota share & Limit:	*The Reassured is obliged to cede and the Reinsurer is obliged to accept an 80% quota share of each and every risk accepted by the Reassured within the scope of this treaty, up to a maximum of US$25m for any one risk. Such cessions deemed to be automatic upon acceptance of the original risk.*

Reinsurers shall follow the settlement of and shall pay as may be paid by the Reassured.

. . .

The Reassured is to be the sole judge as to what constitutes one risk.

This reinsurance is subject to English law and the exclusive jurisdiction of the English Courts.'

The original contract of insurance

3. By a contract of insurance, policy reference no. 789 ('the Property Policy'), in consideration for the payment of premium, the Claimants agreed to insure Jaded Enterprises, subscribing to a line of 100%. The Property Policy contained the following express terms:

'PERIOD:	*24 MONTHS AT 1/1/99*
TYPE:	*PROPERTY*
SUBJECT MATTER:	*TOWER 1 AND TOWER 2, NO. 1 & 2, LIBERTY STREET, ATLANTIS CITY, ATLANTIS*
INSURED PERILS:	*ALL RISKS*
LIMIT OF INDEMNITY:	*US$25,000,000 TOWER 1* *US$25,000,000 TOWER 2*
LAW AND JURISDICTION:	*SUBJECT TO THE LAWS OF ATLANTIS AND THE EXCLUSIVE JURISDICTION OF THE GRAND COURT OF ATLANTIS.'*

4. Pursuant to the terms of the Property Policy, the original risks for Towers 1 and 2 attached on 1st January 1999. The Claimants classified these risks as property business.

Cession of the original risks and sole judgment

5. In the premises, an 80% quota share of the original risks for Towers 1 and 2 was automatically ceded to reinsurance contract reference no. 987 on 1st January 1999 ('the Policy').

6. The Claimants hereby determine in their sole judgment that for the purposes of the Policy, two separate 'risks' were insured under the Property Policy, the first risk being the risk of insured loss or damage to Tower 1, the second risk being the risk of insured loss or damage to Tower 2.

The loss and judgment:

7. Towers 1 and 2 were both skyscrapers located on Liberty Street in the City of Atlantis, some 50 metres apart. On 1st January 2000,

at 09:00 hrs local time Tower 1 was completely destroyed by fire. At 10:00 hrs local time on the same day, Tower 2 was completely destroyed by fire.

8. On 1st December 2000, the Grand Court of Atlantis held that Syndicate 1234 was liable to indemnify Jaded Enterprises Inc. in a total amount of US$50m, comprised of US$25m for each of the Towers, pursuant to the terms of the Property Policy.

9. On 10th December 2000, the Claimants duly indemnified Jaded Enterprises in the sum of US$50m.

10. By reason of the matters aforesaid, the Claimant has suffered reinsured loss and damage and is entitled to an indemnity from the Defendants in an amount of US$40m. Wrongfully, and in breach of the Policy, the Defendants have failed and refused to indemnify the Claimants for the Tower 1 and 2 losses, whether in an amount of US$40m or otherwise. As a result of the Defendants' breach of the Policy, the Claimants have suffered loss and damage in an amount of US$40m. In the alternative, the said sum of US$40m is due and owing from the Defendants to the Claimants under the Policy.

11. The Claimants are further entitled to interest on the amount of US$40m, pursuant to section 35A of the Supreme Court Act 1981, and claim interest at such rate and for such period as the Court deems fit.

AND the Claimants claim:

(1) A declaration that they are entitled to be indemnified by the Defendants.

(2) The aforesaid indemnity.

(3) The sum of US$40m.

(4) Alternatively, damages in an amount of US$40m.

(5) Interest, as set out in paragraph 11 above.

(6) Costs.

(7) Such further or other relief as the Court in its discretion thinks fit.

The Claimants believe that the facts stated in the Particulars of Claim are true.

1 The author would like to acknowledge the Institute of London Underwriters in reproducing the standard JELC clauses.

2 Statement of truth, etc as set out in **Chapter 3, para 3.2**.

CHAPTER 9

Banking

Julian Malins QC
Stephen Cogley

DOCUMENTARY CREDITS

Law and Mercantile Background

9.1 Trading between contracting parties based in different countries or jurisdictions, or which involves goods moving from one country or jurisdiction, inevitably involves a tension between the buyer's desire to receive the goods and the seller's desire to ensure that once the goods have been shipped, or are no longer under his control, he nevertheless can be sure of payment. In International Trade, these objectives are addressed by the parties generally incorporating into their underlying contractual relationship a requirement that enables the seller to have a guarantee of payment from a Bank within his jurisdiction once certain conditions are satisfied. This has the advantage of ease of enforcement and substitutes the Bank as the party primarily responsible for payment to the seller. Such a mechanism historically involved the Bank so substituted accepting Documents presented to it by or on behalf of the seller against which payment would be made – providing the Documents presented complied on their face with the terms of the underlying contract or credit. If the documents were compliant, the Bank would make payment, accept the Documents and forward them to the Buyer – who would then have control of the goods and, usually (payment having been made) property in the same. The credit arrangement between the Bank and the seller is known as a Documentary Credit.

An essential feature of a trading arrangement incorporating Documentary Credits is that the Credit is a self-contained autonomous contract between the Bank and the beneficiary Seller, discrete from the contract between the Buyer and the Seller, and the contract between the Buyer and the Bank, which provides the Credit at the Buyer's request. The Documentary Credit contract is concerned only (bar limited exceptions) with the Documents and the conformity between Documents presented by the Seller to the Bank with the Documents specified in the Letter of Credit.

The increasing complexity, frequency and multi-jurisdictional aspects of International Trade led to the International Chamber of Commerce introducing an international code to govern the operation of Documentary Credits with a view to providing uniformity and certainty for international traders and bankers. The document so introduced – *The Uniform Customs and Practice for Documentary Credits* ('UCP') has gone through many versions since 1933 – being adopted by the USA in 1951, and shortly thereafter the United

Kingdom in 1962. The current edition is UCP 500. UCP 500 does not constitute a legally enforceable regime in domestic law but great weight is given to it whenever questions of banking practice arise[1].

1 Per Rix J in *Glencore International AG v Bank of China* [1996] 1 Lloyds Rep 135 at p 145; per Steel J in *Crédit Industriel et Commercial v China Merchants Bank* [2002] 2 All ER (Comm) 427, [2002] EWHC 973 – in the context of the application of, and weight to be given to, a Policy Statement under UCP in relation to original documents.

Contractual matrix

9.2 As mentioned above, Documentary Credits are autonomous, are concerned only with the documents, and are inevitably part of a series of contracts. Four of the usual five contracts encountered in International Trade involving Documentary Credits were identified by Lord Diplock[1] as: the contract between the Buyer and the Seller – which will stipulate for the issuing of a Letter of Credit; secondly the contract between Buyer and Bank that issues the Letter of Credit and either itself, or through a further Bank ('Confirming Bank'), notifies the credit to the seller and makes payment to the order of the Seller (or pays, accepts or negotiates bills of exchange drawn by the Seller), against presentation of stipulated documents – the Buyer agreeing, in turn, to reimburse the Issuing Bank for payments made under the Credit; thirdly, if payment is to be made through a Confirming Bank, the contract between the Issuing Bank and the Confirming Bank authorising and requiring the Confirming Bank to make payments and to remit the stipulated documents to the Issuing Bank when they are received – in turn the issuing Bank agrees to reimburse the Confirming Bank for payments made under the Credit; and fourthly the contract between the Confirming Bank and the Seller under which the Confirming Bank undertakes to pay to the Seller up to the amount of the Credit against presentation of the stipulated documents. Fifthly, of course, there is the underlying contract between the issuing Bank and the beneficiary – namely the Seller.

A Confirming Bank is a bank which adds its undertaking to pay against presentation of the stipulated documents in accordance with the terms of the Credit. Such an undertaking acts as an additional guarantee to that given by the Issuing Bank. It is quite usual for a Confirming Bank to be the correspondent bank of the Issuing Bank in the Seller's jurisdiction, and often to be the bank which advises the opening of the Credit. The insistence of a Letter of Credit being 'confirmed' is a usual request from a seller, thereby giving it the comfort of a paying party within the jurisdiction with limited risk of insolvency. It is usually the Confirming Bank to whom the stipulated documents are presented.

In practice, most disputes centre around whether the presented Documents comply with the Credit. In reality, the Credit will specify the documents to be presented which are likely to be those stipulated in the contract between the Buyer and the Seller as part of the obligation upon the Buyer to provide the

Credit. UCP 500 contains numerous Articles dealing with the form and content that frequently encountered trade documents must comply with in order for the conditions of the Credit to be satisfied – for example Articles 23, 24 and 25 (Marine bills of lading, non-negotiable sea waybill and charterparty bills of lading), Article 34 (Insurance Documents) and Article 37 (Commercial Invoices). The scope for dispute is extensive: if the Confirming Bank accepts presented documents which are discrepant (i.e. the documents when examined with reasonable care exhibit a discrepancy which is apparent on the face of the same), it is not entitled to reimbursement from the Issuing Bank. Similarly, if the Issuing Bank pays against presentation its right of reimbursement against the applicant Buyer will be lost if the documents are discrepant.

It is noteworthy that providing the presented documents are as stipulated in, and compliant with, the Documentary Credit, the fact that there may be an underlying dispute between the applicant Buyer and beneficiary Seller is irrelevant and founds no ground for refusal to meet the terms of the Credit in favour of the beneficiary. Note that the Autonomy Principle is not offended in the event of the parties expressly agreeing that there should be no draw down against the Credit absent the satisfaction of express conditions: thus in the unusual situation where the beneficiary agreed not to draw on a Letter of Credit without the express consent of the applicant, Jacob J[2] recognised that there could be an exception to the autonomy principle under such circumstances. On the facts, the conditions were satisfied because agreement to draw down was found in a '*Tomlin Order*' entered into between the parties prior to draw down.

The extent of the potential for dispute arises because over half of documents presented contain discrepancies on first presentation – even though the majority of documents are accepted by the Issuing or Confirming Bank[3]. The Autonomy Principle is not, however, inviolate: where the Seller, for the purpose of drawing on the credit, fraudulently presents to the Confirming Bank (or Issuing Bank) Documents that contain, expressly or by implication, material representations of fact that to his knowledge are untrue, the Bank is entitled to refuse payment[4]. The Bank cannot refuse to pay, however, purely because it suspects fraud, or circumstances arise which it contends would put a reasonable banker on notice of fraud[5]: rather actual fraud has to be clearly alleged and established. This means, from a practitioner's perspective, that the Bank that refuses to make payment on this ground should be able to distinctly allege and prove fraud in the classic sense. In practice, this is particularly hard to demonstrate absent forged or falsified documents.

Whilst the American case which forms the root of the 'fraud exception' concerned the successful application for an injunction against the Issuing Bank to prevent payment[6], such injunctions in this jurisdiction are in practice particularly difficult to obtain. Apart from the normal judicial scrutiny accompanying Without Notice Applications under CPR Part 23, conceptually the Buyer may suffer no loss in cases where fraud is made out at trial because he has no obligation to reimburse the Paying Bank, and the courts may well regard the granting of a Freezing Order over the proceeds in the hands of the beneficiary, at the suit of the applicant Buyer, as a more proportionate remedy: even more so bearing in mind the high burden of proof in fraud claims. An additional hurdle is the fact that the Bank has to have knowledge of the fraud – which is notoriously difficult to prove and establish in practice. The overall balance of convenience militates heavily against the grant of such injunctions.

1 *United City Merchants (Investments) Limited v Royal Bank of Canada* [1983] 1 AC 168 at p 182.
2 *Sirius International Insurance Co Limited v FAI General Insurance Limited and others* [2002] EWHC 1611 (Chancery), upheld in the House of Lords [2005] 1 AER (Comm) p 117.
3 *Documentary Credits* (3rd edn) Raymond Jack and Others (preface to 3rd edn); Professor Schmitthoff *Discrepancy of Documents in Letter of Credit Transactions* (1987) JBL p 94.
4 Per Lord Diplock in *United City Merchants (Investments) Limited and Glass Fibres and Equipments Limited v Royal Bank of Canada and others* [1983] 1 AC 168, HL.
5 *Society of Lloyds v Canadian Imperial Bank of Commerce* [1993] 2 Lloyd's Rep at p 579.
6 *Sztejn v J Henry Schroder Banking Corps* 31 NYS 2d 631 (1941).

Pleadings

9.3 The two pleaded illustrations concern a dispute between the Issuing Bank and a beneficiary (1) and a dispute between an applicant Buyer and an Issuing Bank (2).

Assumed facts

9.4 Seller (beneficiary) is based in the UK and Buyer in the USA. They enter into a contract for the purchase of Diesel engines CIF with payment to be made under an irrevocable Letter of Credit opened by Buyer with Z Bank upon presentation and acceptance of certain Documents stipulated in the Credit. Z Bank issued the Letter of Credit and advised Sellers agent, A Bank, of this fact and undertook to pay according to its terms. In the first illustration, Z bank refused to accept the documents upon presentation, whilst in the second Z Bank accepted the same and paid under the credit, but Buyer alleges that Z Bank should have rejected the documents and refuses to reimburse Z Bank. In each illustration it is alleged that the documents are discrepant.

Points of Claim on behalf of Seller against Issuing Bank: refusal to accept stipulated documents and pay

Claim No …………..

IN THE HIGH COURT OF JUSTICE
QUEEN'S BENCH DIVISION
COMMERCIAL COURT

B E T W E E N:

SELLER Ltd

Claimant

- and -

Z INTERNATIONAL BANK INC

Defendant

POINTS OF CLAIM

---

1. Parties

1.1 The Claimant, Seller Ltd, ('Seller') is a manufacturer and exporter of Diesel engines and carries on business from its premises at Ancoats, Manchester and elsewhere in the United Kingdom; and

1.2 Buyer Inc ('Buyer') is a manufacturer of Fire Tenders carrying on its business from premises at Madison, Minnesota USA; and

1.3 The Defendant, Z International Bank Inc ('Z Bank'), is a banker carrying on business as such in the USA and in the United Kingdom.

2. The Contract

2.1 By a contract in writing made on the 1st August 2004 on Seller's standard terms of business it agreed to sell and Buyer agreed to purchase 100 complete Diesel engines type X built to Buyer's specification price £10,000 sterling each unit CIF Boston. Payment was to be in cleared funds under an irrevocable letter of credit upon presentation and acceptance on sight of stipulated shipping documents in accordance with the credit.

2.2 The Letter of Credit was to be opened by Buyer with Z Bank in favour of Seller.

3. Performance

3.1 On 5th August 2004, Z Bank through its London Branch advised Seller by fax and email to Sellers agent, A Bank PLC, that an irrevocable Credit had been opened with Z Bank for the contract sum (£1m) by Buyer in favour of Seller payable on sight of the shipping documents stipulated in the Credit.

3.2 The engines were duly manufactured by Seller and then shipped on board MV Quadrant on 13th August 2004 in accordance with the contract.

4. On 13th September 2004 Seller through its agent A Bank PLC presented to Z Bank at . . . . as stipulated in the Letter of Credit a clean Marine Bill of Lading, Marine Insurance Certificate, Invoice and Inspection Certificate. The Claimant also tendered a Packing List.

5. Breach

5.1 In breach of the contract constituted by the Letter of Credit Z Bank has failed and/or refused to accept the stipulated documents on sight or make payment under the Letter of Credit in the contract sum or any part thereof.

6. Loss

6.1 By reason of the foregoing:

6.1.1 The Claimant is entitled to the contract sum – namely £1m; alternatively

6.1.2 The Claimant has suffered loss and damage in the said sum.

7. Interest

7.1 The Claimant is entitled to and claims to recover interest on the sum of £1m at the rate of x% per month (the contract sum) until judgment or sooner payment totalling £[ ] at the date of issue and continuing at the daily rate of £[ ] alternatively at such rate and for such period as the Court deems fit pursuant to section 35A of the Supreme Court Act 1981.

Accordingly the Claimant claims:

(1) £1m alternatively damages in the said sum;

(2) Interest in the present sum of £[ ] and continuing at the daily rate of £[ ] or as alternatively pleaded.

[Statement of Truth, etc][1]

Hermione Hedonista

Defence by Bank: non acceptance of presented Documents under Letter of Credit

Claim No ....

IN THE HIGH COURT OF JUSTICE
QUEEN'S BENCH DIVISION
COMMERCIAL COURT

B E T W E E N:

SELLER Ltd

Claimant

- and -

Z INTERNATIONAL BANK INC

Defendant

POINTS OF DEFENCE

---

1. It is denied that the Defendant is liable or indebted to the Claimant as alleged or at all.

2. Paragraphs 1 and the sub-paragraphs thereunder are admitted.

3. As regards paragraph 2:

   3.1 Save that it was an express term of the contract that transhipment of the goods was prohibited and that the same were to be shipped direct ship, it is admitted that the contract between Seller and Buyer was on Seller's standard terms of business. The express terms of the contract are contained in the fax dated 1st August 2004 sent on behalf of

Seller to Buyer which in turn accepted the offer made by Buyer in its fax of the 30th July 2004. The fax of 30th July 2004 from Buyer expressly stipulated that Buyer was content to contract upon Sellers standard terms save for transhipment – which was prohibited and that the goods were to be shipped direct ship.

3.2 The remainder of the said paragraph is admitted.

4. Paragraph 3.1 is admitted. The Letter of Credit expressly incorporated UCP 500 as anticipated by Seller's standard terms and as expressly communicated to Seller/its agent, A Bank PLC, by Z Bank's correspondent London Branch when advising that the Credit had been opened in favour of Seller. Further, and as stipulated by Buyer, the Letter of Credit expressly prohibited transhipment.

5. No admissions are made in respect of paragraph 3.2 – the same not being within the knowledge of Z Bank.

6. Save that it is admitted that A Bank PLC presented certain Documents to Z Bank in purported compliance and conformity with the Letter of Credit on 13th September 2004, and that such Documents included those set out in paragraph 4, the remainder of the said paragraph is denied.

Documents

7. The Marine Bill of Lading is not in accordance with the Letter of Credit as it does not demonstrate continuous carriage by direct ship and the Invoice and Packing List are inconsistent – the former referring to complete Diesel engines whilst the latter refers to stripped Diesel engines. The Insurance Certificate refers to Complete Diesel engines and no others.

8. Accordingly:

   8.1 The documents were discrepant and in particular Z Bank was entitled to reject the Documents pursuant to UCP 500, Article 23 as the Letter of Credit prohibited transhipment as did the Marine Bill of Lading; and

   8.2 Did so by conduct – refusing to accept the same, alternatively by fax dated 15th September 2004 alternatively by email of the same date.

9. Without prejudice to the foregoing it is denied that Seller has suffered any loss or that the contract sum or damages in like amount are recoverable: if, which is denied, Z Bank is liable to Seller, it is for no more than the cost of borrowing a like sum from an alternative Bank. In support of this contention, it is Z Bank's case that Seller's rights to claim against Buyer remain intact and so any failure to pay out on presentation of the Documents causes no more than loss of the ability to use the contract sum. The true measure of Seller's loss under these circumstances is the cost of alternative credit.

10. For all of the above reasons Z Bank is not liable to Seller.

[Statement of Truth, etc][1]

Prudence Prufrock

Points of Reply to Banks Defence rejecting Documents under Letter of Credit

Claim No ....

IN THE HIGH COURT OF JUSTICE
QUEEN'S BENCH DIVISION
COMMERCIAL COURT

B E T W E E N:

SELLER Ltd

Claimant

- and -

Z INTERNATIONAL BANK INC

Defendant

POINTS OF REPLY

---

1. Save in so far as the same consists of admissions of matters in the Points of Claim, Seller joins issue with Z Bank upon its Defence.

2. It is denied that the contract included the terms contended for at paragraph 3.1 of the Defence. The fax from Buyer dated 30th July 2004 was not received until 2nd August 2004 and was thus received by Seller after the contract was concluded. Further the fax from Seller dated 1st August 2004 neither referred to or acknowledged implicitly or otherwise the fax of 30th July 2004 or the contents thereof. Accordingly, it is denied that the contract between Seller and Buyer contained any conditions prohibiting transhipment or that the goods had to be shipped direct ship. The

contract was made on Seller's standard terms of business and included no other material terms – thus indirect shipment and transhipment were permitted by virtue of Conditions 10(a) and (b).

3. In addition:

   3.1 even if, contrary to paragraph 2 above, the contract between Seller and Buyer prohibited transhipment, on its true construction the Letter of Credit did not; and

   3.2 the Marine Bill of Lading indicated that the goods would be transhipped; and

   3.3 further the entire ocean carriage is covered by the same Bill of Lading; and

   3.4 in any event the Marine Bill of Lading indicated that transhipment of the goods would take place in Containers;

   3.5 the Packing List is not a Document stipulated for in the contract between Seller and Buyer or in the Letter of Credit and is irrelevant to the Claim. All other Documents are consistent, correspond and are in conformity with the Letter of Credit.

   In these circumstances the Documents complied with the Letter of Credit and the Marine Bill of Lading was compliant and should have been accepted by Z Bank in accordance with UCP 500, Article 23(c) and/or (d), (i).

4. Paragraph 9 of the Defence is denied. In particular, Seller's loss is not limited as set out therein: Seller has at all times been ready able and willing to perform by re-tendering the stipulated Documents and accordingly its loss is the loss of the sum payable under the

Letter of Credit. Further, and for the avoidance of doubt, Seller's rights against Buyer are commercially worthless due to the latter's insolvency.

5. Save as above, the Claimant's case is as stated in the Points of Claim.

[Statement of Truth, etc][1]

Hermione Hedonista

Points of Claim on behalf of Buyer – Claim against Bank for accepting discrepant Documents

Claim No ....

IN THE HIGH COURT OF JUSTICE
QUEEN'S BENCH DIVISION
COMMERCIAL COURT

B E T W E E N:

BUYER Ltd

Claimant

- and -

Z INTERNATIONAL BANK INC

Defendant

POINTS OF CLAIM

---

1. Parties

1.1 The Claimant ('Buyer') is a manufacturer and exporter of Fire Tenders and carries on business from its premises at Walthamstow, London E17 and elsewhere in the UK; and

1.2 The Defendant ('Z Bank') is a banker carrying on business as such in the UK including its Branch at .... London EC4......;

1.3 Seller Inc ('Seller') is a manufacturer and exporter of Diesel Engines and carries on business from its premises at Madison, Minnesota USA.

2. Background

2.1 By a contract in writing contained in an email dated 12th September 2004 from the Seller to the Buyer, Seller agreed to sell and Buyer agreed to buy 100 complete Diesel engines type X built to Buyers specification price £10,000 per unit CIF Boston shipment October at Buyers call.

2.2 It was an express term of the agreement that payment would be made in cleared funds upon presentation of stipulated shipping documents by Seller or its agent under an irrevocable Letter of Credit opened by Buyer in favour of Seller.

2.3 In order to satisfy its payment obligations under the said agreement Buyer duly completed and presented to its Bank, Z Bank, an application to open such a Letter of Credit by utilising Z Bank's standard form 'Application to open a Letter of Credit' (23rd edn).

3. Contract

3.1 Z Bank duly accepted Buyer's Application to open a Letter of Credit in favour of Seller in the contract sum of £1m upon the terms set out in and upon the Application form in consideration of Buyer's Agreement to pay the charges referred to therein and to provide security in favour of Z Bank by the deposit of £300,000 sterling in a blocked account, and a charge over the said account and sums contained therein, and over the Diesel Engines the subject of the agreement between Buyer and Seller.

3.2 It was an express term of the agreement between Buyer and Z Bank that payment under the Letter of Credit would only be made upon presentation by Seller or its agent of conforming shipping documents as stipulated in the Application form, namely:

3.2.1 An original commercial invoice and two copies;

3.2.2 Full set of clean on board Marine Bills of Lading;

3.2.3 Marine Insurance Certificate;

3.2.4 Inspection Certificate.

and that the agreement between Buyer and Z Bank and the Letter of Credit would incorporate and be subject to UCP 500.

4. Breach

4.1 In breach of contract, Z Bank has accepted non-conforming discrepant documents presented on behalf of Seller and has paid to and at Seller's request the contract sum of £1m and further seeks to be reimbursed by Buyer in the contract sum and to claim the credit charges set out in the Application.

PARTICULARS

4.1.1 On 30th September 2004, A Bank PLC as agent for Seller presented to Z Bank at its London Branch shipping documents which were non-conforming and discrepant in that the Bill of Lading was claused and contained a notation that the packing crates containing the Diesel Engines were damaged. The Bill of Lading was thus not clean within UCP 500, Article 32.

4.1.2 Further the Commercial Invoice (and copies) referred to complete Diesel Engines whereas the Packing List referred to stripped Diesel Engines, i.e. stripped into major constituent parts.

5. It was an express term of the agreement between Buyer and Z Bank that the latter's rights to reimbursement and recourse to the security and to claim the credit charges set out the Application would only arise upon acceptance of clean and conforming Documents as stipulated in the Application and the Letter of Credit and payment out of the contract sum. Alternatively, such a term is to be implied in order to give business efficacy to the said agreement.

6. Further, or in the alternative, it was a condition precedent to Z Bank's rights as set out at paragraph 5 above that it should first have accepted and paid out upon clean and conforming Documents as stipulated in the Application and Letter of Credit.

7. In breach thereof and without entitlement, the said condition precedent being unfulfilled, Z Bank on 1st October 2004 transferred to itself the sum of £300,000 in the blocked account and gave notice that it was debiting Buyer's current account with credit charges of £22,000 and exercising its rights over the Diesel Engines under the Charge.

8. Consequences

8.1 By reason of the foregoing:

8.1.1 Buyer is entitled to be repaid the sum of £322,000 so as to effect restitution; alternatively

8.1.2 Buyer has suffered loss and damage in the said sum; and

8.1.3 is entitled to a Declaration that it has no obligation to indemnify or reimburse Z Bank; and

8.1.4 is further entitled to all necessary Orders and Directions cancelling any entry of the Charge in any Books Register or Directory.

9. Interest

9.1 Buyer is entitled to and claims to recover interest at the rate of x% per annum from 2nd November 2004 until judgment or sooner payment of the sum of £320,000 totalling £[ ] at the date of issue and continuing at the daily rate of £[ ] or alternatively at such rate and for such period as the Court deems fit pursuant to section 35A of the Supreme Court Act 1981.

Accordingly Buyer claims:

(1) £320,000, alternatively damages in the said sum.

(2) Interest in the sum of £[ ] and continuing at the daily rate of £[ ] or as alternatively pleaded.

(3) The Declaration and Orders set out at paragraph 8.1.3 and 8.1.4 above.

[Statement of Truth, etc][1]

Hermione Hedonista

Defence by Bank to Buyer's Claim denying acceptance of discrepant Documents

Claim No ....

IN THE HIGH COURT OF JUSTICE
QUEEN'S BENCH DIVISION
COMMERCIAL COURT

B E T W E E N:

BUYER Ltd

Claimant

- and -

Z INTERNATIONAL BANK INC

Defendant

POINTS OF DEFENCE

---

1. It is denied that the Defendant is liable or indebted to the Claimant as alleged or at all.

2. Paragraphs 1 and 2 and the respective sub-paragraphs thereunder are admitted.

3. Paragraph 3.1 is admitted and specifically relied on by Z Bank.

4. As regards Paragraph 4:

    4.1 The Application to open the Letter of Credit expressly recited the notations that were to be regarded as acceptable – and thus not rendering the Bill of Lading foul/unclean, by providing a series of boxes for any applicant to tick, thereby signifying the clauses or notations that could be accepted by Z Bank under UCP 500, Article 32. The said Application contained a tick in the box signifying that a notation indicating damage to the packaging, so long as unaccompanied by any other notation, was acceptable and would not render the Bill of Lading foul/unclean or discrepant. Accordingly, whilst it is admitted that the Bill of Lading when presented contained a notification indicating damage to the packaging of the Diesel Engines, Z Bank was obliged, alternatively entitled to accept the said Bill of Lading and did so;

4.2 The Packing List referred to is not a document stipulated under the Letter of Credit and Z Bank was entitled to, and did, for this reason disregard the same. Further, to the extent that it is contended that the credit contained any terms in relation to packing (which is denied) no documents were stated in the credit in relation thereto and Z Bank was accordingly entitled to disregard any such conditions under UCP 500, Article 13(c). For the avoidance of doubt all other stipulated Documents were compliant and conforming.

5. Paragraphs 5 and 6 are admitted.

6. Save that it was denied that Z Bank was in breach of any term or that any condition precedent was unfulfilled, paragraph 7 is admitted. Z Bank was entitled to so act.

7. Save as above the Points of Claim are denied. Buyer has no Claim against Z bank and is not entitled to the claimed relief against it or any relief.

[Statement of Truth, etc][1]

Prudence Prufrock

1 Statement of truth, etc as set out in **Chapter 3, para 3.2**.

CHAPTER 10

International Trade and Sale of Goods

International Sale of Goods:
Julian Malins QC
Nigel Meeson QC
Stephen Cogley

Sale of Goods:
Simon Croall

INTERNATIONAL SALE OF GOODS: CIF AND FOB CONTRACTS

Law and Mercantile Background

10.1 Contracts for the Sale of Goods between traders in different countries or jurisdictions or which involve goods moving from one country or jurisdiction frequently use standard phrases that have developed through custom and usage to connote specific things. Notwithstanding this practice there are still many disputes that arise revealing a different subjective intention being held by each of the parties. In order to reduce the scope for misunderstanding, and so as to achieve certainty, contracts using such shorthand nowadays frequently incorporate standard terms of trading of one or other of the trade associations pertinent to their business, or the goods in question[1].

Standard terms may be incorporated which govern the whole of the transaction or only specific parts of the transaction – such as the carriage by sea, or the nature and form of the documents to be presented to secure payment. The use of standard terms seeks to address the fact that the buyer and seller are subject to different jurisdictions which may treat the obligations of each party differently, and the fact that the application of the seller's system of law might produce, for example, radically different results from the application of the buyer's. In an international sale each of the buyer and the seller will be satisfying different obligations in different jurisdictions as a result of their different geographical situation – such as accepting the goods and documents and paying the contract sum. In the absence of a clear choice of law clause, the proper law will have to be dealt with by applying conflict of law rules.

This chapter concentrates on international contracts involving two such forms of shorthand – CIF and FOB contracts. It is important to remember that the obligations which commonly arise as a result of using these words can be expressly or implicitly modified by the contract – indeed sometimes modifications change the accepted understanding connoted by the use of this shorthand to such an extent that the concluded contract is of an entirely different nature from that generally understood by the relevant phrase. Thus if the contract between the buyer and the seller reveals that the obligation to pay the price in a contract ostensibly CIF, is in fact dependent upon delivery of the goods[2] or that such delivery is an acceptable discharge of the seller's obligations[3] the contract is not made on CIF terms notwithstanding the parties applying this label.

1 Convention on Contracts for the International Sale of Goods (UNCITRAL); INCOTERMS – published by the International Chamber of Commerce; International Trade Terms Standard Terms of Contracts for the International Sale of Goods (INTRATERMS) terms.
2 *Gardano Giamperi v Greek Petroleum George Mamidakis & Co* [1961] 2 Lloyd's Rep 259.
3 *Holland Colombo Trading Society Limited v Segu Mohamed Khaja Alawdeen* [1954] 2 Lloyd's Rep 45.

FOB

10.2 As a matter of trade usage FOB means 'Free on Board', and in the original strict sense the seller is responsible for all charges up to and including the point at which the goods pass over the rail of the ship[1] nominated by the buyer at the shipping port. Upon passing this point the goods are delivered to the buyer and risk passes. Property may also pass (see below).

The seller is not responsible for any subsequent charges such as stowage or carriage, insurance or charges arising on arrival at the destination port. Thus, if the goods are lost once over the rail there is no claim against the seller in the traditional FOB contract. The seller is usually required to deliver to the buyer a document proving that delivery has taken place in accordance with the contract or the particular custom applying at the port in question or in relation to the goods.

The FOB contract is particularly flexible. It is often varied between the parties to cater for a specific transaction, or by reference to the custom and usage applying in the particular market sector in which the parties function. A strict FOB contract is very often modified by one or other of the parties undertaking additional obligations. It is quite usual, for example, for the seller to arrange shipping and insurance on behalf of the buyer, in which case the court may readily infer that there is a duty on the seller to provide the bill of lading for the buyer, rather than the buyer collecting the bill of lading himself. The FOB contract where such additional obligations are undertaken is generally referred to as '... a FOB contract with additional services or 'an extended FOB'. Regardless, however, of the form of FOB contract, the seller does not undertake or warrant that the goods will arrive safely or at all. The seller's principal obligations in relation to the goods are discharged when they are delivered by being placed on board. Even under an extended FOB contract, as indeed with all FOB contracts, the cost of the freight and insurance ultimately is borne by the buyer[2].

Unless the contract provides to the contrary, it is the responsibility of the buyer to obtain the appropriate licenses and authorities for the import of the goods and to nominate the ship. This is done by providing the name of the ship in which the goods are to be carried, the port and such other information as is necessary for the seller to bring the goods alongside and load in accordance with the contract. The ship has to be suitable – which means ready, able and willing to carry the particular contract goods and able to load the goods within the relevant shipping period. Notice of the foregoing matters has to be given by the buyer within a reasonable time in the absence of there being an express contractual stipulation. If the buyer does not comply with its nomination and notice responsibilities within the stipulated time, or nominates an unsuitable ship, generally the seller can terminate the contract upon accepting these breaches as repudiatory[3]. If a suitable ship is nominated, the buyer, unless the contract provides that a nomination shall be final, is free to nominate a substitute ship in the event of the original nomination failing.

The passing of property under a FOB contract depends upon a combination of the extent to which the goods are ascertained, the express terms of the contract and the Sale of Goods Act 1979 (in the event of English law applying). If the goods are unascertained, property is unlikely to pass until the goods are appropriated, in the case of a bulk consignment, or otherwise become ascertained. If the goods are ascertained, property will pass when the goods are delivered (for example by being placed over the ship's rail) in the absence of an express term to the contrary – such as a '*Romalpa*' clause. If the FOB contract is with additional services, and the seller contracts with the carrier and obtains the bill of lading, passing of property will usually be postponed until the bill of lading is delivered to the buyer, or received on his behalf (for example by the advising bank if a documentary credit/letter of credit is involved).

1 Some judicial latitude is evident regarding this concept: note the observations of Devlin J in '*The Pyrene*' [1954] 2 QB 402 – regarding the unsatisfactory incidence of passing of risk dependent on where the goods are swaying when the loading rope snaps.

2 *NV Handel My J Smits Import-Export v English Exporters Limited* [1957] 1 Lloyd's Rep 517.

3 *Texaco Limited v The Eurogulf Shipping Company Limited* [1987] 2 Lloyd's Rep 54.

CIF

10.3 As a matter of trading usage, CIF means 'Cost Insurance and Freight'. As with FOB contracts there are variants, but the essential ingredients of a CIF contract require the seller to ship the goods and clear them for export to his own account, to procure or enter into a contract of carriage by sea and obtain the bill of lading as evidence of the same; to arrange a contract of marine insurance entitling the buyer to make a claim against the insurer; and to make out an invoice in the precise form required by the contract (or custom and usage) containing specific details in relation to the agreed price, commission charges, freight and insurance. Cardinally, the essential documents – namely the Bill of Lading (in clean form), the Invoice and the Marine Insurance Policy or Certificate have to be delivered to the buyer or his agent.

It is permissible, and not uncommon, for the seller to purchase goods afloat so as to comply with his contractual obligations, and the same goods may in fact be purchased afloat on more than one occasion.

Like the FOB contract, the seller does not undertake or warrant that the goods will arrive. In the CIF contract it is the documents that control the goods, and it is the documents that the buyer can properly be regarded as 'purchasing'. The cardinal significance of the documents does not preclude the buyer from rejecting the goods on arrival for failure to comply with the contract description or because of defects or lack of conformity with the contract. This is distinct from the right to reject the documents – which can be lost when, for example, under a letter of credit the advising bank takes up the documents and pays against them without objection.

The buyer is obliged to take up the documents providing they are in conformity with the contract, bear all risk from the time when the goods pass the ship's rail at the shipment port and receive the goods at the agreed destination port and, with the exception of insurance and freight, pay the costs and charges incurred in the course of transit and on arrival at the destination port, including unloading. The buyer will usually pay the costs of obtaining any other necessary documents – such as consular documents, Import Licences, and Certificates of Origin. Losing the right to reject the documents does not mean that the buyer cannot reject the goods if, on arrival, they are defective, etc. Indeed even the passing of property at an earlier stage to the buyer when the Bill of Lading is delivered does not preclude rejection of the goods, nor does payment of the purchase price on delivery of the shipping documents. The property is regarded as conditional, reverting to the seller if the goods are found to be other than contracted for[1] and payment of the price is said to be subject to a condition subsequent that the goods are as contracted for.

It is usual in CIF contracts for the place of shipment and time to be expressly stipulated in the contract. The contract may cater for the transferring of the goods from one ship to another or may, on the contrary, provide that the goods cannot be so transferred, or that they have to be shipped direct to an identified port. In this latter instance a failure to tender to the buyer a bill of lading demonstrating continuous carriage from the shipping port to the specified destination port without interruption would entitle the buyer to reject the documents in the absence of an express stipulation or practice to the contrary.

1 *Gill & Duffus SA v Berger & Co* [1984] 2 WLR 95.

Pleading

Assumed facts

10.4 Seller is based in USA and Buyer in UK. They have entered into three previous contracts for the same goods within the last 18 months. In the first illustration the contract is on CIF terms whilst the second is FOB. There is a dispute in relation to various matters – not all of which feature in each illustration. The Diesel engines are unique and have been built entirely to the specification provided by Buyer – who has considerable expertise in building and commissioning Fire Tenders. Buyer has contracted with an end user to fit the engines into Fire Tenders and is subject to express stipulations in the contract with the end user in relation to the time for performance of Buyer's obligations. Sundry, other factual matters and disputes are self evident in each illustration.

Points of Claim on behalf of Seller: CIF Contract

Claim No ....

IN THE HIGH COURT OF JUSTICE
QUEEN'S BENCH DIVISION
COMMERCIAL COURT

B E T W E E N:

SELLER INC

Claimant

- and -

BUYER LIMITED

Defendant

POINTS OF CLAIM

---

1. **Parties**

1.1 The Claimant is a manufacturer and exporter of Diesel engines and carries on business from its premises at Madison, Minnesota, USA; and

1.2 The Defendant is a manufacturer of Fire Tenders carrying on its business from premises at Manchester and elsewhere in the United Kingdom.

2. **The Contract**

2.1 By a contract in writing made on the 1st August 2004 on the Claimant's standard terms of business it agreed to sell and the

Defendant agreed to purchase 100 complete Diesel engines type X built to the Defendant's specification price £10,000 sterling each unit CIF Boston payment cleared funds against documents.

3. **Performance**

3.1 The engines were duly manufactured and then shipped on board NV Essex on the 13th of August 2004 in accordance with the contract.

4. On the 13th of September 2004 the Claimant through its agent tendered to the Defendant at .... as stipulated in the contract a clean Bill of Lading, Marine Insurance Certificate, Invoice and Inspection Certificate. The Claimant also tendered a Packing List.

5. **Breach**

5.1 In breach of contract the Defendant has failed and/or refused to accept the documents or take delivery of the same or accept the Diesel engines or pay the total contract price or any part thereof.

6. **Loss**

6.1 By reason of the foregoing:

6.1.1 the Claimant is entitled to the contract price – namely £1m; alternatively

6.1.2 the Claimant has suffered loss and damage in the said sum there being no market for the engines and the same being of no value to anybody other than the Defendant by virtue of the engine's unique design to the Defendant's specification and Patent.

7. **Interest**

7.1 The Claimant is entitled to and claims to recover interest on the sum of £1m at the rate of x% per month (the contract sum) until judgment or sooner payment totalling £[ ] at the date of issue and continuing at the daily rate of £[ ] alternatively at such rate and for such period as the Court deems fit pursuant to section 35A of the Supreme Court Act 1981.

Accordingly the Claimant claims:

(1) £1m, alternatively damages in the said sum;

(2) interest in the present sum of £[ ] and continuing at the daily rate of £[ ] or as alternatively pleaded.

[Statement of Truth, etc][1]

Defence and Part 20 Counterclaim: CIF Contract

Claim No ....

IN THE HIGH COURT OF JUSTICE
QUEEN'S BENCH DIVISION
COMMERCIAL COURT

B E T W E E N:

SELLER INC

Claimant/Part 20 Defendant

- and -

BUYER LIMITED

Defendant/Part 20 Claimant

POINTS OF DEFENCE AND PART 20 COUNTERCLAIM

---

1. It is denied that the Defendant is liable or indebted to the Claimant as alleged or at all.

2. Paragraphs 1 and the sub-paragraphs thereunder are admitted.

3. As regards paragraph 2:

   3.1 It is denied that the contract was made on the Claimant's standard terms of business or that it incorporated the same. In fact the said terms were not brought to the attention of the Defendant until after the dispute herein arose. The express terms of the contract are contained in the fax dated 1st August 2004 sent on behalf of the Claimant to the Defendant. The Defendant further relies on the fact that the said standard terms have never been mentioned or incorporated or formed part of any of the three prior contracts between the parties in relation to identical Diesel engines;

3.2 The remainder of the said paragraph is admitted.

4. The fax dated 1st August 2004 above referred to also recited (amongst other things) that property in the goods remains vested in the Claimant until payment of the full contract price. Accordingly it is denied, pursuant to section 49(1) of the Sale of Goods Act 1979, that the Claimant can maintain a claim for the price for this reason, in addition to those set out below.

5. The Defendant endorsed on the fax prior to transmitting a copy of the same back to the Claimant '*transhipment prohibited*' and '*direct ship*'. These stipulations became terms of the contract when the Claimant thereafter acknowledged receipt of the signed fax containing those endorsements and made arrangements to obtain Certificates of Inspection in relation to the engines after enquiring of the Defendant as to the acceptability of the Inspector.

6. In addition, the contract expressly obliged the Claimant to ship 100 complete Diesel engines. The Defendant contends that by custom and usage and/or the previous course of dealing between the parties this meant Diesel engines capable of being immediately cold started after unpacking and commissioning without fitting further components or assembly.

Breach

7. In breach of the foregoing:

7.1 the Diesel engines were transhipped;

7.2 the Diesel engines were not shipped 'direct ship';

7.3 the Diesel engines were shipped incomplete.

PARTICULARS

After being shipped on board the NV Essex the Diesel engines were transferred on to NV Quadrant at Rotterdam on 1st of September 2004. The Diesel engines were in any event stripped down into major component parts and incapable of being cold started without full assembly.

Documents

8. Further, the Bill of Lading is not in accordance with the contract as it does not demonstrate continuous carriage by direct ship and the Invoice and Packing List are inconsistent – the former referring to complete Diesel engines whilst the latter refers to stripped Diesel engines. The Insurance Certificate refers to Complete Diesel engines and no others.

9. Accordingly:

9.1 the Defendant was entitled to reject the Goods and the Documents; and

9.2 did so by conduct – refusing to accept the same, alternatively by fax dated 15th September 2004, alternatively by email of the same date.

10. In any event and without prejudice to the foregoing:

10.1 It is denied that the Diesel engines had no value as alleged in paragraph 6.1.2;

10.2 The Claimant has no claim for the price (see paragraph 4 above) and in relation to the alleged loss the Claimant has failed to take reasonable steps to mitigate the same – in particular by failing to take any steps to sell the Diesel engines or any of the components thereof whether on the Defendant's behalf or at all.

11. If, which is denied, the Defendant is liable or indebted to the Claimant it will set off its Part 20 Counterclaim hereunder.

<u>PART 20 COUNTERCLAIM</u>

12. The Points of Defence are repeated.

13. The Claimant knew from its previous course of dealing that the Defendant required the Diesel engines complete (as alleged in paragraph 6 above) so that it could incorporate the same expeditiously into Fire Tenders so as to fulfil its contractual obligations to Blankshire Fire Authority. Accordingly, and in any event, it was in the Claimant's actual and/or reasonable contemplation that the Defendant would suffer loss if the Claimant did not comply with the terms of the contract.

14. By reason of the Claimant's breaches of contract above the Defendant has suffered loss and damage in the sum of £300,000 representing the additional expense of obtaining a substituted performance.

<u>PARTICULARS</u>

14.1	Contract price	£1,000,000.00
14.2	Contract price negotiated with Excofor replacement complete diesel engine	£1,300,000.00
	Difference	£300,000.00

15. The Defendant claims interest on the sum of £300,000 at the rate of [ ]% per annum pursuant to section 35A of the Supreme Court Act 1981 totalling £[ ] at the date of service hereof and continuing at the daily rate of £[ ] until judgment or sooner payment alternatively at such rate and for such period as the Court deems fit.

The Defendant counterclaims:

(1) £300,000 or damages in the said sum;

(2) Interest in the sum of £[ ] and continuing at the daily rate of £[ ] or until judgment or sooner payment or as alternatively pleaded

[Statement of Truth, etc][1]

Points of Reply and Defence to Part 20 Counterclaim: CIF Contract

Claim No ....

IN THE HIGH COURT OF JUSTICE
QUEEN'S BENCH DIVISION
COMMERCIAL COURT

B E T W E E N:

SELLER INC

Claimant/Part 20 Defendant

- and -

BUYER LIMITED

Defendant/Part 20 Claimant

POINTS OF REPLY AND DEFENCE TO PART 20 COUNTERCLAIM

---

1. Save in so far as the same consists of admissions of matters in the Points of Claim the Claimant joins issue with the Defendant upon its Defence.

2. It is denied that the contract included the terms contended for at paragraph 5 of the Defence. The fax containing the said handwritten endorsements was received by the Claimant after the contract was concluded. It is denied that the mere acknowledgment of receipt of the fax with the said endorsements thereon by the Claimant varied the agreement already made.

3. The fax sent by the Claimant referred to at paragraph 3 and 4 of the Defence was preceded by a letter dated 14th July 2004 which expressly stated that any contract between the parties was on and incorporated the Claimant's Standard Terms of Business which in turn, by virtue of condition 10 thereof, incorporated the 10th edition of the Diesel Manufacturers Association International Sale of Goods Model Terms ('the Model Terms').

4. The Defendant is aware of the said Model Terms – a copy of the same being provided to the Defendant prior to the parties commencing their previous course of dealing referred to in the Points of Claim.

5. By virtue of condition 8 of the Model Terms (to which full reference will be made):

   5.1 The right to tranship the goods was expressly provided for; and

   5.2 The ship was permitted to call at intermediate Ports.

6. Further, the Bill of Lading expressly provides for transhipment and calling at intermediate Ports and each of the Bill of Lading, Insurance Certificate and Invoice are consistent, correspond and are in conformity with the contract. It is denied, for the avoidance of doubt, that the Packing List is a contractual document.

7. In fact:

   7.1 The Inspection Certificate reveals that the Diesel engines were complete when they left the Claimant's works; and

   7.2 The Diesel engines were in any event complete when shipped.

8. Whilst it is admitted that the fax dated 1st August 2004 from the Claimant to the Defendant reserved the property in the Diesel engines and prohibited the Defendants from disposing of the same until payment of the full contract price the Claimant relies on section 49(2) of the Sale of Goods Act 1979. Alternatively the said provision is solely for the benefit of the Claimant and was waived by service of the Claim Form herein if not earlier in the Claimant's Solicitor's letter before action date 1st November 2004.

9. Save as above the Claimant's case is as stated in the Points of Claim.

POINTS OF DEFENCE TO PART 20 COUNTERCLAIM

10. The Points of Reply are repeated.

11. It is denied that the Claimant is liable to the Defendant as alleged or at all.

12. In any event, and without prejudice to the foregoing:

    12.1 It is denied that the Claimant knew that the Defendant intended to fit the Diesel engines as alleged in paragraph 13; and

    12.2 It is denied that the mere fact of such use in the past informed the Claimant of such use in relation to the immediate consignment or brought the loss contended for within the Claimant's reasonable contemplation.

13. Save as above all matters in the Part 20 Counterclaim are individually denied.

[Statement of Truth, etc][1]

Points of Claim on behalf of Seller: FOB Contract

Claim No ....

IN THE HIGH COURT OF JUSTICE
QUEEN'S BENCH DIVISION
COMMERCIAL COURT

B E T W E E N:

SELLER INC

Claimant

- and -

BUYER LIMITED

Defendant

POINTS OF CLAIM

---

1. **Parties**

1.1 The Claimant is a manufacturer and exporter of Diesel engines and carries on business from its premises at Madison, Minnesota, USA; and

1.2 The Defendant is a manufacturer of Fire Tenders carrying on its business from premises at Manchester and elsewhere in the United Kingdom.

2. **The Contract**

2.1 By a contract in writing contained in an email dated 12th September 2004 from the Claimant to the Defendant the Claimant agreed to sell and the Defendant agreed to buy 100 complete Diesel engines type X built to the Defendant's specification price £10,000 per unit FOB Boston shipment October at buyers call.

2.2 Whilst the contract was 'shipment October at buyers call' the Defendant failed to nominate a vessel within sufficient time to allow for shipment in October: the Defendant by email dated 31st October nominated MV Essex which at that time was one day out from Boston. Essex subsequently docked at Boston on 1st November 2004.

2.3 To cater for the foregoing by an exchange of emails commencing at 14:10 hrs on 31st October 2004 the contract was varied to provide for shipment on MV Essex soonest November 2004.

3. **Performance**

3.1 The Diesel engines were shipped from Boston on 3rd November 2004 on MV Essex and discharged at Glasson Dock on 15th November 2004.

3.2 It was an express term of the contract that the Defendant would pay the full contract price in cleared funds by electronic transfer upon the Diesel engines being loaded on board the vessel. The engines were loaded on board MV Essex on 2nd November 2004.

4. **Breach**

4.1 In breach of contract the Defendant has failed to pay the full contract price or any part thereof.

5. **Loss**

5.1 By reason of the foregoing:

5.1.1 The Claimant is entitled to the contract price – namely £1m; alternatively

5.1.2 The Claimant has suffered loss and damage in the said sum – there being no market for the engines and the same being of no value to anybody other than the Defendant by virtue of the engine's unique design to the Defendant's specification and Patent.

6. **Interest**

6.1 The Claimant is entitled to and claims to recover interest at the rate of x% per annum from 2nd November 2004 until judgment or sooner payment totalling £[ ] at the date of issue and continuing at the daily rate of £[ ] or alternatively at such rate and for such period as the Court deems fit pursuant to section 35A of the Supreme Court Act 1981.

AND the Claimant claims:

(1) £1m;

(2) Interest in the sum of £[ ] and continuing at the daily rate of £[ ] or as alternatively pleaded.

[Statement of Truth, etc][1]

Points of Defence and Part 20 Counterclaim on behalf of Seller: FOB Contract

Claim No ....

IN THE HIGH COURT OF JUSTICE
QUEEN'S BENCH DIVISION
COMMERCIAL COURT

B E T W E E N:

SELLER INC

Claimant/Part 20 Defendant

- and -

BUYER LIMITED

Defendant/Part 20 Claimant

POINTS OF DEFENCE AND PART 20 COUNTERCLAIM

---

1. It is denied that the Defendant is liable or indebted to the Claimant as alleged or at all.

2. Paragraph 2 and 3 of the Points of Claim are admitted.

3. It was an express or alternatively implied term of the contract that the Claimant would ensure that the Diesel engines were loaded on board the carrying vessel free from defect and that the same would be fit for their purpose – namely for incorporation into Fire Tenders without further modification or adaptation, and that the same would be a satisfactory quality.

4. In breach of contract the Diesel engines were not free from defect when loaded and were not fit for their purpose or of satisfactory quality in that each engine exhibited to varying but significant degrees sump case fracturing consistent with significant impact damage when examined on arrival at Glasson Dock.

5. By reason of the foregoing the Defendant has suffered loss and damage as set out in its Counterclaim which it will set off in diminution or extinction of the claim.

6. Save as consistent with the above the Points of Claim are denied.

PART 20 COUNTERCLAIM

7. The Defendant repeats its Defence above.

8. By reason of the Claimant's breaches of contract the Defendant had to incur substantial expenditure in remedying the damage and repairing the defects and is presently subject to a claim from its customer – Blankshire Fire Authority, arising from the Defendant's delay in complying with its contractual obligations to fit the Diesel engines to Fire Tenders the property of The Fire Authority.

PARTICULARS

8.1	Cost of remedying and repairing defects	£[ ]
8.2	Notified claim by Blankshire Fire Authority under its contract	£[ ]

9. Further or alternatively the Defendant claims to be indemnified by the Claimant for, against and in respect of the claim notified by Blankshire Fire Authority including all costs and interest.

10. The Defendant is entitled to and claims to recover interest at such rate and for such period as the Court deems fit pursuant to section 35A of the Supreme Court Act 1981.

AND the Defendant counterclaims:

(1) Damages; and/or

(2) The indemnity pleaded at paragraph 8 above herein;

(3) In any event the interest pleaded at paragraph 10 above.

[Statement of Truth, etc][1]

Points of Reply and Defence to Part 20 Counterclaim on behalf of Seller: FOB Contract

Claim No ....

IN THE HIGH COURT OF JUSTICE
QUEEN'S BENCH DIVISION
COMMERCIAL COURT

B E T W E E N:

SELLER INC

Claimant/Part 20 Defendant

- and -

BUYER LIMITED

Defendant/Part 20 Claimant

POINTS OF REPLY AND DEFENCE TO PART 20 COUNTERCLAIM

POINTS OF REPLY

1. Save in so far as the same consists of admissions of matters in the Points of Claim the Claimant joins issue with the Defendant upon its Defence.

2. As regards paragraph 3:

   2.1 It is denied that there was any obligation on the Claimant in relation to the Diesel engines after they passed over the vessel's rail. The engines from this point onwards were at the Defendant's risk;

2.2 In any event there was no obligation upon the Claimant to stow the goods – any damage which may have occurred (none being admitted) was not caused prior to the Diesel engines being placed on board. Any defects that the Defendant proves were caused after loading and in all likelihood as a result of unsatisfactory stowage;

2.3 It is denied that there was any implied term as contended for in relation to fitness for purpose as the said purpose was never communicated expressly or by implication to the Claimant prior to the contract being made or at all and the Defendant did not rely, alternatively it was unreasonable for the Defendant to rely, on the skill of judgment of the Claimant when ordering the Diesel engines. The Claimant will rely on section 14(3) of the Sale of Goods Act 1979;

2.4 In any event the Diesel engines were defect free and of satisfactory quality when placed on board the vessel.

3. Further it is denied that the existence of defects on examination of the consignment after discharge at Glasson Dock is of any relevance to any obligations upon the Claimant in relation to the engines: as above pleaded after the engines passed over the ships rail for shipment the engines were at the Defendant's risk.

DEFENCE TO PART 20 COUNTERCLAIM

4. The Reply is repeated.

5 It is denied that the Claimant is liable to the Defendant as alleged or at all.

6. It is further denied that any of the matters the subject matter of the Counterclaim can be set off against the claim even if proven. In

particular the Claimant was not responsible for the wellbeing of the Diesel engines once over the vessel's rail for shipment. The engines were defect free up to and over this point.

7. Without prejudice to the foregoing:

   7.1 It is denied that the Defendant can set off a claim to be indemnified against a claim for a debt or liquidated sum; and

   7.2 the Defendant is required to demonstrate that the alleged claim (none being admitted) being advanced or to be advanced by Blankshire Fire Authority is or represents a genuine pre-estimate of the Fire Authority's loss and is not a penalty or otherwise unenforceable;

   7.3 the loss claimed is in any event too remote and was neither foreseen nor reasonably foreseeable.

[Statement of Truth, etc][1]

1 Statement of truth, etc as set out in **Chapter 3, para 3.2**.

SALE OF GOODS: PARTICULARS OF CLAIM AND DEFENCE

Law

10.5 The Sale of Goods Act 1979 ('SOGA 1979') consolidated the law relating to the sale of goods. This is not the place in which to embark upon a detailed analysis of the Act and its effect. Accordingly this brief overview is limited to a short discussion of those terms which frequently arise in typical sale of goods disputes. Particular focus is placed upon the statutorily implied terms as to compliance with description, quality and fitness for purpose.

Under the SOGA 1979, s 13(1), where there is a sale of goods by description, there is an implied term that the goods will correspond with that description. Such a term is deemed to be a condition of the contract[1], with the consequence that any breach of it by the seller will entitle the buyer to reject the goods and treat the contract as repudiated. In contrast to the implied conditions as to satisfactory quality and fitness for purpose, there is no requirement for the seller to be acting in the course of a business and hence the SOGA 1979, s 13 applies to every contract of sale, whether private or commercial. Furthermore, in the ordinary course this term will be incorporated into every contract for the sale of unascertained goods.

Under s 13(1), the relevant description must be one which goes to the identity of those goods, so that goods supplied which did not satisfy that description would be essentially different (i.e. have a different identity) from something which did[2]. It is further necessary for the buyer to show that it is possible to impute to the parties a common intention that it was to be an essential term, or condition, of the contract that the goods would correspond with the description[3].

Once it is established that there is a sale by description, the courts apply a strict test in order to determine whether or not the goods correspond with the description. If they do not, it is no defence for the seller to show that they were of satisfactory quality or otherwise fit for the particular purpose for which they were required[4].

Quality and fitness for purpose are dealt with in SOGA 1979, s 14(2) and (3) respectively, which lay down that where the seller sells goods in the course of a business, there are implied terms that the goods supplied under the contract are of satisfactory quality and reasonably fit for any purpose which the buyer has made known to the seller.

Goods are of a satisfactory quality if they meet the standard that a reasonable person would regard as satisfactory, taking account of any description of the goods, the price (if relevant) and all the other relevant circumstances[5], including but not limited to those set out in SOGA 1979, s 14(2B). There will, however, be no implied term as to satisfactory quality in the situations set out in SOGA 1979, s 14(2C).

In order to rely on the implied term as to fitness for purpose under SOGA 1979, s 14(3), the buyer must have made known to the seller, either expressly or by implication, the particular purpose for which the goods were required. It makes no difference whether or not that is a purpose for which such goods are commonly supplied but the requirement of knowledge will be automatically satisfied where the goods can only be used for one purpose[6]. There will be no implied term as to fitness for purpose in circumstances where the buyer does not rely, or it is unreasonable for him to rely, on the skill or judgment of the seller[7].

Liability for breach of the implied terms as to satisfactory quality or fitness for purpose is strict: it is no defence for the seller to establish that he took all reasonable care and was not in any way at fault[8].

In principle, the Act allows parties to contract out of the obligations imposed by ss 13 to 14. But in the domestic context, the pleader should be aware of the possibility of issues arising under the Unfair Contract Terms Act 1977. This prohibits attempts by the seller to exclude liability under SOGA 1979, ss 13 to

14 by reference to a contract term in the case of a buyer dealing as a consumer. If the buyer has not dealt as a consumer, exclusion is possible but the seller must show that the contract term was reasonable. If a defence is pleaded which deploys an exclusion clause[9], the pleader should acknowledge the statutory provision and the burden of proof, and set out the facts relied upon to show reasonableness. In the Reply, the seller will be able to set out any positive contrary case he may have as to unreasonableness, though care should be taken to make any such assertions expressly without prejudice to the burden of proof.

The above account of the applicable law is only intended to provide an introduction to a few of the relevant areas. There is a large volume of law dedicated to the sale of goods, the discussion of which is beyond the scope of this chapter. For a more detailed exposition of the relevant law, the reader should consult *Benjamin on Sale of Goods* (6th edn) at ch 11 and *Chitty on Contracts* (29th edn) vol 2 at ch 43.

1 Section 13(1A), Sale of Goods Act 1979.
2 *Ashington Piggeries Ltd v Christopher Hill Ltd* [1972] AC 441.
3 *Harlingdon & Leinster Enterprises v Christopher Hull Fine Art Ltd* [1991] 1 QB 564.
4 *Chitty on Contracts* (29th edn), vol 2, para 43-076.
5 Sale of Goods Act 1979, s 14(2A).
6 *Preist v Last* [1903] 2 KB 148.
7 Sale of Goods Act 1979, s 14(3).
8 *Grant v Australian Knitting Mills Ltd* [1936] AC 85 at p 100 and *Henry Kendall & Sons v William Lillico & Sons Ltd* [1969] 2 AC 31 at p 84.
9 I.e. where the buyer deals other than as a consumer; if he did, the clause is useless.

Pleading

Assumed facts

10.6 The claimant buyer, Better Homes Limited, is a company specialising in house building and development. In 2002, the claimant was engaged in the construction of a number of homes at a development at Greenway Fields, Colchester ('the Development'). One of the materials required for the Development was a form of sound insulation material, known as '25mm Gypglass 6405'. Gypglass 6405 conforms to the applicable building regulations which provide that any material used for the purposes of sound insulation must have certain acoustic and compressive properties.

On 28 October 2002, the claimant placed an order with the defendant seller, Shaw Insulation Limited, for 1,400 sq m of '*25 mm Gypglass 6405 or equivalent*'. The following week, the defendant delivered to the claimant 1,400 sq m of a different product, Crown Sound Deadening Quilt ('the Quilt'). The Quilt was delivered in rolls and a delivery note was signed by the claimant's foreman at the Development and forwarded to the claimant's regional office.

Despite the delivery note which accompanied the Quilt identifying the product as 'Crown Sound Deadening Quilt', the claimant did not notice that a different product had been delivered. The Quilt was stored on site until it was needed and then duly incorporated into the Development. Shortly after delivery, the defendant invoiced the regional office for the product supplied.

During mid-2003, it was discovered that not only had the Quilt been installed rather than Gypglass 6405, but also that the Quilt had materially different characteristics to Gypglass 6405 and did not satisfy the acoustic and compressive requirements imposed by the building regulations.

As a result of this, the claimant has had to remove the Quilt and install replacement sound insulation material. The claimant now claims damages for breach of the sale contract. The defendant denies any liability or that in any event the claimant is entitled to recover any damages.

Particulars of Claim

<u>Claim No ....</u>

<u>IN THE HIGH COURT OF JUSTICE</u>
<u>QUEEN'S BENCH DIVISION</u>

BETTER HOMES LIMITED

<u>Claimant</u>

- and -

SHAW INSULATION LIMITED

<u>Defendant</u>

PARTICULARS OF CLAIM

---

1. The Claimant is and was at all material times a national house builder and developer. The Defendant is and was at all material times a supplier of insulation materials and related products.

2. During late 2002, the Claimant was constructing a residential development at a site at Greenway Fields, Colchester ('the Development').

Background

3. On or about 28th October 2002, the Claimant entered into a contract with the Defendant ('the Contract'), for the supply by the Defendant to the Claimant of 1,400 sq m 25mm Gypglass 6405 or its equivalent ('the goods'). The Contract was contained in and/or evidenced by purchase order no. 174588 dated 28th October 2002, a copy of which is attached to these Particulars of Claim at page ** of the appendix.

4. The Claimant relied upon the Defendant's skill and judgment in respect of the properties of the goods in deciding to enter into the Contract.

5. The goods were for installation within each of the residential units in the Development in order to ensure adequate sound insulation in conformity with the applicable building regulations, and in particular Part 2, Para 1 of Regulation 001 of 2000 ('the Regulation')[1].

6. By a telephone conversation between Mr Harwood of the Claimant and Mr Smith of the Defendant on 26th October 2002, the Claimant informed the Defendant that the goods were required for the purposes set out in paragraph 5 above and, in particular, to ensure compliance with the Regulation.

7. In the circumstances, it was an implied term of the Contract that the goods would correspond with the description *'Gypglass 6405 or its equivalent'*.

8. Further and/or alternatively, by reason of the matters pleaded at paragraphs 5 and 6 above, it was an implied term of the Contract that the goods would be reasonably fit for the purpose set out at paragraph 5.

9. Further and/or in the yet further alternative, it was an implied term of the Contract that the goods would be of a satisfactory quality.

Breach of Contract

10. In breach of the implied terms set out in paragraphs 7, 8 and 9 above, the goods delivered pursuant to the Contract failed to correspond with their description and/or were not fit for their intended purpose and/or were not of a satisfactory quality.

PARTICULARS

Sale by Description

10.1 The goods delivered were not Gypglass 6405 but Crown Sound Deadening Quilt ('the Quilt').

10.2 The Quilt was not equivalent to Gypglass 6405 in that the acoustic properties of Quilt were not the same and did not satisfy the requirements of the Regulation.

Fitness for Intended Purpose/Satisfactory Quality

10.3 The Claimant repeats the matters pleaded at paragraph 10.2 above. Further:

10.3.1 the Quilt did not possess the required compressive strength with the result that the floors in the residential units were not settled correctly;

10.3.2 the Quilt failed to provide any or any sufficient sound insulation;

10.3.3 the Quilt was not fit for the purpose for which sound insulation material is commonly supplied.

11. As a result of the matters set out above, the Claimant has suffered loss and damage.

PARTICULARS OF LOSS AND DAMAGE

11.1	Costs of purchasing replacement insulation material	£17,000.00
11.2	Costs of removing and relaying the floor in each residential unit	£85,000.00
	TOTAL	**£102,000.00**

12. Further, the Claimant claims interest pursuant to section 35A of the Supreme Court Act 1981 at such rate and for such period as the Court thinks fit.

AND the Claimant claims:

(1) Damages;

(2) Interest;

(3) Costs;

(4) Further or other relief.

SIGNATURE

[Statement of Truth, etc][2]

Defence

Claim No ....

IN THE HIGH COURT OF JUSTICE
QUEEN'S BENCH DIVISION

BETTER HOMES LIMITED

Claimant

- and -

SHAW INSULATION LIMITED

Defendant

DEFENCE

---

1. Unless otherwise stated, references to paragraph numbers below are references to the corresponding paragraphs of the Particulars of Claim. The Defendant adopts and continues the references used by the Claimant.

The Terms of the Contract

2. Paragraphs 1 and 2 are admitted.

3. Paragraph 3 is admitted. The Defendant will rely on the terms of the Contract for their true meaning and effect.

4. Paragraph 4 is denied.

5. The Claimant is required to prove the facts and matters set out in paragraph 5.

6. Save that it is admitted that, on 26th October, Mr Harwood and Mr Smith had a telephone conversation in which Mr Harwood informed Mr Smith that the Claimant required Gypglass 6405 or similar sound insulation material, paragraph 6 is denied.

7. In particular and without prejudice to the generality of paragraph 6 above:

   7.1 it is denied that at any time the Defendant was provided with any information as to the specific purpose and/or intended use of the goods whether as alleged or at all;

   7.2 it is denied that the Defendant was informed that the goods had to satisfy the requirements of the Regulation.

8. In the premises, the Contract was a contract for the sale of Gypglass 6405 or any similar sound insulation material. Save as aforesaid, paragraph 7 is denied.

9. By reason of the matters pleaded at paragraphs 6 and 7 above and paragraph 10 below, the implied term alleged at paragraph 8 is denied.

10. Further, in any event, it is denied that the Claimant placed any reliance on the skill and judgment of the Defendant when deciding to enter into the Contract.

11. It is admitted that the Contract was subject to the implied term alleged at paragraph 9.

Performance of the Contract

12. On 4 November 2002, and in pursuance of the Contract, the Defendant delivered to the Claimant 1,400 sq m of Crown Sound Deadening Quilt ('the Quilt'). For the avoidance of doubt, it is

expressly averred that this was an equivalent sound insulation material to Gypglass 6504 within the meaning of the Contract.

13. Upon delivery of the Quilt at the Development, the Quilt was accompanied by a delivery note ('the delivery note') which stated as follows:

'Crown Sound Deadening Quilt, 1,400 sq m

25 mm x 1200 mm x 10 m SDQ PFL Grade'

14. The delivery note was signed by the Claimant's foreman, Mr Wilson, for and on behalf of the Claimant and subsequently returned to the Claimant's regional office. The Quilt was then stored for a period of over five months at the Development, until about 12th April 2002, when the Claimant incorporated the Quilt into the residential units in the Development.

The Alleged Breach

15. It is denied that the Defendant was in breach of contract whether as alleged in paragraph 10 or at all. In particular and without prejudice to the generality of this denial:

    15.1 it is admitted that the Defendant supplied the Claimant with Quilt as set out in paragraphs 12 to 14 above;

    15.2 the Claimant is put to strict proof of the facts and matters relied upon in paragraph 10.2;

    15.3 paragraph 10.3 is denied. The Quilt was an equivalent product to Gypglass 6405 in all material and/or relevant and/or necessary respects, being sound insulation material fit for the purpose of providing sound insulation and/or preventing the movement of floors within a building.

16. Further and/or alternatively, if, which is denied, there was any breach by the Defendant of the Contract, the Claimant has waived its right to rely on any such breach as a result of the facts and matters set out in paragraphs 13 and 14 above. In particular, and without prejudice to the generality of the foregoing, the Defendant will say that, in light of the delivery note, the Claimant must have been aware that the Defendant had supplied Quilt and not Gypglass 6405. The Claimant nonetheless accepted the goods and subsequently incorporated it into the residential units in the Development.

17. The Defendant denies that it is liable in respect of any of the losses claimed in paragraph 11. The Claimant is required to prove the existence and the extent of the losses alleged in paragraph 11.

18. In the premises, the Claimant is not entitled to the interest claimed at paragraph 12, or any relief at all.

SIGNATURE

[Statement of Truth, etc][2]

1 This reference is fictional and is not intended to refer to a regulation in force.

2 Statement of truth, etc as set out in **Chapter 3, para 3.2**.

CHAPTER 11

Agency

Yash Kulkarni
Rachel Davies

Law

Introduction

11.1 This short section on the law relating to agency aims simply to provide the reader with some of the principal bullet points in relation to the topic as may be relevant to the drafting of pleadings. For a fuller and more detailed exposition of the topic, the reader is referred to the practitioner texts on agency.

Agency is the fiduciary relationship which exists between two persons, one of whom ('the principal') expressly or impliedly consents that the other ('the agent') should act on his behalf so as to affect his relations with third parties, and the agent similarly consents so to act or does so[1].

1 This is the tentative definition of the concept of agency set out in *Bowstead & Reynolds on Agency* (17th edn) at para 1-001.

Agent's duties to principal at common law

11.2 The first port of call in determining the scope of an agent's duties is the agreement between the parties. In so far as that agreement contains specific terms as to the scope of the agency, these will apply. In the absence of express terms delineating the agent's duties, the law will ordinarily impose the following duties upon an agent:

- A duty to act with due care, skill and diligence;
- A duty to carry out the principal's lawful instructions;
- A duty not to delegate the performance of his functions;
- A duty to act in accordance with fiduciary obligations owed to the principal;
- A duty to account to the principal.

Duty to act with due care, skill and diligence

11.3 An agent must carry out his obligations to his principal with due care, skill and diligence.

If the agency is contractual, the standard of care required by the agent is that which an agent in his position would usually possess and exercise[1]. Failure to meet such a standard will sound in damages for the principal unless the breach can be described as fundamental, in which case the principal will be entitled to terminate the contract and sue for damages. If the agency is gratuitous, the agent nonetheless owes a duty to exercise reasonable skill and care in performing whatever he is engaged to do[2].

1 See *Bowstead & Reynolds on Agency* (17th edn) at para 6-015ff for more detail in this area.
2 *Chaudhry v Prabhakar* [1989] 1 WLR 29, CA.

Duty to carry out principal's lawful instructions

11.4 If the agency is premised in contract, an agent must carry out work in accordance with the terms of that contract – i.e. he must carry out work that he has agreed to perform[1]. If the agency is gratuitous, the agent is not obliged to do anything but will be liable if he does something and does it negligently[2].

If the agent breaches his obligations to carry out his principal's instructions, the principal's remedies will usually take the form of termination of the contract, together with an action for damages in respect of any loss that may have resulted.

1 *Turpin v Bilton* (1843) 5 Man & G 455.
2 *Cohen v Kittell* (1889) 22 QBD 680.

Duty not to delegate

11.5 The general rule is that an agent may not transfer his duties to another without authority from his principal[1]. Exceptions to this rule arise where:

- the principal has either expressly authorised or subsequently ratified the delegation;
- it is within the scope of the agent's authority (e.g. if it is customary in a certain trade); or
- if it is necessary because of some unforeseen circumstance.

Where the duty not to delegate is breached, this may constitute a fundamental breach of contract, entitling the principal to terminate the contract and to sue the agent for any loss caused by the breach.

1 *De Bussche v Alt* (1878) 38 LT 370; *John McCann & Co v Pow* [1974] 1 WLR 1643, CA.

Fiduciary obligations

11.6 An agent, being in a position in which trust and confidence is reposed in him, is a fiduciary and owes certain fiduciary obligations to his principal[1]. Primarily these obligations can be characterised as an obligation not to allow his personal interests to conflict with those of his principal.

An agent is under a duty to disclose any conflict of interest[2]. Furthermore, an agent must not receive any secret commission or bribe[3], make a secret profit[4], or use confidential information acquired in the course of his agency for his own benefit[5].

Broadly speaking, where an agent breaches the above duties, a principal will have the right to terminate the agency and sue the agent for any loss caused and/or require the agent to disgorge any profits made as a result of such breach.

1 See *Bowstead & Reynolds on Agency* (17th edn) para 6-032ff for more detail in this area.
2 *Boardman v Phipps* [1967] 2 AC 46, HL.
3 *Boston Deep Sea Fishing and Ice Co v Ansell* (1888) LR 39 Ch D 339, CA.
4 *Boston Deep Sea Fishing and Ice Co v Ansell* (1888) LR 39 Ch D 339, CA; *Phipps v Boardman* [1965] Ch 992 at p 1018 per Lord Denning MR, CA.
5 *Lamb v Evans* [1893] 1 Ch 218 at p 230.

Duty to account

11.7 Where an agent receives money on behalf of his principal, he will come under a duty to his principal to account for the sums received upon demand by his principal[1]. If the agent fails to account, the principal may either claim an account or, if the amount is known, bring an action for money had and received.

1 See *Bowstead & Reynolds on Agency* (17th edn) para 6-092ff for more detail in this area.

The Commercial Agents (Council Directive) Regulations 1993

11.8 In relation to 'commercial agents', where the agency contract in question was entered into after 1 January 1994, regard ought also to be had to the Commercial Agents (Council Directive) Regulations 1993, implementing the earlier EC Council Directive of 18 December 1986.

A 'commercial agent' is defined in the 1993 Regulations as:

> 'a self-employed intermediary who has continuing authority to negotiate the sale or purchase of goods on behalf of another person ("the principal"), or to negotiate and conclude the sale or purchase of goods on behalf of and in the name of that principal.'

There are a number of exceptions to this definition, perhaps most notably:

- officers of companies or associations authorised to make contracts on behalf of the company or association;
- partners authorised to make contracts on behalf of the partnership;
- where the agency activities are considered 'secondary' to the agent's main activities.

The commercial agent's duties under the 1993 Regulations broadly equate to an agent's common law duties referred to above. Briefly, the agent is required to look after the interests of his principal and to act dutifully and in good faith[1]. He is also required to:

- make proper efforts to negotiate and, where appropriate, conclude the transactions he is instructed to take care of;
- communicate to his principal all the necessary information available to him;
- comply with reasonable instructions given by his principal[2].

In turn the principal also has a duty to act dutifully and in good faith towards his agent[3].

The provisions in the 1993 Regulations cannot be derogated from and will be implied into the contract of any 'commercial agent'.

Those who may be interested in this area are referred to the 1993 Regulations and the practitioner texts on agency law for further information.

1 Commercial Agents (Council Directive) Regulations 1993 reg 3(1).
2 Commercial Agents (Council Directive) Regulations 1993 reg 3(2).
3 Commercial Agents (Council Directive) Regulations 1993 reg 4(1).

Agent's claim for commission

11.9 An agent will only be entitled to commission at common law if he is able to prove that he was the 'effective cause' of the ensuing transaction.

It is a good defence to such a claim if the agent was not the effective cause of the transaction, if he has been guilty of dishonesty[1], or the object of the agency contract is illegal[2]. A further or alternative defence can be raised by way of set off where the principal has suffered loss as a result of any negligence or breach of contractual duty on the part of the agent.

1 *Andrews v Ramsay & Co* [1903] 2 KB 635.
2 *Stackpole v Earle* (1761) 2 Wils KB 133; *Saunders v Soper* [1975] AC 239, HL.

Agent's claim for indemnity

11.10 The general rule, at common law, in the context of a contractual agency, is that an agent is entitled to be indemnified by his principal in respect of all acts done by him in the reasonable performance of the agency[1], or acts done to conform to norms of the market in which he is engaged to operate[2].

An agent who has not complied with his principal's instructions, however, is not entitled to be indemnified[3].

Where an agent has incurred expense outside his ordinary authority he may potentially claim reimbursement from his principal as an 'agent of necessity' if he can show that (1) at the time the expense was incurred it was impossible for him to communicate with his principal[4], (2) that the action was necessary as the only reasonable and prudent course to take[5], and (3) that the agent acted bona fide in the interests of the parties concerned[6].

1 *Lacey v Hill, Crowley's Claim* (1874) LR 18 Eq 182, 30 LT 484.
2 *Chapman v Shepherd, Whitelhead v Izod* (1867) LR 2 CP 228; *Anglo-Overseas Transport Co Ltd v Titan Industrial Corpn (UK) Ltd* [1959] 2 Lloyd's Rep 152.
3 *Barron v Fitzgerald* (1840) 6 Bing NC 201.
4 *Springer v Great Western Rly Co* [1921] 1 KB 257, CA.
5 *Sims & Co v Midland Rly Co* [1913] 1 KB 103.
6 *Prager v Blatspiel, Stamp and Headcock Ltd* [1924] 1 KB 566.

Actions between a third party and the agent/principal

11.11 As a general rule, where an agent contracts on behalf of an undisclosed principal (viz the name or existence of the principal was not disclosed at the time of making the contract) the contract may be enforced by or against the principal[1].

If the agent contracts in his own name for an undisclosed principal, then prima facie the agent will be personally liable on the contracts[2].

Where an agent contracts on behalf of a disclosed principal, the agent cannot, as a general rule, sue or be sued on the contract[3].

Where an agent has acted without authority or has exceeded his authority, he may be sued by a third party for damages for breach of warranty of authority[4]. The want of authority should be specifically pleaded[5].

1 See *Sims v Bond* (1833) 5 B & Ad 389.
2 *Hutchinson v Tatham* (1873) LR 8 CP 482; *Ernest Scragg & Sons Ltd v Perseverance Banking and Trust Co Ltd* [1973] 2 Lloyd's Rep 101, CA.
3 *T P Jordeson & Co and Kahn v London Hardwood Co Ltd* (1913) 110 LT 666.
4 *Collen v Wright* (1857) 8 E & B 647; *Salvesen & Co v Rederi Aktiebologet Nordstjernan* [1905] AC 302, HL.
5 *Byrd v Nunn* (1877) 7 Ch D 284, CA.

Pleading

Assumed facts

11.12 Washwell Limited is a manufacturer and supplier of washing machines. In order to sell its washing machines Washwell Ltd appointed Mr X as its agent for the sale of the washing machines on commission. Mr X was contracted to introduce to Washwell Ltd potential purchasers of the washing machines. It was a term of the contract that Mr X would be paid commission at the rate of 6% of the purchase price of every washing machine sold as a result of Mr X's introduction.

Washwell gave an account of all the sales of washing machines for December and January 20X0, but failed to provide an account or pay the commission due to Mr X arising out of sales in February to April 20X0. Mr X now seeks an account and payment of the commission due to him for the period February to April 20X0.

Particulars of claim by agent for commission and for an account of commission due

Claim No ....

IN THE HIGH COURT OF JUSTICE
CHANCERY DIVISION

B E T W E E N:

Mr X

Claimant

- and -

Washwell Limited

Defendants

PARTICULARS OF CLAIM

---

1. The Claimant is an agent for the sale of goods on commission. The Defendant is and was at all material times a company engaged in the manufacture of washing machines.

2. By a contract in writing dated 1st December 20XY made between the Claimant and the Defendant, the Defendant agreed to pay the Claimant commission at the rate of 6% of the price of each washing machine sold by the Defendant to purchasers introduced to the Defendant by the Claimant.

3. It was an express term of the contract that:

   3.1 The Defendant was to provide the Claimant with a monthly written statement setting out details of all sales effected by the Defendant in the preceding month; and

3.2 The commission due to the Claimant as a result of the sales would be paid to the Claimant by the Defendant on the first day of the month following the monthly written statement.

4. Further or alternatively, it was an implied term that the Defendant would give an account of sales at regular intervals.

5. Pursuant to the contract, between 1st February 20X0 and 1st May 20X0, the Claimant introduced 11 potential purchasers to the Defendant.

PARTICULARS OF INTRODUCTIONS

(State names and addresses of persons introduced)

6. The Claimant understands that during the period February to May 20X0, the Defendant sold some 50 washing machines to Y Limited and Z Limited. It is averred that these sales were effected through the agency of the Claimant.

7. Since March 20X0, in breach of the terms set out at paragraph 3 above, the Defendant has failed to provide the Claimant with written statements of sales made in the preceding month and has not paid to the Claimant any of the commission which is due to him despite requests by the Claimant on 29th April 20X0 and 29th May 20X0 to do so.

8. By reason of the foregoing the Claimant has suffered loss and damage and is entitled to an account of all sales effected by the Defendant through the Claimant's agency since 1st February 20X0 and an order for payment of commission found due upon taking of the account.

9. Further, the Claimant is entitled to and claims to recover interest on the amount found to be due to him pursuant to section 35A of

the Supreme Court Act 1981 at such rate and for such period as the court thinks fit.

AND the Claimant claims:

(1) An account of all sales of washing machines from 1st February 20X0 made by the Defendant through the Claimant's agency.

(2) An order for payment by the Defendant of the sums found due to the Claimant on the taking of such account together with the said interest thereon.

(3) Alternatively, damages.

(4) Interest pursuant to section 35A of the Supreme Court Act 1981.

[Statement of Truth, etc][1]

Defence by principal to a claim for commission and for an account of commission due

Claim No ....

IN THE HIGH COURT OF JUSTICE
CHANCERY DIVISION

B E T W E E N:

Mr X

Claimant

- and -

Washwell Limited

Defendants

DEFENCE

---

1. Paragraphs 1 and 2 of the Particulars of Claim are admitted.

2. As to paragraph 3:

    2.1 It is admitted and averred that it was a term of the contract that the Defendant would provide the Claimant with a monthly written statement setting out details of all sales effected by the Defendant in the preceding month as a result of introductions by the Claimant;

    2.2 It is admitted and averred that the commission due to the Claimant as a result of such sales would be paid to the Claimant by the Defendant as alleged;

    2.3 Save as aforesaid, paragraph 3 is denied.

3. Paragraph 4 is denied. It is denied that the Defendant was liable to provide the Claimant with an account of any sales that did not result from the Claimant's introductions.

4. As to paragraphs 5 to 6:

   4.1 It is admitted and averred that the Defendant sold 26 washing machines to Y Limited and 30 washing machines to Z Limited during the period February to May 20X0;

   4.2 It is denied that the Claimant was the effective cause of the alleged or any sales and/or that these or any sales were effected through the agency of the Claimant during the period February to May 20X0;

   4.3 It is averred that the Defendant has had a long-standing direct relationship with both Y Limited and Z Limited for a number of years and in the case of each of the aforementioned sales the Defendant was approached directly by Y Limited and Z Limited;

   4.4 Save as aforesaid, paragraphs 5 to 6 are not admitted.

5. As to paragraph 7:

   5.1 It is admitted and averred that the Defendant has not provided the Claimant with monthly written statements of sales during the period February to May 20X0. Further it is admitted that the Defendant has not paid the Claimant any commission in respect of the period February to May 20X0;

   5.2 It is denied that the Claimant is entitled to an account or to any commission in respect of the period February to May 20X0 as no sales were effected by the Defendant through the agency of the Claimant during this period;

5.3 In the premises, it is denied that the Defendant is in breach of contract whether as alleged at paragraph 7 or at all.

6. Paragraphs 8 and 9 are denied for the reasons set out in this Defence.

[Statement of Truth, etc][1]

1 Statement of truth, etc as set out in **Chapter 3, para 3.2**.

Pleading

Assumed facts

11.13 Fastcook Ltd is a company that sells boil-in-the-bag rice in supermarkets throughout the land. Mr X was appointed by Fastcook as its agent for purchases of large quantities of rice on behalf of it. In this case, Mr X, seeing the chance to make a tidy sum himself, agreed with one of the potential suppliers, Y Ltd, to purchase large quantities of rice from Y Ltd in return for a kickback from Y Ltd to the tune of 5% of the total value of the sale. Fastcook has recently discovered Mr X's arrangement with Y Ltd and wishes to recover the profits made by Mr X.

Particulars of Claim by principal against agent for receipt of secret profit

Claim No ....

IN THE HIGH COURT OF JUSTICE
CHANCERY DIVISION

B E T W E E N:

X Limited

Claimant

- and -

Mr X

Defendant

PARTICULARS OF CLAIM

---

1. By a written agreement made on 30th January 20X0 the Claimant appointed the Defendant as its agent for purchases of rice and agreed to pay him a commission on such purchases. The commission was calculated by reference to the saving to the Claimant on the purchase price as against the Rice Export Price Index.

2. Pursuant to the agreement the agent acted as a self-employed agent with continuing authority to negotiate and conclude purchases in the name of the Claimant. The Defendant was thereby a commercial agent within the meaning of the Commercial Agents (Council Directive) Regulations 1993 ('the Regulations'). The relationship between the Claimant and the Defendant was governed by the Regulations.

3. By regulation 3, a duty was imposed upon the Defendant to act dutifully and in good faith towards the Claimant.

4. Further the Defendant as an agent undertaking to act for the Claimant in circumstances giving rise to a relationship of trust and confidence owed him a fiduciary duty to prefer his principal's interest to his own. The duty included a duty of loyalty and to act in good faith and not to make a secret profit out of his trust, nor to place himself in a position where his duty and his interest conflicted, nor to act for his own benefit or for that of a third person without the informed consent of his principal.

5. On 19th February 20X0 the Defendant as such agent purchased for the Claimant ….. kg of rice from Y Ltd.

6. Without the knowledge or consent of the Claimant, Y Ltd had agreed with the Defendant to pay him commission at the rate of 5% on such sales as the Defendant negotiated with it pursuant to the agency agreement.

7. The Claimant has paid Y Ltd sums totalling £….. for ….kg of rice. At the rate of 5%, the Claimant estimates that the Defendant will have received £….. .

8. The commission so agreed between the Defendant and Y Ltd constitutes a secret profit and was paid to the Defendant in breach of the duties he owed the Claimant as agent.

9. The commission was also paid in breach of the Defendant's duty of good faith owed pursuant to regulation 3.

10. In the premises, the amount of the commission has become due and payable by the Defendant to the Claimant and the amount of the commission referred to in paragraph 1 above paid by the Claimant to the Defendant has become forfeit.

11. The Claimant is entitled to interest on all sums found due to him at such rate as the Court deems just pursuant to section 35A of the Supreme Court Act 1981.

AND the Claimant claims:

(1) £..... being the amount of the secret commission.

(2) £..... being the amount of commission paid by the Claimant to the Defendant.

(3) Interest pursuant to section 35A of the Supreme Court Act 1981.

[Statement of Truth, etc][1]

Defence by an agent to a claim to recover secret commission

Claim No ....

IN THE HIGH COURT OF JUSTICE
CHANCERY DIVISION

B E T W E E N:

X Limited

Claimant

- and -

Mr X

Defendant

DEFENCE

---

1. It is denied that the Defendant was a commercial agent within the meaning of the Commercial Agents (Council Directive) Regulations 1993.

2. Further it is denied that the agreement between the parties gave rise to a relationship of trust and confidence and/or that the Defendant owed the Claimant a fiduciary duty whether as alleged or at all.

3. It was an implied term of the agreement between the parties by reason of the custom and usage in the trade that the Defendant was entitled to receive commission from suppliers whose goods were purchased by him as the agent of the Claimant. Accordingly it is expressly denied that the Defendant was not permitted to benefit from the payment of commission paid to him by suppliers.

4. Save as aforesaid, paragraphs 1 to 4 of the Particulars of Claim are denied.

5. Further or alternatively, the Claimant knew that the Defendant was to receive commission from Y Ltd as the invoices in which the payment of commission was set out were sent to the Claimant. In the premises, the Claimant agreed to vary and/or waived any term restricting the Defendant's right to receive commission.

6. Paragraph 5 of the Particulars of Claim is admitted.

7. Accordingly, save that it is admitted that Y Ltd agreed to pay the Defendant commission at the rate of 5% on such sales as the Defendant negotiated with it pursuant to the agency agreement, paragraph 6 of the Particulars of Claim is denied.

8. Paragraph 7 of the Particulars of Claim is admitted.

9. For the reasons set out at above, it is denied that the commission paid to the Defendant by Y Ltd constitutes a secret profit and/or it is denied that such sums were acquired by the Defendant in breach of the Defendant's duties to the Claimant. Accordingly, paragraphs 8 to 10 are denied.

10. The claim for interest at paragraph 11 is noted and denied for the reasons set out in this Defence.

[Statement of Truth, etc][1]

1 Statement of truth, etc as set out in **Chapter 3, para 3.2**.

Pleading

Assumed facts

11.14 The Claimant company, Audiotown Ltd are manufacturers and suppliers of musical equipment. Audiotown Ltd contracted X-press Ltd, a road haulage company, to carry a consignment of musical equipment from London to Manchester. Whilst being transported and whilst in the care of X-press Ltd the equipment was stolen. Audiotown presented a written claim to Y Ltd, X-press' local agents at their transport depot in Manchester. In a letter dated 25 April 20X0, Y Ltd accepted that X-press Ltd had a liability for Audiotown's loss and offered them the sum of £8,000 in full and final settlement of the claim. By a letter dated 25 April 20X0 Audiotown accepted the offer made by Y Ltd.

X-press Ltd refused to pay this sum to Audiotown and Audiotown brought proceedings against X-press Ltd in order to recover this sum. X-press Ltd successfully defended the claim on the grounds that in settling the claim with Audiotown, Y Ltd were acting outside the authority given to it by X-press Ltd. Auditown have therefore claimed against Y Ltd for breach of the warranty of authority made by it to Audiotown.

Particulars of Claim by a third party against agent for breach of warranty of authority

Claim No ....

IN THE HIGH COURT OF JUSTICE
CHANCERY DIVISION

B E T W E E N:

Audiotown Limited

Claimant

- and -

Y Limited

Defendant

PARTICULARS OF CLAIM

---

1. The Defendant was at all material times the local agent of X-press Ltd.

2. On 25th April 20X0 the Defendant purported to enter into a compromise agreement with the Claimant on behalf of X-press Ltd, whereby the Claimant agreed that payment of the sum of £8,000 by or to the order of X-press Ltd would be accepted by the Claimant in full and final settlement of all claims which they may have against X-press Ltd.

3. By reason of the aforesaid, the Defendant impliedly warranted that he was authorised by X-press Ltd to enter into the agreement and the Claimant entered into the same in reliance on the said warranty.

4. In breach of the warranty, the Defendant was not authorised by X-press Ltd to enter into any settlement agreement with the Claimant. X-press Ltd by a letter dated 25th May 20X0 repudiated

the same and refused to pay to the Claimant the sum of £8,000 as set out in that agreement.

5. The Claimant has been unable to enforce the compromise agreement and has thereby suffered loss and damage.

<u>PARTICULARS</u>

5.1 The sum of £8,000 being the amount that would have been recoverable by the Claimant from X-press Ltd had they duly authorised the compromise agreement;

5.2 The Claimant was put to the expense of £…… being the costs of unsuccessful legal proceedings reasonably brought by the Claimant against X-press Ltd for the purpose of enforcing the compromise agreement. The aforesaid sum is broken down as follows:

X-press Ltd's costs of the proceedings in the sum of £……….

The Claimant's costs of the unsuccessful proceedings in the sum of £…….

6. Further the Claimant claims interest pursuant to section 35A of the Supreme Court Act 1981 on the amount found to be due to the Claimant at such rate and for such period as the Court thinks fit.

AND the Claimant claims:

(1) £8,000; and

(2) Damages; and

(3) Interest pursuant to section 35A of the Supreme Court Act 1981.

[Statement of Truth, etc][1]

1 Statement of truth, etc as set out in **Chapter 3, para 3.2**.

Chapter 12

Professional Negligence

Lindsay Boswell QC
Marion Smith

Law

12.1 This section deals with claims against professionals based on contractual and tortious duties owed to their clients to exercise reasonable skill and care.

This is a developing area of law. To some extent the precise legal principles depend on the particular area of professional practice being considered. Therefore only general guidelines are set out. For a fuller account the reader should consult the standard references books on professional negligence such as Jackson & Powell *Professional Negligence* (5th edn, 2002), Dugdale and Stanton *Professional Negligence* (3rd edn, 1998) and *Charlesworth on Negligence* (10th edn, 1996).

When formulating a claim against a professional consideration should be given to the range of duties which may be owed: contractual, statutory and fiduciary duties to clients and tortious duties to third parties[1].

Most professionals provide their services pursuant to a contract with the client. As a general rule, professionals owe duties to their clients to exercise reasonable skill and care in contract and in tort (if not expressly stated, a term will usually be implied to the effect that the professional will exercise reasonable skill and care[2]). There may well be advantages in advancing an additional claim in tort, such as the different rules as to limitation and remoteness.

The standard of care expected of any professional is judged objectively, by reference to members of the relevant profession. The classic formulation of the requisite standard is that of MacNair J directing the jury in *Bolam v Friern Hospital Management Committee* [1957] 1 WLR 582 at pp 586–587:

> '... where you get a situation which involves the use of some special skill or competence, then the test as to whether there has been negligence or not is not the test of the man on the top of a Clapham omnibus, because he has not got this special skill. The test is the standard of the ordinary skilled man exercising and professing to have that special skill. A man need not possess the highest expert skill; it is well established law that it is sufficient if he exercises the ordinary skill of an ordinary competent man exercising that particular art.'

Most claimants in professional negligence cases brought in the Commercial Court are seeking to recover pecuniary losses. A claimant seeking to recover such losses in contract or in tort must establish and plead a causal link between the defendant's wrongdoing and the loss claimed. Consideration should be given where appropriate to pleading the claim for damages as a claim for the loss of a chance, see *Allied Maples v Simmons & Simmons* [1995] 1 WLR 1602 (CA).

The defences available to meet such claims are to some extent profession specific (for instance solicitors may be able to assert that they relied on the advice of competent counsel adequately instructed). The general defences such as limitation, contributory negligence and failure to mitigate apply in the usual way.

Many professionals now seek to exclude liability by incorporating a suitable clause or statement in the retainer with the client or in the report or written advice supplied. In addition to the Unfair Contract Terms Act 1977 there may also be applicable specific statutory restrictions such as the Solicitors Act 1974, s 60 (5).

1 Note also the possibility of a third party acquiring a right to enforce contractual obligations under the Contracts (Rights of Third Parties) Act 1999.

2 Supply of Goods and Services Act 1981, s 13.

Pleading

Assumed facts

12.2 Film star Fred Star (FS) was engaged to perform a cameo role in a blockbuster to be known as '101' with a cast of one hundred children aged 3 to 13 years old.

In July 1998, FS asked the producers (Filmbroke Ltd) to arrange illness insurance cover for him, the premium to be deducted from his fee for the film. Filmbroke Ltd instructed an insurance broker (Inbro) to effect insurance against loss of earnings caused by FS being unable to work due to a number of communicable diseases including chicken pox.

Inbro did not arrange insurance cover. The film was shot in August 1998. During the filming, FS misbehaved badly on and off set. FS discovered he had contracted shingles on 27 August 1998. On 30 August 1998, FS attended an audition for the part of Romeo in a forthcoming film of *Romeo and Juliet*, but failed to get the part; he feels that as a result his reputation has been damaged.

On 17 February 2002, having discovered that no insurance was in place, FS instructed Filmbroke's solicitors, Delay and Forget (DF), to act for him.

A claim form was issued against Inbro in July 2003 and served by DF. DF advised FS that the Claim Form had been issued and served. In correspondence, Inbro admitted that it did not effect a policy but disputed all other issues. In August 2004, DF agreed with Inbro a full and final settlement on FS's behalf with no admission of liability. Settlement of £100,000 was agreed subject to FS's agreement. DF advised FS to accept. He acted on this advice and the claim was dismissed by consent in September 2004. DF sent FS a cheque for £90,000 and FS banked and spent it.

Expert evidence showed that, but for the failure to get the role of Romeo, FS would have earned about $5m for three years from August 1998 and continuing substantial earnings for another 20 years whereas in fact he had earned nothing since August 1998.

Particulars of Claim

Claim No ....

IN THE HIGH COURT OF JUSTICE
QUEEN'S BENCH DIVISION
COMMERCIAL COURT

B E T W E E N:

FRED STAR

Claimant

- and -

DELAY AND FORGET

(A Firm)

Defendant

PARTICULARS OF CLAIM

Parties

1. The Claimant ('FS') was at all material times an internationally recognised film actor.

2. The Defendant ('DF') is a firm of solicitors practising from 77 Wardour Street, London, W1.

The Facts

3. In early 1998, FS was engaged by Filmbroke Ltd, the producers of a film to be known as '*101*' ('the Film'), to perform a role in the

Film to be filmed in the United Kingdom starting on 1st August 1998. The Film involved a large number of children aged between 3 and 13 years old.

4. In July 1998, FS orally instructed Filmbroke Ltd to arrange 'illness insurance cover' on his behalf, with any premium payable in respect of such cover to be deducted from the fee payable by Filmbroke Ltd to him.

5. In July 1998, an employee of Filmbroke Ltd orally instructed insurance brokers Inbro to effect insurance against any loss of earnings suffered by FS by reason of his being unavailable for work due to a number of communicable diseases including chicken pox.

6. Inbro did not effect an insurance policy for the benefit of FS prior to the commencement of filming in August 1998 or at any time.

7. The filming involving FS was completed by 8th August 1998.

8. On or about 27th August 1998 FS contracted shingles.

9. On 30th August 1998, FS attended an audition for the role of Romeo in a film to be made of Shakespeare's *Romeo and Juliet*. FS failed to obtain the role following this audition.

10. By reason of the shingles and his consequent failure to obtain the role of Romeo FS's reputation in the film industry and generally was damaged. Since 27th August 1998, he has not been engaged to perform in any film either in the United Kingdom or elsewhere.

11. In February 2002, FS retained DF to act for him in relation to any claims that could properly be made arising out of the events in July and August 1998.

12. It was an implied term of the retainer, alternatively DF was under a duty of care in tort, to act at all times with the skill and care to be expected of competent solicitors.

13. Further, it was an implied term of the retainer that FS would be notified before any steps were taken to issue proceedings.

14. In July 2003, a Claim Form was issued by DF against Inbro claiming damages for negligence. On a date unknown the Claim Form was served on Inbro.

15. By a letter dated 14th November 2003 solicitors acting for Inbro admitted that Inbro had not effected a policy of any nature for the benefit of FS but denied liability and all other allegations.

16. In or about August 2004 DF purported to agree settlement terms with Inbro subject to the approval of FS. The terms were that Inbro would pay £100,000 in full and final settlement of FS's claim with no admission of liability. DF advised FS that this was '*the best settlement possible*'. Consequently, FS accepted the terms.

17. Following receipt of the agreed sum of £100,000 from Inbro's solicitors on 13th September 2004 the action was dismissed by consent with no order as to costs.

18. Under cover of a letter dated 16th September 2004 DF sent FS a cheque for the sum of £90,000.

The claim against DF

19. DF acted negligently and in breach of its retainer.

PARTICULARS

19.1 It failed to obtain full and proper instructions from FS either at the commencement of the retainer or at any time prior to the purported settlement of the claim against Inbro;

19.2 It failed to advise FS that it acted for Filmbroke Ltd and that there was or might be a conflict of interest between the interests of Filmbroke Ltd and FS's interests;

19.3 It failed to commence proceedings against Filmbroke Ltd in respect of its failure to effect proper insurance cover as agreed with FS;

19.4 It failed to obtain the authority of FS either for the commencement of proceedings against Inbro or any other party;

19.5 It obtained the authority of FS for settlement on the basis of its inaccurate advice;

19.6 It purported to settle the claim against Inbro on FS's behalf at an undervalue;

19.7 It procured the dismissal of the claim against Inbro;

19.8 It failed to obtain or consider all of the available evidence in relation to FS's claims arising out of the events in July and August 1998;

19.9 It failed to advise FS properly or at all in relation to his claims arising out of the events in July and August 1998.

Damages

20. By reason of DF's breaches of retainer and/or breaches of duty FS has suffered loss and damage.

<u>PARTICULARS</u>

20.1 FS had a good arguable claim against Filmbroke Ltd in respect of its failure to effect insurance cover on his behalf in July 1998.

20.2 Further, FS had a good arguable claim against Inbro in respect of its failure to effect insurance cover on his behalf in July 1998.

20.3 If proceedings had been issued against Filmbroke Ltd and properly pursued by DF, FS would have recovered in such proceedings damages on the basis set out at paragraph 20.5 below either following a trial or by settlement.

20.4 If proceedings against Inbro had been properly pursued by DF, FS would have recovered in such proceedings damages on the basis set out at paragraph 20.5 below either following a trial or by settlement.

20.5 FS suffered the following damages by reason of Filmbroke Ltd's and Inbro's failure to effect insurance cover in July 1998: Recovery under the policy in respect of:

20.5.1 Loss of earnings from August 1998 to the notional date of trial (December 2004)
$31,666,666

20.5.2 Future loss of earnings.

20.6 By reason of DF's failures FS has lost the opportunity of recovering damages against Filmbroke Ltd and Inbro as set out in paragraph 20.5 above.

21. FS is entitled to claim interest on any sums found to be due and for such period as the Court finds just pursuant to section 35A of the Supreme Court Act 1981.

AND the claimant claims:

(1) Damages; and

(2) Interest pursuant to section 35A of the Supreme Court Act 1981.

FRED BLOGGS

STATEMENT OF TRUTH

[I believe]/[The Claimant believes] that the facts stated in these Particulars of Claim are true.

Signed .... **Position or**
(Legal Representative) **Office held**
(if signing on behalf of a firm or company)

Print
Name .... **Date**

[The Claimant's address for service is: [address]]

Defence

Claim No ....

IN THE HIGH COURT OF JUSTICE
QUEEN'S BENCH DIVISION
COMMERCIAL COURT

B E T W E E N:

FRED STAR

Claimant

- and -

DELAY AND FORGET

(A Firm)

Defendant

D E F E N C E

---

1. Save where otherwise stated:

    1.1 the Defendant adopts the abbreviations used by the Claimant in the Particulars of Claim, and

    1.2 references to paragraph numbers are references to the paragraphs of the Particulars of Claim.

Parties

2. Paragraphs 1 and 2 are admitted.

The Facts

3. Paragraph 3 is admitted.

4. DF does not admit the allegations in paragraph 4. At no time during the course of its retainer did FS inform or advise DF of Filmbroke Ltd's involvement in the arrangement of insurance cover.

5. DF admits that Inbro were orally instructed to effect insurance cover on behalf of FS against loss of earnings suffered by him by reason of his being unavailable for work due to a number of communicable diseases including chicken pox.

6. DF requires FS to prove the allegation in paragraph 5 that instruction was given by an employee of Filmbroke Ltd.

7. In any event, DF denies that it was at any time aware that such instruction was given by an employee of Filmbroke Ltd. FS's instructions were that he had instructed Inbro to effect insurance cover.

8. Paragraph 6 is admitted. DF denies, if it is alleged, that an insurance policy for the benefit of FS could have been effected prior to the commencement of filming in August 1998 or at all. DF will say that insurance policies of this nature are not available in the market. Further, DF will say that no insurer would have offered such terms to FS by reason of the risks inherent in the filming of the Film or insurers would only have offered such insurance on terms that would have been unacceptable to FS.

9. Paragraphs 7 and 8 are admitted.

10. DF does not admit, if it is alleged, that FS contracted shingles as a result of performing in the Film in August 1998.

11. Paragraph 9 is admitted.

12. In relation to paragraph 10, DF denies, if it is alleged, that FS's failure to obtain the role of Romeo was as a result of the contraction of any communicable disease during the filming in August 1998.

13. DF admits that SF's reputation in the film industry and generally was damaged by reason of his failure to obtain the role of Romeo and that FS has not been engaged to perform in any film either in the United Kingdom or elsewhere since August 1998. DF denies that this was caused by the contraction of a communicable disease during the filming in August 1998. DF will say that the most probable reason for FS's failure to obtain the role of Romeo was the publication of reports of FS's behaviour on the set of the Film.

14. In relation to paragraph 11, DF admits that it was retained by FS to act for him in relation to a claim to be made against Inbro for damages arising out of the events in July and August 1998. DF denies that it was at any time retained to act for FS in relation to a claim against Filmbroke Ltd. DF further denies that it was at any material time aware of any facts or circumstances which suggested that FS might have a claim of any nature against Filmbroke Ltd. DF denies that it was at any time aware that there was any conflict of interest between the interests of Filmbroke Ltd and the interests of FS.

15. Subject to the limitations and express terms of the retainer set out at paragraph 14 above, DF admits that it was an implied term of the retainer alleged at paragraph 12 and that DF was under a duty of care in tort to act at all times with the skill and care to be expected of a competent solicitor.

16. Paragraph 13 is denied. DF had been authorised to handle the claim against Inbro, including issue of proceedings and no such consultation was necessary.

17. Paragraph 14 is admitted. The Claim Form was served on Inbro on 17th July 2003.

18. Paragraph 15 is admitted except that this did not occur by a letter dated 14th November 2003. DF avers that by letters dated 14th August 2003 and 17th September 2003 Inbro admitted that it did not effect a policy but denied all other allegations made on behalf of FS. DF will refer to the correspondence for its full terms and effect.

19. Paragraph 16 is denied. On numerous occasions DF sought specific instructions from FS both by letter and by telephone. No detailed instructions were obtained from FS.

20. On 13th July 2004 the solicitors for Inbro offered the sum of £100,000 inclusive of costs in full and final settlement of any and all causes of action arising out of the instruction in July 1998 to effect a policy of insurance for FS's benefit with no admission of liability.

21. On 14th July 2004, DF telephoned FS to obtain instructions on the settlement offer. DF attempted to explain to FS why DF believed that the offer of settlement was reasonable in the light of the difficulties inherent in the claim. FS stated he '*just wanted the money*'.

22. In accordance with FS's express instructions on 2nd August 2004 DF entered into an agreement with Inbro to settle FS's claim.

23. Paragraphs 17 and 18 are admitted. DF deducted £10,000, this being the costs incurred by FS in pursuit of the claim.

The claim against DF

24. It is denied that DF acted in breach of its retainer or negligently as alleged in paragraph 19 or at all.

25. By reference to the subparagraphs of paragraph 19 DF will say:

    25.1 DF was unable to obtain detailed instructions but it acted in accordance with the terms of its retainer and in accordance with its duties at all times.

    25.2 DF was not instructed by FS nor was it otherwise aware of any facts which suggested that FS could or did have a claim of any nature against Filmbroke Ltd. DF was not therefore aware of any conflict of interest.

    25.3 It is admitted that proceedings were not commenced against Filmbroke Ltd. It is denied that DF acted in breach of retainer or negligently in not commencing such proceedings.

    25.4 Authority to commence proceedings against Inbro was obtained from FS.

    25.5 Authority to settle the proceedings against Inbro was obtained from FS.

    25.6 It is denied that DF acted in breach of its retainer or negligently in reaching the settlement against Inbro. It is denied that the settlement was in any event at an undervalue.

    25.7 Paragraph 19.7 is admitted. It is denied that DF acted in breach of its retainer or negligently in this respect.

25.8 It is admitted that full and detailed evidence was not obtained however DF will say that FS refused to provide such information and expressly instructed DF to proceed without it.

25.9 DF properly advised FS in relation to his claim in accordance with the terms of its retainer and its duty.

Damages

26. DF will say that on the basis of the allegations contained in the Particulars of Claim the only good and arguable claim that FS had in relation to the events of July and August 1998 was his claim against Filmbroke Ltd. That cause of action became statute barred at the latest in August 2004. No proceedings were commenced in respect of that cause of action by FS prior to the claim becoming statute barred. DF is not responsible or liable for FS's failure to commence such proceedings within the limitation period. In the premises, in so far as FS has lost the opportunity to recover damages in respect of the events of July and August 1998 such loss was not caused by any failure on the part of DF.

27. In respect of the subparagraphs at paragraph 20 DF will say:

27.1 Paragraph 20.1 is admitted.

27.2 It is denied that FS had a good arguable claim against Inbro as alleged in paragraph 20.2. Such claim was always speculative.

27.3 As to paragraph 20.3, 20.4 and 20.5, DF makes no admissions as to any sum which might have been recovered in any action against Filmbroke Ltd and/or Inbro either at trial or on earlier settlement save that:

27.3.1 DF will say that the sum of £100,000 inclusive of costs recovered by way of settlement from Inbro exceeded any sum which FS was likely to recover at trial from Inbro. FS has suffered no loss of opportunity in respect of any cause of action he may have had against Inbro; and

27.3.2 It is denied that any insurer would have offered terms to FS which would have entitled him to recover loss as alleged in paragraph 20.5, which loss is in any event, not admitted.

27.4 Paragraph 20.6 is denied.

28. Paragraph 21 is denied.

STANLEY MANN

STATEMENT OF TRUTH

[I believe]/[The Defendant believes] that the facts stated in this Defence and Counterclaim are true.

Signed .... **Position or**
(Legal Representative) **Office held**
(if signing on behalf of a firm or company)

PART III

Commercial Court: Other Documents

CHAPTER 13

Appeals

Michael Nolan
Simon Croall

APPEALS: NOTICE OF APPEAL, RESPONDENT'S NOTICE, RESPONDENT'S NOTICE WITH ADDITIONAL GROUNDS

Law

13.1 CPR 52.10 sets out the appeal court's powers in relation to an appeal. On an appeal, the appeal court has all the powers of the lower court and may affirm, set aside or vary any order or judgment made or given by the lower court[1]. The appeal court may also refer any claim or issue for determination by the lower court, order a new trial or hearing, make orders for the payment of interest and make a costs order[2]. Pursuant to CPR 52.11, an appeal will normally be limited to a review of the decision of the lower court and the appeal court will allow an appeal where the decision of the lower court was either wrong or unjust because of a serious procedural or other irregularity in the proceedings in the lower court[3].

1 CPR 52.10(1) and CPR 52.10(2)(a).
2 CPR 52.10(2)(b)–(e).
3 CPR 52.11(1) and (3).

The applicable procedure

13.2 Any party wishing to appeal the decision of the lower court must file and serve an appellant's notice. If permission has not already been granted by the lower court, the appellant's notice must include an application for permission to appeal[1]. The appellant's notice must be in form N161 and must state the grounds of appeal, setting out clearly the reasons why it is said that the decision of the lower court was wrong or was unjust because of a serious procedural or other irregularity in the proceedings. The grounds of appeal must further specify, in respect of each ground, whether the ground raises an appeal on a point of law or is an appeal against a finding of fact[2].

Unless the lower court directs a different period, the appellant's notice must be filed within 14 days of the date of the decision under appeal[3]. The appellant's notice must then be served on each respondent as soon as practicable, and in any event not later than seven days after it is filed[4].

When filing his appellant's notice, the appellant must lodge with the appeal court a bundle of relevant documents, as set out in paras 5.6–5.7 of the Practice

Direction Appeals[5]. The appellant's notice must also be accompanied by the appellant's skeleton argument. Where this is impracticable, the appellant's skeleton argument must be filed and served within 14 days after filing the appellant's notice[6]. A certificate of service of the appellant's notice and the skeleton argument should then be filed as soon as practicable[7].

Any respondent may file and serve a respondent's notice[8]. Such a notice is mandatory in the case of a respondent who is seeking permission to appeal from the appeal court or who wishes to ask the appeal court to uphold the order of the lower court for reasons different from or additional to those given by the lower court[9]. The respondent's notice should be in form N162. Again, the notice must include any application for permission from the appeal court[10].

The time limit for filing a respondent's notice is either that set by the judge whose order or decision is being appealed or within 14 days from the relevant date as set out in CPR 52.5(5)[11]. CPR 52.5(6) states that service on the appellant and any other respondent must be effected as soon as practicable, and in any event not later than seven days after the respondent's notice is filed[12]. There is a discrepancy in this respect between the Rules themselves and the Practice Direction Appeals which, from 30 June 2004, requires that the respondent's notice is served at the same time as it is filed[13]. As at mid-February 2005, this discrepancy has yet to be resolved.

Pursuant to para 7.6 of the Practice Direction Appeals, a respondent must provide a skeleton argument 'in all cases where he proposes to address arguments to the court'. The skeleton argument must either accompany the respondent's notice or else be lodged and served within 14 days of the filing of the notice[14]. Where a respondent does not serve a respondent's notice, his skeleton argument must be filed and served at least seven days before the appeal hearing[15]. If the respondent wishes to rely on any documents in addition to those filed by the appellant, he must make every effort to agree amendments to the appeal bundle with the appellant[16]. If the representatives for the parties are unable to reach agreement, the respondent may prepare a supplemental bundle,[17] in which case, that bundle must then be filed and served together with the respondent's notice or, if a respondent's notice is not filed, within 21 days after the respondent is served with the appeal bundle[18].

The above account of the applicable law and procedure is only intended to provide general practical guidance on a few of the relevant issues. It is not intended to be exhaustive or even complete. For a fuller account, the reader should consult the latest versions of *CPR Part 52* and the *Practice Direction – Appeals*, Supplementing CPR Part 52 together with the accompanying notes in *The White Book*.

1 CPR 52.4(1).
2 CPR 52 PD3.2.
3 CPR 52.4(2).
4 CPR 52.4(3).
5 CPR 52 PD5.6–5.7.

6 CPR 52 PD5.9.
7 CPR 52 PD5.21(2).
8 CPR 52.5(1).
9 CPR 52.5(2).
10 CPR 52.5(3).
11 CPR 52.5(4).
12 CPR 52.5(6).
13 CPR 52 PD7.13.
14 CPR 52 PD7.7.
15 CPR 52 PD7.7(2).
16 CPR 52 PD7.11.
17 CPR 52 PD7.12.
18 CPR 52 PD7.12 and 7.13.

Pleading

Assumed facts[1]

13.3 The claimant appellant, exporters of whisky to Spain, entered into a contract of carriage with Harris Freightways Ltd ('Harris') for the carriage of a consignment of ten cartons of paper tax seals ('the seals') from Malaga in Spain to Glasgow in Scotland. The contract of carriage was subject to the Convention on the Contract for the International Carriage of Goods by Road, as scheduled to the Carriage of Goods by Road Act 1965 ('the CMR'). Harris then sub-contracted the carriage of the seals to the defendant, again subject to the terms of the CMR. At no point, however, did Harris make out a consignment note, with the consequence that the defendant did not become a party to the original contract of carriage. The defendant was not informed of the specific nature of the seals, which were paper tax seals of nominal value used for sealing whisky bottles and which, when affixed to the bottles, indicated that the requisite Spanish excise duty had been paid.

The tax seals were lost by the defendant and the claimant was consequently obliged to pay to the Spanish tax authorities, under a guarantee of which the defendant had no specific knowledge, the sum of €765,000 ('the guarantee payment') which was equivalent to the duty that would have been recovered on the bottles to which the seals should have been attached. Following the insolvency of Harris, the claimant sought to recover the guarantee payment, together with the cost of carriage, from the defendant.

The trial judge at first instance gave judgment for the claimant, holding that the defendant had entered into a sub-bailment of the goods for reward on CMR terms and was therefore liable as sub-bailee to the claimant for the loss of the seals.

Article 23 of the CMR provides that where a carrier is liable for compensation under the provisions of the Convention, that compensation shall be calculated by reference to the value of the goods at the place and time at which they were accepted for carriage subject to a limit of 8.33 Special Drawing Rights per kilogram of the goods' weight. In addition, by art 23.4 of the CMR, the carriage charges, customs duties and other charges incurred in respect of the carriage shall be refunded in full in the case of total loss.

The judge held that the seals had no intrinsic value but that the liability under the guarantee was 'other charges incurred in respect of the carriage' for the purposes of art 23.4 of the CMR. However he awarded damages in the amount only of the carriage charges (€1,000), plus interest, on the grounds that the sums referred to in art 23.4 were only recoverable if English law would not regard them as too remote and that the loss suffered by way of the guarantee payment was too remote to be recovered. Permission to appeal was granted to both the claimant and the defendant.

The claimant now seeks to appeal that part of the trial judge's order relating to quantum whilst the defendant seeks to uphold the judge's order on different or additional grounds.

1 The assumed facts are based loosely on the facts of *Sandeman Coprimar SA v Transitos y Transportes Integrales SA* [2003] QB 1270.

Notice of Appeal

Claim No ....

IN THE COURT OF APPEAL
ON APPEAL FROM THE HIGH COURT OF JUSTICE
QUEEN'S BENCH DIVISION
COMMERCIAL COURT

B E T W E E N:

O'SULLIVAN DISTILLERS LTD

Claimant

- and -

THOMAS TRANSPORT LTD

Defendant

MATTERS TO BE INSERTED IN
THE APPELLANT'S NOTICE

The Notice should be in form N161 and should be lodged in court in a bundle containing the documents listed in section 11. Sections 1 to 3 need to be completed with the details of the parties. Section 4 should be left blank. The following matters should be put in the other sections and the relevant boxes ticked.

Section 5

Name of Judge	Date of Order
The Honourable Mr Justice Browning	24th May 2004

If only part of the order is appealed, write out that part or those parts

That part of the order by which the learned judge ordered:

(1) that there be judgment against the Defendant for Euros 1,000 plus interest at 5% per annum from 18th June 2003 only;

[Insert Track details]

Section 6

Has permission to appeal been granted – Yes

Date of order granting permission	24th May 2004
Name of Judge	The Honourable Mr Justice Browning
Name of Court	High Court of Justice, Queen's Bench Division, Commercial Court

Section 7

The Appellant ('the Claimant') appeals the orders at section 5 because:

(1) Having held correctly that the sums paid by the Claimant to the Spanish Tax Inspectorate under the guarantee were 'other charges incurred in respect of the carriage' for the purposes of article 23(4) of the CMR, the learned judge was wrong to hold that those sums could not be recovered if, as a matter of English domestic law, the loss was too remote. The learned judge should have held that by virtue of article 23(4) 'other charges incurred in respect of the carriage' are recoverable under the CMR in the case of total loss of the goods, regardless of whether or not English domestic law would regard them as too remote. This ground of appeal raises an appeal on a point of law.

(2) Further or alternatively the learned judge was wrong to hold that the loss suffered by the Claimant as a result of being compelled to make payment to the Spanish Tax Inspectorate under its guarantee was too remote and accordingly could not be recovered from the Defendant. The learned judge should have held:

(a) that a loss is not too remote if it is loss of the same kind as a loss which it is reasonably foreseeable that a Claimant will suffer as a result of a negligent act;

(b) that the loss was a loss of the same kind as liability to excise duty and customs duties both of which are losses which it is reasonably foreseeable that a sender of goods by road will suffer if goods are negligently lost in the course of carriage;

(c) that accordingly the loss was not too remote.

This ground of appeal raises an appeal on a point of law.

Section 8

The Appellant's skeleton argument is attached.

Section 9

The Appellant is asking that the order at section 5 be set aside and that the following order be substituted:

(1) That judgment be entered for the Claimant against the Defendant in the sum of Euros 766,000 plus interest at 5% per annum from the 18th June 2003;

(2) That the Claimants' costs of and occasioned by this action be paid by the Defendant.

Section 10

Leave blank.

Section 11

List documents

Dated ....

Respondent's Notice to uphold judgment on additional grounds

Claim No ....

IN THE COURT OF APPEAL
ON APPEAL FROM THE HIGH COURT OF JUSTICE
QUEEN'S BENCH DIVISION
COMMERCIAL COURT

B E T W E E N:

O'SULLIVAN DISTILLERS LTD

Claimant

- and -

THOMAS TRANSPORT LTD

Defendant

MATTERS TO BE INSERTED IN
THE RESPONDENT'S NOTICE

The Notice should be in form N162 and should be lodged in court in a bundle containing the documents listed in section 10. Sections 1 to 2 and 4 to 5 need to be completed with the details of the parties and the order being appealed. Section 3 should be left blank. The following matters should be put in the other sections and the relevant boxes ticked.

Section 6

The Respondent wishes the appeal court to uphold the order on different or additional grounds because:

The trial judge was wrong to find that the loss of the tax seals and consequent liability to pay to the Spanish tax authorities the sum of Euros 765,000, under a guarantee of which the defendant had no specific knowledge, ('the guarantee payment') was a 'charge incurred in respect of the carriage' within the meaning of article 23.4 of the CMR.

This ground of appeal raises an appeal on a point of law.

Section 7

The Respondent's skeleton argument will follow within 21 days of receiving the appellant's skeleton argument.

Section 8

The Respondent is asking that the appeal court uphold the order for the additional reason that loss of the tax seals and consequent liability to pay to the Spanish tax authorities the sum of Euros 765,000, under a guarantee of which the defendant had no specific knowledge, ('the guarantee payment') is not a 'charge incurred in respect of the carriage' within the meaning of article 23.4 of the CMR and hence is irrecoverable by the Appellant.

Section 9

Leave blank.

Section 10

List documents

Dated ....

Respondent's Notice to vary order

Claim No ....

IN THE COURT OF APPEAL
ON APPEAL FROM THE HIGH COURT OF JUSTICE
QUEEN'S BENCH DIVISION
COMMERCIAL COURT

B E T W E E N:

O'SULLIVAN DISTILLERS LTD

Claimant

- and -

THOMAS TRANSPORT LTD

Defendant

MATTERS TO BE INSERTED IN
THE RESPONDENT'S NOTICE

The Notice should be in form N162 and should be lodged in court in a bundle containing the documents listed in section 10. Sections 1 to 2 and 4 to 5 need to be completed with the details of the parties and the order being appealed. Section 3 should be left blank. The following matters should be put in the other sections and the relevant boxes ticked.

Section 6

The Respondent appeals the order because:

The trial judge found that the Defendant had entered into a sub-bailment for reward on Convention terms with the Claimant's implied consent and was therefore liable to the Claimant as sub-bailee for the loss of the seals.

The learned judge was wrong to conclude that the Defendant became a bailee of the seals for the following reasons:

(i) He gave no or insufficient weight to the fact that the Defendant was not aware of the existence of the seals and/or the contents of the containers in which the seals were stored had been misdescribed to it.

(ii) He ought to have concluded that the Defendant, being a person who comes into possession of goods without knowledge that such goods have properties which give them an unforeseeably elevated value, will not be constituted bailee of them.

This ground of appeal raises an appeal on a point of law.

Section 7

The Respondent's skeleton argument will follow within 14 days of filing this notice.

Section 8

The Respondent is asking that the order at section 4 be varied and the following order substituted:

That the claim is dismissed and there be judgment for the defendants in respect of their costs of this action including the costs of this appeal.

Section 9

Leave blank.

Section 10

List documents

Dated ....

CHAPTER 14

Conflict of Laws and Stays

Service out:
Poonam Melwani

Stays:
Charles Haddon-Cave QC
Michael McParland

SERVICE OUT: APPLICATIONS FOR PERMISSION TO SERVE A CLAIM FORM OUT OF THE JURISDICTION

The principles

14.1 The rules and principles in relation to service of Claim Forms are to be found in CPR 6. Where the Defendant is outside the jurisdiction, and the claims against him are claims which the court has power to determine under the Civil Jurisdiction and Judgments Act 1982, then permission to serve out of the jurisdiction is not required (CPR 6.19). In all other cases, however, a Claim Form can only be served out of the jurisdiction with the permission of the court.

The grounds upon which such permission will be granted are set out in the sub-paragraphs of CPR 6.20. Each of the grounds are disjunctive and a Claimant may seek to rely on one or more of the grounds. The burden is on the Claimant to show that every head of claim set out in the Claim Form falls within at least one of the sub-paragraphs, the applicable standard being a good arguable case. Thus, it may be that permission can be obtained for a contractual claim but not for an analogous or related claim in tort.

In addition to showing that the claim falls within one of the sub-paragraphs, the Claimant must also satisfy the court that there is a serious issue to be tried in respect of each cause of action in respect of which permission is sought and further that England and Wales is the proper place (or forum conveniens) for the claim.

A more detailed analysis of the principles applicable can be found in the two leading authorities, *Seaconsar Far East Ltd v Bank Markazi Jomhouri Islam Iran* [1994] 1 AC 438 and *Spiliada Maritime Corp v Cansulex Ltd* [1987] AC 460, as well as in the Notes in the *White Book*. Although CPR 6 is somewhat differently worded to the previous RSC Order 11, the underlying principles are unchanged.

Applicable procedure

14.2 The application is made without notice, with the necessary Application Notice, Supporting Witness Statement, draft Claim Form and draft Order being sent to the Commercial Court judge[1]. If satisfied that permission should be given, the Claim Form will be indorsed by the judge and/or the draft Order initialled. The Claim Form, being for service out of the jurisdiction, is valid for six months[2].

The witness statement in support (usually in the name of the solicitor, based upon knowledge, information and belief) must comply with the particular requirements set out in CPR 6.21(1), the *Admiralty & Commercial Courts Guide*, appendix 15, para 2 and must also be sufficiently full so as to meet the standards of proof outlined above. Thus, in summary, the evidence must:

(1) set out the grounds upon which the application is made and identify (and make good to the good arguable case standard) the sub-paragraph(s) of rule 6.20 relied on;
(2) state the belief that the Claimant's claim has a reasonable prospect of success;
(3) show that there is a serious issue to be tried in respect of each cause of action;
(4) explain why England and Wales is the proper forum for the claim and the matters relied upon as showing that the case is a proper one in which to subject a party outside the jurisdiction to proceedings within it;
(5) be full and frank and draw attention to any features which might reasonably be thought to weigh against the making of the order sought;
(6) set out the Defendant's address or, if not known, what place or country the Defendant is, or is likely, to be found.

Two copies of the draft Order sought must be submitted[3]. The draft Order must specify the periods within which the Defendant may file an acknowledgment of service, file or serve an admission and file a Defence[4]. In the Commercial Court, the time limit for filing an acknowledgement of service is taken from the Table contained within CPR Part 6 – Practice Direction B, with the stipulated number of days running from the date of service of the Claim Form, regardless of whether or not Particulars of Claim are to follow. The time limit for filing a Defence is, if the Particulars of Claim accompanied the Claim Form, the number of days shown in the Table plus 14 days from the date of service of the Particulars of Claim or, if the Particulars of Claim were not included with the Claim Form, 28 days from the date of service of the Particulars of Claim[5]. The Order need not contain the advice, normally required where orders are obtained without notice, that an application to set aside or vary may be made within seven days. Instead, the procedure for setting aside orders for service out of the jurisdiction is as set out in CPR 11[6].

Further detailed provisions in relation to the methods of service, the need for translated documents for service, etc appear in CPR Part 6.25ff. These matters are outside the scope of this work.

1 It appears that litigants in the Commercial Court frequently do not bother with the issue of an Application Notice. However, technically, an Application Notice is required. A generally endorsed Claim Form will suffice – there is no need for full Particulars of Claim at this stage.
2 CPR 7.5(3).
3 Admiralty & Commercial Court Guide, appendix 15, para 4.
4 CPR 6.21(4).
5 See Admiralty & Commercial Court Guide, appendix 15, paras 6 and 7, amending CPR Part 6, Practice Direction B, paras 7.3 and 7.4. A lacuna appears in the Guide which, whilst altering the time limits for acknowledgments and Defences, says nothing about admissions. Technically, therefore, the Part 6 – Practice Direction time limits (as set out in para 7.3) apply.
6 See *Bua International v Hai Hing Shipping Co Ltd* [2000] 1 Lloyd's Rep 300.

Pleadings

Assumed facts

14.3 A group of statues, normally in display in the Décor Museum in London, are loaned to Lovely Jubbly Ltd of Calcutta for a four-month display. Lovely Jubbly Ltd insure the statues with London insurers, Sure Risk Ltd, at a value of £500,000, having used London brokers, Helpful & Co, to assist in placing the insurance. A few weeks after going on show in Calcutta and after closing hours, the statues are stolen. Lovely Jubbly Ltd write to Sure Risk Ltd seeking payment of the insured value. Whilst investigating the claim, Sure Risk Ltd discover that there have been pre-contractual misrepresentations as to the adequacy of the security arrangements in Calcutta and write avoiding the contract of insurance. Sure Risk Ltd wish to institute proceedings in the United Kingdom seeking a declaration that the contract of insurance has been validly avoided for non-disclosure and misrepresentation.

Application form

Grounds for Application and details of remedy

We, Messrs Lawyers & Co on behalf of the Intended Claimants, make this application without notice to the Intended Defendants for an order (a draft of which is attached) that:

1. The Intended Claimants have permission to issue and serve a Claim Form against the Intended Defendants, Lovely Jubbly Limited at their Head Office at 23 ABC Road, Calcutta India; and

2. The time for acknowledgment of service or for filing or serving an admission by the intended Defendants be 23 days after service on it of the said Claim Form; and

3. The time for serving a defence be 28 days after service of the Particulars of Claim herein.

Because

As set out in more detail in the Witness Statement of XY attached, the Intended Claimant's claim falls within CPR 6.20, England is the proper forum for the determination of the Intended Claimant's Claim and this is a proper case for permission to serve out to be granted.

Dated . . . .

Draft Order

<u>Claim No ....</u>

<u>IN THE HIGH COURT OF JUSTICE</u>
<u>QUEENS BENCH DIVISION</u>
<u>COMMERCIAL COURT</u>

<u>In Chambers</u>

<u>Mr Justice ....</u>

B E T W E E N:

SURE RISK LIMITED

<u>Claimants</u>

- and -

LOVELY JUBBLY LIMITED

<u>Defendants</u>

Draft ORDER

Upon reading the papers submitted by the intended Claimants

IT IS ORDERED THAT:

1. The Intended Claimants have permission to issue and serve a Claim Form against the Intended Defendants, Lovely Jubbly Limited at their Head Office at 23 ABC Road, Calcutta India; and

2. The time for acknowledgment of service or for filing or serving an admission by the intended Defendants be 23 days after service on it of the said Claim Form; and

3. The time for serving a defence be 28 days after service of the Particulars of Claim herein.

Dated. . . . .

Witness Statement in Support of Application for Permission to serve Claim Form out of the Jurisdiction

First Witness Statement of XY on behalf of the Intended Claimants dated this . . . day of . . . with exhibits XY 1, XY 2 and XY 3.

Claim No ....

IN THE HIGH COURT OF JUSTICE
QUEENS BENCH DIVISION
COMMERCIAL COURT

B E T W E E N:

SURE RISK LIMITED

Intended Claimants

- and -

LOVELY JUBBLY LIMITED

Intended Defendants

WITNESS STATEMENT OF XY IN SUPPORT OF AN APPLICATION FOR PERMISSION TO SERVE OUT OF THE JURISDICTION

---

1. I am a partner in the firm of . . . . of [address] and I have the conduct of this matter on behalf of the Intended Claimants. I make this witness statement in support of the Intended Claimant's application for permission to issue and serve the draft Claim Form which is attached as Exhibit XY1, out of the jurisdiction. This application is made without notice and I confirm that to the best of my knowledge and belief I have complied with my duty of full and frank disclosure. The facts and matters to which I depose are within my own knowledge, being derived from my conduct of this case, and from information and documents supplied to me by HISS Ltd, loss investigators and are true to the best of my knowledge and belief.

The Background

2. The Intended Claimants are a London based insurance company. The Intended Defendant is an Indian firm, registered in India, specialising in the import of art and sculptures. Their registered address is 23 ABC Road, Calcutta, India.

3. The claim arises out of the insurance arrangements entered into between the parties, in relation to statues borrowed by the Intended Defendants for display in Calcutta.

4. Towards the end of last year, the Intended Defendants secured from the London Company, Décor Ltd, a loan of late 19th Century Statues for a four-month display in the Bontiful Museum in Calcutta.

5. As a term of the loan agreement, the Intended Defendants were required to have in place all risks insurance with reputable international insurers. The Intended Claimants engaged Helpful & Co, of London, to assist in placing the insurance. Helpful & Co contacted the Intended Claimants and the insurance was placed with them. The statues were insured for the sum of £500,000, with a premium of £40,000 being payable by the Intended Defendants. A copy of the contract of Insurance, dated 20th December 2003, is exhibited hereto at XY2. It should be noted that the contract is on a standard London Market Form and that no choice of law or jurisdiction is specified.

6. During the negotiations which pre-dated the contract, Helpful & Co forwarded to the Intended Claimants a copy of a letter written by the Intended Defendants entitled 'Summary of Proposal for Insurance'. This letter stated that the security arrangements at the Calcutta Museum were 'state of the art' and that the museum was 'guarded by experienced security personnel'. A copy of that letter appears at pages 1–3 of XY3.

The Theft of the Statues

7. The statues were shipped to Calcutta and went on display on 24th December. On 4th January 2004, and between the hours of about 01:00 and 03:00, the statues were stolen from the museum. Investigations have revealed that the thief/thieves entered the museum via a back window. The statutes have thus far not been recovered.

8. The Intended Defendants have written to the Intended Claimants seeking payment of the insured sum of £500,000. A copy of their letter, dated 1st February 2004, appears in the run of chronological correspondence exhibited at XY3.

9. However, during the course of investigating the claim, it has come to light that:

   9.1 Rather than being 'state of the art', the security arrangements were old-fashioned and inadequate. The alarm system was fitted over a decade ago, does not comply with any current accredited standard and is not connected to the local police station.

   9.2 The security personnel at the museum consisted, after hours, of a single gentleman who patrolled the museum and the neighbouring shops in the area. Contrary to the impression created by the letter, he was not dedicated to the museum but was regularly off site, patrolling other premises, for periods of up to an hour.

10. Accordingly, by letter dated 14th February 2004, the Intended Claimants wrote to the Intended Defendants avoiding the policy on the grounds of material misrepresentations and/or non-disclosure. That letter, which also sets out the facts as outlined above, appears at pages 7–8 of XY3.

The Application

11. Appended hereto at XY1 is the draft Claim Form which sets out the declaratory relief sought by the Intended Claimants. In summary, a declaration is sought that the Intended Claimants have validly avoided the contract of insurance and are not liable in respect of the theft of the statues. It is submitted that, given the letter written by the Intended Defendants and the true state of affairs as summarised above, there is a serious issue to be tried and, indeed, that the Intended Claimants have a good arguable case.

12. This Application for permission to serve the Claim Form out of the Jurisdiction upon the Intended Defendants is made under CPR 6.20(5) and in reliance on the following sub-paragraphs of that rule:

    12.1 A claim is made in respect of a contract made within the jurisdiction. Given the involvement of London Brokers and the fact that all communications were made between the London Brokers and the Intended Claimants in London, it is submitted that there is a good arguable case that the contract was made in London and therefore, within the jurisdiction, for the purposes of sub-paragraph (a); and/or

    12.2 A claim is made in respect of a contract where the contract was made by or through an agent, namely Friendly & Co, trading or residing within the jurisdiction on behalf of principals, namely the Intended Defendants, trading or residing out of the jurisdiction. Accordingly, the claim falls within sub-paragraph (b) of CPR 6.20(5);

    12.3 A claim is made in respect of a contract where the contract is governed by English Law. This is a contract made in the

London Insurance Market, in a form and incorporating terms in accordance with the practice and usage of the London Insurance Market. This implies that the proper law is English Law so that there is a good arguable case that sub-paragraph (c) is satisfied.

13. Further, it is submitted that in all the circumstances, England is the proper forum for the dispute. The standard of the alarm system in place and of the security guard are, it is believed, matters which can not sensibly be seriously disputed. Certainly, the Intended Defendants have not thus far sought to deny the allegations and assertions which the Intended Claimants have made. In any event, the dispute involves a contract impliedly governed by English Law, where all negotiations and discussions in relation to the contract took place in England. The witnesses will certainly include personnel from the Intended Claimants, who reside in London. In so far as the Intended Defendants intend to call personnel from their own firm then, although they are located in India, I infer from the correspondence and documents in this matter that they speak and read English. Expert evidence will be required as to materiality, the experts being very likely to be located in the jurisdiction. Relevant documents will be in the possession of the Intended Defendants, in India, but also in the possession of the Intended Claimants and Helpful & Co, and therefore within this jurisdiction.

14. I should add that in their letter of 1st February 2004 the Intended Claimants indicated that, if the Claim were not paid, they would seek to commence proceedings in India. However, although the Intended Claimants made clear in their letter of 14th February 2004 that the claim was not being paid, no proceedings have as yet been commenced. Further, the letter of 14th February clearly

states the Intended Claimant's view that the proper forum is England. No response to that letter has yet been received.

Conclusion

15. In all the circumstances, it is submitted that the Court has jurisdiction to grant permission to serve out of the jurisdiction and that England is the appropriate forum for this dispute. A draft order is sent with these papers and the Court is asked to grant the orders sought.

16. I believe that the facts stated in this witness statement are true.

[Statement of Truth, etc][1]

Statement in support of application to set aside Order giving permission to serve process out of the jurisdiction

[Title of action]

WITNESS STATEMENT OF AB IN SUPPORT OF APPLICATION TO SET ASIDE ORDER GIVING PERMISSION TO SERVE PROCESS OUT OF THE JURISDICTION

1. I am an assistant solicitor employed by the firm of . . . of [address] and I have the conduct of this matter on behalf of the Defendants Lovely Jubbly Limited under the supervision of partner Ms CD. I am duly authorised to make this statement on behalf of the Defendants. The facts stated herein are true to the best of my knowledge and belief being either within my own knowledge or derived from documents and information given to me by Mr EF of the Defendants.

2. Without prejudice to such arguments as may be presented by counsel for the Defendants at the hearing of this application to set

aside the Order of Mr Justice Ongat Wilight dated . . ., I shall assume in making this statement that the Claimants are correct in saying that they have a good arguable case that the insurance contract in question was made in England or was made by or though an agent trading or residing within the jurisdiction on behalf of a principal trading or residing outside it. The Defendants do not however accept that the contract was governed by English Law. There was no choice of law clause. One of the parties was Indian. The risks to be run by the Claimants under the policy were to be run in India.

3. I shall also assume that the Claimants are correct in saying that there is a serious issue to be tried as to whether they are liable under the policy.

4. The Defendants submit that this is, nevertheless, not a proper case for an Order giving permission to serve out. At the hearing, the burden will be on the Claimants to make this assertion good, as that will be the first occasion upon which the matter is argued with both parties present.

5. Without prejudice to that, the Defendants submit that the English Court is not the clearly appropriate forum for this suit in that:

   5.1 The contract is not subject to English Law: the only realistic alternative is Indian law, which the Indian court is better placed to apply, and where it need not be proved by expert evidence.

   5.2 There are crucial issues of fact the resolution of which depends entirely upon evidence and witnesses situated in India. The Defendants will say that the security arrangements at the Bontiful Museum were state of the art and that the security patrol was not only dedicated to the Museum but four men strong.

5.3 It will also be necessary for the court to perform a site visit in order to understand the issues, the modus operandi of the thieves and why the theft was extremely difficult to prevent. Realistically this can only happen if the matter is heard and determined by an Indian court.

5.4 The Defendants are Indian and can more readily service the requirements of their legal team if the matter is litigated in their domicile.

5.5 On 16th February 2004, the Defendants began an action as plaintiffs against the Claimants as defendants in the Indian High Court in Calcutta seeking an indemnity or damages for failure to indemnify. The Indian Court has assumed jurisdiction, which the Claimants have not challenged, and will proceed to entertain this suit. If the present English action continues there will be a risk of irreconcilable judgments.

6. It is not presently clear to the Defendants whether XY was aware of the fact stated in 5.5 hereof when making his witness statement but if he was, the Defendants reserve the right to challenge the Order on the ground of non-disclosure of material facts.

[Signed, etc]

1 Statement of truth, etc as set out in **Chapter 3, para 3.2**.

STAYS: JURISDICTIONAL CHALLENGES, FORUM NON CONVENIENS AND ANTI-SUIT INJUNCTIONS

14.4 This part of Chapter 14 is in two parts. The first part looks at challenges to the jurisdiction of the Commercial Court, either on the basis that the court does not have jurisdiction or any jurisdiction that it does have should be declined. The second part considers applications for anti-suit injunctions protecting the Commercial Court jurisdiction.

Part I: Jurisdictional challenges/forum non conveniens – the law

14.5 A defendant who is served with English proceedings (whether within or without the jurisdiction) may choose to challenge the jurisdiction of the court, by arguing that the Claimant's claim to jurisdiction is ill-founded as a matter of fact or law, and/or by contending that English proceedings should be stayed because the defendant has the benefit of a foreign jurisdiction clause (or indeed arbitration clause). Alternatively, it is open for the Defendant to seek to invite the English Court to decline to exercise whatever jurisdiction it possess on the basis that a foreign forum is a clearly and distinctly more appropriate for the hearing of the dispute in question (*forum conveniens*) and/or on the grounds that there are similar proceedings on foot in a foreign jurisdiction which are already well advanced (*lis alibi pendens*). Alternatively, in cases within the scheme of the Council Regulation No. 44/2001 ('The Brussels Regulation') and/or the Brussels or Lugano Conventions (where the doctrines already mentioned have no direct application), the *lis alibi pendens* provisions of the same may be raised to prevent the English proceedings continuing. Such applications arise in a variety of ways and are common in the Commercial Court.

Forum non conveniens: the Spiliada principles

14.6 The principles to be applied are laid down in Lord Goff's judgment in *Spiliada Maritime Corporation v Cansulex Ltd* [1987] AC 460.

The basic principle is set out at p 476 of Lord Goff's speech:

> 'The basic principle is that a stay will only be granted on the ground of forum non conveniens where the court is satisfied that there is some other available forum, having competent jurisdiction, which is [clearly and distinctly]* the appropriate forum for the trial of the action, i.e. in which the case may be tried more suitably for the interests of all the parties and the ends of justice.' [* added from p 477E]

The *Spiliada* principles are usefully summarised by Bingham LJ in *Du Pont v Agnew* [1987] 2 Lloyd's Rep 585 at p 588:

> '(1) The burden of proof rests on the defendant to persuade the court to exercise its discretion to grant a stay (p 476D). It is only if the court

is persuaded that there is another available forum which is *prima facie* the more 'appropriate' forum for the trial of the action, the burden will then shift to the plaintiff to show that there are special circumstances by reason of which justice requires that the trial should nevertheless take place in this country (see (f) below) (p 476E-F).

(2) The initial burden resting on the defendant is not just to show that England is not the natural or appropriate forum for the trial but to establish that there is another available forum which is clearly and distinctly more appropriate than the England forum (p 477E).

(3) Where the defendant's connection with England is a fragile one it should be all the easier for him to prove that there is another clearly more appropriate forum for the trial overseas (p 477F).

(4) The first step is to look at what factors there are which point in the direction of another forum (p 477G). One must look for "connecting" factors which point towards another forum (p 478A). Such factors include (p 478B) e.g. convenience and expense (such as availability of witnesses), the law governing the relevant transaction [or tort], and where the parties respectively reside or carry on business.

(5) If the court concludes at that stage that there is no other available forum which is clearly more appropriate for the trial of the action, it will ordinarily refuse a stay (p 478C).

(6) If however the court concludes at that stage that there is some other available forum which *prima facie* is clearly more appropriate for the trial of the action, it will ordinarily grant a stay unless there are circumstances by reason of which justice requires that a stay should nevertheless be refused (p 478D). The court will look at all the circumstances of the case (p 478D). If the plaintiff can establish objectively by cogent evidence that he will not obtain justice in the foreign jurisdiction, that is a relevant factor (p 478E).

(7) However, the court should not be deterred from granting a stay simply because the plaintiff will be deprived of a legitimate personal or juridical advantage provided it is satisfied that substantial justice will be done in the available appropriate forum (p 482F). An advantage to the plaintiff will ordinarily give rise to a comparable disadvantage to the defendants. To give the plaintiff his advantage at the expense of the plaintiff is not consistent with the objective approach which the court should adopt (p 482D). An English court should not hesitate to grant a stay [eg] merely because a plaintiff may be deprived of a substantially higher award of damages here (p 483C).'

The following useful three-stage analysis was formulated by Hunter JA in *The Adhiguna Meranti* [1988] 1 Lloyd's Rep 384:

'(1) Is it shown that Hong Kong is not only not the natural or appropriate forum for the trial, but that there is another available forum which is clearly or distinctly more appropriate than Hong

Kong. The evidential burden is here upon the applicant. The emphasis is upon "appropriate" rather than "convenient" because this is not simply a matter of practical convenience. The purpose is to identify the forum "with which the action has the most real and substantial connection" per Lord Keith in The Abidin Daver [1984] A.C. 398 at p. 415. The principal factors are enumerated at p. 987D. Failure by the applicant at this stage is normally fatal.

(2) If the answer to (1) is yes, will a trial at this other forum deprive the plaintiff of any "legitimate personal or juridical advantages"? The evidential burden here lies upon the plaintiff.

(3) If the answer to (2) is yes, a court has to balance the advantages of (1) against the disadvantages of (2), Abidin Daver per Lord Brandon at p. 419. Deprivation of one or more personal or juridical advantages will not necessarily be fatal to the applicant provided that the court is satisfied that notwithstanding such loss "substantial justice will be done in the available appropriate forum". The court must try to be objective. Proof of this, which can fairly be called the ultimate burden of persuasion, rests upon the applicant for the stay. By these means he establishes that on balance the other forum is more suitable "for the interests of all the parties and the ends of justice". This may be another way of saying that the plaintiff's choice of forum has been shown to be so inappropriate as to deserve the pejorative description of "forum-shopping" and to be restrained accordingly...'

A simpler 'broad overall view' was favoured by Lloyd LJ in *The Po* [1991] 2 Lloyd's Rep 206 at p 213 citing Bingham LJ, viz:

> 'It does not matter by what route the Judge approaches the basic question, whether there is some other forum which is clearly more appropriate, as long as he gets there in the end, bearing all the relevant factors in mind. Indeed I notice from the brief report in the Harrods case, that Lord Justice Bingham seems to have adopted much of the same approach as the Judge:
>
> > "The court should look to see what factors there were, taking the broad overall view, which pointed in the direction of another forum and then look at such connecting factors as convenience, governing law, availability of witnesses and place of residence and business."'

In *Amchem Products Inc v British Columbia* (1993) 102 DLR 97 at p 110G–H Sopinka J said:

> 'If a party seeks out a jurisdiction simply to gain a juridical advantage rather than by reason of a real and substantial connection with the case to the jurisdiction, that is ordinarily condemned as "forum shopping".'

He also went on to say that in his view:

> '... there is no reason in principle why the loss of juridical advantage should be treated as a separate and distinct condition rather than being weighed in the balance'.

The *forum non conveniens* test is a relative not absolute one. It is to be judged between the two competing *fora*. Thus, it is not necessary to show that the alternative *forum* is the most convenient in the world but merely clearly and distinctly 'more' convenient than the *forum* in respect of which the stay is sought (per Waung J in *The Kapitan Shvetsov* [1998] 1 Lloyd's Rep 199 at p 202).

Lis alibi pendens

14.7 The correct approach where there is a *lis alibi pendens* is to apply the principles in *The Spiliada* set out above (per Clarke J in *The Varna* [1994] 2 Lloyd's Rep 41 at p 47). An important consideration in deciding whether there is another forum which is clearly and distinctly the more appropriate forum is the existence and nature of proceedings elsewhere (per Clarke J, above).

It is not in general a desirable state of affairs for proceedings involving the same issues to be proceedings in different jurisdictions in particular because of the additional cost involved and the risk of inconsistent decisions (per Clark J, above and see Lord Brandon in *The Abidin Daver* [1984] AC 398, pp 411–2).

It is generally undesirable to have concurrent proceedings in different jurisdictions and, accordingly, the policy of the law is to favour the litigation of issues once only in the most appropriate forum (per Bingham LJ *Du Pont v Agnew* [1987] 2 Lloyd's Rep 585, p 589).

The foreign proceedings will be of particular relevance if they have passed beyond 'the stage of the initiating process' and if, by reason of their having reached an advanced stage, they are likely to have an impact on the proceedings which it is sought to stay (see Lord Goff in *de Dampierre v de Dampierre* [1988] 1 AC 92, at p 108).

Text books

14.8 For full details of such challenges see the major works in the field of Conflict of Laws, in particular Dicey & Morris *The Conflict of Laws* (13th edn, 2000, with 2003 supplement) in particular ch 11–13; Briggs & Rees *Civil Jurisdiction and Judgments* (3rd edn, 2002) in particular ch 2–5; Cheshire & North *Private International Law* (13th edn, 1999) in particular ch 10–14.

PROCEDURE FOR JURISDICTIONAL CHALLENGES

14.9 All such claims are brought under the provisions of CPR Part 11 'Disputing the Court's Jurisdiction'. This allows a defendant to dispute the court's jurisdiction to try the claim and/or argue that the court should not exercise its jurisdiction (i.e. a *forum non conveniens* application). Part 11 applies to claims in the Commercial Court list with the modifications set out in CPR

Part 58.7. Thus, this procedure applies both to jurisdiction challenges, claims for a stay, and to *forum non conveniens/lis alibi pendens* applications. The application procedure itself is governed by the provisions of CPR Part 23 as modified by CPR Part 58, and applicant use Form N244 (CC) and the guidance is given in B9 and Section F of the *Admiralty & Commercial Courts Guide*.

Examples

(A): APPLICATION FOR STAY ON GROUNDS OF (a) EXCLUSIVE JURISDICTION CLAUSE, (b) FORUM CONVENIENS AND (c) LIS ALIBI PENDENS

I: APPLICATION NOTICE

Form N244 (CC)

Application Notice

Claim No ....

IN THE HIGH COURT OF JUSTICE
QUEEN'S BENCH DIVISION
COMMERCIAL COURT
ROYAL COURTS OF JUSTICE

B E T W E E N:

AAA Inc

Claimant

- and -

BBB Ltd

Defendants

Part A

The Defendants, BBB Ltd, intend to apply for an order that the proceedings herein be stayed until further order and for an order that the Claimants, AAA Inc., pay the costs of this application

Because:

(a) the proceedings are brought in England by the Claimant, AAA Inc, in breach of an exclusive jurisdiction clause agreed between the parties in favour of Texas, (b) Texas is clearly and distinctly the most convenient forum for this dispute (*forum conveniens*) and (c) there are already proceedings between the parties in the District Court of the Southern District of Texas concerning the identical matters in dispute (*lis alibi pendens*).

Part B

The Defendants, BBB Ltd, intend to rely on the attached witness statement.

II: DEFENDANTS' WITNESS STATEMENT

Heading as in APPLICATION NOTICE

First Witness Statement of **Ben Beetroot**

I, **BEN BEETROOT**, of 10 Upping Street, London WC1, state as follows:

1. I am the Managing Director of BBB Ltd of 10 Upping Street, London WC1. I am duly authorised to make this statement on behalf of the Defendant, BBB Ltd, in these proceedings. The facts stated herein are within my own knowledge and true.

2. I made this statement in support of the Defendant's application dated 1st April 2004 for a stay of these proceedings (2004 Claim No. 333) in favour of Texas on three grounds (a) that the proceedings are brought in England by the Claimant, AAA Inc, in breach of an exclusive jurisdiction clause agreed between the parties in favour of Texas, (b) that Texas is clearly and distinctly the most convenient forum for this dispute (*forum conveniens*) and (c) there are already proceedings between the parties in the District Court of the Southern District of Texas ('the Texas proceedings') concerning the identical matters in dispute (*lis alibi pendens*).

3. BBB Ltd say that Texas is both the contractual choice of jurisdiction and clearly and distinctly the natural and appropriate forum for the trial of this matter and where the matter may be tried more suitably for the interests of all the parties and the ends of justice.

4. I will refer by page number to documents in a bundle of copy documents exhibited to this statement marked '*BBB1*'.

Background facts

5. BBB Ltd is a company specialising in the design and manufacture of computer games. BBB Ltd is registered in London but has its manufacturing base in Texas. In 1997 BBB Ltd was approached by a Texas company, AAA Inc, seeking the exclusive right to sell BBB Ltd's computer games in the USA.

6. By a contract dated 1st April 1997, BBB Ltd granted to AAA Inc the exclusive right to sell its games throughout the USA in consideration of 50% of the net profits of all games sold ('the Agreement'). Clause 15 of the Agreement provided that any disputes were to be referred to the exclusive jurisdiction of the Texas courts. A copy of the Agreement is exhibited at pages 1–10.

7. In 2003, it came to BBB Ltd's attention that AAA Inc had been falsely concealing the profits made from the sale of BBB Ltd's chips for some years.

8. On 1st July 2003, BBB Ltd commenced proceedings for an account in the District Court of the Southern District of Texas pursuant to clause 15 of the Agreement ('the Houston proceedings'). AAA Inc appeared in those proceedings and denied liability. A copy of the pleadings in the Houston proceedings is exhibited at pages 11–20.

9. On 5th November 2003, AAA Inc commenced the present proceedings in England seeking a declaration of non-liability.

Grounds for stay

10. I am advised that AAA Inc's proceedings here are in breach of the exclusive jurisdiction agreement contained in clause 15 of the Agreement.

11. I am also advised that these proceedings should be stayed on the grounds that Texas is clearly and distinctly the most convenient forum for this dispute (*forum conveniens*). The central issue in the case will concern the true profits made by AAA Inc from the sale of BBB's computer games. I draw the court's attention to the following matters in particular:

    11.1 The parties: AAA Inc is registered in Texas and has its headquarters in Houston, Texas. BBB Ltd, whilst registered in London, has its manufacturing base in Botox Valley, Texas.

    11.2 The witnesses: The main witnesses in the case are located in Houston; in particular, Mr Red Pencil, AAA Inc's accountant, and Mr Pull Wool, BBB Ltd's local manager.

    11.3 The documents: Most of the relevant documentation is to be found in Houston, in particular the accounting documents for the period in question, 2000–03.

    11.4 The proper law of the Agreement: The Agreement contains a Texas law clause (clause 14).

12. In contrast, the only real connection this case has with England is that BBB Ltd happens to be registered here; whereas the main operations of the company take place in Texas (see above).

13. I further rely upon the fact that proceedings are on foot and well advanced in Texas which are the mirror image of the present proceedings. Pleadings in the Texas proceedings are now closed and initial disclosure has been made; depositions are scheduled for three months hence and the trial is fixed for January 2005. It is not in the interests of justice for there to be parallel proceedings.

14. Moreover, in these proceedings AAA Inc seek simply a declaration of non-liability. I am advised that this is a case in which the conduct of the AAA Inc deserves the pejorative description of 'forum-shopping'.

15. In these circumstances, I respectfully request this court to grant a stay of these proceedings in the terms of BBB Ltd's application.

[Statement of Truth, etc][1]

III: CLAIMANTS' WITNESS STATEMENT

Heading as in APPLICATION NOTICE

First Witness Statement of **Adam Aardvark**

I, **ADAM AARDVARK**, of 123 Mean Street, Nowheresville, Arkansas, USA state as follows:

1. I am the President of AAA Inc of 123 Mean Street, Nowheresville, Arkansas, USA, a finance and investment company. I am duly authorised to make this statement on behalf of AAA Inc. The facts stated herein are within my own knowledge and true.

2. I made this statement in answer to Ben Beetroot's witness statement dated 1st September 2004 and in opposition to the Defendant's application for a stay of the proceedings herein (Cause No. 638 of 1999 above).

3. In summary, AAA Inc say (a) the Agreement dated 1st April 1997 relied upon by BBB Ltd (and exhibited to Ben Beetroot's statement) was superseded by a fresh agreement which provided for the exclusive jurisdiction of the English courts (see below), and (b) in any event, England is clearly and distinctly the most convenient forum for this dispute (*forum conveniens*).

4. I will refer by page number to documents in a bundle of copy documents exhibited to this statement marked '*AA1*'.

5. Ben Beetroot omits to mention in his statement that in 1999 a dispute arose between AAA Inc and BBB Ltd regarding the quality of the computer games which BBB Ltd was manufacturing. AAA Inc had begun to receive numerous complaints from its customers and distributors that the games

were freezing mid-way or operating too slowly. Negotiations took place between myself and Ben Beetroot which culminated in a fresh agreement being entered into dated 1st April 2000 which reduced BBB Ltd's share of the net profits to 30% ('the New Agreement'). A copy of the New Agreement is exhibited at pages 1–15.

6. It will be noted that Clause 25 of the New Agreement expressly provides for English law and jurisdiction. It is, therefore, quite wrong for Ben Beetroot to assert that the present proceedings have been commenced by AAA Inc in England in breach of contract. On the contrary, AAA Inc have complied with the relevant contract and it is, in fact BBB Ltd themselves who are in breach of contract for commencing proceedings in Texas.

7. Ben Beetroot also omits to mention that the Texas proceedings are currently stayed pending the outcome of AAA Inc's appeal on jurisdictional grounds: AAA Inc sought a stay before the Southern District Court of Texas on the grounds of clause 25 of the New Agreement. AAA Inc are fully confident of winning this appeal. The Notice of Appeal is exhibited hereto at pages 16–30. I should mention that BBB Ltd appear to deny that the New Agreement was ever concluded; it is, however, not clear on what basis.

8. England not Texas is, in any event, the most convenient forum for this dispute because the key issue in the case is clearly going to be whether the New Agreement was concluded and thereby superseded the original Agreement. The negotiations for the New Agreement took place between me and Ben Beetroot in BBB Ltd's offices at 10 Upping Street in London with various witnesses present, including AAA Inc's London agent, Mr Peter Pan, who are resident in England. If AAA Inc are correct in stating that the New Agreement superseded the original Agreement, BBB Ltd's

claim for understated profits (which amounts to about 20%) falls away.

9. For the above reasons, I respectfully request this court to dismiss the application for a stay with costs.

[Signed, etc]

(B): APPLICATION FOR STAY ON GROUNDS OF ARTICLE 2 OF THE REGULATION

I: APPLICATION NOTICE

Form N244 (CC)
APPLICATION NOTICE

Claim No ....

IN THE HIGH COURT OF JUSTICE
QUEEN'S BENCH DIVISION
COMMERCIAL COURT
ROYAL COURTS OF JUSTICE

B E T W E E N:

CCC Ltd

Claimants

- and -

DDD Sarl

Defendants

Part A

The Defendants, DDD Sarl, intend to apply for an order that the proceedings herein be stayed until further order and for an order that the Claimants, CCC Ltd, pay the costs of this application

Because:

(a) the proceedings are brought in England by the Claimant, AAA Inc, in breach of Article 2 of Council Regulation No. 44/2001 ('the Regulation').

Part B

The Defendants, DDD Sarl, intend to rely on the attached witness statement.

II: DEFENDANTS' WITNESS STATEMENT

Heading as in APPLICATION NOTICE

First Witness Statement of **David Dunce**

I, **DAVID DUNCE**, of 1 City Street, London EC2, state as follows:

1. I am a Solicitor of the Supreme Court and partner of the firm of Dunce & Co. I have the conduct of this matter on behalf of the Defendants, DDD Sarl, and am duly authorised to make this statement on behalf of the Defendants. The facts stated herein are within my own knowledge and true.

2. I made this statement in support of the Defendant's application dated 1st April 2004 for a stay of these proceedings (2004 Claim No. 666) in favour of Spain on the grounds that that the proceedings are brought in England by the Claimant, CCC Sarl, in breach of Article 2 Council Regulation No 44/2001 ('the Regulation').

3. This matter is straightforward. The Claimants, CCC Ltd, claim for an alleged breach of contract for the supply of footballs under a contract dated 1st April 2003. It is alleged, in particular, that 10,000 footballs supplied were of the wrong size and shape. This is denied by the Defendants, DDD Sarl.

4. DDD Sarl are a company registered and domiciled in Spain, and have their head office at 1 Real Street, Madrid.

5. Accordingly, by reason of Article 2 of the Regulation, CCC Ltd should have commended proceedings against DDD Sarl in Spain.

6. In these circumstances, I respectfully request this court to grant a stay of these proceedings in the terms of DDD Sarl's application.

[Statement of Truth, etc][1]

III: CLAIMANTS' WITNESS STATEMENT

Heading as in APPLICATION NOTICE

First Witness Statement of **Clive Clever**

I, **CLIVE CLEVER**, of 2 City Street, London EC2 state as follows:

1. I am a Solicitor of the Supreme Court and partner of the firm of Clever & Co. I have the conduct of this matter on behalf of the Claimants, CCC Ltd, and am duly authorised to make this statement on behalf of the Claimants. The facts stated herein are within my own knowledge and true.

2. I made this statement in answer to David Dunce's statement dated 1st December 2003 and in opposition to the Defendants' application for a stay of these proceedings. My ground is that the parties have agreed that the courts of England and Wales would have exclusive jurisdiction in relation to the contract for the supply of this particular shipment of footballs.

3. DDD Sarl are leading manufacturers of footballs and football equipment and have a long-standing relationship with CCC Ltd for over 20 years. Each year DDD Sarl supplies on average 50,000 footballs to CCC Ltd. It became common practice between the parties to vary the jurisdiction clause in the contract each year, so

that in odd years it would be 'home' jurisdiction (England) and in even years it would be 'away' (Spain). After a number of years the parties no longer bothered to draw up a formal contract; but the practice of 'alternating' the jurisdictional clause was understood to continue. 2003 was an odd year and therefore an English jurisdiction year.

4. In April 2003, CCC Ltd complained about a shipment of 10,000 odd-sized and shaped footballs supplied by DDD Sarl (which corresponded more to a 'rugby ball' shape and size). DDD Sarl denied that there was anything wrong with the footballs and, despite demands, refused to take them back or supply round ones.

5. In these circumstances, in accordance with the understanding, CCC Ltd commenced proceedings against DDD Sarl in England. Accordingly, pursuant to Article 23(b), there is a valid agreement conferring exclusive jurisdiction on the courts of England.

6. For the above reasons, I respectfully request this court to dismiss the application for a stay with costs.

[Signed, etc]

1 Statement of truth, etc as set out in **Chapter 3, para 3.2**.

Part II: Anti-suit injunctions – the law

14.10 An 'anti-suit' injunction is an order of the English Court restraining a party from proceeding with an actual or threatened action in a foreign court ('the foreign proceedings'). Such orders are issued when there has been 'wrongful conduct' on the part of a defendant who must be subject to the *in personam* jurisdiction of the English Court and against whom the order would be an effective remedy.

'Wrongful conduct' falls essentially into two categories:

(1) When the defendant has taken (or threatened to take) legal action in breach of a contractual English jurisdiction or arbitration clause covering the dispute in question. In the absence of 'strong reasons' put forward by the defendant for so doing, an anti-suit injunction would normally be issued as damages are regarded as an inadequate remedy for such breaches. *Prima facie* parties to a contract should be held to their contractual bargain on choice of dispute resolution forums.

(2) When where there are existing English proceedings and some of the parties to it need to be protected by from 'unconscionable', 'vexatious' or 'oppressive' conduct by the anti-suit defendant in relation to foreign proceedings[1].

The original equitable jurisdiction to grant anti-suit relief is now contained in the Supreme Court Act 1981, s 37 (1):

> 'The High Court may by order (whether interlocutory or final) grant an injunction ... in all cases in which it appears to the court to be just and convenient to do so.'

This broad discretionary jurisdiction is to be exercised 'when the ends of justice require it'[2], a phrase which has been illuminated in a long line of authorities[3].

1 See, e.g. *Turner . Grovit* [2002] 1 WLR 107, *Airbus Industrie GIE v Patel* [1999] 1 AC 119, pp 138, 140 (HL); *Barclays Bank plc v Homan* [1993] BCLC 680; *Glencore International AG v Exeter Shipping and others* [2002] EWCA 524; *Omega Group Holdings Ltd v Kozeny* [2002] CLC 132.

2 *Sociètè National Industrielle Aèrospatiale v Lee Kui Jak (PC)* [1987] AC 871, p 892.

3 For an overview of the exercise of the jurisdiction, in addition to standard text books see, e.g. *Société Nationale Industrielle Aerospatiale v Lee Kui Jak* [1987] AC 871, (PC); *Airbus Industrie GIE v Patel* [1999] 1 AC 119; *Donohue v Armco Inc* [2002] 2 Lloyd's Rep 425.

Restrictions imposed by the European Court of Justice

14.11 The power of the English Court to issue such injunctions has now been significantly curtailed by two decisions of the European Court of Justice in *Case C-116/02, Erich Gasser GmbH v Misat Srl* [2005] QB 1, and *Case C-159/02, Turner v Grovit* [2005] 1 AC 101. Combined, these decisions effectively hold that in Brussels Convention cases (and thus in Council Regulation 44/2001, and presumably also in Lugano Convention cases) anti-suit injunctions are incompatible with a scheme based on mutual trust which the contracting states accorded to one another's legal systems and judicial institutions. The effect of these decisions will need to be explored in further case law. However, it seems likely that anti-suit injunctions will not be granted by English courts in cases where the 'foreign proceedings' are in EU and/or EEA courts, even if they are manifestly in breach of an exclusive English jurisdiction clause. However, such injunctions will continue to be issued in arbitration clause cases even if the defendant is domiciled in an EU or EEA state and/or the proceedings are in such courts. This is based on the current English law position that anti-suit injunctions are within the 'arbitration' exceptions to the Council Regulation 44/2001[1] and the Brussels and Lugano Conventions[2], thus preventing their application. The latest decisions discussing the issues surrounding the arbitration exception in detail are *The Ivan Zagubanski* [2002] 1 Lloyd's Rep 106 and *Through Transport Mutual v New India Assurance Co* [2004] EWCA Civ 1598, [2005] 1 Lloyd's Rep 67. In relation to all other courts, the traditional English law approach highlighted above will continue to apply.

1 Article 2(d) of the Council Regulation.

2 Article 1(4) of both the Brussels and Lugano Conventions.

Procedure

14.12 In existing Commercial Court litigation in England, an application notice seeking an order can be brought, under the provisions of CPR Part 23 and PD23 as modified by CPR Part 58 and PD58, using Form N244(CC) which has been adapted for use in the Commercial Court[1]. Alternatively, an application can be made under CPR Part 8 for interim or indeed final relief. A Claimant who uses a CPR Part 8 application must use practice form N208(CC), pursuant to PD58 2.4, and *The Admiralty & Commercial Courts Guide*, para B4.1.

In cases involving anti-suit injunctions in support of arbitration, such injunction applications are governed by the provisions of CPR Part 62 and PD62. An Arbitration Claim using Form N8 should be used. See also the Guide.

Obtaining permission to serve the Claim form out of the Jurisdiction is to be made using Form N244(CC) and following the normal application procedure and seeking permission under either the provisions of CPR Part 6 or Part 62.

1 See *The Admiralty & Commercial Courts Guide*, F1.1.

Facts of example: Strong Arms Ships v Ee-Awe Global Insurance

14.13 This is an interim application made before issue of the Arbitration Claim form for an anti-suit injunction in support of an English arbitration clause contained in a bill of lading. The Claimants ('Strong Arm Ships') are the owners of the vessel, the Defendants are all cargo interests insurers whom it is alleged are seeking to start legal proceedings in France in purported breach of the London arbitration clauses. This example is based on an urgent without notice interim injunction before proceedings are issued under the provisions of CPR Part 25.2 where permission is also sought to serve out of the jurisdiction. This example contains (a) an Arbitration Claim Form, (b) the witness statement in support, (c) the interim order of the Court and (d) a response from the Defendants.

I: ARBITRATION CLAIM FORM FOR ANTI-SUIT INJUNCTION

N8 CLAIM FORM

Claim No ....

IN THE HIGH COURT OF JUSTICE (Arbitration)
QUEEN'S BENCH DIVISION
COMMERCIAL COURT
ROYAL COURTS OF JUSTICE

Claimants:

STRONG ARM SHIPS

(A company incorporated under the laws of Bulgaria)

Defendants:

1. EE-AWE GLOBAL INSURANCE

(A company incorporated under the laws of France)

2. A.S.I.E.

(A company incorporated under the laws of Italy)

3. COMBINATION TRANSPORTS

(A company incorporated under the laws of Switzerland).

In the matter of an intended arbitration between

Claimants:

STRONG ARM SHIPS

(A company incorporated under the laws of Cyprus)

Respondents: [*Set of the names and addresses of persons to be served with the claim form stating their role in the arbitration and whether they are defendants.*]

1. **EE-AWE GLOBAL INSURANCE,**
   112 Rue Notre Dame des Victoires, 75042, Paris, France

2. **A.S.I.E.**
   127 Via Cinque Dicembre 3, 16212, Genoa, Italy

3. **COMBINATION TRANSPORTS**
   19 Quai du Mont-Blanc, 12009, Geneva, Switzerland.

All of the above are Defendants herein and are intended to be Respondents to the intended arbitration.

Defendant's name	This claim will be heard on
and address	at am/pm.
[As above]	This claim is made without notice.

Remedy claimed and grounds on which claim is made

The Claimant seeks:

(1) A declaration that the London arbitration clause of a Charterparty in writing dated 21st April 2005 made between the Claimant as Owners and Rock Commodities Limited as Charterers of the Claimant's Vessel 'STRONGBOW' is validly incorporated into all Bills of Lading dated 1st May 2005 issued by the Claimant pursuant thereto and in respect of a cargo of bagged rice shipped at Chiwan, The People's Republic of China aboard the Claimant's said vessel and is binding upon the Defendants and each of them, and

(2) An interim (and subsequently a final) injunction to restrain the Defendants from proceeding with claims arising out of the said Bills of Lading in any other forum or jurisdiction other than London Arbitration as provided for under the said clause.

(3) Permission to serve the Arbitration Claim form, Application Notice and evidence and any Order of this Court, out of the jurisdiction on the Defendants and each of them at the addresses identified herein.

The grounds upon which these remedies are contained are set out in the witness statement of the Claimant's solicitor, Mr Bill Sykes dated 28th June 2005, which gives details of the Defendants, and each of them acting in breach of binding London arbitration clauses contained in bills of lading.

The Claimant seeks an order for costs against

The Defendants to this Arbitration Application and/or each of them.

Statement of Truth

I am duly authorised by the Claimant to sign this statement.

Full name	**BILL SYKES**
Name of Claimant's solicitor's firm	**SYKES & CRYKES**
Position or office held (if signing on behalf of firm, company or corporation)	Claimant's solicitor's address to which documents or payments should be sent if different from overleaf. If you are prepared to accept service by DX, fax or email, please add details.
Partner	**SYKES & CRYKES** Dr Faustus Lodge Humphrey's Street London EC3M 4KJ DX: 2001 London City EC3

II: CLAIMANT'S WITNESS STATEMENT IN SUPPORT – HEADING AS IN ARBITRATION CLAIM FORM

First Witness Statement of **Bill SYKES**
For the Claimant
Dated 28th June 2005

I, **BILL SYKES**, Solicitor of the Supreme Court of England and Wales, of Dr Faustus Lodge, Humphrey's Street, London EC3M 4KJ state as follows:

1. **I am a partner in the firm of Sykes and Crykes of the above address, Solicitors for the Claimants. I have conduct of this matter on behalf of the Claimants and am duly authorised to make this Witness Statement. Save as where otherwise indicated or apparent from the context the facts and matters stated herein are based upon documents and instructions supplied to me by the Claimants' London agent, Mr. Stelios Kourous, and/or by the Claimant's P & I Club, Northern Safety, in particular, Mr Stephen Steel, a director of that company. The Claimants are incorporated under the laws of Bulgaria, and have the benefit of P & I insurance with Northern Safety, based in England. Copies of documents to which I respectfully refer this Honourable Court are exhibited in a paginated bundle marked '*BS1*'. I believe that the facts and matters contained herein are true to the best of my knowledge and belief.**

2. I make this Witness Statement in support of:

   2.1 The Claimant's application for a declaration that the Defendants are obliged to proceed to London Arbitration in respect of all and any claims made by them against the

Claimant arising out of particular Bill of Lading contracts set out below and/or in respect of all and any alleged loss or damage to cargo carried thereunder.

2.2 The Claimant's Application for an interim (and subsequently a final) anti-suit injunction restraining the Defendants from proceeding in respect of all such claims in any jurisdiction or forum other than London Arbitration. This application is presently made on a without notice basis because of the perceived urgency of the situation and the need to prevent the Defendants, or their agents, from taking further steps to involve French Courts in proceedings which are in breach of this injunction.

2.3 The Claimant's Application for permission to issue and serve out of the jurisdiction of this Honourable Court, the Claim Form, Application Notice and evidence and any Order of this Court.

3. The Claim arises out of the following facts and matters.

The Charterparty – London Arbitration/English Law chosen

4. By a Charterparty dated 21st April 2005 on an amended Syncomex 90 form, the Claimants as Owners of the motor vessel 'STRONGBOW' agreed with Rock Commodities Ltd as Charterers to carry a cargo of 20,000 mt of bagged rice from a safe port, China, to three safe ports, Mediterranean, particulars of which are set out in the Charterparty (which appears at pages 1–10 of 'BS1').

5. The Charterparty contained the following dispute resolution/choice of law clause:

> *'17. Arbitration in London, English Law to apply as per the London Maritime Arbitration Association Rules, including short procedure and form of arbitration clause as suggested in current L.M.A.A. handbook to apply.'*

6. This specific choice of English law and arbitration was a typed amendment to the Charterparty that agreed by the parties and inserted after the deletion of the standard printed clause that would have referred any dispute to arbitration in France before and under the rules of the Chambre Arbitrale Maritime de Paris which was governed by French Law.

The Congen Bills of Lading

7. Pursuant to the terms of the Charterparty, the bagged rice was loaded aboard the vessel at Chiwan, China, on or about the 1st May 2005. Ten Bills of Lading (copies of which appear at pages 11–20 of 'BS1') were issued on the Congen Bill 1994 form signed for and on behalf of the Claimants acknowledging each 1000 mt shipment of cargo.

8. The reverse side (page 1) of the Congen Bill 1994 form (a sample of which appears at page 21 of 'BS1') includes as a 'Condition of Carriage' the following:

> *'All terms and conditions, liberties and exceptions to the Charterparty dated as overleaf, including the Law and Arbitration Clause, are herewith incorporated'*.

9. I believe that all the 10 Bills of Lading issued in respect of the relevant voyage of the STRONGBOW included this Clause. On the face of each of the Bills of Lading it is stated:

'*Charterparty dated 21/04/2005*'.

10. In the circumstances, the Claimant respectfully contends that, as a matter of English law, all disputes arising out of the Bills of Lading contracts are subject to London Arbitration in accordance with the Arbitration Clause of the Charterparty.

The Voyage of the STRONGBOW

11. On or about the 15th May 2005, the vessel sustained damage after an explosion and resulting fire that occurred at sea in the Indian Ocean. The fire was put out and the STRONGBOW proceeded to the Port of Ancona, Italy to discharge the cargo carried under Bill of Lading reference nos SOX1-4. The vessel arrived in port on or about the 30th May 2005.

12. Damage to the cargo was alleged and Mr Stephen Steel of the Claimant's P & I Club, Northern Safety, was contacted by M Victor Hugo of Groupe Concordat of Paris. It is believed that M Hugo and his firm, Groupe Concordat, are insurance brokers and/or claims handlers acting on behalf of various cargo interests, namely cargo underwriters and their insured.

13. After discussions between M Hugo and Mr Steel, it was agreed that the cargo interests would be allowed to send surveyors, including English fire and cargo experts on board the vessel at Ancona to investigate the casualty. However, I am informed by Mr Steel that there was a dispute at Ancona as to the scope of the intended investigation and to date M Hugo has contended that the vessel has not been fully inspected. Details of the dispute as to what happened in Ancona can be seen from correspondence at pages 38–43 of 'BS1'. I reiterate that the Claimants remain willing to co-operate with any proper investigations by the cargo interests.

14. On or about the 10th June 2005, M Hugo requested security for the cargo interest's claims in respect of alleged loss and damage

to cargo. Mr Steel drew M Hugo's attention to the terms of the Bills of Lading incorporating the London Arbitration Clause of the Charterparty, and proposed to M Hugo that the Claimant's Club should provide security in the form of a Letter of Undertaking in respect of any arbitration award in favour of cargo interests in London Arbitration. Mr Steel expressly confirmed that the Claimant's Club remains ready, willing and able to provide security for cargo interests claims by this proposed Letter of Undertaking in respect of an Award in London Arbitration.

15. M Hugo was not satisfied with this and asked for security in a form which indicated that the claims by cargo interests should be litigated in the Paris Commercial Court. Mr Steel refused to sign this and re-iterated the Club's position in correspondence. The relevant correspondence is at pages 22–26 of 'BS1'.

The Defendants Subsequent Actions in France

16. On or about the 22nd June 2005, M Hugo gave notice to Mr Steel and the Club that the cargo interests had obtained an Order from the President of the Tribunal de Commerce de Paris for the appointment of a Court Surveyor.

17. This was an application '*Requete Afin De Designation D'Un Expert Judiciaire*' pursuant to Article 106 of the French Code of Commerce. A copy of the application was attached at pages 27–33 of 'BS1'. I apologise because of the urgency of this application that no full translation has yet been produced. I undertake to provide to the Court as soon a possible a full and completed translation of the same in advance of the resumed hearing of this matter.

18. It appears from this Application to the French Court that the three applicants are all the named Defendants in this application. Their addresses indicate that they are probably domiciled in France, Italy, and Switzerland.

19. Furthermore, the relief that has been obtained from the French Court shows that the appointment of a legal surveyor and supporting experts is for the express purpose of investigating the facts to enable a competent 'court' to determine liability for all and any damage to the entire cargo (when, under the terms of the Arbitration clause, this should be a matter to be determined in London arbitration). This, I respectfully contend can be seen from the final paragraphs of the Application which was put in the following terms:

'C'est pourquoi les requérantes sont bien fondées, Monsieur le Président, en application de l'article 106 du Code de Commerce, à demander qu'il vous plaise désigner tel expert judiciaire qu'il vous plaira avec mission de:

Se rendre à bord du navire dès que possible, et faire toutes constatations entendre tous sachants.

- *Déterminer les circonstances du sinistre, en rechercher les causes et établir celles-ci.*
- *Déterminer le montant des dommages, de tous ordres, subis par la cargaison et ses ayants-droit, chiffrer ces dommages et, le cass ácháant, procéder à toute mesure de sauvetage qui pourrait sa révéler opportune.*
- *Se faire assister, pour accomplir sa mission, par tout sapiteur de son choix, notamment sapiteur nautique, sapiteur feux/explosions.*
- *Rassembler tous les éléments propres à parmettre aux juridictions compétentes de déterminer les responsibilitiés dans la survenance du sinistre et en attributer réparation.*
- *Et du tout, dresser rapport.'*

20. I have been advised by Giles de Laval, a French advocate in Paris, that he believes that the only logical basis for making such an application to the French Court in these circumstances is to try and involve the French Court in the merits of the cargo claims with a view to avoiding London arbitration. Indeed, my clients fear that this application to the French Court is intended to frustrate London arbitral proceedings.

Further contact

21. After the Club received this information, I contacted M Hugo on 24th June 2005 by fax, inviting him to agree to London arbitration on behalf of his clients, and pointing out that this was the contractually chosen forum for any dispute. This fax also gave notice of the Claimant's appointment of Mr Roger Rabbit QC as their arbitrator in respect of each contract. I also invited M Hugo to confirm that the cargo interests would not take any other action other than in London arbitration. As such, I pointed out the appointment of the French Court surveyor was unnecessary and asked for that court appointment to be terminated by agreement. A copy of this letter is at pages 34–35 of 'BS1'.

22. I heard nothing until the 28th June 2005, when I received a short fax in which M Hugo refused to contemplate agreeing to arbitration in London and repeated a request for security in the sum of US$3m for alleged damage to cargo. M Hugo threatened to take 'all steps necessary' by way of 'legal measures' to obtain security. By this I fear both an arrest of STRONGBOW and/or sister vessels of STRONGBOW and/or further court proceedings being taken in France.

This application

23. This application is made as a matter of urgency and without notice to the Defendants because of the risk of vessel arrest(s) taking

place and/or to prevent the French Court becoming further involved in these matters. I respectfully contend that the Claimants have, as a matter of English law, a good arguable case that the arbitration clause in the charterparty is incorporated into the bills of lading and that the Defendants, and each of them, are bound by such clauses. However, I understand from M Laval that French Courts have taken a different view of the question of whether or not a party is bound by a jurisdiction/arbitration clause unless it has been expressly agreed by them (See pages 36–37 of 'BS1'). In such circumstances, there is very considerable doubt as to whether the French Court will properly give effect to these arbitration clauses.

24. I also respectfully contend that England is a proper and convenient forum for such an order. England is the seat of the proposed arbitration and English Law governs the contractual relationship. In the circumstances of this case it is contended that it is just and convenient for such an order to be made at this stage.

Is the Court entitled to grant such relief?

25. As is readily apparent from the Defendant's addresses, all three are I believe domiciled in Brussels Regulation or Lugano Convention Contracting States. I respectfully remind the Court of the decision of the European Court of Justice in *Case C-159/02, Turner v Grovit* [2005] 1 AC 101. However, this application is based upon the submission (upheld in previous English authorities) that the relief sought in this Claim is within the scope of the 'Arbitration' exception to the ambit of both the Council Regulation and the Lugano Convention. In such circumstances this Honourable Court has jurisdiction.

The Current Defendants

26. At this stage the Claimants have not sought to join the Charterers to this application as it is unclear whether or not they have any involvement in the French proceedings. The Claimant's respectfully reserve the right to apply to the Court to join the Charterers, Rock Commodities Ltd, if this proves to be necessary.

Permission to serve out of the jurisdiction

27. Permission to serve the Arbitration Claim form out of the jurisdiction is sought under the provisions of CPR Part 62.16(1). The grounds for which permission are sought is set out above. As already indicated I respectfully contend that the Claimant had a good arguable case and reasonable prospects of success and that English a proper place and convenient forum for the granting of the proposed relief. The addresses of all three Defendants (at which it is intended to serve them) are:

    (a) **EE-AWE GLOBAL INSURANCE,**
    112 Rue Notre Dame des Victoires, 75042, Paris, France

    (b) **A.S.I.E.**
    127 Via Cinque Dicembre 3, 16212, Genoa, Italy

    (c) **COMBINATION TRANSPORTS**
    19 Quai du Mont-Blanc, 12009, Geneva, Switzerland.

28. Translations of the Arbitration Claim Form will be prepared in accordance with CPR Part 6.28.

29. I respectfully ask for the anti-suit injunctive relief on an interim basis.

Signed,

Bill SYKES, etc.

III: ORDER FOR INTERIM INJUNCTION made on a without notice application

HEADING as in Claim Form above

BEFORE MR. JUSTICE FLOGGER

ORDER OF 1st JULY 2005

UPON HEARING Counsel for the Claimant

AND UPON READING the first witness statement of Bill Sykes and its accompanying exhibit 'BS1' dated 28th June 2005

AND UPON the Claimant undertaking by Counsel to:

1. Issue forthwith an Arbitration Claim Form and Application Notices in the form attached and pay the appropriate fees;

2. Notify the Defendants forthwith by fax to M Victor Hugo, of Groupe Concordat, Paris of the Claim Form, the Application Notice, the witness statement and exhibit and this Order and to serve the same on the Defendants as soon as reasonably practicable;

3. Abide by any order this Court may make as to damages in case this Court shall hereafter be of the opinion that the Defendants shall have sustained any by reason of this order which the Claimant ought to pay; and

4. As soon as practicable serve on the Defendants an Application for the return date together with a copy of the witness statement and exhibit containing the evidence relied on by the Claimant.

IT IS ORDERED AND DIRECTED that the Claimant be given permission to issue the Claim Form and Application Notice and to serve the Arbitration Claim Form, Application Notice, witness statement and exhibit and Order in the form attached out of the jurisdiction on the Defendants at the addresses set out in the Claim Form or elsewhere where the Defendants can be found.

AND THAT the Defendants whether by themselves, their servants or agents, or howsoever otherwise be restrained in respect of all or any claims against the Claimant arising out of or in connection with the bills of lading ('the Bills of Lading') or any of them, issued by the Claimant pursuant to a charterparty in writing dated 21st April 2005 and made between the Claimant as Owners and Rock Commodities of Sunshine City, Venezula as Charterers of the Claimant's vessel 'STRONGBOW' and in respect of a cargo of bagged rice shipped by or about May 2005 at Chiwan, People's Republic of China, aboard the Claimant's said vessel, the First to Third Defendants be restrained, and an injunction is hereby granted restraining them, until final trial herein, whether by themselves, their servants or agents, or howsoever otherwise, from:

(1) Continuing or prosecuting or taking any further steps in or assisting in the continuation or prosecution or taking of further steps in or otherwise participating in any legal proceedings before the Tribunal de Commerce de Paris, Palais du Justice, Paris, France, against the Claimant;

(2) Commencing any further or other proceedings as against the Claimant in any Court or Tribunal wherever situated, other than before a London arbitration tribunal constituted in accordance with the arbitration clause incorporated into the Bills of Lading or some one or more of them.

AND THAT there be a further hearing of the Claimant's Application Notice on

Claimant to provide a realistic time estimate by …. July 20054.

AND THAT the Defendants be at liberty meanwhile to apply to set aside this order by giving at least 24-hour notice to the Claimant's solicitors, Sykes & Crykes, telephone number 44 207 555 4454, or out of hours care of Mr Bill Sykes on 44 208 993 1298.

AND THAT the costs of and occasioned by this application be reserved.

IV: DEFENDANT'S STATEMENT IN RESPONSE

[Heading as above]

First Witness Statement of **FERGAL FEARLESS**
For the Defendants
Dated 21st July 2005

I, **Fergal Fearless**, Solicitor of the Supreme Court of England and Wales, of 10 Houndsworth Close, London EC3A 70R, state as follows:

1. I am a Partner in the firm of Fearless and Smart of the above address, Solicitors for the Defendants. I have the conduct of this matter on behalf of the Defendants and am duly authorised by them to make this Witness Statement. Save as where indicated or apparent from the context, the facts and matters stated herein are based on documents and instructions received by me from M Victor Hugo, of Groupe Concordat, Paris, who is instructed as a loss adjuster on behalf of the Defendant cargo interests. Copies of documents that I refer to in this Witness Statement are exhibited in a paginated bundle marked '*FF1*'.

2. I make this application in response to the anti-suit injunction made by the Honourable Mr Justice Flogger on 1st July 2005 2000 and

in answer to the first witness statement of Mr Bill Sykes dated 28th June 2005.

3. On behalf of the Defendants, it is contended that the Order of 1st July 2005 should be discharged and the relief sought in the Claimant's Arbitration Claim form should be refused. The Defendants will contend that:

   3.1 This Honourable Court has no jurisdiction to make the order sought; and/or

   3.2 If the jurisdiction exists, then it should not be exercised as a matter of the exercise of this Honourable Court's discretion, and/or

   3.3 Leave to serve the proceedings out of the jurisdiction should be set aside; and/or

   3.4 There are no proper grounds for the granting of the relief sought in the Arbitration Claim form, and this should be refused.

The Defendants

4. As Mr Sykes accepts all the Defendants are domiciled in Brussels Regulation and/or Lugano Convention countries. All are entitled not to be sued in countries other than their domicile unless there are proper grounds under either the Regulation or the Lugano Convention for doing so.

Damage to the Cargo

5. Contrary to what Mr Sykes contends in paragraph 12 of his First Witness Statement that '*damage to the cargo has been alleged*', the Defendants respectfully contend that it is clear beyond doubt

that the cargo of Chinese rice has been extensively damaged. This has been confirmed both by independent experts and by the Claimant's Master himself: see the correspondence at pages 1–10 of 'FF1'.

6. However, the suspicions of the Defendants arose because no notification was given until some 17 days after the fire occurred, and then only shortly before the vessel arrived in Italy. The Defendants were naturally anxious to have the damage to the cargo examined for damage and the cause of the explosion properly investigated. It appears that the Claimant might already have used the time when they had not provided information on the explosion to put their own 'rice experts' 'on the spot' in Italy where the arrival of the Vessel was imminent.

7. Hugo's firm was instructed on behalf of the Defendants, who gave instructions for various experts to attend. However, when they arrived in Italy, there were problems obtaining access and in conducting the investigations that they wished to perform. The substance of this dispute is set out at correspondence at pages 11–25 of 'FF1'. The Defendants maintain that they have not been given proper access to the vessel, and are anxious to do so as it appears that repairs are already underway that might well disguise the true cause of the explosion on the vessel.

The Order of the French Court

8. As a result of the impasse that appeared to arise between the parties, M Hugo sought an order of the French Court for the appointment of experts.

9. I have discussed the legal position in France with Professor Pierre Boulangerie, Professor of Marine Law at the Sorbonne, and a very experienced French Marine Lawyer of international reputation.

10. Professor Boulangerie informs me that the obtaining of a court order in France appointing and sanctioning the use of an expert to establish and preserve evidence is extremely common and is crucial in a case such as this where there has been substantial damage to perishable cargo. Under French law, any legally admissible measures of investigation may be ordered at the request of any interested party, by *ex parte* request or *référé*, pursuant to Article 145 of the French New Code of Civil Procedure. These are not 'substantive' proceedings, and are not regarded as such by the French Courts. Indeed, it is perfectly acceptable for such a procedure to be adopted in support of foreign proceedings and indeed arbitration.

11. Professor Boulangerie pointed out that the French Courts naturally apply the provisions of the Brussels Regulation and Lugano Conventions when appropriate. However, the Claimant owner is a Bulgarian entity not domiciled within Convention territory. Accordingly, the competence of the French Court over the Claimant is governed by Article 14 of the French Civil Code which provides that '*...a foreigner, even one not resident in France, may be summoned before the French courts . . . for the obligations contracted by him in a foreign country towards French people*'. That entitled the Paris Court to make the procedural order that they did make.

12. Professor Boulangerie suggests that, with respect, the connection with France is (as least as great) as the connection with England which is apparently based on the interests of insurance interests.

13. Thus, at this stage, there can be no proper suggestion that the Defendants have acted in breach of contract by seeking this Order. There is thus no proper basis for seeking the relief that the Claimants have sought and obtained.

No jurisdiction in any event

14. In any event, the Defendants contend that this Honourable Court has no jurisdiction to make orders or make declarations of the kind sought in this claim over Defendants domiciled in Brussels Regulation and/or Lugano Convention States. The relief sought does not fall within the '*Arbitration*' exception to those Conventions. Accordingly, the Defendants are entitled to the protection of the respective Regulation and / or Convention and have to be sued in their own states of domicile.

15. The last time this issue was before the Court of Appeal in *Toepfer International GmbH v Cargill France SA* [1998] 1 Lloyd's Rep 379, it was decided that the issues of jurisdiction were not clear and referred the question to the European Court of Justice, namely:

> '*1. Does the exception in art. 1.4 of the Brussels Convention extend to proceedings commenced before the English Courts seeking: (a) a declaration that the commencement and continuation of proceedings before a French Court constitutes a breach of an arbitration agreement; (b) an injunction restraining the appellants from continuing the proceedings before the French Court, or instituting any further proceedings before any other Court, in breach of the arbitration agreement?*'

16. That case was settled and there has been no ruling on the question from the European Court of Justice. There is manifestly no material distinction between this case and the *Toepfer International GmbH v Cargill France SA* on the jurisdiction question under the Regulation/Convention. The material difference is that there are even fewer grounds for the exercise of

the Court's power (if jurisdiction existed) than in that case. In the light of the recent decisions of the European Court of Justice, it will be contended that the matter needs to be looked at afresh.

Discretion

17. If such a power existed, then the Defendants contend that it should not be exercised as a matter of discretion. It is, with respect, not only an affront to the comity principles of the EEA but also manifestly unnecessary on the facts where no substantive proceedings have been commenced, and in the light of the existence of the 1958 New York Convention.

The Attitude of the French Court System to Anti-Suit Injunctions

18. Professor Boulangerie informs me that the concept of an anti-suit injunction is unknown in France:

'The position in French law on this point is totally the opposite of that under English law. The latter accepts the possibility of the judge granting an injunction to stop proceedings started abroad while there is no such possibility under French law which would regard such an intervention as an intrusion in the functioning of the foreign legal system.'

19. Professor Boulangerie is of the opinion that the imposition of an anti-suit injunction by an English Court is a grossly offensive intrusion of its own functioning. This is particularly so in the case of international arbitration where French Courts have a long-standing adherence to the provisions of the 1958 New York Convention.

The New York Convention

20. France is a party to the New York Convention 1958, which entered into force in France on 24th September 1959. Indeed, France was

among the first countries to place the New York Convention in force.

21. French Law follows the letter and spirit of the New York Convention. For example, Article II.3 of the New York Convention provides:

'The court of a Contracting State, when seized of an action in a matter in respect of which the parties have made an agreement within the meaning of this article, shall, at the request of one of the parties, refer the parties to arbitration, unless it finds that the said agreement is null and void, inoperative or incapable of being performed'.

22. Article II.3 and its requirements are found in French Law by Article 1458 of the New Code of Civil Procedure. Article 1458 applies to both domestic and international arbitration as laid down by the décret of 12 May 1981 (which was the equivalent of s. 1 of the English Arbitration Act 1975). Article 1458 states:

'When a dispute, of which an arbitration tribunal is seised by virtue of an arbitration clause, is referred to a State Court, the latter must declare itself incompetent. If the arbitration tribunal has not yet been seised, the court must equally refuse competence unless the arbitration agreement is patently null and void. In both cases, the court cannot raise incompetence of its own motion.'

23. Accordingly, if any substantive proceedings were brought in France, it is open for the Claimants to ask the French Court to decline jurisdiction under Article 1458. That is a proper remedy that reflects international comity concerns rather than the grant of anti-suit relief.

24. In the circumstances, I respectfully ask that the Orders of 1st July 2005 be discharged, leave to serve out of the jurisdiction be set aside and no relief granted on the Claimant's Arbitration Claim Form.

25. I believe the facts stated in this Witness Statement to be true.

[Statement of Truth, etc][1]

1 Statement of truth, etc as set out in **Chapter 3, para 3.2**.

CHAPTER 15

Search and Freezing Orders

Chirag Karia
Jo Cunningham

FREEZING INJUNCTIONS

The freezing injunction as a remedy

15.1 Although the remedy of freezing another's assets originated as a judicial innovation to assist in the administration of justice[1], it now has statutory recognition by s 37(3) of the Supreme Court Act 1981. Freezing injunctions (formerly known as Mareva injunctions) are now governed largely by CPR 25, which deals with interim remedies and security for costs. CPR 25.1(f) empowers the court to issue an injunction to restrain a party from removing from the jurisdiction, assets located there or to restrain a party from dealing with any assets whether those assets are located within the jurisdiction or not, the latter being known as a 'worldwide freezing injunction'.

The function of the freezing injunction is to prevent the defendant or prospective defendant from frustrating justice by dissipating his assets so as to avoid the enforcement of any judgment against him. However, given the draconian nature of the relief, the court will require good proof of a real risk of dissipation before granting the order sought.

Applications for a freezing injunction must ordinarily be made in the High Court, since the County Court does not have jurisdiction to make such orders[2], unless the application is made to a specialist court sitting within the County Court, such as the Mercantile List, or unless the purpose of the order is to preserve or detain property which is the subject of the proceedings or to aid execution of a judgment[3].

To obtain a freezing injunction, the applicant must demonstrate to the court that:

(i) it has a legal or equitable right against the respondent;
(ii) the English court has jurisdiction over the claim or s 25 of the Civil Jurisdiction and Judgments Act 1982 applies;
(iii) it has a good arguable claim against the respondent;
(iv) the respondent has assets within or outside the jurisdiction;
(v) there is a real risk that those assets may be dissipated so as to render any judgment in the applicant's favour unenforceable;
(vi) it can provide an enforceable undertaking in damages; and
(vii) it is just and convenient in all the circumstances to grant the injunction sought[4].

Obviously, where there is a real risk of dissipation, the prospective claimant does not want to put the prospective defendant on notice of his intention to obtain judgment against him by issuing proceedings and then seeking a freezing injunction. For this reason, the application can be, and usually is, made before the commencement of litigation[5], even if the litigation is intended to take place in a foreign jurisdiction[6].

1 *Nippon Yusen Kaisha v Karageorgis* [1975] 2 Lloyd's Rep 137 (CA); *Mareva Compania Naviera SA v International Bulkcarriers SA* [1975] 2 Lloyd's Rep 509 (CA).
2 County Court Remedies Regulations 1991.
3 County Court Remedies Regulations 1991, reg 3(3).
4 Goldrein, *Commercial Litigation: Pre-Emptive Remedies* (4th edn, 2003), paras A2-098–A2-099.
5 CPR 25.2(b) allows this, provided 'the matter is urgent' or 'it is otherwise necessary to do so in the interests of justice'.
6 Civil Jurisdiction and Judgments Act 1982, s 25; CPR 25.4.

Special rules concerning without notice applications

15.2 For the same reason, the application will also generally be made without notice[1] although the reasons why the application is without notice should still be expressly stated in the filed written evidence[2]. However, in those unusual cases where there is no need to proceed without notice, the applicant must make the application on notice. A freezing injunction granted on a without notice application is liable to be discharged if the applicant was not justified in proceeding without notice[3].

When making an application without notice, the applicant must demonstrate the utmost good faith and must make full, fair and accurate disclosure of all material information to the court and must draw the court's attention to all significant factual, legal and procedural aspects of the case. A skeleton argument and a draft order must be lodged with the court prior to the oral hearing[4]. The applicant must make proper inquiries before making the application, as its duty of disclosure applies not only to material facts known to it but also to any additional facts which it would have known if it had made such inquiries. The court, and not the applicant or its legal advisors, is the ultimate judge of what information is material and should have been disclosed[5]. The applicant must identify the crucial points for *and against* its application, and must point out any likely defences that the absent defendant might assert. In short, the applicant must disclose all facts that a judge could reasonably take into account in deciding whether or not to grant the application[6].

A failure by the applicant to make full and fair disclosure of all material facts that it knows or ought reasonably to have discovered will generally lead to the immediate discharge of the *ex parte* order obtained 'without examination of the merits', though the court has a discretion not to discharge the order despite the material non-disclosure. The fact that the non-disclosure was innocent, in the sense that the applicant either did not know the information or did not appreciate its relevance, though an important consideration, will not necessarily prevent the court from discharging the *ex parte* order[7]. Given the severity of the sanction for material non-disclosure, the applicant's lawyers would be well advised to resolve all doubts about materiality in favour of disclosure.

1 The applicant must demonstrate 'good reasons for not giving notice': CPR 25.3(1).
2 CPR 25.3(3) and 25 PD3.4.
3 *The P* [1992] 1 Lloyd's Rep 470 (Evans J).
4 *Memory Corporation plc v Sidhu (No. 2)* [2001] 1 WLR 1443 (CA).
5 *Brink's Mat Ltd v Elcombe* [1988] 1 WLR 1350 (CA).
6 *Siporex Trade SA v Comdel Commodities Ltd* [1986] 2 Lloyd's Rep 428, (Bingham J).
7 *Brink's Mat Ltd v Elcombe* [1988] 1 WLR 1350 (CA).

The applicable procedure

15.3 The application for a freezing injunction is generally made on Form N224 and a sworn affidavit must be served in support of the application[1]. The application should also be accompanied by a draft of the order sought. Pro-forma freezing injunction orders are set out in the Annex to the Practice Direction – Interim Injunctions supplementing CPR Part 25 and in Appendix 5 to *The Admiralty & Commercial Courts Guide.*

Importantly, the pro-forma order does not put a total freeze on the respondent's assets and some allowance is made at para 11 of the Order for reasonable or ordinary living and trading expenses and for legal costs. This caveat enables the respondent to pursue legitimate activities, whilst preventing him from deliberately dissipating his assets.

Finally, the court will also require the applicant to give at least some of the undertakings contained in Sch B to the Order.

Upon granting the freezing injunction, the court will set a return date at which the respondent will be able to argue that the injunction should be discharged or varied. In considering any such application, the court will generally give considerable weight to any failures by the applicant to give full and frank disclosure at the time that the order was sought.

The order will cease to have effect if, on application by the respondent, the court so orders, or if the respondent pays into court sufficient security[2]. In any event, the injunction will cease to have effect upon the entry of judgment. Accordingly, upon entry of judgment, the claimant/applicant should take steps to ensure that a further order is sought continuing the injunction until he is able to effectively enforce the judgment.

1 CPR 25 PD3.1; CPR 32 PD1.4(2).
2 See para 11(4) of the Pro Forma Order.

Committal for wilful breach of the injunction

15.4 The pro-forma freezing injunction order contains a penal notice and should the respondent fail to comply with the terms of the order, the applicant may apply to the court for the respondent to be fined or to be imprisoned for his contempt[1], provided that the applicant can demonstrate beyond reasonable doubt a deliberate or wilful breach of the order by the respondent[2].

An application to commit the respondent for contempt must comply with the detailed provisions contained in RSC O.52 and the accompanying Practice Direction. Where the application is made to a Divisional Court, permission to apply must first be obtained[3]. In the context of non-compliance with a freezing order, the application will be made by way of an application notice stating that the application is being made in the context of the ongoing proceedings[4]. The application notice must state the grounds upon which the committal is sought and contain a prominent notice stating the possible consequences of the court making a committal order[5]. A form of notice that can be used on the application notice is annexed to O.52[6]. The application must also be supported by an affidavit[7]. Finally, the application together with the supporting documents must be served personally upon the respondent[8], although the court does have power to dispense with service altogether in certain circumstances.

The hearing will not generally take place less than 14 days after service of the application, unless the court otherwise directs[9]. O.52 PD52.10 recognises the court's power to waive any procedural defects in the commencement or conduct of a committal application, however, given the seriousness of the application, care should be taken to ensure that the correct procedure is followed.

1 RSC O.45.
2 *Deborah Building Equipment v Scaffco* The Times 5 November 1986 and O.52 PD1.4
3 O. 52.2.
4 O.52 PD2.2(2) and (3).
5 O.52 PD2.6.
6 This notice is reproduced in the Application Notice to Commit for Contempt below.
7 O.52 PD3.
8 O.52 PD2.6.
9 O.52 PD52.4.

SEARCH ORDERS

15.5 Section 7 of the Civil Procedure Act 1997 provides the statutory basis by which a party may apply for a search order (formerly known as an 'Anton Piller order'[1]) requiring the respondent to admit the applicant to his premises for the purpose of preserving evidence. The search order is a form of interim relief expressly recognised by CPR 25.1(h) and the application for a search order should be made in accordance with CPR 25.

Pro-forma search orders are set out in the Annex to the Practice Direction – Interim Injunctions supplementing CPR Part 25 and in Appendix 5 to *The Admiralty & Commercial Courts Guide*.

In common with the application for a freezing injunction, the application for a search order can, and usually will, be made before the commencement of proceedings and without notice to the respondent. Obviously, to put the respondent on notice of the application would defeat the purpose of surprising the respondent before he disposes of the relevant evidence. All the principles discussed above in relation to without notice applications for a freezing injunction apply equally for a without notice application for a search order.

An application for a search order must be supported by affidavit evidence[2] disclosing: the address of the premises to be searched; whether those premises are private or business in nature; the reason the search order is sought; and the probability that the relevant material might disappear if the order is not granted[3]. To obtain a search order, the applicant must demonstrate to the court that:

(i) it has an extremely strong prima facie case on the merits;
(ii) the respondent's activities have caused or are likely to cause serious harm to the applicant's interests;
(iii) there is clear evidence that incriminating documents or materials are in the respondent's possession;
(iv) there is a real possibility that those items may be destroyed before any application on notice can be made; and
(v) the harm likely to be caused to the respondent and his business by the execution of the search order will not be excessive or out of proportion to the order's legitimate objective[4].

The brief summary set out above is only intended to provide general practical outline of a few of the issues that need to be considered in relation to freezing injunctions and search orders. It is not intended to be a complete account of the applicable law. For a fuller account, the reader should consult the standard reference books, such as Gee *Commercial Injunctions* (5th edn, 2004) and Goldrein *Commercial Litigation: Pre-Emptive Remedies* (4th edn, 2003), and the latest versions of *CPR Part 25* and the *Practice Direction to Part 25*.

1 From Anton Piller *KG v Manufacturing Processes Ltd* [1976] Ch 55 (CA).
2 CPR 25 PD3.1; CPR 32 PD1.4(2).
3 CPR 25 PD7.3.
4 Goldrein, *Commercial Litigation: Pre-Emptive Remedies* (4th edn, 2003), paras A3-006–A3-007.

Pleading

Assumed facts

15.6 Mr Smith's yacht LADY II was insured under a policy of insurance underwritten by Insurers UK. In April 2004, Mr Smith made a claim under the insurance policy in respect of his yacht, which he claimed had been stolen. Insurers UK paid out £200,000 under the policy. Later, in July 2004, unbeknown to Mr Smith, Insurers UK discovered that LADY II was being stored by Mr Smith in a local boatyard, the Super Yacht Club. Mr Brown of the Super Yacht Club has sought to assist Insurers UK in providing documents relating to LADY II, however, whilst Mr Brown is certain that there is a storage agreement signed by Mr Smith in April 2004, he is unable to find a copy but is certain that Mr Smith will have a copy. Mr Brown has also been able to confirm that the storage has to date been paid by cheque drawn on an account of Mr Smith held with the British Bank plc.

Having investigated Mr Smith's background further, it has now come to light that Mr Smith also has a criminal conviction for fraud, for which he spent time in prison in 1998. This is in stark contrast to his answer on the proposal form completed in 2003, where he stated that he had no previous criminal convictions.

Insurers UK wishes to bring proceedings against Mr Smith to recover the monies which it has paid to Mr Smith. However, it is concerned that in the light of his fraudulent activities, he might dissipate his assets in order to avoid the enforcement of any judgment that might be entered against him. Insurers UK has therefore, sought to issue an application to freeze his assets in England and Wales.

Insurers UK also wishes to obtain a search order against Mr Smith because it believes that he will, if given the opportunity, destroy the contract of storage and deny all knowledge of the whereabouts of the yacht and of the storage arrangements made in respect of LADY II.

Note that whilst the application for a freezing and search order would in these circumstances be made jointly, for illustration purposes the two applications will be drafted separately. Also note the change in the parties from applicant/respondent to claimant/defendant, after the assumed issue of the claim form and commencement of proceedings.

Application for Freezing Injunction

Application Notice N244

The Applicant, Insurers UK

Intends to apply for an order (a draft of which is attached) pursuant to CPR Rule 25(1)(f), that the Respondent Barry John Smith be restrained from dealing with his assets located within the jurisdiction.

Because there is a real and significant risk that if the order is not granted, the Respondent will dissipate his assets.

Affidavit in Support of Application for Freezing Injunction

Affidavit on behalf of the Applicant
Peter Jones
1st Affidavit
Exhibit PJ1
Sworn on the [date]

Claim No ....

IN THE HIGH COURT OF JUSTICE
QUEEN'S BENCH DIVISION
COMMERCIAL COURT

B E T W E E N:

INSURERS UK

Applicant/Claimant

- and -

BARRY JOHN SMITH

Respondent/Defendant

AFFIDAVIT OF PETER JONES

I, **PETER JONES**, of 1 High Street, London EC1M 4AA, will say as follows.

1. I am a Solicitor of the Supreme Court and a partner in the firm of Jones and Jones of the above address, Solicitors for the Claimant and the Applicant in this matter. I am duly authorised by the Applicant to make this Affidavit on its behalf.

2. All facts and matters in this statement are from my own knowledge or, where specified, are derived from my review of the documents

exhibited hereto and/or from the instructions or information I have received from Mr Roy Brown of the Super Yacht Club and Mr Lee of London Investigations Ltd. Where the facts are within my knowledge, they are true. Where they are not within my knowledge, they are true to the best of my information and belief.

3. There is now shown to me a bundle of copy documents. the contents of which are true to the best of my knowledge and belief and marked exhibit 'PJ1'. References in this statement to, for example (**tab 1, page 1**), are references to the tabs and pages within 'PJ1'.

THE RELIEF SOUGHT

4. This statement is made in support of the Claimant's application pursuant to CPR part 25 for a freezing order over the Respondent's assets within the jurisdiction namely:

   4.1 the vessel known as 'LADY II' with hull identification no. 4567;

   4.2 the property known as 123 Low Road, London N14;

   4.3 any bank account held solely or jointly in the name of the Respondent at British Bank plc.

PAYMENT UNDER POLICY NO. GEN-99-43194

5. On 4th June 2003, the Respondent completed a standard Brokers United proposal form to obtain insurance for his vessel, 'LADY II' ('the Vessel') in the sum of £175,000. On that form, in response to the question 'have you or anyone who will be in charge of the vessel been convicted of a criminal offence?', the Respondent answered 'no' (**tab 1, page 1**). An insurance policy was effected by the Applicant and allocated a policy number XYZ ('the policy'). The insurance was effective for a period of 12 months commencing 10th June 2003.

6. On 28th April 2004, the Respondent made a claim under the policy for £175,000. In completing the Brokers United standard claim form, the Respondent stated that the Vessel and its contents had been stolen from outside his premises on the night of 26th April 2004. The Respondent further represented that a full search for the Vessel had been made, but without success. The alleged theft had also been reported to the police and a crime number: ABC007 had been allocated to the incident. The claim form was signed by the Respondent (**tab 3, pages 5 and 6**).

7. On 9th June 2004, Brokers United, sent to the Respondent a cheque, No. 004171, drawn on their account in the sum of £175,000 and made payable to the Respondent (**tab 4, pages 7–9**). On 15th June 2004, the cheque cleared (**tab 4, page 11**). In turn, the Applicant accounted to Brokers United for the £175,000 paid to the Respondent (**tab 4, pages 12–15**).

THE MISSING VESSEL

8. Mr Brown of Super Yacht Club states (**tab 6, page 5**), that the Respondent became a member of the Super Yacht Club on 1st March 2004. In or about the first week of April 2004, the Respondent telephoned Mr Brown to inquire whether or not it would be possible to store his vessel at the Super Yacht Club since the marina where he had previously berthed her was too far away. Mr Brown's recollection of this conversation and of subsequent events are set out in his statement.

9. The boat apparently arrived at the Super Yacht Club on 26th April 2004 (**tab 6, page 17**). Invoices were tendered by the Super Yacht Club on a monthly basis commencing 1 May 2004 (**tab 6, pages 18–20**). Payment was made by the Respondent by cheques which Mr Brown's records show were all drawn on a bank account in the

name of the Respondent and held with the British Bank plc. Unfortunately, Mr Brown is unable to locate any further records which would identify the number of the account on which the cheques were drawn (**tab 6 page 21**).

10. I am advised and believe that the vessel stored by the Respondent at the Super Yacht Club is the same vessel as that which the Respondent reported as stolen and in respect of which the claim was made in April 2004. I refer to a letter dated 9th July 2004 in which Mr Lee confirms how he came to find the Vessel at the Super Yacht Club and how it is the same vessel as that said to have been stolen in April 2004 (**tab 7, page 22**). I also refer to photographs taken at the time by Mr Lee, which clearly demonstrate that the vessel being stored bears the name LADY II and has a hull identification number No. 4567 (**tab 8, page 23**). I refer to the proposal form completed by Mr Smith in June 2003 which clearly states the Vessel's particulars, including her name LADY II and hull identification No. 4567.

RESPONDENT'S DISHONEST CONDUCT

11. Since the discovery of the Vessel on 7th July 2004, my firm has conducted further investigations into the Respondent's background and I now believe that the representation made by the Respondent on the proposal form in June 2003, namely that he had no criminal convictions, is untrue. Mary Brown of this firm made inquiries of Southwark Crown Court and received from them a certificate of conviction which certifies that the Respondent was convicted of fraud in 1998 and was sentenced to six months imprisonment (**tab 10, page 31**).

RESPONDENT'S ASSETS

12. As a result of discussions with Mr Brown of the Super Yacht Club, it has come to the Applicant's attention that the Respondent

appears to have operated bank accounts with the British Bank plc although I do not know the account numbers or whether the accounts are still operational.

13. A land registry search has also indicated that the property known as 123 Low Road, London N14 is owned by the Respondent and a Mrs June Smith, whom I assume to be his wife (**tab 12, page 35**). In addition, the Vessel remains in the custody of the Super Yacht Club.

POTENTIAL DISSIPATION OF ASSETS BY THE RESPONDENT

14. I believe that there is a significant risk that the Respondent will act dishonestly and will dissipate his assets in order to impede the enforcement of a judgment against him, should a freezing injunction not be granted. I base my belief on the following:

    14.1 The Respondent has a criminal record evidencing dishonest behaviour. He was convicted of a count of fraud in 1998 for which he received a six-month custodial sentence;

    14.2 The Respondent lied about his criminal record on the proposal form in order to obtain insurance;

    14.3 The Respondent fraudulently induced the Applicant to pay to him, the sum of £175,000 on the basis of a false theft claim, as set out in this Affidavit.

APPLICANT'S CLAIM AGAINST THE RESPONDENT

15. The Applicant intends to bring an action against the Respondent to recover the monies paid over to him. The Applicant is entitled to recover the monies from the Respondent either on the basis that they were paid pursuant to a fraud committed on the Applicant or alternatively, by avoiding the policy of insurance for misrepresentation or material non-disclosure.

16. In addition to £175,000 paid to the Respondent in satisfaction of his insurance claim, the Applicant has also suffered consequential losses including the costs of the investigation, which it will seek to recover. As such, the Respondent's liability to the Applicant is likely to be in the region of about £225,000 plus costs.

THE PRESENT APPLICATION

17. This application is made pursuant to CPR part 25 and is made without notice to the Respondent because I believe that the Respondent would take steps to dissipate his assets if he became aware of this application.

18. The Applicant is prepared to give a cross-undertaking in damages and will undertake to serve a Claim Form and Particulars of Claim upon the Defendants as soon as practicable. The Applicant is a substantial publicly traded UK insurance company and, I believe, has the means to satisfy that undertaking.

19. For the reasons which I have set out above, I seek the relief sought in the draft order attached to the Application Notice.

Sworn by : ....

Peter Jones

Sworn at : ....

....

....

....

This day of

Before me : ....

Qualification : ....

This Affidavit is filed on behalf of the Applicant.

Application to Vary the Freezing Order

The Respondent

Intends to apply for an order (a draft of which is attached) that paragraph 11(1) of the Order of Mr Justice Judge dated .... be varied so as to permit the Respondent to spend £350.00 per week towards his ordinary living expenses.

Because the Respondent's reasonable weekly living expenses exceed the sum £175.00 provided for in paragraph 11(1) of the Order.

Witness Statement in Support

Statement on behalf of the Defendant
Barry John Smith
1st statement
Exhibit BJS1
[date]

Claim No ....

IN THE HIGH COURT OF JUSTICE
QUEEN'S BENCH DIVISION
COMMERCIAL COURT

B E T W E E N:

INSURERS UK

Applicant/Claimant

- and -

BARRY JOHN SMITH

Respondent/Defendant

WITNESS STATEMENT OF BARRY JOHN SMITH

I BARRY JOHN SMITH of 123 Low Road, London N14 will say as follows.

1. I am a Director of Smiths Enterprises Limited and am the Respondent in the matter. The above address is my home

address. I make this statement in support of my application to vary the Order of Mr Justice Judge dated 12th July 2004 ('the Order').

2. All facts and matters in this statement are from my own knowledge or, where specified, are derived from my review of the documents exhibited hereto. Where the facts are within my knowledge, they are true. Where they are not within my knowledge, they are true to the best of my information and belief.

3. There is now shown to me a bundle of copy documents. the contents of which are true to the best of my knowledge and belief and marked exhibit 'BJS1'. References in this statement to, for example (**tab 1, page 1**), are references to the tabs and pages within 'BJS1'.

4. I refer to the Order and in particular to paragraph 11(1), which provides (**tab 1, page 4**):

   '11(1) This order does not prohibit the Respondent from spending £175.00 a week towards his ordinary living expenses and also a reasonable sum on legal advice and representation. But before spending any money the Respondent must tell the Applicant's legal representatives where the money is to come from.'

5. As can be seen from the table which I have compiled and attached hereto (**tab 2, page 9**), my weekly living expenses far exceed £175.00 and are much closer to £350.00. In particular, the monthly mortgage repayment on 123 Low Road, London N14 is approximately £900.00 per month as can be seen by the mortgage statement issued by The Mortgage Company Limited (**tab 3, page 11**). The present allowance of £175.00 per week will not enable me to keep up repayments on the mortgage of 123 Low Road. If, which I do not accept, the Applicant is entitled to judgment against me, it is clearly in the Applicant's interest that I maintain the

mortgage repayments so as to provide security against which any judgment might, in due course, be enforced against the property.

6. In addition to the mortgage repayments, I have calculated my ordinary living expenses which include an allowance for utilities, for food and general groceries and for clothing for both my wife and myself. I attach hereto the utilities bills for 123 Low Road over the last 12 months (**tab 4, pages 15–27**), which I have used to arrive at the figures in my table (**tab 2**). I do not have any children and no allowance need be made for school fees, etc.

7. As regards income, I receive a monthly salary of £4,110.17 net of tax. I attach hereto, pay slips from Smiths Enterprises Limited dating from January 2004 to date (**tab 5, pages 30–37**).

8. The figure in the table produced at **tab 2**, shows a weekly figure of £309.27. I respectfully ask the Court to vary the figure in paragraph 11(1) Order to £350.00 so as to permit me some flexibility to enable me to pay additional and irregular expenses such as minor repairs to 123 Low Road, without recourse to the Court on each occasion.

I believe that the facts contained in this witness statement are true.

Signed: ....

Application to Commit the Defendant for Contempt

Application Notice N244

The Claimant

Intends to apply for an order in these proceedings, for the committal of the Defendant pursuant to RSC Order 45, r 5(1)(a).

Because the Defendant has failed to comply with paragraph 9(1) of the Order of Mr Justice Judge dated 12th July 2004, which was endorsed with a penal notice addressed to the Defendant. The Defendant has failed to comply with paragraph 9(1) in that it required him to provide within 48 hours of service an affidavit disclosing details of his assets. The Order was served personally on the Defendant on 12th July 2004, the deadline of 48 hours has now passed and the Defendant has not served an affidavit.

IMPORTANT NOTICE The Court has the power to send you to prison and to fine you if it finds that any of the allegations made against you are true and amount to contempt of court. You must attend court on the date shown on the front of this form. It is in your own interest to do so. You should bring with you any witnesses and documents which you think will help you put your side of the case. If you consider the allegations are not true you must tell the court why. If it is established that they are true, you must tell the court of any good reason why they do not amount to a contempt of court, or, if they do, why you should not be punished. If you need advice you should show this document at once to your solicitor or go to a Citizens' Advice Bureau.

Affidavit in Support of Application to Commit the Defendant for Contempt

Affidavit on behalf of the Claimant
Mary Brown
1st Affidavit
Exhibit MB1
Sworn on [date]

Claim No ....

IN THE HIGH COURT OF JUSTICE
QUEEN'S BENCH DIVISION
COMMERCIAL COURT

B E T W E E N:

INSURERS UK

Applicant/Claimant

- and -

BARRY JOHN SMITH

Respondent/Defendant

AFFIDAVIT OF MARY BROWN

I, **MARY BROWN**, of 1 High Street, London EC1M 4AA, will say as follows.

1. I am a Solicitor of the Supreme Court and am employed by Jones and Jones of the above address, Solicitors for the Claimant and the Applicant in this matter. I have the conduct of this matter under

the supervision of Peter Jones, a partner in the firm of Jones and Jones and I am duly authorised by the Claimant to make this Affidavit on its behalf.

2. All facts and matters in this statement are from my own knowledge or, where specified, are derived from my review of the documents exhibited hereto and/or from the instructions or information I have received from Bob Speed of Speedy Deliveries Limited. Where the facts are within my knowledge, they are true. Where they are not within my knowledge, they are true to the best of my information and belief.

3. There is now shown to me a bundle of copy documents, the contents of which are true to the best of my knowledge and belief, marked exhibit 'MB1'. References in this statement to, for example (**tab 1, page 1**), are references to the tabs and pages within 'MB1'.

4. This Affidavit is made in support of the Claimant's application made pursuant to RSC Order 45, r. 5(1)(a) and in accordance with RSC Order 52 to seek the committal of the Defendant for breach of the Order of Mr Justice Judge dated 12th July 2004 ('the Order').

5. The Order was granted pursuant to an application made by the Claimant dated 12th July 2004 which was supported by the Affidavit of Peter Jones and the exhibit thereto, dated the same. The Order was endorsed with a penal notice addressed to the Defendant (**tab 1, page 1**).

6. Upon the Order having been sealed, I instructed Bob Speed of Speedy Services Limited to serve the Order together with a copy of the Affidavit of Peter Jones and its exhibit and a copy of the Application Notice dated 12th July 2003, personally upon the Defendant at his home address 123 Low Road, London N14.

7. At about 10:00 hrs on 13th July 2004, Mr Speed attended 123 Low Road and served the aforementioned documents on the Defendant in person. Service of the documents is evidenced by way of an Affidavit of Mr Speed sworn on 13th July 2004 (**tab 2, page 8**).

8. The Order provided at paragraph 9:

   '(1) Unless paragraph 2 applies, the Respondent must within 48 hours of service of this order and to the best of his ability inform the Applicant's Solicitors of all his assets in England and Wales exceeding £350,000 whether in his own name or not and whether solely or jointly owned, giving the value, location and details of all such assets.'

9. Service of the Order and accompanying documents having taken place at about 10:00 hrs on 13th July 2004, the Defendant had until 10:00 hrs on 15th July 2004 by which to inform this firm of his assets.

10. I can confirm that at the time of swearing this Affidavit, this firm has not received any information from the Defendant as to his assets situated in England and Wales, nor have I been contacted by the Defendant or by any representative of his.

11. For the reasons which I have set out, the Defendant is in breach of the Order and I seek the relief sought in the attached draft order.

Sworn by: ....

Mary Brown

Sworn at: ....

....

....

....

This day of July 2004

Before me: ....

Qualification: ....

This Affidavit is filed on behalf of the Claimant.

Application for Search Order

The Applicant, Insurers UK

Intends to apply for a search order (a draft of which is attached) pursuant to CPR Rule 25.1(h) in respect of the private residence of the Respondent, Barry John Smith, at 123 Low Road, London N14.

Because there is a real possibility that incriminating documents or materials in the Respondent's possession may be destroyed.

Affidavit in Support of Application for Search Order

Affidavit on behalf of the Applicant
Peter Jones
1st Affidavit
Exhibit PJ1
Sworn on [date]

<u>Claim No ....</u>

<u>IN THE HIGH COURT OF JUSTICE</u>
<u>QUEEN'S BENCH DIVISION</u>
<u>COMMERCIAL COURT</u>

B E T W E E N:

INSURERS UK

<u>Applicant/Claimant</u>

- and -

BARRY JOHN SMITH

<u>Respondent/Defendant</u>

AFFIDAVIT OF PETER JONES

I, **PETER JONES**, of 1 High Street, London EC1M 4AA, will say as follows.

1. I am a Solicitor of the Supreme Court and a partner in the firm of Jones and Jones of the above address, Solicitors for the Claimant and the Applicant in this matter. I am duly authorised by the Applicant to make this Affidavit on its behalf.

2. All facts and matters in this statement are from my own knowledge or, where specified, are derived from my review of the documents exhibited hereto and/or from the instructions or information I have received from Mr Roy Brown of the Super Yacht Club and Mr Lee of London Investigations Ltd. Where the facts are within my knowledge, they are true. Where they are not within my knowledge, they are true to the best of my information and belief.

3. There is now shown to me a bundle of copy documents. the contents of which are true to the best of my knowledge and belief and marked exhibit 'PJ1'. References in this statement to, for example (**tab 1, page 1**), are references to the tabs and pages within 'PJ1'.

THE RELIEF SOUGHT

4. This statement is made in support of the Claimant's application pursuant to CPR Rule 25.1(h) for a search order in respect of the Respondent's private residence at 123 Low Road, London N14.

5. The Claimant seeks documents evidencing or relating to the Respondent's possession and dealings with the vessel 'LADY II' after 28th April 2004, including a contract of storage with the Super Yacht Club concluded on or around April 2004 and bank statements and chequebooks evidencing payments made by the Respondent relating to the storage of that vessel.

PAYMENT UNDER POLICY NO. GEN-99-43194

6. On 4th June 2003, the Respondent completed a standard Brokers United proposal form to obtain insurance for his vessel 'LADY II' ('the Vessel') in the sum of £175,000. On that form, in response to the question 'have you or anyone who will be in charge of the vessel been convicted of a criminal offence?', the Respondent answered 'no' (**tab 1, page 1**). An insurance policy was effected by the Applicant and allocated a policy number XYZ ('the

policy'). The insurance was effective for a period of 12 months commencing 10th June 2003.

7. On 28th April 2004, the Respondent made a claim under the policy for £175,000. In completing the Brokers United standard claim form, the Respondent stated that the Vessel and its contents had been stolen from outside his premises on the night of 26th April 2004. The Respondent further represented that a full search for the Vessel had been made, but without success. The alleged theft had also been reported to the police and a crime number: ABC007 had been allocated to the incident. The claim form was signed by the Respondent (**tab 3, pages 5 and 6**).

8. On 9th June 2004, Brokers United, sent to the Respondent a cheque, No. 004171, drawn on their account in the sum of £175,000 and made payable to the Respondent (**tab 4, pages 7–9**). On 15th June 2004, the cheque cleared (**tab 4, page 11**). In turn, the Applicant accounted to Brokers United for the £175,000 paid to the Respondent (**tab 4, pages 12–15**).

THE MISSING VESSEL

9. Mr Brown of the Super Yacht Club states (**tab 6, page 5**), that the Respondent became a member of the Super Yacht Club on 1st March 2004. In or about the first week of April 2004, the Respondent telephoned Mr Brown to inquire whether or not it would be possible to store his vessel at the Super Yacht Club since the marina where he had previously berthed her was too far away. Mr Brown's recollection of this conversation and of subsequent events are set out in his statement.

10. The boat apparently arrived at the Super Yacht Club on 26th April 2004 (**tab 6, page 17**). Invoices were tendered by the Super Yacht

Club on a monthly basis commencing 1 May 2004 (**tab 6, pages 18–20**). Payment was made by the Respondent by cheques which Mr Brown's records show were all drawn on a bank account in the name of the Respondent and held with the British Bank plc. Unfortunately, Mr Brown is unable to locate any further records which would identify the number of the account on which the cheques were drawn (**tab 6, page 21**).

11. I am advised and believe that the vessel stored by the Respondent at the Super Yacht Club is the same vessel as that which the Respondent reported as stolen and in respect of which the claim was made in April 2004. I refer to a letter dated 9th July 2004 in which Mr Lee confirms how he came to find the Vessel at the Super Yacht Club and how it is the same vessel as that said to have been stolen in April 2004 (**tab 7, page 22**). I also refer to photographs taken at the time by Mr Lee, which clearly demonstrate that the vessel being stored bears the name LADY II and has a hull identification number No. 4567 (**tab 8, page 23**). I refer to the proposal form completed by Mr Smith in June 2003 which clearly states the Vessel's particulars, including her name LADY II and hull identification No. 4567.

RESPONDENT'S DISHONEST CONDUCT

12. Since the discovery of the Vessel on 7th July 2004, my firm has conducted further investigations into the Respondent's background and I now believe that the representation made by the Respondent on the proposal form in June 2003, namely that he had no criminal convictions, is untrue. Mary Brown of this firm made inquiries of Southwark Crown Court and received from them a certificate of conviction which certifies that the Respondent was convicted of fraud in 1998 and was sentenced to six months imprisonment (**tab 10, page 31**).

APPLICANT'S CLAIM AGAINST THE RESPONDENT

13. The Applicant intends to bring an action against the Respondent to recover the monies paid over to him. The Applicant is entitled to recover the monies from the Respondent either on the basis that they were paid pursuant to a fraud committed on the Applicant or alternatively, by avoiding the policy of insurance for misrepresentation or material non-disclosure.

14. In addition to £175,000 paid to the Respondent in satisfaction of his insurance claim, the Applicant has also suffered consequential losses including the costs of the investigation which it will seek to recover. As such, the Respondent's liability to the Applicant is likely to be in the region of about £225,000 plus costs.

15. I believe that the applicant has an extremely strong prima facie case against the respondent for the recovery of about £225,000 plus costs. The Respondent's fraudulent insurance claim has, I believe, caused serious harm and loss to the applicant.

RESPONDENT'S POSSESSION OF INCRIMINATING DOCUMENTS

16. Based on the information provided by Mr Brown of Super Yacht Club, I believe that it is highly likely that the Respondent has crucial incriminating documents in his possession, including the contract of storage with the Super Yacht Club concluded on or around April 2004 and bank statements and chequebooks evidencing payments made by the Respondent for the storage of that vessel.

REAL POSSIBILITY OF DESTRUCTION OF THOSE DOCUMENTS

17. I believe that there is a real possibility that the Respondent will act dishonestly and will destroy the crucial incriminating documents described above. I base my belief on the following:

17.1 The Respondent has a criminal record evidencing dishonest behaviour. He was convicted of a count of fraud in 1998 for which he received a six-month custodial sentence;

17.2 The Respondent lied about his criminal record on the proposal form in order to obtain insurance;

17.3 The Respondent fraudulently induced the Applicant to pay to him, the sum of £175,000 on the basis of a false theft claim, as set out in this Affidavit.

THE PRESENT APPLICATION

18. This application is made pursuant to CPR part 25 and is made without notice to the Respondent because I believe that the Respondent would take steps to destroy incriminating documents in his possession if he became aware of this application.

19. The Applicant is prepared to give a cross-undertaking in damages and will undertake to serve a Claim Form and Particulars of Claim upon the Defendants as soon as practicable. The Applicant is a substantial publicly traded UK insurance company and, I believe, has the means to satisfy that undertaking.

20. For the reasons which I have set out above, I seek the relief sought in the draft order attached to the Application Notice.

Sworn by : ....

Peter Jones

CHAPTER 16

Arbitration Applications

Stay of legal proceedings:
Nick Craig

Time extensions:
Nathan Tamblyn

Challenging an award for serious irregularity/permission to appeal:
Peter Ferrer
Thomas Macey-Dare

Interim remedies in support of arbitration:
Chirag Karia

STAY OF LEGAL PROCEEDINGS: SECTION 9, ARBITRATION ACT 1996

Law

16.1 The Arbitration Act 1996, s 9 enables a party to an arbitration agreement to apply to the court for a stay of proceedings brought (in either the High Court of the County Court: see the Arbitration Act 1996, s 82(1)) in breach of this agreement. Such an application can be brought, notwithstanding the fact that the seat of the arbitration is outside the jurisdiction.

Timing is crucial in relation to such an application. An application cannot be made:

(1) until service of the proceedings has been acknowledged; or
(2) after the taking of any step to answer the substantive claim.

See the Arbitration Act 1996, s 9(3).

In relation to (2), an application for security for costs has been held to bar a defendant from obtaining a stay (see *Adams v Cattley* (1892) 66 LT 687) as has the failure in resisting an application for summary judgment to issue such an application for a stay until after the first (adjourned) hearing of the summary judgment application (see *Turner & Goudy v McConnell* [1985] 1 WLR 898). However, the burden rests upon the Claimant to show that the dispute ought not to be referred to arbitration. This is the effect of s 9(4), which provides that:

> 'On an application under this section the court shall grant a stay unless satisfied that the arbitration is null and void, inoperative or incapable of being performed.'

Procedure

16.2 A Defendant should apply by way of ordinary application notice (in accordance with CPR Part 23) to the court in which the legal proceedings are pending.

The above account of the applicable law is only intended to provide general practical guidance on a few of the relevant issues. It is not intended to be exhaustive or even complete. For a fuller account, the reader should consult the standard reference books on arbitration such as Mustill & Boyd *Commercial Arbitration: 2001 Companion Volume to the Second Edition* (2001), pp 268-272; St John Sutton & Gill *Russell on Arbitration* (22nd edn, 2003), p 298 and *Bernstein's Handbook of Arbitration and Dispute Resolution Practice*, s 2–152. The reader should also consult the latest versions of *CPR Part 62* and the *Practice Direction – Arbitration, Supplementing CPR Part 62* for the applicable procedural rules.

Pleading

Assumed facts

16.3 The Claimant, Swinburne Limited, agreed to buy and the Defendant, Rosetti GmbH, agreed to sell a total of 100,000 mt of coal to be delivered FOB in ten monthly instalments. Prior to the contract being concluded the Defendant had pressed for an arbitration clause as follows:

> 'This contract shall be governed by English law. Any dispute arising out of this contract shall be referred to arbitration in London.'

During the negotiations, the Claimant indicated that it was agreeable to this; however, the fixture re-cap sent by the Claimant to the Defendant the day the contract was concluded (9 December 1998) did not refer to the arbitration clause. The Claimant subsequently sought to renegotiate the terms of delivery. It alleged that the Defendant was in breach of these amended terms and commenced proceedings in the Commercial Court. The Defendant acknowledged service of these proceedings and then issued an application for security for costs.

Application for Stay of Legal Proceedings

Application Form – PF244

Part A:- I,/We, the [solicitor on behalf of the] Defendant apply for an order, a draft of which is attached, that these proceedings be stayed pursuant to section 9 of the Arbitration Act 1996.

Part B:- I/We wish to rely upon the attached witness statement.

Dated

Signed (name) position or office held

Witness Statements

FIRST WITNESS STATEMENT OF GABRIEL DANTE IN SUPPORT OF AN APPLICATION PURSUANT TO SECTION 9 OF THE ARBITRATION ACT 1996

I, GABRIEL DANTE of Browning House, 6 Morris Street, Barrettville state as follows:

1. I am a solicitor and partner in the firm of Christina Dante & Co of the above address. I have conduct of this matter on behalf of the Defendant and am duly authorised to make this statement. I make this statement on the basis of copy documents and correspondence supplied to me by the Defendant and from the facts known to me by virtue of handling this case. The facts stated herein are true to the best of my knowledge, information and belief.

2. I make this statement in support of the Defendant's application for an order that these proceedings be stayed pursuant to Section 9 of the Arbitration Act 1996.

3. There is now produced and shown to me marked 'GB1' a paginated bundle containing true copies of relevant documents to

which I shall refer by page number in the course of this witness statement. Numbers in square brackets appearing in this witness statement refer to page numbers in this bundle.

(1) The contract

4. The Defendant, based in Germany, is a coal-trader. Pursuant to a contract in writing dated 9th December 1998, the Defendant agreed to sell and the Claimant agreed to buy 100,000 mt coal by instalments.

5. In its Particulars of Claim the Claimant has alleged that the Defendant was in breach of the terms of this contract in failing to deliver the coal in accordance with an alleged variation of the shipment dates under the contract. This is denied by the Defendant.

(2) The arbitration clause

6. However and in any event, the contract provided, amongst other things, as follows:

   'Clause 10: This contract shall be governed by English law. Any dispute arising out of this contract shall be referred to arbitration in London.'

7. It is clear from the Particulars of Claim that the claim advanced by the Claimant in these proceedings arises from the contract. Accordingly, this claim should have been referred to arbitration and the Claimant is in breach of this term in bringing them.

Accordingly, I would ask that the Court grant the Defendant a stay in the terms of the draft order attached to the application notice.

[Signed, etc]

FIRST WITNESS STATEMENT OF EDMUND GOSSE IN RESPONSE TO AN APPLICATION PURSUANT TO SECTION 9 OF THE ARBITRATION ACT 1996

I, EDMUND GOSSE of Butler Cottage, The Green, Erewhon state as follows:

1. I am a solicitor and partner in the firm of Gosse & Co of the above address. I have conduct of this matter on behalf of the Claimant and am duly authorised to make this statement. I make this statement on the basis of copy documents and correspondence supplied to me by the Claimant, from instructions received from Charles Algernon, the Managing Director of the Claimant, and from the facts known to me by virtue of handling this case. The facts stated herein are true to the best of my knowledge, information and belief.

2. I make this statement in response to the Defendant's application for an order that these proceedings be stayed pursuant to Section 9 of the Arbitration Act 1996.

3. There is now produced and shown to me marked 'EG1' a paginated bundle containing true copies of relevant documents to which I shall refer by page number in the course of this witness statement. Numbers in square brackets appearing in this witness statement refer to page numbers in this bundle.

(1) No arbitration clause

4. As is clear from the Particulars of Claim and as is accepted by the Defendants, the Claimant contracted with the Defendant to buy 100,000 mt of coal in instalments. However, I am advised by

Charles Algernon that the Claimant did not agree to the arbitration clause. In this regard, I refer to the fixture re-cap dated 9th December 1998 sent by the Claimant to the Defendant in which there is no reference to an arbitration clause.

5. In addition, I refer to the pre-contractual exchanges which make clear that:

   (i) the Defendant proposed on a number of occasions an arbitration clause in the terms set out in paragraph 6 of the First Statement of Gabriel Dante; and

   (ii) the Claimant was not prepared to accede to this request.

(2) Substantive step taken by the Defendant

6. In any event, I believe that the Defendant cannot now make this application because it has taken a step in these proceedings to answer the substantive claim.

7. Last week the Defendant lodged an application for security for its costs pursuant to CPR Part 25.12 (such application has yet to be listed). I believe that this bars the Defendant from obtaining the order that it seeks.

Accordingly, I would ask that the Court dismiss the Defendant's application.

[Signed, etc]

TIME EXTENSIONS: THE ARBITRATION ACT 1996

Extending time for beginning arbitral proceedings

16.4 The Arbitration Act 1996, s 12(1) provides:

> 'Where an arbitration agreement to refer future disputes to arbitration provides that a claim shall be barred, or the claimant's right extinguished, unless the claimant takes within a time fixed by the agreement some step–
>
> (a) to begin arbitral proceedings, or
> (b) to begin other dispute resolution procedures which must be exhausted before arbitral proceedings can be begun,
>
> the court may by order extend the time for taking that step.'

This section expressly applies to arbitration agreements to refer future disputes and therefore appears not to cover agreements to refer existing disputes[1]. It seemingly does not apply to time limits imposed other than by agreement. It also appears that where a time limit provides a substantive defence, but otherwise does not prohibit the claimant from bringing arbitral proceedings, no relief is available under this section[2].

Any party to the arbitration agreement may apply on notice to the other parties for an order extending time, but only after a claim has arisen and after exhausting any available arbitral process for obtaining the extension[3]. The court may extend time whether or not the time previously fixed by agreement or by a previous order has expired[4]. An order under this section does not affect the operation of the Limitation Acts[5]. Permission of the court is required for any appeal from a decision of the court under this section[6], and that means permission is only available from the Court of First Instance[7].

The Arbitration Act 1996, s 12(3) provides:

> 'The court shall make an order only if satisfied–
>
> (a) that the circumstances are such as were outside the reasonable contemplation of the parties when they agreed the provision in question, and that it would be just to extend the time, or
> (b) that the conduct of one party makes it unjust to hold the other party to the strict terms of the provision in question.'

There appears to be no residual discretion for the court to grant an extension outside the conditions of s 12(3). While s 12(1) is couched in discretionary terms, it would be surprising if no extension were granted if either of the conditions of s 12(3) be met.

This section has been considered recently in *Harbour & General Works v Environment Agency* [2000] 1 Lloyd's Rep 65 (CA), and *Thyssen v Calypso Shipping* [2000] 2 Lloyd's Rep 243 (David Steel J)[8]. The test of what is 'just' replaced the previous test of 'undue hardship' under the Arbitration Act 1950, s 27, and previous case law on that phrase might not be reliable[9].

As part of the application, alternative relief could be sought in the form of a declaration that a time extension is not needed, for example because the proceedings have been instituted within time. This is expressly permitted by CPR 62.4(3), and its use (under the similar previous regime of CPR PD49G, para 21) is discussed in *Grimaldi Co v Sekimyo Line (The Seki Rolette)* [1998] 2 Lloyd's Rep 638, [1998] 3 All ER 943 (Mance J). If the tribunal is itself considering whether proceedings have been correctly started within time, it may be appropriate either to stay the application to the court, or for the court to continue on the assumption that proceedings have not been started.

1 This point was considered under previous legislation in *Navigazione Alta Italia v Concordia Maritime (The Stena Pacifica)* [1990] 2 Lloyd's Rep 234 (Evans J), where it was held that an option to arbitrate was an agreement to refer future disputes.
2 See *Babanaft v Avant Petroleum (The Oltenia)* [1982] 2 Lloyd's Rep 99 (CA), and *Mariana Islands Steamship v Marimpex (The Medusa)* [1986] 2 Lloyd's Rep 328 (CA).
3 Arbitration Act 1996, s 12(2).
4 AA 1996, s 12(4).
5 AA 1996, s 12(5).
6 AA 1996, s 12(6).
7 AA 1996, s 105(1), see also *Inco Europe v First Choice Distribution* [2000] 1 WLR 586 at 590 (HL).
8 See also *Vosnoc v Transglobal Projects* [1998] 1 Lloyd's Rep 711, [1998] 1 WLR 101 (Judge Jack QC); *Cottiship v Allansons (The Catherine Helen)* [1998] 2 Lloyd's Rep 511, [1998] 3 All ER 714 (Geoffrey Brice QC); *Fox & Widley v Graham* [1998] 1 EGLR 91 (Clarke J); *Grimaldi Co v Sekihyo Line (The Seki Rolette)* [1998] 2 Lloyd's Rep 638, [1998] 3 All ER 943 (Mance J); and *Union Trans-Pacific v Orient Shipping* [2002] EWHC 1451 (16 July 2002) (Nigel Teare QC).
9 See DAC Report (February 1996) para 62ff.

Extending time in arbitral proceedings

(1) Under Arbitration Act 1996, s 79

16.5 The Arbitration Act 1996, s 79(1) provides:

> 'Unless the parties otherwise agree, the court may by order extend any time limit agreed by them in relation to any matter relating to the arbitral proceedings or specified in any provision of this Part having effect in default of such agreement. This section does not apply to a time limit to which section 12 applies…'

This section does not apply to time limits provided by the Arbitration Act 1996 which apply other than in default of agreement by the parties, as held in *Kalmneft v Glencore* [2002] 1 Lloyd's Rep 128 [2002] 1 All ER 76 (Colman J). Seemingly, it does not apply to time limits imposed by the arbitral tribunal.

An application may be made by any party to the arbitral proceedings on notice to the other parties and the tribunal, or by the tribunal on notice to the parties[1]. The court's power may be exercised whether or not the time has already expired[2]. Again the permission of the court is required for any appeal from a decision of the court under this section[3].

The Arbitration Act 1996, s 79(3) provides:

> 'The court shall not exercise its power to extend a time limit unless it is satisfied–
>
> (a) that any available recourse to the tribunal, or to any arbitral or other institution or person vested by the parties with power in that regard, has first been exhausted, and
> (b) that a substantial injustice would otherwise be done.'

The test of 'substantial injustice' is also found in s 50(3) (extension of time for making award) and in s 68(2) (challenging the award for serious irregularity). This is in contrast to the test of whether the extension would be 'just' in s 12(3), which was originally also 'substantial injustice' in the July 1995 Bill, and which itself replaced a test of 'undue hardship' in the Arbitration Act 1950, s 27. The language of 'substantial injustice' suggests that a consideration of the merits of the dispute, as well as purely procedural matters, may be relevant in determining whether to grant the extension.

1 AA 1996, s 79(2).
2 AA 1996, s 79(4).
3 AA 1996, s 79(6).

(2) Under Arbitration Act 1996, s 80(5)

16.6 The Arbitration Act 1996, s 80(5) provides:

> 'Where any provision of this Part requires an application or appeal to be made to the court within a specified time, the rules of court relating to the reckoning of periods, extending or abridging of periods, and the consequences of not taking a step within the period prescribed by the rules, apply in relation to that requirement.'

It was held in *Ranko Group v Antarctic Shipping*, an unreported decision of Toulson J of 12 June 1998, that s 80(5) applies to time limits which are set by the Arbitration Act 1996 other than in default of the agreement of the parties, and is not restricted by s 79. It therefore covers at least that one loophole left by s 79. The availability of s 80(5) and the court's general case management powers under CPR 3 was confirmed in *Kalmneft*[1].

1 *Kalmneft v Glencore* [2002] 1 Lloyd's Rep 128, [2002] 1 All ER 76 (Colman J).

(3) Under CPR 62.9

16.7 In addition, CPR 62.9 empowers the court to extend the time for challenging an award under s 67 (substantive jurisdiction) or s 68 (serious irregularity) or for appealing against an award under s 69 (point of law) from the standard 28 days fixed by s 70(3). Such an application may be made without notice if made before the period expires[1], and then in the usual CPR 23 application form[2], but if the period has expired then the application must be contained in the arbitration claim form, and the defendant may file evidence opposing the application within seven days of service[3].

1 CPR 62.9(2).
2 CPR PD62.11.
3 CPR 62.9(3).

CPR procedure

16.8 Specialist provisions appear in CPR 62 and its accompanying Practice Direction.

Save for an application under CPR 62.9 made before expiry of the time period (as above), an application to the court under the Arbitration Act 1996 for a time extension is to be started by the issue of an arbitration claim form in accordance with the CPR Part 8 procedure[1]. The arbitration claim form means that set out in the practice direction[2] which currently appears to be Form N8. It must be served within one month of the date of issue unless the court orders otherwise[3].

The required contents of the arbitration claim form are set out in CPR 62.4(1), which provides:

> 'An arbitration claim form must–
>
> (a) include a concise statement of–
>   (i) the remedy claimed; and
>   (ii) any questions on which the claimant seeks the decision of the court;
>
> (b) give details of any arbitration award challenged by the claimant, identifying which part or parts of the award are challenged and specifying the grounds for the challenge;
>
> (c) show that any statutory requirements have been met;
>
> (d) specify under which section of the 1996 Act the claim is made;
>
> (e) identify against which (if any) defendants a costs order is sought; and
>
> (f) specify either–
>   (i) the persons on whom the arbitration claim form is to be served, stating their role in the arbitration and whether they are defendants; or
>   (ii) that the claim is made without notice under section 44(3) of the 1996 Act and the grounds relied on.'

Where the Arbitration Act 1996 requires any application to be on notice to a party to the arbitration, then that party must be made a defendant[4]. In contrast, notice to an arbitrator need only be given by sending him the arbitration claim form and evidence in support[5]. A hearing concerning the granting of a time extension will be heard in private unless the court orders otherwise[6], although applications to extend the 28 days time period of s 70(3) – if not most time extension applications – will usually be determined without a hearing[7]. Automatic case management directions are set out in CPR PD62.6.

Pursuant to the High Court and County Courts (Allocation of Arbitration Proceedings) Order 1996 (SI 1996/3215), proceedings under the Arbitration Act 1996 for a time extension may be commenced in the Mercantile List of the Central London County Court as well as in the High Court. The financial value of the dispute and the general importance of the legal issues raised are relevant factors. Ordinarily, if the value of the dispute exceeds £200,000, the proceedings should be taken in the High Court unless they do not raise questions of general importance[8].

1 CPR 62.3(1).
2 CPR 62.1(2)(f), CPR PD62.2.2.
3 CPR 62.4(2).
4 CPR 62.6(3).
5 CPR 62.6(2).
6 CPR 62.10.
7 CPR PD62.10.
8 SI 1996/3215, art 5(4).

Pleading

Assumed facts

16.9 The parties entered into a contract which required arbitration pursuant to the Widget Association Arbitration Rules. At the time of contracting, they required the appointment of an arbitrator within 12 months. A dispute arose and the Applicant appointed an arbitrator within 12 months. However, prior to the dispute arising but after contracting, the Widget Association issued new Arbitration Rules which required the appointment of an arbitrator within nine months. There is a dispute as to whether the new Rules were incorporated into the contract and the conduct of the parties once the dispute arose.

Claim Form (Arbitration) – N8
Grounds of application

1. The Applicant seeks an order that time for the appointment of an arbitrator be extended by one month pursuant to the Arbitration Act 1996, s 12.

2. Alternatively, the Applicant seeks a declaration pursuant to CPR 62.4(3) that no such order is needed on the basis that arbitral proceedings have already been correctly commenced.

3. By a contract dated 1st January 2000, the parties agreed to refer all future disputes under the contract to arbitration, pursuant to the Widget Association Arbitration Rules. At the time of entering into the contract, clause 10 of those Rules required the Applicant to commence arbitration proceedings by appointing an arbitrator within one year of the cause of action arising, failing which its claim shall be barred.

4. A claim has arisen under the contract, brief details of which are set out in the letter appointing the Applicant's arbitrator.

5. The claim arose on 1st April 2003. The Applicant sought to appoint Mr I M Partial as an arbitrator within time on 30th January 2004 by a letter of the same date. The Applicant contends that this letter constituted proper appointment within the terms of the contract. Accordingly, the Applicant seeks the decision of the Court on the question of whether arbitral proceedings have been correctly commenced.

6. However, the Respondent denies that this constituted timely appointment. In December 2002, the Widget Association amended its Arbitration Rules such that appointment was required

within nine months of the cause of action arising. Pursuant to the Arbitration Act 1996, s 12(3)(a), those circumstances were outside the reasonable consideration of the parties when they agreed the contract.

7. Further, it would be just to extend time because the parties had corresponded heavily before the Applicant's appointment of the arbitrator such that the Respondent was well positioned to investigate the matter and protect itself by claiming down the contractual chain if necessary, and because the size of the claim is material to the continued existence as a trading concern of the Applicant, a significant employer in Dolesville.

8. Further or alternatively, and pursuant to the Arbitration Act 1996, s 12(3)(b), the conduct of the Respondent makes it unjust to hold the Applicant to the strict terms of the arbitration clause in the contract. The Respondent knew of the change in the Rules but in correspondence told the Applicant that it had 12 months in which to bring its claim.

9. Upon receipt of the Respondent's denial that the letter constituted proper appointment, the Applicant made this application to the Court. At the same time, it also applied to the arbitrator for determination of the preliminary issue of whether or not he was properly appointed within time. The learned arbitrator has indicated that he will not consider that application pending this application to the Court, in agreement with the parties to the arbitration. In such circumstances, it is submitted that the Applicant has exhausted the available arbitral process pursuant to the Arbitration Act 1996, s 12(2).

10. It is requested that this application be determined without a hearing, pursuant to CPR PD62.10.

11. This Arbitration Claim Form is to be served on the Respondent, who is also the intended respondent in the intended arbitration proceedings, and the other party to the contract. The Respondent's address for service is set out above. Notice of this application has also been given to the learned arbitrator.

12. The Applicant seeks a costs order against the Respondent, who has refused to grant any time extension despite being fully informed of the above circumstances.

The Arbitration Claim Form should be accompanied by witness statement(s) and evidence in support.

Witness statement in support

1. I make this witness statement in support of the Applicant's application for an order that time for the appointment of an arbitrator be extended by one month pursuant to the Arbitration Act 1996, s 12, alternatively, for a declaration pursuant to CPR 62.4(3) that no such order is needed on the basis that arbitral proceedings have already been correctly commenced.

2. The parties entered into a contract dated 1st January 2000 ('the contract'), a copy of which is attached. They agreed to refer all future disputes under the contract to arbitration, pursuant to the Widget Association Arbitration Rules. At the time of entering into the contract, clause 10 of those Rules required the Applicant to commence arbitration proceedings by appointing an arbitrator within one year of the cause of action arising, failing which its claim shall be barred.

3. A claim has arisen under the contract. I wrote to Mr I M Partial on 30th January 2004 seeking to appoint him as arbitrator, and setting out the details of the claim. A copy of that letter is attached.

4. The claim arose on 1st April 2003. In the circumstances, the Applicant contends that this letter constituted proper appointment within the terms of the contract.

5. However, the Respondent denies that this constituted timely appointment. In December 2002, the Widget Association amended its Arbitration Rules such that appointment was required within nine months of the cause of action arising. Accordingly, the Respondent contends that the appointment should have been made by 31st December 2003. This is disputed by the Applicant on the basis the contract only incorporated the old Rules and made no reference to any future modifications. The Applicant contends that the old Rules still apply contractually so that appointment was to occur within 12 months.

6. Alternatively, pursuant to the Arbitration Act 1996, s 12(3)(a), the change of Rules was outside the reasonable consideration of the parties when they agreed the contract. This is because both parties wrote to the Widget Association shortly prior to contracting enquiring whether any new Arbitration Rules might be brought out, and the Association replied that they did not intend this to occur. A copy of their letter is attached.

7. Further, it would be just to extend time. The parties had corresponded heavily before the Applicant's appointment of the arbitrator. Copies of the correspondence are attached. The Respondent was well positioned to investigate the matter and protect itself by claiming down the contractual chain if necessary. Also, the size of the claim is enormous with the result of the arbitration likely to decide whether or not the Applicant remains solvent. The Applicant is the only major employer in the greater Dolesville region, with many livelihoods dependent upon the success of the company.

8. Further or alternatively, and pursuant to the Arbitration Act 1996, s 12(3)(b), the conduct of the Respondent makes it unjust to hold the Applicant to the strict terms of the arbitration clause in the contract. The Respondent knew of the change in the Rules, because the managing director of the Respondent is on the committee of the Widget Association. However, in correspondence he told the Applicant that it had 12 months in which to bring its claim. A copy of his letter is attached.

9. Upon receipt of the Respondent's denial that the letter constituted proper appointment, the Applicant made this application to the Court. At the same time, it also applied to the arbitrator for determination of the preliminary issue of whether or not he was properly appointed within time, on the basis that the contract only incorporated the old Rules. The learned arbitrator has stated that he will not consider that application pending this application to the Court, in agreement with the parties to the arbitration. A copy of the arbitrator's letter is attached. In such circumstances, it is submitted that the Applicant has exhausted the available arbitral process pursuant to the Arbitration Act 1996, s 12(2).

10. It is requested that this application be determined without a hearing, pursuant to CPR PD62.10, in order to save costs.

Witness statement in opposition

1. I make this witness statement in opposition to the Applicant's application for a time extension, alternatively, for a declaration that no such order is needed.

2. It is admitted that the parties entered into a contract dated 1st January 2000 ('the contract'), and that they agreed to refer all future disputes under the contract to arbitration, pursuant to the Widget Association Arbitration Rules. It is admitted that at the

time of entering into the contract, clause 10 of those Rules required the Applicant to commence arbitration proceedings by appointing an arbitrator within one year of the cause of action arising, failing which its claim shall be barred.

3. The parties are in dispute under the contract, although the Respondent strongly denies that it is in breach. The Applicant did seek to appoint its arbitrator on 30th January 2004. However, the date of alleged breach is 1st April 2003, and the current Widget Association Arbitration Rules require any appointment to be within nine months. The Applicant's appointment is therefore out of time.

4. These new rules were modified in December 2002. The Respondent contends that the new Rules apply. While it is accepted that the arbitration clause in the contract did not expressly refer to possible future modifications of the Rules, nevertheless the contract was annually renewable, with each new annual order to be expressly placed on the Widget Association Standard Order Form 'currently in force'. There were two changes of Order Form during the currency of the contract, and always did the Applicant respond by placing its order on the appropriate new form.

5. It is denied that the change to the Rules was beyond the contemplation of the parties. Modifications of the Order Form were commonplace prior to contracting. The Arbitration Rules were on their third issue. While both parties wrote to the Widget Association asking if any new Rules were likely to be introduced, and the response from the Association was negative, the question posed was not whether this would ever happen, but whether it would be likely in the two years, the originally anticipated duration of the contract. A copy of the letter to the Widget

Association is attached. The new Rules were introduced after two years.

6. It would not be just to extend time. The Respondent would have been able to institute proceedings down the contractual chain only within nine months, and that opportunity has now passed. It should also be pointed out that the Applicant is not the only employer in Dolesville; the Respondent's largest factory is based there, and its local economic impact is considerable.

7. It is denied that the Respondent has deceived the Applicant as to the change in the Rules. I am chairman of the committee of the Widget Association. I was only appointed to this role in February 2004, after the time for appointing an arbitrator had expired. Prior to that, I did not know there was any change in the Rules.

8. When the Applicant first complained to the Respondent of an alleged breach, in April 2003, it threatened Court proceedings. The Respondent replied that only arbitration proceedings were available under the Widget Association Arbitration Rules. Reference was made to the old Rules (because I did not know about the new Rules), but not to any time period for instituting proceedings, only to make the point that Court proceedings were inappropriate. The Applicant cannot rely on that letter to extend time.

9. It is requested that this application be determined with a hearing. This is an important dispute of considerable financial value. The allegations made against the Respondent are serious and complicated and require oral presentation.

CHALLENGING AN AWARD FOR SERIOUS IRREGULARITY/PERMISSION TO APPEAL: SECTIONS 68 AND 69, ARBITRATION ACT 1996

Law

Section 68

16.10 The Arbitration Act 1996, s 68 provides that a party to an arbitration may apply to the court to challenge an award on the grounds of serious irregularity affecting the tribunal, the proceedings or the award[1]. Serious irregularity is defined in the Act as an irregularity of one or more of the following kinds which the court considers has caused or will cause substantial injustice to the applicant:

(a) failure by the tribunal to comply with s 33 (general duty of tribunal);
(b) the tribunal exceeding its powers (otherwise than by exceeding its substantive jurisdiction);
(c) failure by the tribunal to conduct the proceedings in accordance with the procedure agreed by the parties;
(d) failure by the tribunal to deal with all the issues that were put to it;
(e) any arbitral or other institution or person vested by the parties with powers in relation to the proceedings or award exceeding its powers;
(f) uncertainty or ambiguity as to the effect of the award;
(g) the award being obtained by fraud or the award or the way in which it was procured being contrary to public policy;
(h) failure to comply with the requirements as to the form of the award; or
(i) any irregularity in the conduct of the proceedings or in the award which is admitted by the tribunal or by any arbitral or other institution or person vested by the parties with powers in relation to the proceedings or award[2].

Should the court consider that there was a serious irregularity affecting the tribunal, the proceedings or the award, the court may:

(a) remit the award to the tribunal in whole or in part for reconsideration;
(b) set the award aside in whole or in part;
(c) declare the award to be of no effect, in whole or in part[3].

The court will not exercise its power to set aside or declare an award to be of no effect, unless it is satisfied that it would be inappropriate to remit the matters in question to the tribunal for reconsideration. Any application has to be brought within 28 days of the award or termination of the appeal process[4]. The court does have a general power to extend time however under s 79 of the Arbitration Act. Section 68 is subject to the restrictions contained in s 70(2). A party may therefore lose the right to apply if it has not first exhausted any available arbitral process of appeal or review and any available recourse under s 57[5].

The court will only exercise its powers under s 68 if it considers that the irregularity has caused or will cause substantial injustice. The Report of the Departmental Advisory Committee[6] in defining 'substantial injustice' stated:

> 'The test of "substantial injustice" is intended to be applied by way of support for the arbitral process, not by way of interference with that process. Thus it is only in those cases where it can be said that what has happened is so far removed from what could reasonably be expected of the arbitral process that we would expect the Court to take action. The test is not what would have happened had the matter been litigated. To apply such a test would be to ignore the fact that the parties have agreed to arbitrate, not litigate. Having chosen arbitration, the parties cannot validly complain of substantial injustice unless what has happened simply cannot on any view be defended as an acceptable consequence of that choice. In short, Clause 68 [which is now s 68] is really designed as a long stop, only available in extreme cases where the tribunal has gone so wrong in its conduct of the arbitration that justice calls out for it to be corrected[7].'

The threshold for satisfying the test of substantial injustice is therefore high.

1 Arbitration Act 1996, s 68(1).
2 Arbitration Act 1996, s 68(2).
3 Arbitration Act 1996, s 68(3).
4 Arbitration Act 1996, s 70(3).
5 *Torch Offshore LLC & v Cable Shipping Inc* [2004] 2 Lloyd's Rep 446.
6 DAC report February 1996, para 280.
7 For a discussion on s 68, see *The Petro Ranger* [2001] 2 Lloyd's Rep 348; *Hussman (Europe) Ltd v Al Ameen* [2000] 2 Lloyd's Rep 83 and *Ascot Commodities v Olam* [2002] CLC 277.

Section 69

16.11 The Arbitration Act 1996, s 69 gives the parties to an arbitration a limited right (which can be excluded by agreement) to appeal from an award to the Court on a point of law. Unlike an application under s 68, an appeal under s 69 can only be brought either with the agreement of all other parties to the proceedings or with the leave of the court[1]. It is usual for the court to determine the application for permission to appeal without an oral hearing (although in the example below, because it is combined with an application under s 68, an oral hearing will take place). The right to appeal is also subject to ss 70(2) and (3). Section 69(3) provides as follows:

> '(3) Leave to appeal shall be given only if the Court is satisfied:
> (a) that the determination of the question will substantially affect the rights of one or more of the parties,
> (b) that the question is one which the tribunal was asked to determine
> (c) that, on the basis of the findings of fact in the award–
> (i) the decision of the tribunal on the question is obviously wrong, or
> (ii) the question is one of general public importance and the decision of the tribunal is at least open to serious doubt, and
> (d) that, despite the agreement of the parties to resolve the matter by arbitration, it is just and proper in all the circumstances for the court to determine the question.'

The criteria set out in s 69(3) follow broadly the guidelines outlined by Lord Diplock in *The Nema* [1982] AC 724. However, the criteria are now statutory and there is no scope for the court to amplify or adapt them[2].

An application to court under ss 68 or 69 must be started with the issue of an arbitration claim form in accordance with the CPR Part 8 procedure[3]. The arbitration claim form must contain a concise statement of the remedy claimed and the grounds for challenging the award[4]. It is usual practice for the claim form to attach a more detailed statement of the grounds for challenging the award, though whether this is appropriate will depend on the facts of each particular case.

This is intended as a brief outline only. For a more detailed exposition of the law, the reader should consult Mustill & Boyd, *Commercial Arbitration* (2nd edn, 2001), Robert Merkin *The Arbitration Act 1996* (2000) and St John Sutton & Gill, *Russell on Arbitration* (22nd edn, 2003). The reader should also consult the latest versions of CPR Part 62 and the *Practice Direction – Arbitration, Supplementing CPR Part 62* for the applicable procedural rules.

1 Arbitration Act 1996, s 69(2).
2 *The Northern Pioneer* [2002] 1 Lloyd's Rep 212.
3 CPR 62.3(1).
4 CPR 62.4(1).

Pleading

Assumed facts

16.12 JFR Offshore Ltd ('Charterers') chartered a vessel RAINBOW BLUE ('the Vessel') from Panama Shipping Inc ('Owners') a SUPPLYTIME 89 form dated 30 April 2003. Prior to entering into the charterparty, Owners made various representations including a representation that the Vessel's deck strength throughout was 10 t/sqm and that the Vessel could carry a deep water cable laying system without modification to the Vessel. It became apparent during the course of the charterparty that the Vessel's deck strength was in fact substantially less and that the Vessel would require modification to carry the cable laying system. Charterers purported to terminate the charterparty in December 2003 for breach of contract. Owners brought a claim in arbitration for hire due and owing and damages for wrongful termination. Charterers defended the claim on the basis that the representations were false and that they were therefore entitled to rescind the charterparty, alternatively to recover damages for misrepresentation under s 2(1) of the Misrepresentation Act 1967. Alternatively, Charterers claimed to be entitled to terminate for breach of condition. The Tribunal held that Charterers' termination of the charterparty was wrongful and found that Charterers were not induced by the misrepresentations to enter the charterparty. Respondents sought to challenge the award pursuant to ss 68 and 69 of the Arbitration Act 1996.

In the drafts below, the use of a Part 8 Claim Form is assumed and the Addendum thereto is set out. Provided that this is verified by a statement of truth, it is unnecessary for a separate supporting witness statement to be used (and in the example, such a statement on behalf of the Charterers would be mere duplication).

The statement on behalf of the Owners in opposition is then set out.

ADDENDUM TO ARBITRATION CLAIM FORM

REMEDY CLAIMED AND GROUNDS ON WHICH CLAIM IS MADE

Introduction

1. This claim is made in relation to the Interim Final Award dated 2nd April 2004 of Mr Joseph Smith ('the Tribunal'). The Award is attached to this claim form as Annexe 1.

2. The Claimants ('JFR Offshore') were the respondents in the arbitration and were the charterers of the Vessel RAINBOW BLUE (the 'Vessel').

3. The Defendants ('Owners') were the claimants in the arbitration and owners of the Vessel.

4. The following documents are attached to this Arbitration Claim Form:

   (1) Annexe 1 – Award

   (2) Annexe 2 – Claim Submissions

   (3) Annexe 3 – Defence Submissions

   (4) Annexe 4 – Reply Submissions

   (5) Annexe 5 – JFR Offshore's written opening submissions

   (6) Annexe 6 – Owners' written opening submissions

   (7) Annexe 7 – JFR Offshore's written closing submissions

   (8) Annexe 8 – Owners' written closing submissions

   (9) Annexe 9 – transcript of the oral closing submissions.

Remedies Claimed

Serious Irregularity

5. There is a serious irregularity in the Award in that the Tribunal failed to address one of the central issues put to it, namely, whether the second misrepresentation as defined below induced JFR Offshore to enter the charterparty.

6. JFR Offshore seeks an order, pursuant to sections 68(2)(d) and (3) of the Arbitration Act 1996 (the 'Act'), setting aside and/or varying the Award and/or remitting the Award to the Tribunal.

Questions of law

7. JFR Offshore seek leave, pursuant to section 69(2)(b) of the Act, to appeal on two questions of law, namely,

   (i) whether the Tribunal erred in law by failing to apply the correct legal test in deciding that the first misrepresentation (defined below) did not induce JFR Offshore to enter the charterparty;

   (ii) whether the Tribunal erred in law in deciding that JFR Offshore was barred from rescinding the contract by reason of lapse of time.

Relief sought

8. If permission is granted, JFR Offshore will seek an order that pursuant to section 69(7) of the Act:

   (i) that the finding in the Award that JFR Offshore's rescission of the charterparty was wrongful be set aside and/or varied to hold that the said rescission was lawful;

(ii) that the Award be remitted to the Tribunal to assess the financial consequences of such lawful rescission;

(iii) alternatively that the Award be remitted to the Tribunal for reconsideration of the finding that JFR Offshore's rescission was wrongful.

Costs

9. JFR Offshore seeks an order that the Owners pay the costs of this arbitration claim.

Grounds

10. The dispute arose out of charterparty on an amended SUPPLYTIME 89 form.

11. A summary of the background is set out at paragraphs 4 to 20 of the Reasons for the Award and in the parties' written submissions and is not repeated here.

12. The issue, for the purposes of this claim, is whether by reason of two misrepresentations made prior to the charterparty being entered into, JFR Offshore were entitled to rescind the charterparty on 24th December 2003.

13. The misrepresentations were that:

(1) the deck strength of the vessel throughout its deck area was 10 mt/sqm ('the first misrepresentation'); and

(2) the vessel's deck could support a deep water cable laying system without modification to the Vessel (the 'second misrepresentation').

Serious Irregularity

14. Owners' position had been from the outset that the first misrepresentation had been made and that it was false. In relation to the second misrepresentation, Owners conceded that it had been made but asserted that it was true. During the course of the hearing, Owners also conceded that the second misrepresentation was false. The Tribunal, having apparently misunderstood the scope of the admission in relation to the making of the misrepresentations, then proceeded to analyse inducement and reliance as if there had been only one misrepresentation.

15. It is plain from a consideration of the award at paragraph 32 to 49 that the Tribunal was only considering the first misrepresentation. It is of paramount importance that the second misrepresentation was made by the Owners in response to a specific enquiry by JFR Offshore at the very outset of negotiations. This was not a representation which JFR Offshore lighted on after the event to seek to justify termination. It was at the heart of their enquiries. Yet none of these factors were addressed by the Tribunal which focused solely on the first misrepresentation.

16. This serious irregularity has caused a serious injustice to the Claimants. JFR Offshore say that it is plain that they did rely on the second misrepresentation, yet the Tribunal failed to consider it.

Remedy

17. Generally a failure by the Tribunal to consider an issue put to it would result in the decision being remitted for reconsideration to the Tribunal.

18. However in this case as there is also an application to appeal on questions of law and as the answer is plain, the Court is entitled to vary the Award to hold that JFR Offshore were entitled to rescind the charterparty.

PERMISSION TO APPEAL

Inducement/reliance

19. The Tribunal's findings in respect of this issue are to be found at paragraphs 32 to 49 of the Award.

20. In paragraph 32, the Tribunal sets out some of the authorities which deal with the test to be applied.

21. JFR Offshore accepts that in that paragraph the test is properly stated. The question is whether the representation was a 'real and substantial part of what induced' JFR Offshore to enter the charterparty. The Tribunal did state in its conclusion at paragraph 48 that it was not persuaded that the warranted deck strength could be properly categorised as a 'real and substantial part' of what induced JFR Offshore. However while the conclusion is couched in the language of the proper test, it is plain from the reasoning that led to the conclusion that the proper test was not applied.

Failure to apply the presumption

22. If a statement is material (that is that the statement is such that a person in the position of the representee could be expected to rely on it) there is a presumption of fact that it was relied upon. The matter was put as follows by Jessel MR in *Mathias v Yetts* (1882) 46 LT 497 that:

    'If a man has a material misstatement made to him which may from its nature induce to enter into the contract, it is an inference that he is induced to enter into the contract by it. You need not prove it affirmatively . . .'

23. In this case, the first representation was plainly material. Indeed the Tribunal stated as much as paragraph 45 of its Reasons where it acknowledged that a charterer would prefer a stronger deck.

24. However the Tribunal erred in failing to consider the effect of the presumption in this case.

Decision of the Tribunal obviously wrong

25. If one considers how the representation came to be made, it is obvious that the Tribunal has misdirected itself as a matter of law. The misrepresentation was made by the Owners in response to specific enquiries on the issue of deck strength. The finding that the answers did not form a real or substantial part of the decision-making process therefore flies in the face of reason.

26. The conclusion can only demonstrate that the Tribunal despite referring to the proper test did not apply it and must have misdirected itself as a matter of law.

Lapse of time

27. The Tribunal found in paragraphs 52 and 53 that the right to rescind had been lost by lapse of time.

28. The Claimants contend that the Tribunal was wrong in law to hold that:

    (1) Any lapse of time can be a bar to rescission as opposed to evidence of affirmation or estoppel other than by the doctrine of laches.

    (2) A lapse of time of the order considered in this case could constitute a bar in the light of the findings of fact in relation to affirmation and estoppel.

29. The Claimants contend that mere lapse of time is not a bar to rescission. Lapse of time only bars rescission if it give rise to laches.

30. The Tribunal erred in finding to the contrary as a matter of law.

31. Applying the proper law to the facts of this case, it is clear that there was no ground for holding that the remedy should be barred.

General public importance

32. There is uncertainty in the leading textbooks as to whether mere lapse of time not amounting to affirmation, estoppel or laches is a bar to recission.

33. This uncertainty renders it a question of general public importance to bring clarity to this area of the law.

Remedy

34. JFR Offshore contends that it is clear that there was sufficient inducement/reliance and that the right to rescind was not lost through lapse of time. In the premises, the first sentence of paragraph 6 of the Award should be set aside and the Award varied to hold that JFR Offshore's rescission of the charterparty was lawful.

35. The matter should be remitted to the Tribunal to assess the sums that need to be paid to the parties to effect restitution.

Dated this day of 2004

[Title from Part 8 Claim Form]

STATEMENT OF EUSTACE PRENDERGAST IN OPPOSITION TO CHARTERERS' APPLICATIONS UNDER SECTIONS 68/69

1. I Eustace Prendergast am a partner in the firm of Scuttle and Butt, solicitors of 33 Bilge Lane, London EC4. I have the conduct of this matter on behalf of the Owners of the RAINBOW BLUE, Panama Shipping Inc, and I am duly authorised by them to make this statement on their behalf. I do so in response to the contents of the Claim Form Addendum which has been verified by the statement of truth of my opposite number, Sally Anne Wilberforce of solicitors Bitter and End who act for the Charterers. I attended the arbitration hearing in question and was present throughout. The facts stated herein are within my own knowledge and true.

2. **Serious Irregularity** References to Annexes 2 to 8 of the attachments to the Claim Form show that both parties addressed the tribunal at length upon both alleged misrepresentations. I recall that the arbitrator, Mr Joseph Smith, asked several questions of counsel for each side about the second misrepresentation. It is extremely unlikely that the Tribunal did not fully consider the issue of the second misrepresentation. I produce a copy extract marked '*EP 1*' from my notebook to support this. Although the court will take a view as to the extent to which the Tribunal's consideration of these arguments is explicitly reflected in the reasons for the award, I submit that passages in paragraphs 40, 42 and 43 are consistent with its having done so.

3. **Permission to appeal** It is not necessary or appropriate for the Owners as respondents to the application to adduce evidence. They reserve the right to present argument at the hearing, if called upon. Briefly however the Owners' position is as follows:

disclosure of all material information to the court and must draw the court's attention to all significant factual, legal and procedural aspects of the case. A skeleton argument and a draft order must be lodged with the court prior to the oral hearing[2]. The claimant must make proper inquiries before making the application, as its duty of disclosure applies not only to material facts known to it but also to any additional facts which it would have known if it had made such inquiries. The court, and not the claimant or its legal advisors, is the ultimate judge of what information is material and should have been disclosed[3]. The claimant must identify the crucial points for *and against* its application, and must point out any likely defences that the absent defendant might assert. In short, the claimant must disclose all facts that a judge could reasonably take into account in deciding whether or not to grant the application[4].

A failure by the claimant to make full and fair disclosure of all material facts that it knows or ought reasonably to have discovered will generally lead to the immediate discharge of the *ex parte* order obtained 'without examination of the merits', though the court has a discretion not to discharge the order despite the material non-disclosure. The fact that the non-disclosure was innocent, in the sense that the claimant either did not know the information or did not appreciate its relevance, though an important consideration, will not necessarily prevent the court from discharging the *ex parte* order[5]. Given the severity of the sanction for material non-disclosure, the claimant's lawyers would be well advised to resolve all doubts about materiality in favour of disclosure.

The claimant's counsel and solicitors must make a full note of the hearing either at the time or soon thereafter, and must provide a copy of that note with all expedition to any party affected by the grant of relief[6].

1 CPR 62.4(1)(f)(ii) and 25.3.
2 *Memory Corporation plc v Sidhu (No 2)* [2001] 1 WLR 1443, (CA).
3 *Brink's Mat Ltd v Elcombe* [1988] 1 WLR 1350, (CA).
4 *Siporex Trade SA v Comdel Commodities Ltd* [1986] 2 Lloyd's Rep 428, (Bingham J).
5 *Brink's Mat Ltd v Elcombe* [1988] 1 WLR 1350, (CA).
6 *Interoute Telecommunications (UK) Ltd v Fashion Gossip Ltd,* The Times, 10 November 1999 (Lightman J).

Service out of the jurisdiction

16.17 If the defendant is resident outside England and Wales, the claimant may also ask the court to grant permission to allow the arbitration claim form to be served on the defendant out of the jurisdiction under CPR, Rule 62.5(1)(b). Such an application must be supported by written evidence showing the place or country where the defendant is or probably may be found[1]. Alternatively, in an appropriate case, the court may exercise its powers under CPR, Rule 6.8 to permit service of an arbitration claim form at the address of the defendant's solicitor or representative acting for him in the arbitration[2].

The brief summary above is only intended to provide a general practical outline of some of the relevant issues that should be considered in connection with an application under s 44. It is not intended to be an exhaustive or even complete account of the applicable law. For a fuller account, the reader should consult the standard reference books on arbitration, such as Mustill & Boyd *Commercial Arbitration: 2001 Companion Volume to the Second Edition* (2001), pp 192 and 323–4 and St John Sutton & Gill *Russell on Arbitration* (22nd edn, 2003), paras 7-129–7-144, pp 350–7, and the latest versions of CPR Part 62 and the Practice Direction to Part 62.

1 CPR 62.5(2)(b).
2 *Practice Direction – Arbitration,* Supplementing CPR Part 62, para 3.1.

Pleading

Assumed facts

16.18 The Claimant buyer, Beans & Co Inc, purchased a quantity of soya beans from the Defendant seller, Soya Export Ltd, C&F Zadar, Croatia or Koper/Rijeka in the buyer's option. The seller shipped the cargo on a vessel it had time chartered. On arrival at the discharge port, a portion of the cargo was found to be hardened and damaged. The facilities at that port would not allow the damaged cargo to be discharged there. The vessel therefore had to deviate to Venice, where the damaged cargo was discharged after being dug out by mechanical diggers.

The buyer sold the cargo by way of salvage sale at Venice. The seller is now purporting to exercise a lien over the damaged cargo for the costs of the deviation to Venice and is refusing to deliver the damaged cargo to the sub-buyer. The seller is demanding that the sum of US$68,000.00 be paid directly to it as a precondition for the release of the damaged cargo.

The cargo is continuing to deteriorate and the sub-buyer is threatening to terminate the sub-sale and sue the buyer for breach of the sub-sale contract.

Application for Delivery Up Order

Claim Form (Arbitration) – N8

Grounds for application and details of remedy claimed:

1. This is an application made without notice for:

   (1) An order pursuant to section 44 of the Arbitration Act 1996 directing the Defendant to deliver a cargo of Brazilian soya beans ('the damaged cargo') being wrongfully held by it to the Claimant; and

   (2) Permission, pursuant to CPR, Rule 62.5, to serve this Arbitration Claim Form and any Order issued by the Court on the Defendant out of the jurisdiction at its offices at [address].

2. This dispute arises from a contract of sale between the Claimant and the Defendant that provides for arbitration in London.

3. This is a case of urgency for the purpose of preserving assets under section 44(3) of the Arbitration Act 1996. The present application is being made without notice to the Defendant because of, *inter alia*, the ongoing deterioration of the damaged cargo, the danger of losing the salvage sale to the sub-buyer and the upcoming bank holiday weekend.

4. The arbitration reference has not yet been commenced, and therefore there is no arbitral panel able for the time being to act.

5. The Claimant is willing to undertake to commence arbitral proceedings within a reasonable time or, alternatively, within a period specified by the court.

6. The Claimant hereby seeks an order that the Defendant pay the Claimant's costs.

Statement in Support of Application for Delivery Up Order

Claimant
[Buyer's Solicitors' Name]
First, AB1
[Date]

Claim No ....

IN THE HIGH COURT OF JUSTICE
QUEEN'S BENCH DIVISION
COMMERCIAL COURT

IN THE MATTER OF THE ARBITRATION ACT 1996
IN AN ARBITRATION APPLICATION BETWEEN:

[BEANS & CO INC.]

Claimant

- and -

[SOYA EXPORT LTD]

Defendant/
Intended Respondent

WITNESS STATEMENT OF [AB] IN SUPPORT OF APPLICATION UNDER SECTION 44 OF THE ARBITRATION ACT 1996

THE RELIEF SOUGHT

1. I am a partner in the firm of [name & address], and I have the conduct of this matter on behalf of the Claimant. I make this statement in support of the Claimant's application for:

1.1 An order pursuant to section 44 of the Arbitration Act 1996 directing the Defendant to deliver a cargo of Brazilian soya beans ('the damaged cargo') wrongfully held by it to the Claimant;

1.2 Permission, pursuant to CPR, Rule 62.5, to serve this Arbitration Claim Form and any Order issued by the Court on the Defendant at its offices out of the jurisdiction at [address]; and

1.3 An order that the Defendant do pay the Claimant's costs.

2. This statement and the information that I rely on herein are from my own knowledge of the matter and that provided to me by [name] of the Claimant. Where the facts are within my knowledge, they are true. Where they are not within my knowledge, they are true to the best of my information and belief.

3. There is now produced and shown to me marked 'AB1' a paginated bundle containing true copies of relevant documents, to which I shall refer by page number in the course of this Statement. Numbers in brackets appearing in this Statement refer to pages in that bundle.

THE PURCHASE CONTRACT BETWEEN THE PARTIES

4. On [date], the Claimant entered into a contract (pp.__) to purchase from the Defendant 20,000 mts, 5% more or less at seller's option, of Brazilian soya beans 'suitable for oil extraction, sound, loyal, merchantable and free from any foreign smell' at a price of US$185 per metric ton ('the Purchase Contract').

5. The Purchase Contract provided for delivery C&F 'Zadar, Croatia or Koper/Rijeka in Buyers option'. The Claimant elected to take

delivery in Zadar. The Purchase Contract provides that all disputes arising from that contract must be resolved by arbitration in London.

6. The Claimant has paid the purchase price due under the Purchase Contract in full. Attached at 'AB1', p.__ is a confirmation from [name of bank] of the transfer of the purchase price to the Defendant.

THE DAMAGED CARGO, DEVIATION AND SALVAGE SALE

7. At the discharge port, it was found that part of the cargo was rotting, lumpy and giving off an unpleasant odour. The sound cargo was discharged at the discharge port, but lumpy damaged cargo could not be discharged using the suction system available at that port.

8. The Vessel therefore had to divert to Venice, where the damaged cargo was discharged after being dug out from the hold using mechanical diggers.

9. The Claimant has sold the damaged cargo to a sub-buyer at Venice by way of sub-sale at a very favourable price of US$115 per ton (pp.__).

THE DEFENDANT'S REFUSAL TO RELEASE THE CARGO

10. However, the Defendant has refused to release the damaged cargo to that sub-buyer, despite instructions from the Claimant that it do so. Instead, the Defendant has claimed to be entitled to receive an additional US$68,000.00 from the Claimant for alleged costs associated with the deviation of the Vessel and has purported to exercise a lien on the damaged goods to enforce that claim (pp.__).

11. The Claimant denies that the Defendant is entitled to that sum, or any sum. Given that the Claimant has already paid the full purchase price for the goods to the Defendant, the Claimant further denies that the Defendant is entitled to exercise any lien over the damaged goods.

12. In accordance with the Claimant's duty of full and frank disclosure, I should point out that the Defendant's argument against the granting of the relief sought by the Claimant in this application would likely be that it is entitled to exercise its purported lien over the damaged cargo to secure payment of its claim and the Court should not deprive it of that right. However, in my submission, it is clear that the Defendant can have no lien over the damaged cargo given that it has received payment of the purchase price in full and has already released the bills of lading relating to the damaged cargo to the Claimant.

THE URGENCY JUSTIFYING A WITHOUT NOTICE APPLICATION

13. I am informed by [name] of the Claimant, and believe, that the sub-buyer is pressuring the Claimant to deliver the damaged cargo in accordance with the sub-sale. I am also informed by [name], and believe, that the cargo is continuing to deteriorate.

14. There is a danger that, unless the Claimant delivers the damaged cargo to the sub-buyer very soon, the Claimant will not only lose the salvage sale (which is at a very favourable price for the Claimant), but will also face liability to the sub-buyer for breach of contract. It is not clear how much of that potential liability the Claimant might be able to recover from the Defendant in the intended arbitral proceedings.

15. The Defendant is fully aware that the Claimant has concluded a favourable salvage sale with the sub-buyer and that the damaged cargo is continuing to deteriorate (pp.__).

16. The present application is being made without notice to the Defendant under section 44(3) of the Arbitration Act 1996 because of the urgency of the matter, including the ongoing deterioration of the damaged cargo, the danger of losing the salvage sale to the sub-buyer and the upcoming bank holiday weekend.

THE ABSENCE OF A CONSTITUTED ARBITRAL TRIBUNAL

17. Given the urgency of the matter and the fact that negotiations with the Defendant were continuing until very recently, the Claimant has not been able to commence arbitral proceedings in accordance with the terms of the Purchase Contract. It is for that reason that there is at present no arbitral panel able to act in accordance with section 44(5) of the Arbitration Act 1996.

18. The Claimant is willing to undertake to commence arbitral proceedings within a reasonable time or, alternatively, within a period specified by the court.

PERMISSION TO SERVE OUT OF THE JURISDICTION

19. The Defendant has its offices out of the jurisdiction at [address]. I submit that this is a proper case for the Court to give the Claimant permission, pursuant to CPR, Rule 62.5, to serve the Arbitration Claim Form and any order that the Court might make on the Defendant at its offices out of the jurisdiction.

20. For the reasons set out above, I respectfully ask the Court to grant the Claimant the relief listed in paragraph 1 above.

21. I believe the facts stated in this witness statement are true.

Signed: ____________________

[AB]

Dated ____________________

Statement in Opposition to Application for Delivery Up Order

Defendant
[Seller's Solicitors' Name]
First, YZ1
[Date]
Claim No ....

IN THE HIGH COURT OF JUSTICE
QUEEN'S BENCH DIVISION
COMMERCIAL COURT

IN THE MATTER OF THE ARBITRATION ACT 1996
IN AN ARBITRATION APPLICATION BETWEEN:

BEANS & CO INC

Claimant

-and-

SOYA EXPORT LTD

Defendant/
Intended Respondent

WITNESS STATEMENT OF [YZ] IN OPPOSITION TO CLAIMANT'S APPLICATION FOR DELIVERY UP ORDER

---

1. I am a partner in the firm of [name & address], and I have the conduct of this matter on behalf of the Defendant. I make this statement in opposition to the Claimant's application under Section 44 of the Arbitration Act 1996 for delivery up of the

damaged cargo to the Claimant. For convenience, I have used in this Statement the abbreviations adopted in [AB]'s statement.

2. This Statement and the information that I rely on herein are from my own knowledge of the matter and that provided to me by [name] of the Defendant. Where the facts are within my knowledge, they are true. Where they are not within my knowledge, they are true to the best of my information and belief.

3. There is now produced and shown to me marked 'YZ1' a paginated bundle containing true copies of relevant documents, to which I shall refer by page number in the course of this Statement. Numbers in brackets appearing in this Statement refer to pages in that bundle.

4. The description of the background to the present dispute set out in [AB]'s statement is substantially accurate.

5. However, in my submission, [AB] is wrong in asserting that the Defendant has no lien over the damaged goods. It is the Defendant's position that it has such a lien and is entitled to exercise it over the damaged cargo, as it has done.

6. The Purchase Contract imposed a duty on the Claimant to discharge all the goods on the vessel at Zadar. In breach of contract, the Claimant failed to discharge the damaged goods at Zadar.

7. As a result of that breach of the Purchase Contract, the Vessel had to divert to an alternative port where the damaged cargo was ultimately discharged. The Defendant suffered a loss of at least US$68,000.00 (consisting of, *inter alia*, additional hire payable to the owners of the vessel, bunkers consumed and port dues) as a result of that deviation (pp.__).

8. The Defendant is entitled to recover that loss from the Claimant. Furthermore, in my submission, the Defendant is entitled to exercise a lien over the damaged goods in respect of that loss. The Defendant's right to a lien arises from the true construction of the following clauses of the Purchase Contract and/or by virtue of an implied term in those clauses (to be implied therein for business efficacy and/or to reflect the intentions of the parties):

   '[Quotations from the relevant clauses of the Purchase Contract]'

9. It is therefore the Defendant's case that it is fully entitled to exercise a lien over the damaged cargo to secure payment of its claim. I therefore respectfully ask the Court to dismiss the Claimant's application with costs.

10. Alternatively, without prejudice to the aforesaid, if the Court is nevertheless minded to issue a delivery up order in favour of the Claimant, I respectfully submit that it should make any such order conditional upon the Claimant paying the sum of US$68,000.00 into court. Such a course would allow the Claimant to perform its sub-sale, whilst at the same time allowing the Defendant to retain the benefit of its security interest in the damaged goods.

11. In my submission, it would be inappropriate for the court to summarily deprive the Defendant of its lien over the damaged cargo in these urgent proceedings under section 44. Instead, it should leave the question of the validity of the Defendant's lien to be resolved by an arbitral tribunal appointed in accordance with the arbitration clause in the Purchase Contract.

12. I believe the facts stated in this witness statement are true.

Signed: ____________________

[YZ]

Dated ____________________

Assumed facts 2

16.19 The Claimant charterers, Oil Trading Ltd, chartered the vessel 'TITAN' from the Defendant owners, Tankers International Inc., for carriage of crude oil from Nigeria to the US Gulf. Whilst the vessel was sailing towards the loadport, the owners informed the charterers that the vessel would be unable to perform the voyage as they had just discovered an oil leak from one of the cargo tanks into an adjacent water ballast tank and the vessels' classification society had ordered the vessel to go into dry-dock for inspection and urgent repairs.

The charterers replied that the owners were in repudiatory breach of the charter, that they accepted that repudiatory breach as bringing the charter to an end, and that they held the owners liable for all their losses resulting from the non-performance of the charter. The owners argued that they were not liable to the charterers because the leak resulted from a latent defect which they could not have discovered by the exercise of due diligence.

The charterers sent a surveyor to inspect the vessel in dry-dock on their behalf. The owners allowed the charterers' surveyor partial access to the vessel, but refused to allow him to inspect tanks not directly affected by the leak or the vessel's gas detection system. The charterers therefore applied under s 44 of the Arbitration Act 1996 for an order requiring the owners to permit the surveyor to inspect the vessel fully.

Application for Inspection of Vessel

Claim Form (Arbitration) – N8

Grounds for application and details of remedy claimed:

1. This is an application made with notice for:

   (1) An order pursuant to section 44 of the Arbitration Act 1996 directing the Defendant to allow the Claimant's nominated surveyor free and full access to the vessel 'THE TITAN' ('the Vessel') for the purposes of inspection; and

   (2) Permission, pursuant to CPR, Rule 62.5, to serve this Arbitration Claim Form and any Order issued by the Court on the Defendant out of the jurisdiction at its offices at [Defendant's address].

2. This dispute arises from a charterparty between the Claimant and the Defendant that provides for arbitration in London.

3. This is a case of urgency for the purpose of preserving evidence under section 44(3) of the Arbitration Act 1996. The present application is being made with notice to the Defendant.

4. The arbitration reference has not yet been commenced, and therefore there is no arbitral panel able for the time being to act.

5. The Claimant is willing to undertake to commence arbitral proceedings within a reasonable time or, alternatively, within a period specified by the Court.

6. The Claimant hereby seeks an order that the Defendant pay the Claimant's costs.

Statement in Support of Application for Inspection Order

Claimant
[Charterer's Solicitors' Name]
First, CD1
[Date]

Claim No ....

IN THE HIGH COURT OF JUSTICE
QUEEN'S BENCH DIVISION
COMMERCIAL COURT

IN THE MATTER OF THE ARBITRATION ACT 1996
IN AN ARBITRATION APPLICATION BETWEEN:

OIL TRADING LTD

Claimant

- and -

TANKERS INTERNATIONAL INC

Defendant/
Intended Respondent

WITNESS STATEMENT OF [CD] IN SUPPORT OF APPLICATION UNDER SECTION 44 OF THE ARBITRATION ACT 1996

THE RELIEF SOUGHT

1. I am a partner in the firm of [name & address], and I have the conduct of this matter on behalf of the Claimant. I make this statement in support of the Claimant's application for:

1.1 An order pursuant to section 44 of the Arbitration Act 1996 directing the Defendant to allow the Claimant's nominated surveyor free and full access to the vessel 'TITAN' ('the Vessel') for the purposes of inspection;

1.2 Permission, pursuant to CPR, Rule 62.5(1)(b), to serve this Arbitration Claim Form and any Order issued by the Court on the Defendant at its offices out of the jurisdiction at [address]; and

1.3 An order that the Defendant do pay the Claimant's costs.

2. This statement and the information that I rely on herein are from my own knowledge of the matter and that provided to me by [name] of the Claimant. Where the facts are within my knowledge, they are true. Where they are not within my knowledge, they are true to the best of my information and belief.

3. There is now produced and shown to me marked 'CD1' a paginated bundle containing true copies of relevant documents, to which I shall refer by page number in the course of this Statement. Numbers in brackets appearing in this Statement refer to pages in that bundle.

THE CHARTERPARTY AND ITS TERMINATION

4. On [date], the Claimant entered into a charterparty ('the Charterparty') on the amended STB VOY form (pp.__) for a laden voyage carrying crude oil from Nigeria to the US Gulf.

5. On or around [date], the Defendant informed the Claimant that a leak of oil from one of the vessel's starboard cargo tanks to an adjacent ballast tank had been detected and that, as a result, the Vessel would be proceeding immediately to a suitable shipyard for

repairs and would be unable to perform the voyage under the Charterparty (pp.__).

6. On [date] the Claimant sent a Notice of Protest to the Defendant stating that the Defendant's refusal to perform the voyage constituted an anticipatory and/or repudiatory breach of contract, which the Claimant accepted as terminating the Charterparty (pp.__). In that Protest, the Claimant also claimed damages from the Defendant for breach of the Charterparty and requested permission for a surveyor to be allowed on board to inspect the Vessel on its behalf.

THE DEFENDANT'S REFUSAL TO ALLOW FULL INSPECTION OF THE VESSEL

7. On [date] the Defendant informed the Claimant that the Vessel would be available for inspection for seven days at Gibraltar Bay, Spain. The Claimant's surveyor, [name] of [company], attended the Vessel on [date] whilst she was in dry-dock.

8. Although the Claimant's surveyor was permitted to enter the number 4 starboard ballast tank that suffered from the leak, he was unable to get a close up view of the crack from the cargo tank side due to the absence of staging.

9. The Claimant's surveyor then asked to inspect number 4 port water ballast tank, as it is normal procedure to inspect 'mirror image' tanks in the event of a structural failure. The Defendant, however, refused to allow that inspection. No specific reason was given for this refusal.

10. Further, the Claimant's surveyor also asked to inspect the Vessel's gas detection system, but the Defendant again refused to allow the surveyor to carry out that inspection.

HOW A FURTHER SURVEY WILL ASSIST THE ARBITRAL TRIBUNAL

11. The Defendant's defences will presumably be (a) that it exercised due diligence to make the Vessel seaworthy and/or (b) the Charterparty was frustrated. Therefore, the dispute between the parties will turn on the cause of the leakage and the extent to which it could have been prevented if the Defendant had exercised due diligence. Thus, the Vessel will be the subject matter of the proceedings to be issued.

12. A full and thorough inspection of the Vessel is necessary in the interests of justice, because the Claimant's surveyor cannot determine the cause of the leak and whether the leak could have been prevented by the exercise of due diligence without such an inspection.

13. In my submission, it is in the interests of both parties that this crucial evidence be collected before the defect is repaired. This evidence will enable the arbitral tribunal to determine whether or not the Claimant has a valid claim against the Defendant under the Charterparty.

14. Further, if the Claimant's surveyor is not given the opportunity to conduct a proper and full investigation the Claimant will have been deprived of the chance to prove its claim.

THE BALANCE OF CONVENIENCE

15. The Vessel is undergoing special survey, repairs and tests and therefore is out of service in any event. It will not cost the Defendant anything to allow the Claimant's Surveyor full access to the Vessel.

16. This application is urgent, as the Claimant's surveyor needs to have access to the relevant parts of the Vessel while she is still in dry-dock and before the defects in the Vessel are repaired. I therefore believe that the Surveyor needs to attend the Vessel immediately.

THE ABSENCE OF A CONSTITUTED ARBITRAL TRIBUNAL

17. Given the urgency of the matter, the Claimant has not been able to commence arbitral proceedings in accordance with the terms of the Charterparty. It is for that reason that there is at present no arbitral panel able to act in accordance with section 44(5) of the Arbitration Act 1996.

18. The Claimant is willing to undertake to commence arbitral proceedings within a reasonable time or, alternatively, within a period specified by the court.

PERMISSION TO SERVE OUT OF THE JURISDICTION

19. The Defendant has its offices out of the jurisdiction at [address]. I submit that this is a proper case for the Court to give the Claimant permission, pursuant to CPR, Rule 62.5, to serve the Arbitration Claim Form and any order that the Court might make on the Defendant at its offices out of the jurisdiction.

20. For the reasons set out above, I respectfully ask the Court to grant the Claimant the relief listed in paragraph 1 above.

21. I believe the facts stated in this witness statement are true.

Signed: ___________________

[CD]

Dated ___________________

Statement in Opposition to Application for Inspection Order:

Defendant
[Owner's Solicitors' Name]
First, GH1
[Date]

Claim No ....

IN THE HIGH COURT OF JUSTICE
QUEEN'S BENCH DIVISION
COMMERCIAL COURT

IN THE MATTER OF THE ARBITRATION ACT 1996
IN AN ARBITRATION APPLICATION BETWEEN:

OIL TRADING LTD

Claimant

- and -

TANKERS INTERNATIONAL INC

Defendant/
Intended Respondent

WITNESS STATEMENT OF [GH] IN OPPOSITION TO CLAIMANT'S APPLICATION FOR INSPECTION ORDER

---

1. I am a partner in the firm of [name & address], and I have the conduct of this matter on behalf of the Defendant. I make this statement in opposition to the Claimant's application, pursuant to section 44 of the Arbitration Act 1996, for an order for the inspection of the Vessel. For convenience, I have used in this Statement the abbreviations adopted in [CD]'s statement.

2. This Statement and the information that I rely on herein are from my own knowledge of the matter and that provided to me by [name] of the Defendant. Where the facts are within my knowledge, they are true. Where they are not within my knowledge, they are true to the best of my information and belief.

3. There is now produced and shown to me marked 'GH1' a paginated bundle containing true copies of relevant documents, to which I shall refer by page number in the course of this Statement. Numbers in brackets appearing in this Statement refer to pages in that bundle.

4. The description of the communications between the parties set out in [CD]'s statement is substantially accurate. Attached at 'GH1' pp__ are copies of additional relevant correspondence not attached to [CD's] statement.

THE FURTHER INSPECTION REQUESTED BY THE CLAIMANT

5. As [CD] acknowledges in his statement, the Defendant has already allowed the Claimant's surveyor free and unhindered access to the site of the leak, namely, No. 4 starboard water ballast tank. The Claimant's surveyor has been allowed to, and has, inspected that site as much as he wanted.

6. It is true that the Claimant's surveyor was not allowed to inspect No. 4 port water ballast tank. I have been advised by [name] of the Defendant, and therefore believe, that such inspection was refused because: (i) there is no defect in No. 4 port water ballast tank; (ii) that tank played no role in the Vessel's inability to perform the Charterparty; (iii) it is neither necessary nor helpful to inspect No. 4 port water ballast tank in order to determine the nature and cause of the defect in No. 4 starboard water ballast tank; (iv) unnecessary inspections of the Vessel, such as the one requested

by the Claimant, will hinder the work being carried out on the Vessel and thereby delay her departure from dry-dock; and (v) it was obvious from the Claimant's surveyor's attitude whilst on board that he was simply 'fishing' for defects in the Vessel, even though there is no evidence to suggest that any defect other than that openly disclosed by the Defendant exists.

7. As regards the Claimant's surveyor's request to inspect the Vessel's gas detection system, I have been advised by [name] of the Defendant, and therefore believe, that: (i) there is no defect in that system; (ii) an inspection of that system can provide no information as to the nature and cause of the leak in No. 4 starboard water ballast tank; and (ii) such an inspection would hinder the work being carried out on the Vessel and thereby delay her departure from dry-dock.

THE BALANCE OF CONVENIENCE

8. For the reasons set out above, the Defendant is strongly of the view that the further inspection requested by the Claimant will not assist the arbitral tribunal. All such an inspection will do is to hinder ongoing repairs to the Vessel and thereby delay her departure from dry-dock and ultimate return to profitable employment.

9. Therefore, I submit that the balance of convenience favours the rejection of the Claimant's application the relief listed, and I respectfully ask the court to do just that. I also ask the Court to award the Defendant its costs.

10. I believe the facts stated in this witness statement are true.

Signed: __________________

[GH]

Dated __________________

ENFORCEMENT OF AN ARBITRAL AWARD: SECTIONS 66 AND 101, ARBITRATION ACT 1996

Law

16.20 The Arbitration Act 1996, ss 66 and 101 empower the court to give leave to (i) enforce an arbitral award in the same manner as a judgment or order of the court to the same effect and/or (ii) enter a judgment in terms of the award[1]. Section 66 can be used for the enforcement of both domestic and foreign arbitral awards[2]. Section 101 specifically deals with those foreign awards enforceable under the New York Convention[3].

A court cannot give leave to enforce a domestic award if the defendant shows that the arbitral tribunal lacked substantive jurisdiction, unless the defendant has lost the right to raise that objection pursuant to s 73 of the 1996 Act[4]. Although lack of substantive jurisdiction is the only defence expressly mentioned in s 66, since that section does not *require* a court to allow enforcement but merely empowers it to do so, the court has a discretion to refuse leave where, for example, the award is defective in form or substance or enforcement would be contrary to public policy[5].

The bases upon which a court may refuse to enforce a foreign award under the New York Convention are set out in s 103 of the 1996 Act. They include the incapacity of a party to the arbitration agreement, the invalidity of the arbitration agreement, the absence of proper notice of the commencement of the arbitration, the award having being set aside or suspended by a competent authority, and the enforcement of the award being contrary to English public policy. The court must allow enforcement of the award unless one of the bases listed in s 103 is established. Unlike under s 66, the court has no general discretion to refuse leave to enforce an award under s 101[6].

1 Arbitration Act 1996, ss 66(1)–(2) and 101(2)–(3).
2 Arbitration Act 1996, s 2(2).
3 *The Convention on the Recognition and Enforcement of Foreign Arbitral Awards* adopted by the United Nations Conference on International Commercial Arbitration on 10 June 1958.
4 Arbitration Act 1996, s 66(3).
5 St John Sutton & Gill, *Russell on Arbitration* (22nd edn, 2003), para 8-003, p 363.
6 St John Sutton & Gill, *Russell on Arbitration* (22nd edn, 2003), paras 8-012–14, pp 369–371.

The applicable procedure

16.21 The procedure to be followed to obtain leave to enforce an award as a judgment and/or enter it as a judgment is set out in Section III of CPR, Part 62. In summary, the application must be supported by written evidence (usually in the form of a statement): (i) exhibiting the original or a copy (duly authenticated or certified in the case of an application under s 101) of the arbitration agreement and the award; (ii) stating the name and address of the claimant and the defendant; and (iii) stating that the award has not been complied with or setting out the extent to which it has not been complied with[1].

The application must be made on an arbitration claim form. It may be made without notice, though the court may specify parties to the arbitration upon whom the claim form must be served[2]. The court can give leave for such service to be made out of the jurisdiction, irrespective of where the award was made[3].

The court's order giving permission to enforce the award as a judgment may itself be served out of the jurisdiction without permission in accordance with CPR, Rules 6.24–6.29 as if the order were an arbitration claim form[4]. A defendant served with the order may apply to have it set aside within 14 days of service or, if the order was served outside the jurisdiction, within such period as the court may set[5]. The order must inform the defendant of its right to apply to have the order set aside and that the order cannot be enforced until the time period for making such an application has expired or the application has been finally disposed of[6].

The above is only a brief summary of some of the relevant issues that need to be considered when applying to enforce an arbitral award or opposing such enforcement. For a fuller account of the applicable law and procedure, the reader should consult the standard reference books on arbitration, such as St John Sutton & Gill *Russell on Arbitration* (22nd edn, 2003), paras 8-002–27, pp 361–79, and the latest version of CPR Part 62 and the Practice Direction to Part 62.

1 CPR, Rule 62.18(6).
2 CPR, Rule 62.18(1)–(3).
3 CPR, Rule 62.18(4).
4 CPR, Rule 62.18(8).
5 CPR, Rule 62.18(9).
6 CPR, Rule 62.18(9)–(10).

Pleading

Assumed facts

16.22 The Claimant, International Commerce Ltd and the Defendant, Worldwide Trading Inc, were parties to an International Agency Agreement. The Claimant claimed commission from the Defendant under that Agreement. The Defendant denied liability and rejected the Claimant's claim. The Claimant commenced arbitration by appointing its arbitrator and inviting the Defendant to appoint its arbitrator in response. The Defendant refused to appoint an arbitrator or have anything to do with the arbitration, arguing that the claim fell outside the scope of the arbitration clause in the Agreement. The Claimant's arbitrator became the sole arbitrator and issued an award in the Claimant's favour. The Defendant has refused to comply with the award. The Claimant therefore wishes to obtain an order from the court allowing (i) the award to be enforced as a judgment of the court and (ii) entering a judgment in the terms of the award.

Application to Enforce Award as Judgment and Enter Judgment in Terms of the Award

Claim Form (Arbitration) – N8

Grounds for application and details of remedy claimed:

1. This is an application made without notice pursuant to Section 66 of the Arbitration Act 1996 for:

   1.1 Leave of the court to enforce the award of the arbitral tribunal published on [date] in the arbitration held in London between the Claimant and the Defendant ('the Award') against the Defendant in the same manner as a judgment or order of the court to the same effect;

   1.2 Leave of the court to enter judgment in terms of the Award;

   1.3 Directions from the court pursuant to CPR, Rule 62.18(2) as to the parties upon which this arbitration claim form must be served; and

   1.4 If necessary, leave pursuant to CPR, Rule 62.18(4) to serve this arbitration claim form on the Defendant out of the jurisdiction at its offices at [address].

2. Pursuant to CPR, Rule 62.18(1), the present application is being made without notice to the Defendant.

3. The Claimant hereby seeks an order that the Defendant pay the Claimant's costs, to be assessed if not agreed.

Statement in Support of Application to Enforce Arbitral Award

Claimant
[Claimant's Solicitors' Name]
First, JK1
[Date]

Claim No ....

IN THE HIGH COURT OF JUSTICE
QUEEN'S BENCH DIVISION
COMMERCIAL COURT

IN THE MATTER OF THE ARBITRATION ACT 1996
IN AN ARBITRATION APPLICATION BETWEEN:

INTERNATIONAL COMMERCE LTD

Claimant

- and -

WORLDWIDE TRADING INC

Defendant

WITNESS STATEMENT OF [JK] IN SUPPORT OF APPLICATION TO ENFORCE AWARD & ENTER JUDGMENT IN TERMS OF AWARD

---

1. I am a partner in the firm of [name & address], and I have the conduct of this matter on behalf of the Claimant. I make this statement in support of the Claimant's application for:

1.1 Leave of the court to enforce the award of the arbitral tribunal published on [date] in the arbitration held in London between the Claimant and the Defendant ('the Award') against the Defendant in the same manner as a judgment or order of the court to the same effect;

1.2 Leave of the court to enter judgment in terms of the Award;

1.3 Directions from the court pursuant to CPR, Rule 62.18(2) as to the parties upon which this arbitration claim form must be served;

1.4 If necessary, leave pursuant to CPR, Rule 62.18(4) to serve this arbitration claim form on the Defendant out of the jurisdiction at its offices at [address]; and

1.5 An order that the Defendant do pay the Claimant's costs.

2. This statement and the information that I rely on herein are from my own knowledge of the matter and that provided to me by [name] of the Claimant. Where the facts are within my knowledge, they are true. Where they are not within my knowledge, they are true to the best of my information and belief.

3. There is now produced and shown to me marked 'JK1' a paginated bundle containing true copies of relevant documents, to which I shall refer by page number in the course of this Statement. Numbers in brackets appearing in this Statement refer to pages in that bundle.

4. Attached hereto at 'JK1', pp.__, is a true and correct copy of the Award of the arbitral tribunal (consisting of Mr [name] as sole arbitrator) published on [date] in the arbitration held in London between the Claimant and the Defendant.

5. Attached hereto at 'JK1', pp.__, is a true and correct copy of the International Agency Agreement between the Claimant and the Defendant. The arbitration agreement between the parties appears at clause 28 of that contract (p.__) and provides as follows:

   [Quote Arbitration Clause]

6. The Claimant's name is International Commerce Ltd. Its place of business is located at [address].

7. The Defendant's name is Worldwide Trading Inc. Its last known place of business is at [address].

8. Despite the fact that the Award was published over nine months ago, the Defendant has not complied with it at all.

9. For the reasons set out above, I respectfully ask the Court to grant the Claimant the relief listed in paragraph 1 above.

10. I believe the facts stated in this witness statement are true.

Signed: ________________

[JK]

Dated ________________

Statement in Opposition to Application to Enforce Arbitral Award

Defendant
[Defendant's Solicitors' Name]
First, MN1
[Date]

Claim No ....

IN THE HIGH COURT OF JUSTICE
QUEEN'S BENCH DIVISION
COMMERCIAL COURT

IN THE MATTER OF THE ARBITRATION ACT 1996
IN AN ARBITRATION APPLICATION BETWEEN:

INTERNATIONAL COMMERCE LTD

Claimant

- and -

WORLDWIDE TRADING INC

Defendant

WITNESS STATEMENT OF [MN] IN OPPOSITION TO APPLICATION TO ENFORCE AWARD & ENTER JUDGMENT IN TERMS OF AWARD

---

1. I am a partner in the firm of [name & address], and I have the conduct of this matter on behalf of the Defendant. I make this statement in opposition to the Claimant's application for leave to enforce the award of the arbitral tribunal published on [date] ('the

Award') against the Defendant as a judgment and to enter judgment in terms of the Award.

2. This statement and the information that I rely on herein are from my own knowledge of the matter and that provided to me by [name] of the Defendant. Where the facts are within my knowledge, they are true. Where they are not within my knowledge, they are true to the best of my information and belief.

3. There is now produced and shown to me marked 'MN1' a paginated bundle containing true copies of relevant documents, to which I shall refer by page number in the course of this Statement. Numbers in brackets appearing in this Statement refer to pages in that bundle.

4. I respectfully submit that the court cannot give the leave sought by the Claimant because the arbitral tribunal lacked substantive jurisdiction: see section 66(3) of the Arbitration Act 1996.

5. As the summary set out in the Award demonstrates, the commission claimed by the Claimant related to real property transactions allegedly undertaken by the Claimant in London. The sums purportedly awarded to the Claimant in the Award are in respect of that claim.

6. However, the International Agency Agreement, under which the Claimant's claim was purportedly advanced before the arbitral tribunal, is exclusively concerned with the provision of agency services by the Claimant in relation to the Defendant's sale and purchase of bulk goods, particularly crude oil and petroleum products, on the international market. The arbitration agreement at clause 28 of the International Agency Agreement only covers those agency services. I submit that it does not, on its true construction in the context of the Agreement as a whole and the

commercial relationship between the parties, cover agency services relating to alleged real property transactions that form the basis of the Award.

7. As a result of the arbitral tribunal's lack of substantive jurisdiction over the claim asserted by the Claimant, the Defendant expressly refused to nominate its arbitrator (pp.__) and took no part whatsoever in the reference. The Defendant thereby preserved its right to challenge any award based on lack of jurisdiction: see section 72 of the Arbitration Act 1996.

8. For the reasons set out above, I respectfully ask the Court to dismiss the Claimant's application in its entirety and award the Defendant its costs.

9. I believe the facts stated in this witness statement are true.

Signed: ____________________

[MN]

Dated ____________________

CHAPTER 17

Case Memorandum and List of Issues

Christopher Smith

Generally

17.1 It is a requirement of the Commercial Court, pursuant to para 10 of the Commercial Court Practice Direction, that in advance of a case management conference, all the parties must file and serve a completed case management information sheet, and the Claimant must prepare, in consultation with the other parties to the case, a case memorandum and a list of issues. All of these documents must be included in the case management bundle which has to be lodged at least seven days before the hearing, see para 10.8 of the Commercial Court Practice Direction.

The requirements of the Mercantile Courts are slightly less demanding, and all that is required in advance of a case management conference in the Mercantile Courts is for the parties to file and serve a case management information sheet and to agree a short list of the principal issues in the case, see para 7.7 of the Practice Direction to CPR 59.

As regards the case memorandum and list of issues, it must be remembered at the outset that the purpose of these documents is simply to expedite the case management conference by ensuring that the judge understands the issues in the case and hence is in a position to make the appropriate directions, see para D5.1 of the *Admiralty & Commercial Courts Guide*. These documents are not pleadings and are not binding on either party. Accordingly, it is not necessary for the parties to set out their entire case in these documents, and they should not be regarded as being part of the 'battleground' in the dispute.

Case Memorandum

17.2 Typically, this should be split up into two sections:

(1) a summary of what the case is about; and
(2) a summary of the case's history.

A summary of the dispute

17.3 Paragraph 10.8 of the Commercial Court Practice Direction states that the Case Memorandum should be 'short and uncontroversial'. Further guidance is given by para D5.5 of the *Admiralty & Commercial Courts Guide* which states:

'(a) It should be clearly understood that the only purpose of the case memorandum is to help the judge understand broadly what the case is about. The case memorandum does not play any part in the trial. It is unnecessary therefore for parties to be unduly concerned about the precise terms in which it is drafted, provided it contains a reasonably fair and balanced description of the case.'

The key to drafting the case summary section of the Case Memorandum is to imagine that you are trying to explain the case to a third party in a neutral and objective manner. First, there should be a summary of the facts which form the background to the dispute, explaining who the parties are, what their relationship is, and what the key events are which caused the dispute to crystallise.

Once this background has been established, the parties' respective positions and allegations should be explained. The starting point for this should be setting out what the Claimant's cause of action in respect of each Defendant is, along with any necessary accompanying factual allegations. This should be followed by an explanation of the defence of each Defendant in respect of the above allegation. Finally, any germane points made in Reply by the Claimant should be set out. All of the above should be on the basis of the pleadings. Any allegations or matters which are not contained in the pleadings should not be included.

A procedural summary

17.4 This should be kept very simple. The Case Memorandum should simply state when the Claim Form was issued; when an Acknowledgment of Service was filed and what its contents were; when Particulars of Claim were served; when a Defence was served; and when a Reply was served. Details of any other procedural steps, such as applications that have been issued and orders made by the court, should also be included.

List of issues

17.5 Again, this should be split up into two sections:

(1) a list of matters not in issue; and
(2) a list of those matters in issue.

The first section should incorporate any *important* matters that have been admitted in the pleadings. It is to be stressed that it is not necessary to put in every single admission contained in the pleadings, only those which will have an impact on how the case will be progressed and ultimately decided.

The second section should attempt to set out succinctly what the key issues in the case are. As is made clear by para D6.1 of *The Admiralty & Commercial Courts Guide*, only the important issues in the case should be included in this section. It is not necessary to include every matter which has not been admitted in the pleadings, otherwise the list of issues will end up resembling a re-hashed version of those pleadings and will not serve to assist the judge any better than had he simply read them. This is also the case for List of Issues in the Mercantile Court, see para 7.7 of the Mercantile Court Practice Direction which refers to a list of 'the principal issues'.

Case management information sheet

17.6 The standard form for the case management information sheet (which can be found in Appendix 6 to the *Admiralty & Commercial Courts Guide*), expressly states that the form should be completed with the involvement of the advocate(s) instructed for the trial.

The questions which have to be filled in are for the most part self-explanatory, and require the relevant party to state by when they can give standard disclosure, serve signed witness statements, etc.

One useful feature of the case management information sheet is that it allows the parties to make various applications at the case management conference without having to issue a formal application notice. Certain applications the parties might wish to make, for instance applying for permission to amend their statement of case, are expressly dealt with by the case management information sheet. For those matters not expressly dealt with, question 16 of the sheet states 'What other applications will you wish to make at the Case Management Conference?'. Paragraph D8.5(c) of the *Admiralty & Commercial Courts Guide*, states that if the relevant application does not require written evidence then it is not necessary to issue an application notice and the seven day notice given by entering the application on the information sheet will suffice.

Case Memorandum (based on pleadings to be found in Chapters 7 and 10)

Claim No ....

IN THE HIGH COURT OF JUSTICE
QUEEN'S BENCH DIVISION
COMMERCIAL COURT

B E T W E E N:

PROPERTY INSURANCE LIMITED

Claimant

- and -

CLOTHES SHOP LIMITED

Defendant

CASE MEMORANDUM

Case Summary

1. The Claimant is and was at all material times a company carrying the business of underwriting property insurance. The Defendant company is a ladies' fashion retailer operating from premises at 2–4 Main Street, Townville ('the Premises').

2. By a policy of insurance dated 1st June 2003, the Claimant agreed to insure the Premises and its contents against certain risks, including accidental damage by fire, for a period of 12 months commencing on 1st January 2003 ('the policy').

3. Clause 3 of the policy provided that, in the event of hot work being carried out, certain minimum precautions have to be taken, including appointing a fire safety employee, removing all combustible materials from the area where the hot works are being carried out, provision of a sufficient number of fire extinguishers, and making sure the individual carrying out the works is aware of the location the fire alarms and fire-fighting equipment. Clause 3 further provided that the taking of these precautions is a condition precedent to the Claimant's liability under the policy.

4. On or around 14th September 2003, the premises and all its content were destroyed by fire ('the fire'). The Defendant has made a claim under the Policy against the Claimant in respect of the fire ('the claim').

5. At the time of the fire, the Defendant had engaged a workman, Mr Sawyer, to carry out repairs to a felt roof over the premises. It is the Claimant's case that the fire was caused when, during work being carried out by Mr Sawyer with a blowtorch, a pile of old cardboard boxes and polythene bags ignited. No admissions have been made by the Defendant as to the cause of the fire.

6. The Claimant contends that the work being carried out by Mr Sawyer constituted hot work, and that the Defendant was obliged to take the minimum precautions set out in clause 3 of the policy. The Claimant avers that the Defendant in fact took none of the minimum precautions, and hence was in breach of the condition precedent contained in clause 3 of the policy.

7. Accordingly, the Claimant seeks a declaration that it is not obliged to indemnify the Defendant in respect of the claim.

8. The Defendant admits that the minimum precautions were not taken, but avers that on a true construction of clause 3 of the

policy, it was only obliged to take the minimum precautions listed therein if it had actual or constructive knowledge that Mr Sawyer intended to use a blowtorch to carry out the repairs.

9. It is the Defendant's case that it had no such knowledge, and hence was under no obligation to comply with the minimum precautions.

10. Therefore, the Defendant contends that the Claimant's rejection of the Claim is wrongful and constitutes a breach of contract, and the Defendant has counterclaimed for the full amount of the claim.

11. In Reply, the Claimant has contended that, on a true construction of clause 3 of the policy, there is no requirement of knowledge on the part of the Defendant that the hot works are taking place to trigger the obligation to take the minimum precautions. Further, had the Defendant exercised common care, it would have known that hot work would have been carried out, and accordingly the Defendant is in breach of the terms of the policy.

Procedural History

Claim Form served	12th January 2004
Acknowledgement of Service filed stating intention to defend the claim	24th January 2004
Particulars of Claim served	8th February 2004
Defence served	20th February 2004
Reply Served	3rd March 2004

List of Issues

Claim No ....

IN THE HIGH COURT OF JUSTICE
QUEEN'S BENCH DIVISION
COMMERCIAL COURT

B E T W E E N:

PROPERTY INSURANCE LIMITED

Claimant

- and -

CLOTHES SHOP LIMITED

Defendant

LIST OF ISSUES

Common Ground

1. The Claimant is an insurance company. The Defendant is a ladies' fashion retailer, operating from premises at 2–4 Main Street, Townville ('the premises').

2. By a policy of insurance dated 1st June 2003, the Claimant agreed to insure the premises and its contents against accidental damage by fire for a period of 12 months commencing 1st January 2003 ('the policy').

3. Clause 3 of the policy provided that in the event of hot work being carried out at the premises, certain minimum safety precautions had to be taken.

4. On or around 14th September 2003, the premises burnt down destroying both the building and all its contents.

5. At or around the time of the fire, the Claimant had engaged a workman, Mr Sawyer, to perform repairs to a felt roof over the premises.

6. The Defendant and/or Mr Sawyer failed to take the minimum precautions listed in clause 3 of the policy.

7. The Defendant has made a claim under the policy for its losses arising out of the fire, and the Claimant has rejected that claim.

In Issue

8. What was the cause of the fire, in particular was it caused by Mr Sawyer using a blowtorch whilst carrying out the repairs and thereby igniting a pile of old cardboard boxes and polythene bags?

9. On a true construction of clause 3 of the policy, was the Defendant only obliged to take the minimum precautions if it knew or ought to have known that hot work was taking place?

10. Did the Defendant know, and/or ought the Defendant to have known, that hot work was taking place?

11. Is the Claimant liable to the Defendant under the policy for the Defendant's losses arising out of the fire?

Claim No ....

IN THE HIGH COURT OF JUSTICE
QUEEN'S BENCH DIVISION
COMMERCIAL COURT

B E T W E E N:

SELLER INC

Claimants

- and -

BUYER LIMITED

Defendants

CASE MEMORANDUM

Case Summary

1. The Claimants are an American company involved in the business of manufacturing and exporting diesel engines. The Defendants are an English company involved in the business of manufacturing Fire Tenders.

2. By a contract in writing concluded on or around 12th September 2004, the Claimants agreed to sell and the Defendants agreed to buy 100 complete diesel engines at a price of £10,000 per unit FOB Boston shipment October at buyers' call.

3. It was an express term of the contract that the Defendants would pay the Claimants the full contract price upon the engines being loaded on board the nominated Vessel.

4. The contract was subsequently varied to provide for shipment on the motor vessel 'ESSEX' soonest November 2004, and the engines were in fact shipped from Boston on the 3rd November 2004, and were discharged at Glasson dock on the 15th November 2004.

5. The Claimants contend that, wrongfully and in breach of contract, the Defendants have failed to pay the Claimants the price of the engines in accordance with the terms of the contract. As such, the Claimants are claiming for the full contract price of £1m, said sum is said to be the true measure of the Claimants' loss and damage as the engines were manufactured to the Defendants' unique specification, and there is no other market for them.

6. The Defendants do not deny that the contract price has not been paid, but aver that it was a term of the contract that the engines would be loaded on board the vessel free from defect, of satisfactory quality and fit for their purpose, namely incorporation into Fire Tenders without modification.

7. The Defendants contend that, in breach of contract, the engines were in fact loaded on board the Vessel in a defective state in that each engine exhibited sump case fracturing. As such, the Defendants are counterclaiming for their expenditure in repairing the damage, and such losses as they will suffer by their inability to supply the engines to their own customer.

8. In response, the Claimants contend that the engines were free from defect when they were placed on board the Vessel, and that any damage to them occurred after the engines had passed the ship's rail and/or during stowage, and that under the terms of contract the engines were at the Defendants' risk at these points in time. The Claimants further deny that there was a term in the contract as to the engines' fitness for purpose.

9. The Claimants in any event further deny that the Defendants are entitled to set off a claim to be indemnified against a claim for a debt or a liquidated sum.

Procedural History

Claim Form issued	1st December 2004
Acknowledgment of Service filed	10th December 2004
Particulars of Claim served	24th December 2004
Defence and Counterclaim served	8th January 2005
Reply and Defence to Counterclaim served	20th January 2005

<u>**Claim No ....**</u>

<u>**IN THE HIGH COURT OF JUSTICE**</u>
<u>**QUEEN'S BENCH DIVISION**</u>
<u>**COMMERCIAL COURT**</u>

B E T W E E N:

SELLER INC

<u>**Claimants**</u>

- and -

BUYER LIMITED

<u>**Defendants**</u>

LIST OF ISSUES

Common Ground

1. The Claimants are an American company involved in the business of manufacturing and exporting diesel engines. The Defendants are an English company involved in the business of manufacturing Fire Tenders.

2. By a contract in writing concluded on or around 12th September 2004, the Claimants agreed to sell and the Defendants agreed to buy 100 complete diesel engines at a price of £10,000 per unit FOB Boston shipment October at buyers' call.

3. It was an express term of the contract that:

   3.1 the Defendants would pay the Claimants the full contract price upon the engines being loaded on board the nominated Vessel;

3.2 the engines would be free from defects up to the point of their passing the ship's rail on loading.

4. The Defendants did not nominate a vessel in time for an October shipment, and accordingly the parties agreed to vary the contract to provide for shipment on the motor vessel 'ESSEX' soonest November 2004.

5. The Defendants have not paid the Claimants for the engines in accordance with the terms of the contract.

In Issue

6. Whether it was a term of the contract that the engines would be fit for their purpose, namely incorporation into Fire Tenders without modification or adaptation?

7. Whether the engines were in a defective state in that each of them exhibited sump case fracturing?

8. If the engines were in a defective state as aforesaid, when did they become damaged, and at whose risk under the contract of sale were they at this time?

9. If the engines were damaged whilst they were at the Claimants' risk, what losses have the Defendants suffered as a result, and are the Defendants entitled to set those losses off against the Claimants' claim for the contractual price?

CHAPTER 18

Offers to Settle and Payments into Court

Nigel Cooper

Introduction

18.1 The procedures for making offers to settle and payments into court are laid down in Part 36 of the Civil Procedure Rules and the accompanying Practice Direction. With the introduction of the Civil Procedure Rules, claimants as well as defendants are now able to make offers to settle.

Rule 36.1 makes clear that Part 36 is not intended to prevent a party making an offer to settle in whichever way that party chooses. However, it is only if the offer is made in accordance with Part 36 that the offer will have the consequences laid down in that Part (unless the court otherwise orders).

Part 36 offers and payments can be made both in respect of first instance proceedings and in respect of appeal proceedings. However, a claimant's offer made for the purposes of the original proceedings will not continue to be effective in respect of an appeal. A claimant has to make a separate offer to cover any appeal proceedings (*East West Corporation v DKBS* [2003] 1 Lloyd's Rep 265 and *Cel Group Ltd v Nedlloyd Lines UK Ltd* [2004] 1 Lloyd's Rep 388).

The formalities required in relation to Part 36 offers and payments are set out below. It is important to stress that a failure to comply with those formalities may render the offer or payment invalid so that it does not offer the party making it the expected protection in relation to costs. The court does have a discretion to waive compliance with the mandatory requirements, but it will only exercise this discretion if it can be shown that the other party has not been misled or suffered any prejudice as a consequence of the failure (*Mitchell v James* [2004] 1 WLR 158 and *Neave v Neave (No. 2)* [2002] EWHC 966 (QB)).

A Defendant's offer to settle a money claim needs a Part 36 payment – CPR 36.3

18.2 The provisions of Part 36 apply to both money claims and non-money claims. However, if a defendant wishes to make an offer in respect of a money claim, he must make a Part 36 payment if he wishes to obtain the costs protection offered by Part 36 (the position may be different if the defendant is a public body, which will inevitably be good for the money offered; see *Crouch v King's Healthcare NHS Trust* [2004] EWCA Civ 1332). A Part 36 payment can only be made after the commencement of proceedings, but the court will take into account any offer made before the commencement of proceedings when making any order as to costs provided that the terms of Rule 36.10 are complied with. A Part 36 offer may consist of a proposal to settle for a specific sum or for some other remedy (Part 36 PD2.3)

Defendant's offers to settle a money claim and a non-money claim – CPR 36.4

18.3 Where a defendant wishes to make an offer under Part 36 in respect of proceedings for a money claim and a non-money claim, he must make a Part 36 payment in respect of the money claim and a Part 36 offer in respect of the non-money claim. The Part 36 payment notice must identify the document that sets out the terms of the Part 36 offer and state that if the claimant gives notice of acceptance of the Part 36 payment he will be treated as also accepting the Part 36 offer. If the claimant then gives notice of acceptance of the Part 36 payment, he will be treated as giving notice of acceptance of the Part 36 offer in respect of the non-money claim.

Form and content of a Part 36 offer – CPR 36.5

18.4 A Part 36 offer has to be in writing, must state that it is a Part 36 offer and be signed by the offeror or his legal representative. Where a Part 36 offer is made by a company or other corporation, it can be signed on the offeror's behalf by a person holding a senior position in the company or corporation but the signatory must state his position (CPR 36 PD5). For a registered company or corporation, a person holding a senior position is a director, the treasurer, secretary, chief executive, manager or other officer of the company or corporation. For corporations that are not registered companies, the mayor, chairman, president, town clerk or similar officer are also officers in a senior position.

A Part 36 offer can relate to the whole claim or to part of it or to any issue that arises in it. The offer must state:

- whether it relates to the whole of the claim or to part of it or to an issue, and if so, which part or issue;
- whether it takes into account any counterclaim;
- if it is not expressed to be inclusive of interest, whether interest is offered and if so at what rate and for what period.

If a Part 36 offer is made not less than 21 days before the start of the trial, it must be expressed to remain open for acceptance for 21 days from the date that it is made and must state that after 21 days the offeree can only accept it if the parties agree the liability for costs or the court gives permission.

A Part 36 offer made less than 21 days before the start of the trial must state that the offeree can only accept it if the parties agree the liability for costs or the court gives permission.

A Part 36 offer must not include as part of the offer any terms relating to the costs of the proceedings (*Mitchell v James* [2004] 1 WLR 158 and *Ali Reza-Delta Transport Co Limited v United Arab Shipping Co SAG (No. 2)* [2003] 2 Lloyd's Rep 455).

Where a party on whom a Part 36 offer, a Part 36 payment notice or a notice of acceptance is to be served, is legally represented, the Part 36 offer, Part 36 payment notice and notice of acceptance must be served on the legal representative. This applies in respect of both Part 36 offers and payments by a defendant and Part 36 offers by a claimant (CPR 36 PD11).

If a Part 36 offer is withdrawn, it will not have the consequences set out in Part 36. A Part 36 offer can be withdrawn at any time prior to acceptance (*Scammell v Dicker* [2001] 1 WLR 631).

Form of Part 36 Payment – CPR 36.6

18.5 A Part 36 payment can relate to the whole claim or part of it or to an issue that arises in it. A defendant who makes a Part 36 payment must file with the court a notice that states:

- the amount of the payment;
- whether the payment relates to the whole claim or to part of it or to any issue that arises in it and if so to which part or issue;
- whether it takes into account any counterclaim;
- if an interim payment has been made, that the defendant has taken into account the interim payment; and
- if it is expressed not to be inclusive of interest, whether interest is offered and if so at what rate and for what period.

The court form for notice of a payment into court under CPR Part 36 is presently Form N242A. The offeror must serve the Part 36 payment notice on the offeree and file a certificate of service of the notice. The payment must be sent to the Court Funds Office together with a sealed copy of the claim form and Court Funds Office Form 100 (CPR 36 PD4.1). There are, however, special rules for litigants in person without a current account bringing proceedings in a County Court or District Registry.

Money can be paid into court in a foreign currency when it is a Part 36 payment and the claim is in a foreign currency or under a court order. The court can direct that the money be placed in an interest bearing account in the currency of the claim or any other currency. If a Part 36 payment is made in a foreign currency and has not been accepted within 21 days, the defendant may apply under CPR Part 23 for an order that the money be placed in an interest bearing account (CPR 36 PD10).

Unlike a Part 36 offer, a part 36 payment can be withdrawn or reduced only with the permission of the court. A party seeking to withdraw or reduce a Part

36 payment should apply for permission in accordance with CPR Part 23 stating the reasons for wishing to withdraw or reduce the payment. (CPR 36 PD3.5). The circumstances in which a court will be prepared to permit a withdrawal or reduction of a Part 36 payment are discussed in *MRW Technologies Limited v Cecil Holdings Limited* (Garland J, All England Official Transcripts, 22 June 2001 as well as in *Capital Bank plc v Peter Strickland* [2004] EWCA Civ 1677 and *Flynn v Scougall* [2004] 1 WLR 3069).

Offer to settle a claim for provisional damages – CPR 36.7

18.6 A defendant can make a Part 36 payment in respect of a claim, which includes a claim for provisional damages. If he does so, the Part 36 Notice must state whether or not the defendant is offering to agree to the making of an award of provisional damages. If the defendant is offering to agree to the making of such an award, the payment notice must also state:

(i) that the sum paid into court is in satisfaction of the claim for damages on the assumption that the injured person will not develop the disease or suffer the type of deterioration specified in the notice;
(ii) that the offer is subject to the condition that the claimant must make any claim for further damages within a limited period; and
(iii) what that period is.

If the Part 36 payment is made in the required form and accepted within the normal 21-day period, it will have the usual costs consequences unless the court orders otherwise. If the claimant accepts the Part 36 payment, he must, within seven days of doing so, apply to the court for an order for an award of provisional damages under CPR 41.2.

Date when a Part 36 offer or Part 36 payment is made and accepted – CPR 36.8

18.7 A Part 36 offer is made when it is received by the offeree. A Part 36 payment is made when written notice of the payment into court is served on the offeree. Similarly, an improvement in a Part 36 offer is made when it is received by the offeree and an increase in a Part 36 payment is made when notice of the increase is served on the offeree. A Part 36 offer or Part 36 payment is accepted when notice of its acceptance is received by the offeror. The current court form for Notice of a Part 36 Payment is Form N242A. The current form for giving notice of acceptance and making a request for payment is Form N243A/Form 201.

Seeking clarification of a Part 36 offer or a Part 36 payment notice – CPR 36.9

18.8 An offeree can request clarification of a Part 36 offer or payment within seven days of it being made. If the offeror does not give the clarification requested within seven days of receiving the request, the offeree can, unless the trial has started, apply for an order that the offeror gives the requested clarification. The application should be made pursuant to CPR Part 23 and should state the respects in which the Part 36 offer or payment notice requires clarification. If an order for clarification is made, the court must specify the date when the offer or payment is to be treated as having been made. It should be noted that the courts have stressed the need for parties to give full and prompt disclosure of all relevant information and that a failure to do so may render the offer or payment ineffective for the purposes of protecting the offeree in relation to costs; see, for example, *Ford v GKR Construction Ltd* [2000] 1 WLR 1397 and *Jetoil v Okta* [2003] 1 Lloyd's Rep 42.

Offers to settle made before the commencement of proceedings – CPR 36.10

18.9 If a person makes an offer to settle before proceedings begin that complies with the requirements of CPR 36.10, the court will take that offer into account when making any order as to costs (*Huck v Robson* [2002] 3 All ER 263 and *Jetoil v Okta* [2003] 1 Lloyd's Rep 42, p 47). The offer must be expressed to be open for at least 21 days after the date it was made. If made by a person who would be a defendant were proceedings to be commenced, the offer must also include an offer to pay the costs of the offeree incurred up to the date 21 days after the date it was made. Finally, it must otherwise comply with Part 36.

If the offeror is a defendant to a money claim, he must make a Part 36 payment within 14 days of service of the claim form for an amount not less than the sum offered before proceedings began.

Once proceedings have begun, an offeree cannot accept an offer or payment made in accordance with CPR 36.10 without the permission of the court. An offer under this rule is made when it is received by the offeree.

Time for and consequence of acceptance of a defendant's Part 36 offer or a Part 36 payment – CPR 36.11, 36.13 and 36.16

18.10 A claimant may accept a Part 36 offer or payment that is made not less than 21 days before the start of the trial without needing the court's permission provided he gives the defendant written notice of acceptance not later than 21 days after the offer or payment was made. If the claimant accepts the offer or payment, he will be entitled to his costs of the proceedings up to the date of serving notice of acceptance. If the Part 36 offer or payment relates only to part of the claim and the claimant abandons the balance of his claim at the time of serving notice of acceptance, the claimant will be entitled to his costs of proceeding up to the date of serving notice of acceptance unless the court otherwise orders.

If a defendant's Part 36 offer or payment is made not less than 21 days before the start of the trial or the claimant does not accept it within the permitted 21-day period, the claimant can still accept the offer or payment without needing the permission of the court provided the parties agree the liability for costs. If the parties do not agree the liability for costs, then the claimant needs the permission of the court to accept the offer. If the court's permission is needed, and it is given, the court will make an order as to costs. If permission is sought before the trial has started, the application should be made under CPR Part 23. If it is made after the trial has started, the application is made to the trial judge.

Where the claimant accepts a Part 36 payment, he obtains payment out of the sum in court by making a request using the relevant practice form (presently Form N243A/Form 201).

Time for and consequence of acceptance of a claimant's Part 36 offer – CPR 36.12 and 36.14

18.11 A defendant can accept a Part 36 offer made not less than 21 days before the start of the trial without needing the court's permission if he gives the claimant written notice of acceptance no more than 21 days after the offer was made.

If a claimant's Part 36 offer is made less than 21 days before the start of the trial; or the defendant does not accept it within the 21-day period, the defendant can still accept the offer without needing the permission of the court provided that the parties agree the liability for costs. If the parties do not agree the liability for costs, the defendant requires the permission of the court to accept the offer. If permission is required, the court will, if it gives permission, make an order for costs. It should not be assumed, however, that the court will always give permission (see *Capital Bank plc v Peter Strickland* [2004] EWCA Civ 1677).

If the defendant accepts a claimant's Part 36 offer without needing the permission of the court, the claimant is entitled to his costs of the proceedings up to the date on which the defendant serves notice of acceptance.

The effect of accepting a Part 36 offer or Part 36 payment – CPR 36.15

18.12 If a Part 36 offer or payment relating to the whole claim is accepted, then the claim is stayed. Where a Part 36 offer has been accepted, the stay will be on the terms of the offer and either party can apply to enforce those terms without the need for a new claim. A Part 36 payment is accepted by the claimant obtaining payment out of court of the sum in court by making a request for payment using the practice form (presently Form N243A/Form 201).

If the Part 36 offer or payment that is accepted relates to only part of the claim, then the claim will be stayed as to that part and unless the parties have agreed costs, the liability for costs will be decided by the court.

If the approval of the court is required before a settlement can be binding (for example in cases involving children or patients), any stay will only take effect once that approval has been given.

Any stay arising under this rule will not affect the power of the court to enforce the terms of a Part 36 offer, to deal with any question of costs or to order payment of court of any sum paid into court. In particular, where a Part 36 offer has been accepted and a party alleges that the other party has not honoured the terms of the offer and that he accordingly has a remedy for breach of contract, that party can claim the remedy without starting a new claim (unless the court orders otherwise).

Acceptance of a Part 36 offer or payment made by one or more, but not all, defendants – CPR 36.17

18.13 A situation may arise where the claimant wishes to accept a Part 36 offer or payment made by one or more, but not all of a number of defendants. If the claimant is suing the defendants jointly or in the alternative, then he can only accept the payment without the permission of the court if he discontinues his claim against those defendants who have not made the offer or payment and those defendants give their written consent to the acceptance of the offer or payment. If the claimant alleges that the defendants have a several liability to him, the claimant can accept the offer or payment in accordance with the ordinary rule (CPR 36.11(1)) and continue with his claims against the other defendants if he is entitled to do so. In every other case, the claimant must apply to the court for:

(i) an order permitting a payment out to him of any sum in court; and
(ii) such order as to costs as the court considers appropriate.

Where the court gives a claimant permission to accept a Part 36 offer or payment after the trial has started, any money in court may only be paid out with a court order and the court must deal in the order with the whole costs of the proceedings. Similarly, if the claimant accepts a Part 36 payment after a defence of tender before claim has been put forward, the money can only be paid out after an order of the court.

Restrictions on disclosing a Part 36 offer or a Part 36 payment – CPR 36.19

18.14 A Part 36 offer is treated as being made 'without prejudice save as to costs'. The fact that a Part 36 offer or payment has been made is not to be communicated to the trial judge until all questions of liability and the amount of money have been decided. This rule does not apply:

(i) if the defence of tender before claim has been raised;
(ii) where the proceedings have been stayed under CPR 36.15 following acceptance of a Part 36 offer or payment; or
(iii) where the issue of liability has been determined before any assessment of the money claimed and the fact that there has or has not been a Part 36 payment may be relevant to the question of the costs of the issue of liability.

If an offer or payment is disclosed in breach of CPR Part 36.19, it is for the trial judge to determine what the consequence of the disclosure is to be. If the judge thinks it proper or necessary for the due administration of justice, he may refuse to hear the action any further and direct it to be tried before another tribunal. On the other hand, if he is satisfied that no injustice will be done, he may allow the matter to proceed and, if he adopts this course, that will not in itself afford any ground for an appeal from the order, which is ultimately made; see *Garratt v Saxby* [2004] 1 WLR 2152 approving the guidance given in *Millensted v Grosvenor House (Park Lane) Ltd* [1937] 1 KB 717.

Costs consequences in the event that the claimant fails to do better than a Part 36 offer or a Part 36 payment – CPR 36.20

18.15 If a claimant fails at trial to better a Part 36 payment or obtain a judgment that is more advantageous than a defendant's Part 36 offer, then he will be ordered to pay any costs incurred by the defendant after the latest date on which the payment or offer could have been accepted without needing the permission of the court unless the court considers it unjust that the claimant should do so. For a discussion of the circumstances where the court might consider it unjust to follow the usual rule; see *Ford v GKR Construction* [2000] 1 WLR 1397, *Uttley v Uttley* [2001] All ER (D) 240 (July) and *Factortame v Secretary of State* [2002] 1 WLR 2438.

Costs and other consequences where a claimant does better than he proposed in his Part 36 offer – CPR 36.21

18.16 If a defendant is held liable at trial for more or the judgment against a defendant is more advantageous to the claimant than the proposals contained in a claimant's Part 36 offer, the court has a considerable discretion as to the consequences that follow in terms of interest and costs. The court may order interest on the whole or part of any sum of money (excluding interest) awarded to the claimant at a rate not exceeding 10% above base rate for some or all of the period starting with the latest date on which the defendant could have accepted the offer without needing the permission of the court. The court can also order that the claimant is entitled to his costs on an indemnity basis from the latest date when the defendant could have accepted the offer without needing the permission of the court and interest on those costs at a rate not exceeding 10% above base rate. If the court awards interest under this rule and awards interest on the same sum and for the same period under any other power, the total rate of interest cannot exceed 10% above base rate. It should be noted, however, that the fact that a Claimant makes a successful Part 36 offer under CPR 36.21 does not prevent the court making an issue-based costs order under its powers under CPR 44.3; see *Kastor Navigation Co Limited v Axa Global Risks (UK) Limited* [2004] Lloyd's Rep 481.

The court will make orders for an enhanced rate of interest, indemnity costs and interest on those costs unless it considers that it would be unjust to do so (see *Jetoil v Okta* [2003] 1 Lloyd's Rep 42 for an example of a case where the court did consider such orders unjust). In considering whether such orders would be unjust, CPR 36.21 requires the court to take into account the circumstances of the case including:

(i) the terms of any Part 36 offer;
(ii) the stage in the proceedings when any Part 36 offer or payment was made;
(iii) the information available to the parties at the time when the Part 36 offer or payment was made; and
(iv) the conduct of the parties with regard to the giving or refusing to give information for the purposes of enabling the offer or payment into court to be made or evaluated.

In *Huck v Robson* [2002] 3 All ER 263, the Court of Appeal offered some guidance in applying these factors. Although not mandatory, it would be prudent for a judge to expressly consider the four factors in CPR 36.21. A judge will be entitled to exercise his discretion and refuse indemnity costs if the offer is made purely tactically in order to obtain the benefit of CPR Part 36. The court should look at the question of justice by reference to the facts of the individual case before it and not look to questions of justice in general or issues of social policy.

Unlike an order for indemnity costs made under CPR Part 44, an award of indemnity costs under CPR 36.21 is not intended to be penal or carry any stigma with it. It is simply one of the incentives offered to the claimant to make an offer to settle his claim; see *McPhilemy v Times Newspapers (No. 2)* [2001] 4 All ER 861 and *Petrotrade Inc v Texaco Ltd* [2002] 1 WLR 947.

Some guidance on determining the appropriate interest rate for the purposes of CPR 36.21 was offered obiter by Lord Woolf MR in *Petrotrade Inc v Texaco Ltd* [2002] 1 WLR 947[1]. In that case, Lord Woolf rejected the approach of starting with an interest rate of base rate plus 10% and working down. He offered the following factors as guiding his view that in that case an appropriate interest rate would have been 4% above the base rate:

- That the claimant had not provided all the information necessary for the defendant to consider properly the offer made.
- That so far as interest in commercial cases is concerned, the going rate is now 1% above base rate.

- That, if there is cause to criticise a party's conduct, it would not justify increasing the rate of enhanced interest to punish that party. It would, however, mean that, because the party had behaved in that way, it had forfeited the opportunity of achieving a reduction in the rate of additional interest payable.
- That the court would have to take into account all the circumstances in considering whether it would be just to make an order for enhanced interest.
- That if a claim is small, enhanced interest has to be at a higher rate than if the claim is large.

Examples of the application of the principles of CPR 36.21 by the court include:

– *McPhilemy v Times Newspapers (No. 2)* [2001] 1 WLR 934, in which the Court of Appeal awarded interest of 4% above base rate on costs.
– *Various Claimants v Bryn Alyn Community (Holdings) Ltd & Ors* [2003] EWCA Civ 383 in which the judge at first instance awarded interest of 8% above base rate on the general damages.
– *East West Corporation v DKBS 1912 and AKTS Svendborg Utaniko v P & O Nedlloyd BV* [2002] 2 Lloyd's Rep 222, in which Thomas J awarded enhanced interest of 2% above the US dollar prime rate on sums due under the judgment.
– *The Vergina (No. 3)* [2002] 1 Lloyd's Rep 238, in which Aikens J awarded interest of LIBOR plus 3% on damages and costs.
– *Ali Reza-Delata v United Arab Shipping* [2003] 2 Lloyd's Rep 455 in which the Court of Appeal allowed an enhanced interest rate of 3% above prime rate.
– *Cel Group Ltd v Nedlloyd Lines UK Ltd* [2004] 1 Lloyd's Rep 388 in which the Court of Appeal allowed an enhanced interest rate of 2% above base rate, which was a reduced rate to take account of the fact that the successful claimant's solicitors' fees were the subject of a conditional fee agreement.

1 In this case, Lord Woolf was not applying the principles laid down in CPR 36.21 directly because the case was decided on a summary judgment application. However, by analogy, he applied similar principles under CPR Part 44.

Interest – CPR 36.22

18.17 Any claimant's Part 36 offer which offers to accept a sum of money and any Part 36 payment notice will be treated as being inclusive of interest until the last date on which it could be accepted without needing the permission of the court unless it indicates to the contrary. If a claimant's Part 36 offer or a Part 36 payment notice is expressed not to be exclusive of interest, the offer or notice must state whether interest is offered and, if so, the amount offered, the rate or rates offered and the period or periods for which it is offered.

Offers to settle in collision cases – CPR 61.4(10)–(12)

18.18 Special provisions governing the making of offers to settle in collision claims (other than a claim for loss of life or personal injury) are found in CPR 61.4(10)–(12). The rules apply where a party to a claim to establish liability for a collision claim (other than a claim for loss of life or personal injury) makes an offer to settle in the appropriate form not less than 21 days before the start of the trial, the offer is not accepted and the maker of the offer obtains at trial an apportionment that is equal to or more favourable than his offer. In this circumstance, the parties will, unless the court considers it unjust, be entitled to the following costs:

- The maker of the offer will be entitled to all his costs from 21 days after the offer was made and his costs before then in the percentage to which he would have been entitled had the offer been accepted.
- All other parties to whom the offer was made will be entitled to their costs up to 21 days after the offer was made in the percentage to which they would have been entitled had the offer been accepted but will not be entitled to their costs thereafter.

An offer in the appropriate form must be in writing and must contain:

(i) an offer to settle liability in the stated percentages;
(ii) an offer to pay costs in accordance with the same percentages;
(iii) a term that the offer remains open for 21 days after the date it is made; and
(iv) a term that unless the court orders otherwise, on expiry of that period, the offer remains open on the same terms except that the offeree should pay all the costs from that date until acceptance.

Offers to settle in arbitrations

18.19 The powers of arbitrators in relation to the award of costs and interest are laid down in s 59 to 65 and s 49 of the Arbitration Act 1996 respectively. Essentially, subject to the agreement of the parties, arbitrators have a discretion as to the award of costs, which they must exercise judicially; see *The 'Maria'* [1993] 2 Lloyd's Rep. 168 and *Stotesbury v Turner* [1943] 1 KB 370. The ordinary principle is that, in the absence of circumstances justifying some other order, costs should follow the event so that the winner recovers his assessed or agreed costs and the loser pays them (s 61(2), Arbitration Act 1996). One circumstance that may justify the arbitrators making a different offer is the making by one party of a 'sealed offer' or 'open offer' that exceeds the amount eventually awarded by the arbitrators. A simple 'without prejudice' offer will be insufficient to affect the exercise by an arbitration tribunal of its discretion as to costs; see *Tramountana Armadora SA v Atlantic Shipping Co SA* [1978] 1 Lloyd's Rep 391 at p 396.

An 'open' offer is one which the parties make known to the arbitrators. A 'sealed' offer is the equivalent in arbitration to a payment into court.

Essentially, the party making the offer provides the arbitration tribunal with a sealed envelope containing a copy of the offer it has previously made to the other party. The tribunal should only look at the offer after it has reached its decision on all matters in dispute other than costs and should not revise its decision in light of the terms of the sealed offer once it has looked at them. To allay concerns that even alerting a tribunal to the fact that a sealed offer has been made by a respondent may adversely affect the tribunal's assessment of the strength of a respondent's case, there are two possible procedures that might be adopted. Firstly, the tribunal can be asked to make an interim final award on the substantive dispute and then at a later date a final award as to costs. This, of course, means that the overall cost of the arbitration is likely to be increased. The second alternative, although it is not one that appears to be in common usage, is for the tribunal to invite or require a respondent to give it a sealed envelope at the end of the hearing in any event. The envelope would contain either a statement that no sealed offer has been made or the sealed offer itself; cf *Tramountana Armadora SA v Atlantic Shipping Co Ltd* [1978] 2 Lloyd's Rep 391 at p 397.

If a respondent makes an open or sealed offer and the tribunal decides to take it into account, then the question for the tribunal in exercising their discretion is similar to that for a court considering a payment-in, namely whether the claimant has achieved more by rejecting the offer and going on with the arbitration than he would have achieved if he had accepted the offer; see *The 'Maria'* [1993] 2 Lloyd's Rep 168 at pp 173, 177 and 180. In the same case, the Court of Appeal held that in answering this question, the tribunal should have regard only to the amount awarded to the claimant by way of principal and interest and should not have regard to the amount of costs incurred by the claimant in going on with the arbitration rather than accepting the offer.

Although a tribunal will ordinarily take a sealed or open offer into account in reaching its decision on costs, it is not bound to do so. Provided its reasons for not giving effect to the offer demonstrate a proper exercise of a tribunal's judicial discretion, a court will not interfere with a refusal to take account of the offer; see *The 'Angeliki'* [1982] 2 Lloyd's Rep 594.

Arbitrators have no express statutory powers analogous to the powers given to the court by CPR Part 36 in relation to offers to settle by a claimant. Nevertheless, a practice is developing for claimants to make offers in arbitrations by analogy with the provisions CPR Part 36. As yet there appears to be no reported authority confirming whether such offers are effective. However, as arbitrators have a general power to award costs on such basis as they think fit (s 63(3), Arbitration Act 1996), an arbitration tribunal would seem to have the power to award costs on an indemnity basis for an appropriate period when a claimant's offer has been rejected and the claimant has subsequently recovered more in the arbitration than it had offered to accept. The position may be more difficult in relation to the award of an enhanced rate of interest on the principal claimed and on costs. However, s 49, Arbitration Act 1996, does give the tribunal the power to award simple or compound interest at such rates and with such rests as it considers meet the justice of the case:

- on the whole or part of any amount awarded by the tribunal in respect of any period up to the date of the award;
- on the whole or any part of any amount claimed in the arbitration and outstanding at the commencement of the arbitral proceedings, but paid before the award was made, in respect of any period up to the date of payment;
- on the outstanding amount of any award (including any award of interest under subsection (3) and any award as to costs), from the date of the award or any later date until payment.

These powers would accordingly seem wide enough to allow arbitrators a discretion to award enhanced rates of interest on any principal claimed in line with the rates set down in CPR Part 36.21 and to allow similar rates to be awarded on any award of costs, at least from the date of the award on costs.

PRECEDENTS

18.20 These precedents are intended to give the reader guidance as to the form and content of various types of Part 36 offer. They will clearly need adapting to the circumstances of the individual case. In particular, the level of information that a Part 36 offer letter will need to contain as to how the offer has been calculated will vary depending on the complexity of the case.

Given that defects in the form of a letter can render an offer ineffective for the purposes of later relying on the provisions of CPR Part 36, it is essential that any Part 36 offer letter complies with the mandatory requirements as to form found in the provisions of CPR Part 36.

Part 36 offer in respect of the whole or part of a money claim made more than 21 days before trial

The present court form for notice of a payment into court is Form N242A

Notice of acceptance and request for payment in respect of a payment into court made under CPR 36

The present court form for giving notice of acceptance and request for payment is Form N243A/Form 201.

Part 36 offer by a Defendant in respect of the whole of a non-money claim made more than 21 days before trial

Dear Sirs,

Re: *Craggy Trading Ltd v Selborne Property Limited*

We refer to the above action, in which we represent the Defendant. Our client has instructed us to make an offer to settle the whole of your client's claim.

This is an offer made in accordance with Part 36 of the Civil Procedure Rules, by which our client offers to settle your client's claim on the following terms:

[*insert full terms of the proposed offer*]

[This offer takes into account/does not take into account our client's counterclaim against you for [*identify the counterclaim*].]

This offer is made more than 21 days before trial. Accordingly, it is open for acceptance for 21 days from the date you receive this letter. If your client accepts our client's offer by giving notice of acceptance within this period, then our client will pay your client's costs of the proceedings (assessed on the standard basis, if not agreed) up to the date of service of the notice of acceptance. If your client does not accept our client's offer within the period of 21 days, then your client can only accept it thereafter if the parties can agree liability for costs or if the court gives permission.

[If the above offer is acceptable to your client, we would propose that the terms are included in a consent order and enclose a draft for your consideration].

Yours, etc

Part 36 Offer relating to the whole of a non-money claim made less than 21 days before the trial

Dear Sirs,

Re: *Craggy Trading Ltd v Selborne Property Limited*

We refer to the above action, in which we represent the Defendant. Our client has instructed us to make an offer to settle the whole of your client's claim.

This is an offer made in accordance with Part 36 of the Civil Procedure Rules, by which our client offers to settle your client's claim on the following terms:

[*insert full terms of settlement*]

[This offer takes into account/does not take into account our client's counterclaim against you for [*identify the counterclaim*].]

Your client may accept this offer at any time before the trial begins. However, as this offer is made less than 21 days before the trial, your client can only accept the offer if the parties can agree the liability for costs or if the court gives permission.

We would make the following proposal in relation to the costs of the proceedings, namely [*insert proposed terms*]. If this proposal is not acceptable to your client then it is open to them to seek the permission of the court to accept the offer. In this circumstance, our client will contend that, if the court gives its permission, an appropriate order for costs would be [*insert terms*].

If the above offer is acceptable to your client, we would propose that the terms are included in a consent order. We will provide a draft for your consideration once your client has indicated the basis on which it is accepting our client's offer.

Yours, etc

Part 36 offer relating to part of the claim/a particular issue made more than 21 days before the trial

Dear Sirs,

Re: *Craggy Trading Ltd v Selborne Property Limited*

We refer to the above action, in which we represent the Defendant. Our client has instructed us to make an offer to settle [part of your client's claim/a particular issue arising in the claim], namely [*insert details of the part of the claim/particular issue that is to be settled*]. This offer is made in accordance with Part 36 of the Civil Procedure Rules.

Our client offers to settle the [part of your client's claim/particular issue arising] on the following terms:

[*insert full terms of the offer being made*]

[This offer does/does not take account of our client's counterclaim.]

This offer is made more than 21 days before trial. Accordingly, it is open for acceptance for 21 days from the date you receive this letter. If your client accepts our client's offer by giving notice of acceptance within this period and at the same time abandons the balance of its claim, then [our client will pay your client's costs of the proceedings (assessed on the standard basis, if not agreed) up to the date of service of their notice of acceptance][1].

If your client serves notice of acceptance within the required 21 days from the date you receive the offer, but does not abandon the balance of his claim, then the claim will be stayed as to that [part of the claim/particular issue] and the court will have to decide the liability for costs. Our proposal so far as costs are concerned, and the order we will ask the court to make in the event that it is not possible to agree costs, is [*insert terms of the proposal on costs*].

If your client does not accept our client's offer on either of the bases proposed above within the period of 21 days, then your client can only accept it thereafter if the parties can agree liability for costs or if the court gives permission.

If the above offer is acceptable to your client, we would propose that the terms are included in a consent order. We will provide a draft for your consideration once your client has indicated the basis on which it is accepting our client's offer.

Yours, etc

1 It is open to the defendant to apply for a different order for costs to that laid down in CPR 36.13(2). If the defendant wishes to apply for a different order, then the words in square brackets should be replaced with text along the following lines:

> '...our client will apply to the court for a different order as to costs from that laid down in CPR 36.13(2). The order as to costs that we propose is [insert details of the costs order proposed]'

Claimant's Part 36 offer relating to the whole of a money claim made more than 21 days before the trial

Dear Sirs,

Re: *Navlax Chartering Limited v Tanker Ship Limited*

We refer to the above action in which we represent the Claimant. Our client has instructed us to make the following offer to settle this action. This is a claimant's offer made in accordance with Part 36 of the Civil Procedure Rules.

Our client claims the following relief from yours in the action, namely [*insert details of the relief claimed*] plus interest. Our client is however prepared to settle his whole claim against your client for the sum of [£ ....]. This sum has been calculated in the following manner: [*insert details of the basis on which the sum has been calculated*]. It is inclusive of interest until 21 days from now, which has been calculated using a commercial rate of [*insert details of rate*].

This offer remains open for acceptance for 21 days from the date you receive it. If your client accepts our client's offer by giving notice of acceptance within this period, then our client will be entitled to his costs of the proceedings (assess on the standard basis if not agreed) up to the date upon which your client serves notice of acceptance.

If your client does not accept the offer within the 21-day period, then the offer can be accepted thereafter, if we can agree the liability for the costs of the proceedings or the court gives permission.

If your client does not accept this offer and is held liable at trial for a sum greater than that which our client has offered to accept, then our client will ask the court to exercise its power under CPR 36.21 to make appropriate orders against your client in respect of interest and costs.

Yours, etc

Claimant's Part 36 offer relating to part of a money claim made more than 21 days before the trial

Dear Sirs,

Re: *Navlax Chartering Limited v Tanker Ship Limited*

We refer to the above action in which we represent the Claimant. Our client has instructed us to make the following offer to settle this action. This is an offer made in accordance with Part 36 of the Civil Procedure Rules.

Our client has claimed the following relief from your client, namely [*insert details of the relief claimed*]. One part of that claim relates to [*insert relevant details*]. Our client is prepared to make the following offer to settle that part of his claim, namely [*insert details of the offer*]. This sum has been calculated in the following manner: [*insert details of the basis on which the sum has been calculated*]. It is inclusive of interest until 21 days from now, which has been calculated using a commercial rate of [*insert details of rate*].

This offer remains open for acceptance for 21 days from the date that you receive it. If your client accepts this offer by giving notice of acceptance with that period, the claim will be stayed in relation to that part of the claim. The court will further have to decide liability for costs unless we are able to agree costs.

If your client does not accept our client's offer within the 21-day period, it can be accepted thereafter if we can agree the liability for the costs of the proceedings or if the court gives permission.

If your client does not accept this offer and is held liable at trial for a sum greater than that which our client has offered to accept, then our client will ask the court to exercise its power under CPR 36.21 to make appropriate orders against your client in respect of interest and costs.

Yours, etc

Pre-action offer by a defendant in a money claim

Without prejudice save as to costs

Dear Sirs,

Re: *Navlax Chartering Limited v Tanker Ship Limited*

We refer to the above matter in which we act for the proposed Defendant. Your client has given notice of its intention to pursue a claim against our client for the sum of [*insert details*] plus interest arising from [*insert brief description of the nature of the claim*].

Our client is prepared to make the following offer to settle the whole claim, namely a payment to your client of the sum of [£ . . .]. This sum is inclusive of interest/This sum is exclusive of interest, which the Defendant offers to pay at a commercial rate of . . . % pa from [*insert date*] to [*insert date*]. [It takes account/does not take account of the potential counterclaim that our client has against your client.]

Our client also offers to pay your client's reasonable costs incurred up to 21 days from the date you receive this letter.

This offer is open for acceptance for 21 days after you receive this letter. [It takes account/does not take account of our client's potential counterclaim [details of which you already have/[*insert brief details of the counterclaim*]].]

If your client does not accept this offer and subsequently commences proceedings against our client, our client will pay the above-mentioned sum into court within 14 days of service of the claim form. Our client will then rely on the provisions of CPR 36.10.

Yours, etc

Claimant's pre-action offer in a money claim

Without prejudice save as to costs

Dear Sirs,

Re: *Navlax Chartering Limited v Tanker Ship Limited*

We refer to the above matter in which we act for the proposed Claimant. As you are aware, our client has a claim against your client for [*insert brief details of the claim including the nature of the claim and the sums claimed*].

Our client is willing to settle the whole claim for a sum of [*insert the amount*]. [This sum includes interest/This sum is exclusive of interest, which the Claimant will accept at a rate of . . . % pa from [*insert date*] to [*insert date*]].

The Claimant also expects your client to pay his reasonable costs that have already been incurred as well as those reasonable costs that will be incurred in the period up to 21 days from the date when you receive this letter.

[This offer takes account/does not take account of the counterclaim that you have suggested your client may have].

This offer remains open for 21 days from the date when you receive it.

Should your client choose not to accept our client's offer so that it becomes necessary for him to issue proceedings, it will be the claimant's intention to rely on the provisions of CPR 36.21 in the event that the court gives judgment against your client for an amount greater than the claimant's present offer.

Yours, etc

Letter with offer to settle in respect of a claim to establish liability for a collision claim (other than a claim for loss of life or personal injury)

Dear Sirs

Re: *Black Box Shipping Co Ltd v White Cap Shipping Co SA*

We write in relation to the collision action presently ongoing between our respective clients. Please accept this letter as an offer to settle made pursuant to the provisions of CPR 61.4(10)–(12).

Having reviewed the statement of case served on behalf of your client and the evidence now available, our client is prepared to settle the issue of liability in this action on the basis that our client will accept [40%] of the liability for the collision and your client will accept [60%] of the liability for the collision.

Our client further offers to pay costs in accordance with the same percentages.

This offer remains open for acceptance for 21 days after the date on which you receive this letter. Should your client fail to accept the offer within this period, the offer will remain open for acceptance on the same terms except that your client will pay all the costs from that date until acceptance.

Yours, etc

Respondent's offer to settle a money claim in arbitration proceedings

Without prejudice save as to costs

Dear Sirs,

Re: *Navlax Chartering Limited v Tanker Ship Limited*

We refer to the above arbitration, in which we represent the Respondent. Our client has instructed us to make an offer to settle the whole of your client's claim.

Our client makes the following offer in full and final settlement of your client's claim in this arbitration:

[*insert full terms of settlement including details of (i) any proposal made in relation to interest and (ii) any allowance that has been made in relation to a counterclaim*]

[This offer remains open for acceptance until [allow a reasonable time for acceptance].]

In the event that your client fails to accept our client's offer, we shall hand a sealed copy of this letter to the Tribunal when they come to consider the question of costs. Should your client fail to recover more than our client has offered, we shall invite the Tribunal to award our client its costs of the arbitration from the last date when your client could have accepted our client's offer.

Yours, etc

Claimant's offer to settle a money claim in an arbitration

Without prejudice save as to costs

Dear Sirs

Re: *Navlax Chartering Limited v Tanker Ship Limited*

We refer to the above action in which we represent the Claimant. Our client has instructed us to make the following offer to settle its claims in this arbitration. This is an offer made by analogy with Part 36 of the Civil Procedure Rules.

Our client has claimed the following relief from your client, namely [*insert details of the relief claimed*]. Our client is prepared to make the following offer to settle that claim. This sum has been calculated in the following manner: [*insert details of the basis on which the sum has been calculated*]. It is inclusive of interest until 21 days from now, which has been calculated using a commercial rate of [*insert details of rate*].

This offer remains open for [21 days] from the receipt of this letter by you.

In the event that this offer is not accepted by your client, it is our intention to hand a sealed copy of this letter to the tribunal when they come to consider the question of costs. We will then invite the tribunal to exercise its discretion in relation to the question of interest and costs arising in relation to this arbitration in line with the powers granted to the courts by CPR Part 36 Rule 21, which allow a court to award enhanced interest at up to 10% above base rate together with indemnity costs and to award interest at an enhanced rate on those costs.

Yours, etc

Index

[*all references are to paragraph number*]

D